THE AMERICAN ALPI

2019

[Front Cover] **David Lama summiting Lunag Ri in Nepal (see p.12).** *Sean Haverstock / Red Bull Content Pool* [This page] **Tiphaine Duperier skiing the northwest face of Laila in Pakistan, with the Gondokhoro Glacier far below (see p.290).** *Boris Langenstein*

2019   VOLUME 61 ISSUE 93

CONTENTS

RECON

[Photo] Jeremy Collins finishing Moonshadow (1,100', 5.11b), a new route on Moonlight Buttress in Zion National Park, Utah (see p. 133). *Dan Krauss*

CLIMBS & EXPEDITIONS

The American Alpine Journal, 710 Tenth St. Suite 100, Golden, Colorado 80401

E-mail: aaj@americanalpineclub.org; www.publications.americanalpineclub.org

ISBN: 978-0-9998556-4-5
ISBN: (hardcover edition): 978-0-9998556-6-9

FIND MORE AT THE AAJ WEBSITE. Our online stories frequently contain additional text, photographs, videos, maps, and topos. Look for these symbols at the end of a story indicating additional resources at *publications.americanalpineclub.org*.

FULL-LENGTH REPORT	ADDITIONAL PHOTOS	MAPS OR TOPOS	VIDEO OR MULTIMEDIA

[Photo] Ice cave inside the Kaparoqtalik Glacier on southern Bylot Island, Nunavut, Canada (see p.182). *Grant Dixon*

FRIENDS OF THE AAJ

Richard Bickel
Robert M. Branch
Yvon & Malinda Chouinard
Carla L. Firey
Richard E. Hoffman M.D.
Louis Kasischke
Louis Reichardt
Eivind Rynning
Samuel Silverstein M.D.
Timothy Wilt

[Photo] Tom Livingstone exploring the east face of Jezebel in Alaska (see p.151). *Uisdean Hawthorn*

2018 GREAT RANGES FELLOWSHIP

[EIGER]

Nancy Bender
Yvon & Malinda Chouinard
Kevin & Leanne Duncan
Timothy Forbes
Gerald E. Gallwas
Louis Kasischke

Scott McCaffrey
Craig McKibben & Sarah Merner
Garry Menzel
Miriam Nelson & Kinloch Earle
Edith Overly
Mark & Teresa Richey

Janet Schlindwein
Steve & Paula Mae Schwartz
Cody J Smith
Travis Spitzer
Roger & Sha Sha Walker

[ALPAMAYO]

Warren Adelman
Jim Ansara
Edmund & Betsy Cabot Foundation
Bill Campbell
Philip Duff

James M. Edwards & Michele Mass
Dan Emmett
Bruce Franks
Rocky Henderson
Randy Luskey

Naoe Sakashita
Jo Ann Silverstein
Lawerance True & Linda Brown
Heidi Wyle

[ROBSON]

Lisa Abbott
Mark Aiston
Gordon A. Benner M.D.
Sumit Bhardwaj
Mitch Campbell
John Catto & The
    Alpenglow Foundation
Jeffrey Cohen
Christopher Croft
Joseph Davidson

The Duckworth Family
Philip Erard
Chas Fisher
Chuck & Lisa Fleischman
Charlotte Fox
Jim Frush
Eiichi Fukushima
James & Franziska Garrett
David Goeddel
Eric Green

Doug Henderson
Richard E. Hoffman M.D.
James Holmes
Thomas Hornbein M.D.
George Lowe III
Peter & Kathleen Metcalf
Michael W. Morgan
Paul Morrow
Brian Peters
Louis Reichardt

Wolf Riehle
David Riggs
John & Rebecca Soebbing
Theodore "Sam" Streibert
Duncan Stuart
Steven Swenson & Ann
    Dalton
Bill Thompson
Maggie Walker

[TEEWINOT]

Anonymous(3)
Jon Anderson
Joseph Andreotti
Conrad & Jenni Lowe-Anker
Michael Ashley
William Atkinson
Deborah Augsburger
Mia Axon
Carol Baker & Mark Stein
George Basch
Bob Bechaud
Rich Beeson
Vaclav Benes
John Berry
John Bird
Ronald H. Bixby
Stephen Bonowski
Audrey Borisov
Steve Bott
Tanya Bradby & Martin
    Slovacek
Martin Brigham
Lisa Brown
Pete Brownell
Paul Brunner & Coleen Curry
Jennifer Bruursema
Deanne Buck
Thomas Burch
Will Butcher
Mark Butler
R.J. Campbell
Marjorie Campbell
Kevin Capps
Diana Choi
Brianna Chrisman
Eric Christu
Dan & Ilene Cohen
Brendan Conway
Kevin & Ann Cooney
John Costello
Stephen Creer
Matt & Charlotte Culberson

Jim Davidson
Scott Davis
Kit DesLauriers
Ed Diffendal
John Donlou
Melvyn Douglas
Jeff Dozier
Richard & Martha Draves
Bill Egger
Charles Eilers
Stuart Ellison
Keith Fleischman
Jared Fox
Joanne Galka
Steve Gaykan
Marilyn Geninatti
Clark Gerhardt JR.
Michael Gibbons
Evan Green
Wayne & Cynthia Griffin
George Grzyb
Robert Hall
Roger Hartl
John Hebert
Scot Hillman
Mark Hingston
Michael Hodges
Marley & Jennifer Hodgson
Robert P. Hoffman M.D.
Scott Holder
Reynold Hoover
Peter Horan
Stephanie Hutchins
John Hutchinson
Jeremiah Johnson
Chris Johnson
Lorraine Kan
Steven Kasoff
Ben Katz & Becky Carmen
Diane Kearns
Joel G. Kinney
James Kunz III

Phil Lakin Jr.
Michael Lederer
Paul Lego
Daniel Lochner
Dave Lonack
Chris Lynch
Jessica Maly
Brent Manning
Robert Mascarenas
John Mastro
Patrick Mauro
Lisa Mckinney and Alex
    Intermill
Brad McQueen
Richard Merritt
Scott Milliman
Halsted "Hacksaw" Morris
Mie Nakane
Don Neer
John Nicholson
Sean O'Brien
Vanessa O'Brien
Chris O'Connell
Jeanne O'Connell
Matt Ochs
Bob Palais
Charles Peck
Samuel Perlik
Keenan Pope
Mark Powers
John & Barb Pugh
John & Mitzi Raaf
John Rehmer
Drummond Rennie
John Reppy
Jodi Richard
Jim Richards
Michael Riley
Carey Roberts
Joel Robinson
Mark Robinson M.D.
Jeffrey Rueppel

Vik Sahney
Dennis Sanders
Lauren Sanders
Jeb Sanford
Stephen Schofield
Raymond VJ Schrag
Ulrika & Mark Schumacher
    M.D.
Stephen Scofield
George Shaw
Lauren Sigman
Samuel Silverstein M.D.
Fred Simmons
John Sirois
David Skyer
George N. Smith
Jay Smith
Joy Souligny
Katelyn Stahley
Robert & Jennifer Stephenson
William & Barbara Straka
Bob & Pamela Street
Bruce Sullivan
Pavan Surapaneni
Lewis Surdam
Jack & Pat Tackle
Steve & Krista Taylor
David Thoenen
John Townsend
Dieter Von Hennig
Erik Weihenmayer
Jim Wickwire
Mark Wilford
Douglas Wilson
Todd Winzenried
Fred L. Wolfe
Keegan Young
Alina Zagaytova
James Zahn
Rob Ziegler

THE AMERICAN ALPINE JOURNAL

EDITOR
Dougald MacDonald

ART DIRECTOR
David Boersma

SENIOR EDITOR
Lindsay Griffin

ASSOCIATE EDITORS
Andy Anderson, Chris Kalman, Erik Rieger

CONTRIBUTING EDITORS
Whitney Clark, Damien Gildea, David Stevenson (Book Reviews), Drew Thayer

ILLUSTRATIONS AND MAPS
Dallin Carey, Anna Riling, Marty Schnure

PROOFREADERS
Rolando Garibotti, Damien Gildea, Bruce Normand and the AAC headquarters crew

TRANSLATORS
Guillaume Cossette, Emily Laskin, Oh Young-hoon, Pam Ranger Roberts, Maria Samsonova, Sonia Szczesna, Dmitry Zagorovskiy, Xia Zhongming

INDEXERS
Ralph Ferrara, Eve Tallman

REGIONAL CONTACTS
Steve Gruhn, Mark Westman, *Alaska*; Ian Welsted, *Canada*; Sevi Bohorquez, Sergio Ramirez Carrascal, *Peru*; Luis Pardo, *Colombia*; Damien Gildea, *Antarctica*; Rolando Garibotti, Camilo Rada, Marcelo Scanu, *Argentina-Chile*; Robert Rauch, Alex von Ungern, *Bolivia;* Harish Kapadia, Nandini Purandare, *India*; Rodolphe Popier, Richard Salisbury, *Nepal*; Tamotsu Nakamura, Hiroshi Hagiwara, *Japan*; Peter Jensen-Choi, Oh Young-hoon, *Korea*; Elena Dmitrenko, Anna Piunova, *Russia, Tajikistan, and Kyrgyzstan*; Xia Zhongming, *China*

ADVISORY BOARD
Whitney Clark, Alison Criscitiello, Kelly Cordes, Damien Gildea, Colin Haley, Mark Jenkins, Chris Weidner, Graham Zimmerman

SKI MOUNTAINEERING TEAM
Brody Leven, *chair*, Adrian Ballinger, Kit DesLauriers, Adam Fabrikant, Beau Fredland, Caroline Gleich, Pica Herry, Juan Señoret, Peter Schön, Forrest Shearer

WITH HEARTFELT THANKS TO...
Christine Blackmon, Brian Block, Elizabeth Cromwell, Colin Haley, Stephanie Hileman, Anna Riling, Marty Schnure, members of the American Alpine Club, and our hundreds of authors, photographers, and supporters

MILESTONES

THE CLIMBS FEATURED IN the AAJ don't happen in a vacuum—they are part of the broader evolution of climbing performance. The following achievements in 2018 provide additional context for the big-wall and mountaineering ascents documented in our pages. – The Editors

JANUARY

FILIP BABICZ (Italy) dry-tooled a 62-meter cave route in Poland that he called Oświecenie and rated M16/D16, the first in Europe of the grade. In December, Darek Sokołowski (Poland) completed Parallel World in the Italian Dolomites, also longer than 60 meters and also rated D16. Notably, both climbs also were rated DTS or "dry-tool style," meaning no figure-four moves were used during the ascents. Gord McArthur (Canada) proposed the world's first D16, in August 2017, for Storm Giant in British Columbia.

FEBRUARY

ADAM ONDRA (Czech) flashed Super Crackinette at Saint-Léger, France, the first flash of 9a+ (5.15a) route. Ondra had been attempting this feat since 2012, when he tried to flash Biographie (9a+) in France and flashed Southern Smoke Direct at the Red River Gorge in Kentucky (then given 5.15a but downgraded by Ondra to 5.14d). Visiting the U.S. in the fall of 2018, Ondra onsighted Just Do It (5.14c) at Smith Rock, Oregon, and made a strong attempt to onsight-free the Salathé Wall on El Capitan.

MAY

ALEX MEGOS (Germany) redpointed Perfecto Mundo at Margalef, Spain, making him the second person to do the first ascent of a 9b+ (5.15c) route. (Adam Ondra was the first to free climb 9b+ and 9c routes.) Stefano Ghisolfi (Italy) repeated Perfecto Mundo in December.

JUNE

KATRIN "KADDI" LEHMANN (Germany) completed Kryptos in the Basler Jura, Switzerland, becoming the second woman to boulder 8C (V15). In 2016, Ashima Shiraishi (USA) climbed two problems graded V15.

OCTOBER

FREE SOLO, the documentary film featuring Alex Honnold's solo of El Capitan, opened in theaters and soon became the highest grossing climbing film ever made, with over $21 million in box office sales. Directed by Elizabeth Chai Vasarhelyi and Jimmy Chin, the documentary won a BAFTA (U.K.) award and an Oscar in early 2019.

ALONE ON LUNAG

THREE YEARS AND FINALLY SUCCESS ON A HIGH PEAK IN NEPAL

DAVID LAMA

EDITOR'S NOTE: Just as the *AAJ* went to press in April, we learned of the tragic loss of Hansjörg Auer, David Lama, and Jess Roskelley in the Canadian Rockies. We hope this story, and others about these men throughout this year's *AAJ*, will be lasting tributes to three extraordinary climbers.

Conrad Anker (left) and David Lama attempted Lunag Ri in 2015 and 2016. When Anker could not return for another try, the author was determined to finish the job himself. *Martin Hanslmayr | Red Bull Content Pool*

"It's either the lung or the heart," Conrad Anker said between gasps. He was suffering from severe pain in his chest. The temperature of around -20°C wasn't helping. It was November 2016, and we were about 450 meters up on our second attempt on Lunag Ri, an unclimbed summit on the Nepal-Tibet frontier, southwest of Cho Oyu. The line we had picked was demanding. In our discussions, Conrad had prevailed with his preferred alternative, which might have been objectively safer but also was harder than a line through the icefield to our right. He wasn't having a great day and had asked me to lead. The higher we climbed, the more his condition worsened, to the point where it could only be described as alarming. But he didn't want to give up. It was time to make a decision—if necessary, against his wishes. Was the summit of Lunag Ri really that rock tooth sticking out from the wall like a diving board high overhead? We probably weren't going to find out this time either.

"We need to turn around," I told Conrad. He asked me to wait a few more minutes to see if his condition improved. "Maybe we can build a little platform for our tent up on that icy rib over there and see how things go tomorrow," he said. "You've got five minutes," I told him. In reality, I don't think I granted him more than three minutes. I started to build the first rap anchor, and when it was ready, Conrad finally gave in without protest. I had tried to convince him to call a helicopter that could pick him up as soon as we got to the base of the wall, but he refused. At least we were heading down. The steep, difficult terrain was now to our advantage, and we descended without incident.

In our advanced base camp, Conrad still didn't want a helicopter, but he wasn't doing any better. Where is the line between respecting a friend's wish and assuming responsibility for his survival? I took a decision and called our agency in Kathmandu. They immediately arranged to send a chopper our way. We didn't talk much while waiting for the rescue, but I vividly remember this one sentence, which Conrad half panted, half murmured: "It's on you now, David!"

Finally, the clattering chuf-chuf of the helicopter drew nearer, and they quickly loaded Conrad aboard and flew off down the valley. Soon we received news from Kathmandu: Conrad had suffered a heart attack. Thanks to his great physical condition, he was doing well after emergency surgery. He was in good hands; his condition was stable. However, he wouldn't return to Lunag Ri. There was nothing I would rather have done than finish the climb with him, but that wasn't going to happen. I sat in base camp, almost not daring to tell anyone: I was going to try alone. The chances were slimmer, the risk was bigger. Well, so be it.

CONRAD AND I already had tried Lunag Ri in 2015, and we reached a point about 300 meters below the summit, starting on the same vertical pillar on the lower wall. It was extremely cold. Even though we had rigorously packed, taking only the utmost necessities, I had to remove my pack on the very first pitch, as leading the steep, icy rock just seemed impossible with it. Every pitch cost us precious time.

We reached a saddle and veered right to climb along the knife-edge northwest ridge. The climbing was exposed, right on the border of Tibet and Nepal, and also right on the fine line between bold and stupid. On several sections, the snow was so unstable that the only protection was for each of us to stay on opposite sides of the ridge. Sometimes we'd have to traverse down as much as 20 meters off the ridge to find solid snow to support our crampons. When it was time to set up our bivy, the summit was still so far away that we kept going into the night to have a shot at the top the next day. We had underestimated this ridge.

Under a boulder, we found a little crevasse that we dug out until our tent somehow fit inside. We melted some snow, cooked, ate, and left at two in the morning for the summit push, without our tent and sleeping bags. The terrain stayed difficult, and gradually it dawned on us that,

Looking to the southwest during the 2015 attempt on Lunag Ri. The high peaks in the center background are Menlungtse (left) and Gaurishankar. Directly behind the climber is Little Lunag. *David Lama*

Lunag Ri from the southwest. (A) Summit (ca 6,907m). (B) Southeast top, reached by French climbers in 2010, via the southeast face. (1) Line followed in 2015 and 2016. (2) Line of Lama's solo ascents. (H1) High point with Anker in 2016. (H2) High point of 2015 attempt and 2016 solo attempt. *David Lama*

although we might have a chance to reach the summit, it would come at a price: We would have to bivouac on the descent, without any bivy gear. At temperatures between -20° and -30°, coupled with strong winds, losing fingers or toes was not just a theoretical worst-case scenario but the certain toll of a high-stakes game—one that we were both unwilling to play. My friend Peter Ortner, who was my partner on Cerro Torre and on Masherbrum in 2013 and 2014, had lost several toes while climbing and paragliding in Alaska, and I was acutely aware of the danger. We turned around and decided we'd return the next year. In fact the conditions were much better in 2016 and we were having a great time. Then came Conrad's heart attack.

And there I was, knowing that I would try alone, knowing that my chances had not exactly increased, but also that it wasn't impossible. I had to adapt my plan to the fact that I was soloing: Our original line was too hard to climb without a belay, and self-belaying all those pitches would take too long. I thus chose to climb the icefield to the right of the pillar, getting an early start to reach its top before sunrise and the inevitable falling rock and ice that would come with it. After the icefield, I planned to angle left to reach the ridge on our original line. I anticipated two bivvies on the way up and hoped to descend without needing a third bivouac. That was the plan.

Conditions were good on the icefield, but on the ridge the climbing was too hard for ropeless soloing while carrying the backpack. Leading, self-belaying, rappelling, and climbing back up with the pack took so much effort; the cold bit my bronchi, and a painful and worrisome cough was the result. I climbed a bit past the previous year's high point and somewhat precariously pitched my tent on a small, icy balcony right on the ridge. I spent the night psyching myself up for the next day's task of descending safely. The summit was far out of reach. All that counted was getting back down.

BACK IN AUSTRIA, I stayed in touch with Conrad, monitoring his recovery at home in Montana. When he boarded that helicopter at the base of Lunag Ri, he had said good-bye to extreme alpinism. He'd had enough; it was a dignified decision. At the same time, it felt odd: Conrad had always been there, kind of like the mountains themselves. He had done first ascents long before I was born. When he climbed the amazing west face of Latok II with the Huber brothers and Toni Gutsch in 1997, I was busy with learning multiplication in second grade. Of all his first ascents around the globe, the one that stuck out for me was Badlands on Torre Egger. This climb rings a bell only to a few connoisseurs, but there aren't many lines like it.

Jimmy Chin, a close friend of Conrad's, had connected us after a film festival in Spain around 2014. After completing a couple of smaller climbing projects together, we set our sights on unclimbed Lunag Ri. [*In 2010, a French team climbed the southeast face of Lunag; they finished on a point atop the face and descended without traversing to the higher main summit as planned.*] Then came our two expeditions to the mountain, the heart attack, and my solo attempt. Conrad recovered well, and in the summer of 2018, he and I climbed a couple of nice routes in the Dolomites. Those days meant a lot to me, but he had taken his decision. He was done with climbs like Lunag Ri. A few strong climbers asked if I wanted to try the mountain with them. Sorry guys, but no way. It wasn't that I wanted to make it harder or more spectacular—it was just that, given Conrad wasn't joining me, the second-most beautiful option I could imagine was to complete the project by myself. And so I declined all offers and returned to make an attempt alone in October 2018.

"The third time is the charm," Conrad had said to me in the Dolomites. But once in Nepal, a few long, nerve-wracking weeks went by before I could set off. Weather windows came and went, each too short for a promising attempt. I was focused and ready. Ready in a way I had rarely been before. Time after time, Charly Gabl, a world-renowned mountain meteorologist from Innsbruck, warned me the good weather wouldn't last long enough to descend, that the wind would be too strong. Twice I went to advanced base camp, backpack ready. Both times I turned around because of Charly's warnings. I trusted him.

Still, the back and forth tormented me. Soon, some friends from Tirol would turn up in base camp. I had promised them and my cameraman friend, Martin "Mungo" Hanslmayr, that we all would climb Cholatse together. I felt

[Top] During his climb of Lunag Ri, Lama rested for 24 hours at the first bivouac before heading toward the summit. [Bottom] Dry-tooling on Lunag's steep headwall in 2015. *David Lama (both photos)*

Lama alone on the frontier between Nepal and Tibet. A drone operated from advanced base captured images of his solo ascent, including the summit photo on our cover. *Sean Haverstock | Red Bull Content Pool*

committed to this promise. Then, at the last moment, I got a forecast that would at least provide a real chance. Finally!

Just after midnight on the morning of October 23, I set off. I climbed through the night as the temperature plummeted to 30 below. There were wind squalls, but they didn't hit me quite as hard as they would if I'd already been up on the ridge. At 8 a.m., I put my tent on a small, flat platform and rested. Inside the tent, the cold was less biting. The ice between my two socks, which had frozen solid inside my boots, began to melt. My airways got some relief as I drank a few sips of warm water. I rested all day and the following night. Had I continued that day, I might have gotten past the Toblerone, a prominent rock tower on the ridge, but I could not have made the summit, and the bivy options higher up were not as good. And so I stayed in the tent for about 24 hours before starting again.

In the morning of October 24, I continued along the fabulous ridge, passing some incredible

pitches on which I could hear the lovely sound of my crampons' teeth grating against the granite, finding a hold, and coming to halt. I saved time and energy by belaying only on the trickiest sections. Some 200 meters below the top, I stopped again and set up my tent on a wildly overhanging cornice.

The third day could have started better. I hadn't even gotten out of my sleeping bag yet when I threw up my entire breakfast. Even before setting off on the first pitch, my feet were completely numb. I self-belayed more frequently, not only because the headwall was so steep, but also because I could rest in my harness at the belay, which briefly brought some warm blood back into my toes. It took four hours of painstakingly slow climbing to crest the headwall. Gradually I could see the summit ridge ahead, and my thoughts shifted from *I am so, so slow* to a more confident *I am moving up, slowly but surely.* The rock tooth that Conrad and I had guessed might be the summit was indeed the highest point, sticking into the abyss. Around 10 a.m., I carefully strode out to the tip. I would have loved to share this moment with Conrad.

Less than two weeks after standing on top of Lunag Ri, my friends and I reached the summit of Cholatse. Even though the two ascents were very different, they each had their own appeal. While Lunag Ri will be engraved in my memory for the exposure, the difficulty, the cold and the loneliness, and for a successful conclusion to a personal project, sharing my friends' joy on their first Himalayan 6000er and seeing the happiness in their eyes made the ascent of Cholatse a great pleasure.

SUMMARY: First ascent of Lunag Ri (Lunag I) in the Rolwaling Himal of Nepal, by the southwest face and northwest ridge (approximately 1,500m vertical gain), by David Lama, October 23–25, 2018. Lama descended by rappel, mostly along the route of ascent, and returned to advanced base camp late on October 25. Lunag Ri's elevation is variously quoted at 6,895m and 6,907m; however, based on his mobile phone's GPS and his climbing distance, Lama believes the peak is closer to 7,000m.

ABOUT THE AUTHOR: *Born in 1990, David Lama lived in Innsbruck, Austria. In January 2012, Lama and Peter Ortner made the first free ascent of Cerro Torre's southeast ridge.*

K2 ON SKIS

THE FIRST DESCENT OF THE WORLD'S SECOND-HIGHEST PEAK

BY THE EDITORS

K2 from Concordia to the south (June 2006 photo). The face is approximately 3,400 meters high. The red line (3) shows the route traced by Andrzej Bargiel to make the first complete ski descent of the mountain. (1) General area climbed by the Magic Line (1986). (2) Kukuczka-Piotrowski Route. (4) Cesen Route (south-southeast spur). (5) Abruzzi Ridge (continuing up the right skyline). *Alan Arnette*

On July 22, 2018, just before 11:30 a.m., Andrzej Bargiel from Poland reached the summit of K2 (8,611 meters). That day and the day before, more than 60 other people summited K2—a record for a single season—but unlike the large majority of them, Bargiel was not breathing supplementary oxygen. And unlike almost anyone else in history, he was carrying skis. About seven hours later he skied onto the Godwin-Austen Glacier, about 3,400 meters below the summit, having finished the first complete ski descent of the mountain.

Bargiel, age 30 at the time of the descent, had climbed three other 8,000-meter peaks from 2013 to 2015: the central summit of Xixabangma (a.k.a. Shishapangma), Manaslu, and Broad Peak. The latter was the first complete ski descent from the summit of Broad Peak (8,051 meters). In 2017, he attempted K2 without success. (He reached about 6,500 meters on his planned ski route.) Other mountaineers who had attempted to ski K2 before Bargiel included Hans Kammerlander (Italy), Dave Watson (USA), who skied through the Bottleneck in 2009, starting about 250 meters below the summit, and Luis Stitzinger (Germany), who skied from around 8,050 meters in 2011. (He downclimbed about 200 meters near Camp 3 on the Cesen Spur.) At least two mountaineers had died during their attempts to climb and ski K2.

Previous skiers had envisioned descending a line similar to the Cesen route on the south-southeast spur, left of the Abruzzi Ridge, but it was very unlikely this route would ever be covered with enough snow to allow a continuous descent. From the slopes of Broad Peak in 2015, Bargiel spotted a better way. "None of the descent lines directly from the summit was entirely viable, so I had to link them," he said at a press conference in Poland, recorded by *Góry* magazine. "From Broad Peak, [I saw] the right combination of snowy lines to allow for an actual attempt at descending."

Bargiel had custom-made skis, including top sheets emblazoned with the initials of his parents and ten siblings. His extremely light carbon boots, made in France by Pierre Gignoux, were comfortable enough for both climbing and skiing. "When others see me in these, they're shocked because the boots are small and not as warm as Himalayan ones," Bargiel said at the press conference. "But I have a few methods which ensure that the temperatures in the boots are comfortable—for example, inside I have heated insoles, and outside I have neoprene boots which protect me from wind and moisture." His ski bindings had no brakes or leashes, and on the summit he experienced a moment of panic when the skis nearly slipped away as he worked to get his neoprene-covered boots into the bindings. During the descent, he used lightweight ski poles, sometimes wielding an ice tool in one hand.

Before the summit push on K2, Bargiel spent some time acclimatizing on Gasherbrum II and a little time on K2. On his second trip up K2, he went up the Abruzzi almost to the Shoulder, at nearly 8,000 meters, and back down again in a long day.

Bargiel had hoped to summit the peak with Janusz Gołąb, a fellow Pole, but at Camp 3, Gołąb suddenly developed severe back pain. He was unable to climb up or down. Contacted by radio at base camp, a doctor said the only way for Gołąb to recover was to lie motionless on his back for two days. Bargiel's brother, Bartek, who was operating drones to film the climb and descent, flew anti-inflammatories to Camp 3 (at around 7,000 meters) to help. Together, the two men there decided Bargiel should try to reach the summit alone. He had forgotten his GoPro and was worried he might make the first ski descent of K2 without any point-of-view footage to show for it. So, Bartek made two drone flights to deliver the gear, first the camera and then a battery. (Previously, he had flown the drone to 8,500 meters to scope the planned line of descent.)

On July 21, Bargiel headed for Camp 4 carrying all of his own gear (tent, sleeping bag, skis, etc.) and spent the night there. Early in the morning, heating water with the stove between his legs, he set his high-altitude suit on fire. "Luckily, I put it out quickly," he said. "There were really a lot of weird things going on." He left for the summit at 4 a.m.

On top there were light winds and intermittent clouds, but as Bargiel started down he entered thick fog. He had worried the descent from the summit to the Shoulder would be the crux, but a continuous line of deep snow made it feel quite reasonable. "Somewhere around 8,400 meters, I was all alone, far from the path. It was incredible to have the whole wall to myself." At one section, above the Bottleneck, he made use of a 50-meter length of fixed rope, but only because he worried about knocking loose snow onto climbers below. "That was the main challenge," he explained,

[Top] **Point-of-view video capture, looking down to the Godwin-Austen Glacier.** [Middle] **Alongside the fixed ropes through the Bottleneck on the Abruzzi Ridge. In some spots, Bargiel skied with both poles in one hand and an ice tool in the other for security.** [Bottom] **Nearing the bottom of the face.** *Marek Ogień | Red Bull Content Pool*

"because the terrain wasn't difficult enough to warrant descending with a rope."

Peering through a powerful spotting scope, photographer Marek Ogień directed Bargiel over the radio. "This ended up being key, just as the drone was," Bargiel said. "There was a heavy fog in Camp 4, which was problematic because below that was a part [of the descent] that I didn't entirely know." This was the section of his route where he left the Abruzzi route, starting from a little before Point 7,722m. From here, Bargiel planned to stay to skier's right of the Cesen spur, but he had to wait about an hour for the fog to clear. "So, I'm lying on the snow and I didn't know what to do, because it's about 1,000 meters of pretty steep wall and then a bowl into which all the slopes empty—if there was an avalanche there, it would be a massacre. The descent had to be very precise. Marek told me where I could hide behind rocks, where there are fissures. For him, it was probably really stressful, because by saying what I should do, he took on some responsibility for [my life]."

At Camp 3 on the Cesen, Bargiel was thrilled to find Gołąb waiting and ready to descend to base camp on his own. This "filled me with optimism," he said. Moreover, "I felt that I had the descent under control, because I felt it get colder after Camp 3. At the same time, I realized it was still going to be difficult, because I had to do the 'Messner Traverse.' I had gone down that way during my acclimatization, and I prepped by placing a screw and putting up a line. During the final push, I took a different way, but from the 200-meter serac above it was raining blocks of ice."

This descending traverse beneath the great serac barrier, beginning at around 6,800 meters, was the link-up between the Cesen spur and the Kukuczka-Piotrowski Route (1986)—it was the key to Bargiel's carefully crafted route. Afterward, this line was widely misreported as the "Messner Traverse," even though Reinhold Messner never went near it nor had any intention of doing so. (He briefly explored this area of

"At the bottom I was totally exhausted.... I lay on the snow for an hour. *Marek Ogień | Red Bull Content Pool*

the mountain in 1979, hoping to climb what eventually became the Magic Line, but only went to around 6,200 meters before switching to the Abruzzi Ridge.) The traverse has been ascended at least twice during attempted climbs of K2, but perhaps never to the summit.

In this area, Bargiel used a rope for only the second time during the 3,400-meter descent, securing himself for about 10 meters. Once across the traverse, Bargiel skied down the Kukuczka-Piotrowski to a point at around 6,200 meters, where that route heads off to skier's right and Bargiel skied more directly toward the glacier below.

Although the skiing appeared more straightforward here, the enormous temperature swing between early in the day on the upper mountain and the evening at below 6,000 meters now came into play, as the soft, warm snow continuously threatened to slide. "The terrain looked like it would be OK, but as it turned out, I needed to do some ski cuts to [release dangerous snow and] conquer these slopes," Bargiel said. "There was always something falling, and I thought that I would get knocked into a crevasse."

Bargiel finally reached the glacier and stopped skiing about seven hours after leaving the summit (including rests). He was about ten minutes away from base camp. "At the bottom I was totally exhausted, and I had enough of everything," he said. "I lay on the snow for an hour. I still had the skis on my feet."

After his first attempt in 2017, Bargiel hadn't been sure if he wanted to return to K2. But his desire to accomplish the feat was compounded by a sense of urgency: "An important factor is that the climate is changing rapidly," he explained. "If I waited a few years, everything would have changed, and I would have to start from scratch."

Returning to a hero's welcome in Poland, Bargiel soon visited the family farm, where his father told him, "Well, you had a nice little holiday, but now it's time to do some work."

ABOUT THE SOURCES: *Visual documentation of Andrzej Bargiel's descent is mostly in video footage captured by his GoPro or by distant telephoto or drone cameras. A five-minute video of the highlights can be seen at the AAJ website, and a longer film is in the works. This account was compiled by AAJ editors Dougald MacDonald and Lindsay Griffin, using published interviews with Bargiel, along with Griffin's notes from a talk that Bargiel gave at the Ladek Mountain Film Festival in Poland in September 2018. Most of the direct quotes are drawn from an article published in the Góry Magazyn in Poland, which in turn was developed from the press conference and interviews with Bargiel. The AAJ thanks Piotr Drożdż, editor of Góry, and Sonia Szczesna, translator of the Góry article, for their generous assistance.*

THREADING THE NEEDLE

SKIING LHOTSE'S DREAM LINE

HILAREE NELSON

On September 30, at about 2 p.m., Jim Morrison and I pulled off our overboots, clicked into our ski bindings, and laboriously buckled our boots. Our oxygen masks were off, making every action at 27,940 feet, on the summit of Lhotse, extremely slow and difficult. I reached for my backpack, so much lighter now that my skis were on my feet, and swung it over my right shoulder, then slowly buckled the waist and chest straps. I slid my oxygen mask back over my face, stuck my right hand on the summit cornice, and soaked up the view one last time.

Exactly four weeks earlier, on August 31, our team of four—Jim and I, along with photographers Dutch Simpson and Nick Kalisz—left the U.S. from various points and convened at the Kathmandu airport. Jim and I went straight from the hotel to the Nepal Ministry of Tourism to register for our expedition, pay garbage fees, meet our liaison officer, and finalize the two necessary permits for Lhotse: one for climbing and one for skiing back down. We took another full day to organize in Kathmandu before heading to the airport to fly into the Khumbu and begin our trek to base camp.

Our goal for this expedition was simple: Jim and I wanted to ski the Lhotse Couloir from the summit in as pure a fashion as we could muster. Forming a super-direct narrow line from the upper Lhotse Face to the summit, the couloir was a dream line for skiing and the complete descent had been attempted several times. Jamie Laidlaw came closest in the spring of 2007, when he climbed solo to just 200 meters below the top before his oxygen regulator failed and he was forced to turn around and descend from there.

Jim and I had chosen the autumn for our attempt, knowing there would be more snow on the mountain in the post-monsoon season and that it was unlikely there would be other climbers on the Lhotse Face (also a crucial part of the South Col route on Everest). If other climbers were on the mountain, we risked endangering them by sending down avalanches or rocks as we skied, and their tracks and fixed ropes might adversely affect our ski descent. However, our decision to climb in the post-monsoon also made the objective much more challenging. Having climbed Everest and Lhotse in the spring of 2012, during one of the busiest seasons on record, it felt very strange to be alone at base camp. Each day

Hilaree Nelson exiting the Lhotse Couloir with Everest behind. *Nick Kalisz | The North Face*

Lhotse (8,516m) seen from the southeast ridge of Everest. The slender Lhotse Couloir drops directly from the summit down the shadowed northwest face. The ski descent then continued another vertical mile down the vast Lhotse Face (lower right) to Camp 2 in the Western Cwm. *Paul Pottinger*

we were reminded of what it meant to have no help from other expeditions, whether it be building a trail through the moraine, breaking trail in deep snow, or fixing all the rope for our route.

Our puja ceremony was held on September 11, five days after we arrived at base camp. The next day, all five of the Sherpa climbers we had hired—our sirdar Palden Namgje, his brother Fu Tashi, his son Ila Nuru, Urken Lendu, and Phura Chettin—along with icefall doctors Yangda Sherpa and Nim Dorchi Sherpa, started into the dangerous maze of the Khumbu Icefall,

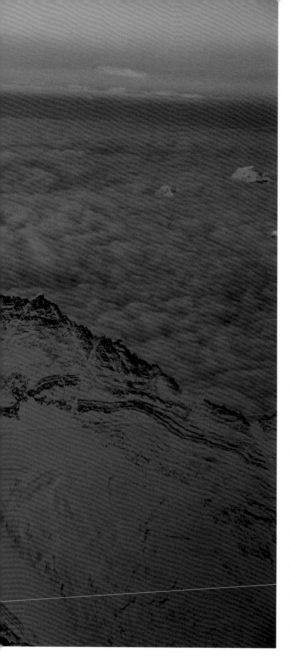

the gateway to the upper reaches of the Western Cwm. Jim and I did our best to help, carrying loads of rope and pickets to drop for the Sherpa, but they are so strong and efficient that we mostly drafted on their work. The conditions were optimal, and it took them only four days to put in the route, including one rest day. We followed the route from the previous spring, on the climber's right of the icefall, and the route to Camp 1 at 19,000 feet required only one ladder to bridge a crevasse. In 2012, on a route more to the climber's left, I had crossed 15 to 20 ladders.

With such a small team and no one else on the mountain, we took many measures to ensure a lightweight approach to this objective, knowing that we wanted to limit our passes through the icefall and simultaneously be poised for a summit attempt in a very short timeframe of two weeks. Compared with the usual team in the Western Cwm, we carried a minimal setup, with only one set of sleeping bags and pads for Camp 2 and beyond and a super-lightweight single-wall tent for Camp 3. To save weight and time, we planned to skip Camp 4 altogether. Jim and I decided not to wear down suits but chose a layering system that was less bulky and more versatile. On our final push from base camp, we wore our ski boots the whole way to avoid carrying any excess gear.

We reached Camp 2 for the first time on September 16 just as darkness descended. This was the most surreal experience of the entire expedition. There were dozens of ghost camps where Everest outfitters had left behind huge bundles of colorful and messy gear from the spring season—I spent the first night there having zombie nightmares.

On September 18 we descended to base camp, passing the Sherpa climbers and our Camp 2 cook on their way up to drop loads. We hoped we'd have good news at base camp about our ski equipment. Due to the complications of the heavy monsoon season, none of our ski gear had reached base camp yet, so it was a huge relief to learn that the porters had just arrived with the missing equipment. We were now green-lighted to don our ski boots and begin our final push toward the fourth-highest peak in the world.

Skinning up the Western Cwm, en route to Camp 3. *Dutch Simpson | The North Face*

Only four days later, we were back on the move. The weather had been very unsettled, and there was nearly four feet of new snow between 18,000 feet and 19,000 feet. The Sherpa carried monstrous loads, Jim and I were both carrying our skis, and we all did our best to take turns breaking trail. Just before reaching Camp 1, we were relieved to see Urken and Ang Karma Sherpa (our Camp 2 cook) descending to help us break trail and uncover the fixed lines. Still, it was a crushing day, taking us more than 12 hours from BC to C2. Fortunately, the monsoon storm had brought very little snow and only light winds above Camp 2, which meant the upper mountain, particularly the Lhotse Face, would still be safe to climb.

After a full rest day, Jim and I started pushing higher. We set the route to the bergschrund at the base of the Lhotse Face, carrying our skis and making our first turns of the expedition. I was astonished to see enough snow filling the bergschrund that we would be able to ski across it with no rappel—the schrund often requires up to 15 meters of vertical climbing in the spring season. The conditions on the lower Lhotse Face appeared to be a mix of hard snow and ice. This would be a huge bonus because it meant the climbing would be straightforward and the avalanche danger significantly low, yet we would still be able to ski.

Over the next two days the Sherpa moved through the bergschrund and all the way to Camp 3 at 23,800 feet with ropes, pickets, and oxygen bottles. On the second day, we followed with tents and everything needed to spend a night at C3. This is one of the more incredible spots in the Himalaya, and we were the only climbers on the face. In the morning, we waited for the sun to hit our tents at around 9:30 a.m. before gearing up to ski the 2,700 feet back to Camp 2. Skiing this section so close to our summit push was risky, because it meant we would tire ourselves and that we'd have to carry our skis all the way back up. But other than the relatively easy terrain we'd skied below the 'schrund, I hadn't been on skis in more than three months. We knew the lower Lhotse Face would be one of the toughest sections of the whole descent, and I needed to feel confident about skiing a 50°-plus slope in exposed terrain on very firm and variable snow.

Back at Camp 2 on the afternoon of the 27th, we received a weather report confirming that the jet stream was going to drop in elevation on the afternoon of September 30. This is typically an indicator that the fall climbing season is coming to an end. The wind would be increasing to as high as 50kph (31mph) above 26,000 feet and even more in the following days, reaching highs over 100kph—conditions too challenging for a summit attempt. Moreover, the high winds could blow away the snow we needed for skiing. As a result, we'd have time for only one rest day before moving back up to Camp 3 and then on to the summit.

We hatched a plan that left very little room for error and relied heavily on the hard work of our Sherpa team and our two cinematographers, both of whom were new to climbing above 20,000 feet. On the morning of September 29, all five Sherpa headed up the Lhotse Face at about 3 a.m. The four of us followed a few hours later. The plan was for the Sherpa to climb past Camp 3 as a group of five and fix lines through the Yellow Band. At that point, Tashi and Ila would descend to C3, spend the night, and then climb back up with the four of us the following morning. Meanwhile, Palden, Urken, and Phura would continue fixing the more difficult stretches above the Yellow Band and through the Lhotse Couloir, and then descend to Camp 3 for the night, break down that camp the following morning, and carry much of the gear down to Camp 2.

From Camp 3 we watched as the Sherpa above us moved up. Beyond the Yellow Band, it was painfully obvious that conditions had become more difficult, as their pace slowed dramatically. Tashi and Ila turned around at this point, as planned, while the others continued upward. Urken was the only one of the three that had not summited Lhotse before and, because the weather was good, they pushed hard to get him to the top. Through our radios, we heard that Urken had summited at about 6 p.m., just before sunset. By 8 p.m., everyone was back at C3 in high spirits, ready to take on the next day.

[Top] Deep snow mostly covered the summit cliffs, allowing a ski descent from the very top. *Jim Morrison*
[Bottom] Jim Morrison (front) and teammates on top of Lhotse. *Hilaree Nelson*

Our alarms went off at 12:30 on the morning of September 30. By 2 a.m., the six of us—Tashi, Ila, Dutch, Nick, Jim, and I—were geared up and ready to head out. The tracks above Camp 3 that the Sherpa had left only hours before were completely filled in, and we all had to break trail again. After eight hours of climbing, we moved from the top of the face into the Lhotse Couloir. At this point, the conditions became increasingly difficult, with deep snow and a breakable wind crust that slowed Jim and me to a crawl. The two of us were climbing without oxygen, but at this point it became pretty obvious that we wouldn't reach the summit at this pace. We decided that skiing was more important than a no-O's ascent, so we donned masks and tapped into the oxygen bottles that Ila had been carrying to this point.

Though the oxygen helped, it still took another four hours to reach the summit. We climbed through the choke of the couloir and were relieved to see that it would be wide enough to ski without a rappel. In 2012, on my first climb of Lhotse, this section of the route was entirely rock and only about 80cm (31 inches) wide. Before continuing up, we pulled the rope that had been fixed through the choke so it wouldn't be in our way during the descent. (Some fixed ropes were left on the mountain at the end of the expedition.) The last 100 feet of the summit block steepened

Jim Morrison drops off the summit of Lhotse. Deep snow allowed careful hop turns until a small cliff band, which he shot directly over to reach easier terrain. *Nick Kalisz | The North Face*

to 60°, and we wallowed in waist- to chest-deep snow. Again, this section had been mostly rock in 2012 and required climbing a 20-foot cliff. Now, seeing the mountain with this much snow, I knew we would be able to make our ski descent from the very top.

After 12 hours and 4,300 feet of climbing, our entire group was planted on the summit. We had a clear view of the southeast ridge of Everest and over to Makalu and Cho Oyu. The north-facing Lhotse Couloir had been in full shade, but the summit was sunny and we soaked up the warmish rays, trying to muster the energy to gear up for our descent. Exactly as forecasted, the wind began to pick up in early afternoon and we knew it was time to start down.

I was relieved to feel energized and excited once I put on my skis. The massive descent ahead was daunting, but knowing that we would be able to keep our skis on the entire time simplified things and made Jim and I eager to get started. That deep sugar snow that covered the summit block, which had been so strenuous to climb, now proved to be a blessing. Jim made the first move from the summit, sinking into waist-deep snow with each turn. Because it was so steep, he would fall some 10 to 15 feet between each turn, taking them meticulously slow, one hop at a time. I chose to arm-wrap a rope for extra security for the first 100 feet off the top before kick-turning around a small cliff band and skiing the final turns off the bottom of the summit pyramid.

At this point the skiing eased up and we were able to lean into the slope and wait for the rest of our team to descend to us. The next section would be the most challenging, as the slope narrowed into the choke of the couloir. The snow was a crazy mixture of bulletproof wind slab, breakable crust, and sugar snow, and each turn had to be calculated and controlled. The choke lasted about 100 feet and was just barely wide enough for us to side-slip through, our skis' tips and tails scraping the rock on either side. Jim and I were still using oxygen at this point, but even with this help we

Lining up for the choke of the couloir, where the skiers' tips and tails scraped rock on both sides. *Jim Morrison*

could only make two or three turns at a time, and then we would have to stop and catch our breath, doubling over our poles and gasping.

Once out of the couloir, we skied a long traverse into the vast Lhotse Face, leaving the main route and the rest of our team behind to continue their descent. More consistent snow allowed us to ski a little faster and link more turns. Zigzagging back and forth across the massive expanse of the face, we laughed and enjoyed the simple freedom of skiing.

At Camp 3, Palden was waiting with hot water. We loaded up our packs with the remainder of the camp and pressed on to the final challenge, the lower 1,500 feet of the Lhotse Face, with the steepest pitch toward the bottom. The sun had left the face, making it much harder to discern skiable snow from ice. Jim and I took our time, and because we'd already skied this section a few days earlier, we were pretty comfortable with the descent despite the flat light.

Our full descent took about four hours. In total, we skied 1,800 feet of the Lhotse Couloir, about 4,200 feet on the Lhotse Face, and another 1,000 feet below the bergschrund. When we ran out of snow, we popped of our skis and fell onto the ground, too tired to talk. Eventually we pulled ourselves together, strapped our skis to our packs, and walked back into Camp 2 around 6 p.m., in total a 16-hour day. The others made it to camp soon after, and the next day we all hiked down through the icefall with huge loads and massive grins.

SUMMARY: First ski descent of Lhotse (8,516m/27,940') by Jim Morrison and Hilaree Nelson, September 30, 2018. Supported on summit day by two Sherpa climbers and two cameramen, and using fixed ropes and supplemental oxygen to climb and descend the upper mountain, the two skied the Lhotse Couloir and Lhotse Face to Camp 2 (ca 6,400m), a descent of more than 2,100 meters.

ABOUT THE AUTHOR: *Born and raised in Seattle, Hilaree Nelson began her career as a professional ski mountaineer in 1999, as an athlete for the North Face and Clif Bar. She has lived in Telluride, Colorado, for almost 20 years and is the mom of two wild little boys, Quinn and Grayden, ages 9 and 11.*

L A T O K

TWO EXTRAORDINARY ASCENTS

STORIES

ALEXANDER GUKOV & TOM LIVINGSTONE

LATOK: THE NORTH RIDGE

A FAMOUS LINE IS FINALLY CLIMBED BUT WITH NO SUMMIT AND A HEAVY COST

ALEXANDER GUKOV

The original plan was for three of us to attempt Latok I: me and Glazunov brothers, Evgeny and Sergey. We had never climbed together, but we knew one another. I thought we would make a great team for a mountain like this. Although I'm already old compared to them, I believed that with their speed and my experience and knowledge of the route, we would quickly get to the summit. I had attempted the north ridge the summer before, reaching about 6,700 meters with Anton Kashevnik and Valery Shamalo, the highest anyone had climbed since the famous first attempt in 1978.

But at the last moment Evgeny could not go. Everything was ready, but now there were only two of us. Sergey was in a fighting mood. But me—I'm not a superstitious person, but somewhere deep in my soul something was off. It didn't feel right to take on such a route as a pair. Yet what if I was wrong? What if everything was not so bad, what if Sergey was ready and we would make a great team? Who can answer these questions in advance?

So, we decided to go together. Some friends from Russia arrived at the base camp a week before us, but they were planning to draw another line to the summit, directly up the north face. On July 7, two days after Sergey and I arrived at BC, we started acclimatization. There was an uncomplicated snow shoulder nearby at 5,875 meters. We spent one night at 5,200 meters and two nights on the shoulder. We realized this was not enough, but we didn't know any easy way to reach a higher point to acclimatize in that area.

On July 10 we were back in base camp. The weather was perfect, but at the same time it was too warm and sunny, and the mountains came to life. At first Sergey and I planned to start on July 12, the same day as the guys from the second group, but in the morning we realized our packs were too heavy and we would never get to the summit.

We went through everything and set aside the third ice tool, a couple of pitons, a couple of cams, and one ice screw. We took no spare clothes except for mittens. I cut down my wide Thermarest pad so it was the same as Sergey's, removed the central anti-balling plates on the crampons, shortened the toothbrush handles, cut off extra packaging from our Mountain House food and poked holes in it with a needle to avoid inflation at height. We removed a Tibloc, part of the shovel handle, the only snow picket, one gas canister, and some dried fruits and peanuts. In this way we stripped about six kilograms from the loads, leaving backpacks that weighed 20 kilograms each, including food for 10 days and five 240-gram gas canisters.

Meanwhile, we kept looking through binoculars all day long for the guys who had approached the north wall that morning. It was in the evening, just before sunset, before I saw them again, heading back down. "So things are pretty bad up there," I thought.

In the morning of July 13 I chatted with them before leaving. "There was rockfall all day long, no chance of getting out of the bergschrund," the guys said. "What are your plans?" I asked. "We'll think about it, maybe we'll follow you later," they answered. Although the thought of all five of us joining forces for the north ridge crossed my mind, I did not mention it. We we were all geared up to go as a pair. We were ready to go.

(A) Latok I (7,145 meters) from the north. (B) Latok II. (1) Russian attempt to the top of the north ridge at approximately 7,050 meters. (R) Approximate site where Alexander Gukov was stranded and eventually rescued by helicopter. (2) Slovenian-British Route (second ascent of Latok I), passing through the col between Latok I and II to finish by the southern slopes. See story on p.40. *Sergey Glazunov* [Previous pages] Ales Česen searching for the line on Latok I's north side. *Tom Livingstone*

Sergey Glazunov nearing the finish of his last lead atop the north ridge of Latok I. *Alexander Gukov*

We started our route in the same way I had the previous year, on the left side of the ridge. The higher the sun rose, the more wet avalanches descended. We mostly managed to hide from them, but by the end of the day all the equipment and clothes were wet. We spent the first night at 5,360 meters.

The next day we crossed over the north ridge, but we could not reach the bivy spot at 5,800 meters as I had planned. We had to traverse over a lot of snowy ridges, which took quite a while. However, we found a good serac at 5,640 meters where we spent the night. We finally reached the planned bivouac at 5,800 meters, where a snow ridge butts into the steeper face, at 3 p.m. the next day. Here we decided to stop for a day, dry out, and try to make our packs even lighter. We counted out a daily supply of food, ate the extra, and dropped one gas canister, the extra mittens, Sergey's wet pants, and some other trifles. In all we were down two kilograms.

Over the coming days, we continued directly up, either right on the ridge or on the face to its right. We worked in turns: One day I was the leader, the other day Sergey led. Much of the time we were simul-climbing, if there were no traverses. But there were a lot of them. Compared with the previous year, the route had melted out a lot, but our line was relatively safe from rockfall and avalanches. There were two scary falls on vertical snow, first by me and then Sergey. Everything turned out OK, but Sergey lost his GoPro camera with the footage we had managed to shoot.

On July 19 we reached the huge snowy "flatiron" at 6,800 meters. I hadn't climbed any higher than this—we did not know what would come next. We had tried to study this section through the binoculars during acclimatization, and it didn't look too bad. It seemed we might summit within a day. But there was a nasty turn in the weather in the evening, and the wall above was no longer visible.

For three nights we were stuck on the "flatiron" because of the bad weather. Sometimes the fog cleared, but not long enough to study the line ahead. Finally, it cleared up in the evening and we managed to see what was ahead of us, although part of the wall was concealed by a serac. We ate only one freeze-dried dinner over two days, leaving us with only one breakfast packet as a full meal.

On July 22 we reached the top of the snowy "flatiron" and saw there was no simple way through the wall above. We climbed two pitches (one of which required aid climbing), fixed our ropes, and descended for the night.

The next morning we decided to leave all the bivouac equipment, try to reach the summit, and return. It was a bad idea, in my opinion. But it was Sergey's turn to lead, and he convinced me that he could do it. We ate the last pack of food and started our summit push.

The rocks were technically hard and the weather started getting worse, so our progress was slow. The last position I registered on our satellite tracker was at 6,980 meters, at 2:40 p.m., approximately 70 meters below the top of the north ridge. After that the tracker turned off by itself because its battery was low.

By 4 p.m. I began to realize that we might not make it to the summit on time and that we needed to descend. The weather was getting worse and worse. But we really wanted to reach the top, so we delayed our turnaround. At 7 p.m., Sergey climbed up to a tiny col between a snow-covered rock buttress and a serac. I was standing ten meters below him. The snow was almost vertical. I started shooting video, commenting for the camera that we had climbed up "somewhere."

"What do you mean 'somewhere'"? It's Latok I, Sanya," Sergey shouted.

"Bring me up!" I shouted to him.

"It's unrealistic, Sanya. It's nothing but ice mushrooms and debris," he answered and started to descend.

In such terrain, and not able to see anything higher around, we declared this to be the top, got everything on camera, and started down together. I am not too good at navigation at night-time, but Sergey assured me he would find the way. And he did. We descended straight to our tent late at night.

I do not remember what happened the next day. I remember that the weather was good when we woke up and we spent half the day at our high camp. I think we may have descended a bit before bivouacking again on the night of July 24. I remember sharing my doubts with Sergey as to whether he'd actually been on the summit. I am still in doubt today. Perhaps some-one would bend the facts and say that he had been there, but not me. I don't remember the pre-summit ridge; we did not stand together and hug one another as I had dreamed. I think that it was the top of the north ridge or the western "top" of Latok I. Today I can see on Google Earth that the main summit was only about 360 meters away and a little higher, but we could not see this in the fog.

Looking up at the difficult climbing above the "flatiron" bivouac at 6,800 meters. *Alexander Gukov*

Sergey and I decided that we would not lie. He believed it was the summit, I believed it was not. If we had taken the tent with us and bivouacked near our high point on the mush-rooms, we might have found out for sure the next day. But we did not take the tent.

On July 25 we began to descend again. We saw a helicopter and thought that it was aiding the other Russian team, as we knew they had been injured by rockfall during their attempt. As we found out later, those guys were okay and the helicopter was search-ing for us, with Victor Koval from the other Russian team on board as a spotter. They saw us and threw off some food and a gas can. How Sergey caught it, I have no idea. There

[Top] Rescue helicopter approaching the perch at nearly 6,300 meters where Gukov (in red) was stranded for six days. *Maj. Fakhar-e-Abbas* [Left] Sergey Glazunov relaxing on the north ridge. *Alexander Gukov*

wasn't much, though.

After that we rappelled a few more times, Sergey going first and making anchors with an ice screw and Abalakov threads. So far, there had been enough ice for Abalakov anchors using 6mm cord. I would rappel to him, back up the V-thread with the screw, give him all the extra equipment, and pull the ropes.

On our last rappel, one rope was fixed to the Abalakov cord, and the second one was backing up Sergey with the ice screw. He used a Grigri to rappel the single strand. Below was a snow and ice slope, which ended with a rock face. Sergey rappelled over the rock and that was the last I saw of him.

The backup rope fixed to the screw went tight, and I yelled down to Sergey that he was at the end of the rope. One rope seemed to be unweighted and free, the other one didn't. I shouted to Sergey several times, but there was no answer.

I rearranged the ropes to rappel on both strands, left the ice screw combined with the cord just in case, and started down. When I reached the edge I saw that Sergey was gone.

There was one poorly hammered, beak-style piton, and the ends of both ropes were secured to it. Nothing else. I hammered this piton as hard as possible, but I was not confident it was enough.

Now what? I was alone at somewhere around 6,300 meters, still about 1,700 meters above the glacier.

The rock where I found myself ended about five meters below, and then there was another snow slope, continuing a long way down. I couldn't see Sergey anywhere. He probably had fallen over the next rock wall. Later, looking at the photos and the estimated scene of the accident, I could see that Sergey likely fell over a huge wall below. But I did not know it at that time.

Sergey had fallen with almost all of our gear. I had the bad piton at this anchor and one short ice screw at the anchor above. I thought, *You can ascend the rope to get the screw.* But would the 6mm cord rub through and break as I ascended? Had I used the ropes or the cord to connect the V-thread to the screw? *I think it was with the cord. Fuck.* And even if I could retrieve the screw, what would it give me? I still wouldn't have nearly enough material to rappel 1,700 meters.

OK, keep thinking. The satellite tracker's battery was down to two percent, but maybe the SOS button would still work? I took it out, pressed the button to trigger the SOS, and sent a message that I was stranded and needed help.

Soon, my friend Anna Piunova in Moscow sent a message that a helicopter had taken off, and Julia Krisanova, my wife, advised me to find a ledge nearby where I could wait. *Yes, I thought, hanging here is really not an option.*

There were a couple of rocks on the snow slope a little lower, and I thought I could arrange a place there to wait for a helicopter. I had a piece of cord that was tied to the food bag they had thrown to us. It gave me just enough of a tether to get to those rocks. I hung the tent from the cord like a sack and got inside. And I began to wait. My satellite communicator stopped working completely in three days. The weather was awful throughout. I was constantly digging out from avalanches. It calmed me down to think that if there was a big avalanche it would fly over me, and that tomorrow the weather would be fine and the helicopters would reach me. But the helicopters were only able to get up in the air and rescue me after six days. But you already know that.

To be honest, it does not matter to me whether we climbed to the summit of Latok. I am sure that we climbed the north ridge to its top. It was a good climb. We took turns leading and worked well together, even though this was our first climb together. You were a good person, Sergey! I'm very sorry that it all happened on the descent, when most of the work had already been done. Please forgive me if I did something wrong.

Summary: Ascent of the north ridge of Latok I (7,145m) in the Panmah Muztagh of the Karakoram, reaching the top of the ridge at approximately 7,050 meters, by Alexander Gukov and Sergey Glazunov, July 13–23, 2018. During the descent, Glazunov fell to his death. Gukov was rescued six days later.

This account is adapted from a story originally published at Mountain.ru and translated by Maria Samsonova and Dmitry Zagorovskiy, with additional assistance from Emily Laskin. In early 2019, Anna Piunova, editor of Mountain.ru, published a multi-part account of Gukov's rescue, available in English at that website.

About the Author: *Born in 1976, Alexander Gukov lives in St. Petersburg, Russia, and works as chief mate aboard oceangoing ships. He recovered from his ordeal and married his partner, Julia Krisanova, soon after returning home from Pakistan.*

Luka Stražar pauses during the ascent. The high peak in back left is Bobisghir (6,414m). *Tom Livingstone*

LATOK I: THE SECOND ASCENT

A CLEVER WORKAROUND YIELDS THE FIRST SUMMIT ROUTE FROM THE CHOKTOI GLACIER

TOM LIVINGSTONE

Slovenian alpinists have a strong reputation. Straight-talking, quiet, and solid climbers, they regularly climb hard alpine routes without any fuss. When Luka Stražar attended a BMC International Winter Meet in Scotland a few years ago, I shared a couple of beers and belays with him. We never tied in together, but we crossed paths in Europe and Alaska over the following years, and in early 2018 he approached me with the idea of a trip to Pakistan. Along with Aleš Česen, we'd travel to the Choktoi Glacier in the Karakoram, with the infamous Latok I (7,145m) in mind. I met the two of them in Slovenia in February for some bitterly cold days of climbing on the dark walls of the Julian Alps, and there they set the hook: "We think there is a better way than the full north ridge," Aleš said.

Latok's most famous feature, the north ridge, runs nearly straight from the glacier to the summit, about 2,500 meters higher. Its reputation was cemented in 1978, when four Americans spent 26 days on the ridge, climbing higher and higher, battling storms, only to retreat a few hundred meters below the summit. In the following 40 years, dozens of teams had tried to better their impressive effort, but without success. A Japanese team summited the mountain from the south in 1979, but their route remains unrepeated. In fact, Latok I hadn't been climbed by any route in nearly 40 years.

Just one year earlier, in 2017, a team of three Russian climbers had a 15-day epic on Latok's north ridge, enduring several storms and poor conditions. They reached the highest point on the ridge since 1978. Afterward, two of the climbers had digits amputated due to frostbite. I knew my Slovenian friends were tough, but thankfully we all agreed we didn't want to risk any epics.

I joined them en route to Pakistan in July. After four days of walking through the barren, dusty Karakoram mountains, we finally rounded a corner of the glacier and glimpsed the biggest mountain objectives I'd ever seen. "Oh shit, this is the real deal!" I exclaimed. Luka and Aleš have climbed many times in the Greater Ranges, but this was my first time in the Karakoram, where routes were measured in days, not pitches. I could stack two of the mountains I'd previously climbed into one of these—it was two Grandes Jorasses or two Cerro Fitz Roys. The impressive mountains around our base camp—the Latok group and Ogre I and II—needed little introduction.

In mid-July, just as we arrived in base camp, two Russian teams started separate attempts on the north face and north ridge. We wished them luck but tried not to think about them as we acclimatized on a nearby peak. We didn't want to be pressured into starting before we were fully prepared. One team bailed in the face of severe rockfall, but two other climbers, Alexander Gukov, a veteran of the 2017 attempt, and Sergey Glazunov, continued for 10 days, battling storms and deep snow up to around 7,000 meters. We tried to watch from base camp as they made several attempts from their high camp. Once they began to retreat, Sergey fell to his death in a rappelling accident, leaving Alexander stranded at nearly 6,300 meters, with no means to descend. Impressively, Alexander survived a six-day storm before he was rescued by a Pakistani helicopter on his 19th day on the mountain.

Aleš summed up our feelings: "You wouldn't be human if you didn't feel something about this accident." But, after a brief discussion, we confirmed our intentions. We were still motivated to attempt Latok, but via a different style and route to the Russians. "Let's keep an open mind," I said. "We can start climbing without too much commitment." We all agreed and anxiously watched the weather forecast. A stable window looked to be arriving in a couple of days.

On August 5 we left base camp at 1 a.m., the bright stars creating a patchwork of light above. The north side of Latok stood in total darkness, tall and ominous. As we soloed over the bergschrund, I was absorbed by the white circle of light from my headlamp, my pack pulling against my shoulders. We carried a small tent and a snow hammock for bivouacs, a double sleeping bag and one single bag for the team, and food and fuel for about seven days. Our rack felt small for such a huge face: eight screws, a set of cams, a few pins, and six wires.

The author feeling the altitude at around 6,400 meters, headed toward the west col. *Ales Česen*

We started to the right of the true north ridge and stayed on that side for most of the climb. I swung and kicked into chewy, soft ice, trying to be as efficient as possible, trying to ignore the enormous amount of climbing towering above my head. We stopped to bivy in midmorning, finding a small flat section in a notch on the ridge, about 800 meters up, safe from rockfall as the sun moved onto the face.

The alarm chimed merrily at around 3 a.m. on the second day, and we collectively started the motions of getting ready. The stove burst into life, then porridge, water, pack our bivy. I led us up and right, over ridges of snow and through deep runnels of ice. We took turns leading simul-climbing blocks for a hundred meters or more, then quickly pitching harder steps. Warily, we weaved and ducked under cornices and snow mushrooms along one section of the ridge. In late afternoon we found a poor bivy on a snow mushroom at around 6,000 meters, barely big enough for the three of us to lie down.

The third day took us higher up the north ridge, threading couloirs of ice. At each corner or bulge, I peered round in anticipation of a dead-end. *Where would this path lead?* Luck remained with us, and we flowed through sections of white névé and concrete, pick-blunting ice. At about 6,300 meters, we saw snow slopes leading out right toward our goal, the west col, between Latok I and II. From there we planned to continue up the south side of the peak to reach the summit. [*Josh Wharton (U.S.), who traveled to the Choktoi Glacier four times to attempt Latok I, had envisioned the west col crossover and hoped to attempt it in 2012; however he was unable to make an attempt that summer and eventually joined Kyle Dempster and Hayden Kennedy for a new route up the Ogre.*] We started moving away from the north ridge, and at 1 p.m. we chopped a spacious bivy beneath a small serac, halfway between the ridge and the col.

We crested the western col, at over 6,700 meters, around noon on August 7. I slumped headfirst into the snow, gasping for breath; it felt like I had a plastic bag over my head. We all had studied countless photos of the north side of Latok I, but the far side of the col was much less known; sections of the upper mountain were hidden in the few photos we'd found. Fortunately, there were no nasty surprises. Aleš led as we sidestepped across easy-angled snow until we all began to bonk, hanging from the single ice screw belays and breathing heavily. Now only 300 meters below the summit, we were so close but felt emptied of energy. A bergschrund gave us enough flat ground to pitch the tent, and we collapsed inside.

As the fifth day began to brighten, I turned to Luka. "I haven't slept," he said, wide eyes staring at the ceiling. Heavy spindrift and gusts had rocked our single-skin tent all night, and we constantly hit the walls to shed the new snow. By morning, about eight inches had fallen. Luka had nearly been trapped on Phola Gangchen in Tibet a few years earlier, and was worried we'd have a repeat experience. All thoughts of the summit had gone, and we simply debated, between heavy breaths, how we might get down safely in the storm.

Livingstone digging out on the fifth morning of the climb. "All thoughts of the summit had gone." *Aleš Česen*

By midmorning, however, the clouds had thinned and the summit looked to be within reach again. In silence, Luka began re-racking and then started kicking steps away from the tent, ignoring the heavy spindrift avalanches that tumbled down snow grooves on either side of him. Aleš and I followed on the other end of the rope, exhausted but determined. Wind-blown snow and clouds crashed over the summit. It looked like a stormy day in the Scottish Highlands, I thought grimly, except we were above 7000 meters in the Karakoram.

When I took my turn on the summit cornice, I couldn't see the view because of the racing clouds. But

the satisfaction of being here was all I needed, and the relief was absolute. Up until a few hours earlier, I still hadn't dared to believe we could climb this mountain—the biggest route I'd ever tried. I knew this point only marked halfway, and that arriving safely back in base camp was our true goal. But right then, on the summit, I was totally content.

After another uncomfortable night in our high camp, our fifth on the mountain, we reversed our route back to the west col and then angled back down toward the north ridge. Only with the safety of colder temperatures at night did we then plunge down into the darkness, abseiling again and again from V-threads in the ice. I weighted each anchor with caution, watching it carefully, before sliding down the ropes, over and over and over again. Eventually, the sky began to brighten and we reached our first bivy site at the notch of the north ridge.

[Top] Traversing the upper south side of Latok I, with Latok II behind. [Bottom] Česen and Stražar reaching the summit in blowing snow. *Tom Livingstone (both)*

We slumped on the bivy platform, facing the imminent sunrise, waiting for warmth and light and relief. Aleš fell straight to sleep, but Luka and I lay awake despite our exhaustion and laughed as our brains exaggerated the shapes and colors, the snow looking brighter and faces appearing in the lichenous patterns in the granite. Finally the morning sun burst over the horizon, flooding us with heat. I felt the sunlight prickle my cheeks, and I wriggled my cold toes. We slipped into a deep, satisfied sleep for a few hours, dreaming of base camp and of home.

SUMMARY: New route and second ascent of Latok I (7,145m), by Ales Česen and Luka Stražar (Slovenia) and Tom Livingstone (U.K.), August 5–12, 2018. The climbers started from the Choktoi Glacier on the north side of the mountain, generally followed the right side of the north ridge to around 6,400m, then traversed to the west col (ca 6,700m), between Latok I and II, followed by a traverse up the southern slopes to the summit (2,500m, ED+). They descended approximately the same line. Livingstone and Stražar discussed this climb in depth in episode 11 of the *AAJ's* Cutting Edge podcast.

ABOUT THE AUTHOR: *Born in southern England in 1990, Tom Livingstone now lives in North Wales and enjoys climbing in all its forms.*

HEART OF THE MOUNTAIN

A SUMMER OF SEARCHING ON ALASKA'S JUNEAU ICEFIELD

BRETTE HARRINGTON

In mid-March I glided my skis across a snow-covered glacier of the Juneau Icefield. A short distance away, near base camp, four of my closest friends were scattered on rocky outcroppings, watching the sun set over the Mendenhall Towers. The seven summits of the towers cast dark shadows down their cold north faces where snowshed had accumulated at the base. It was here that just a few days earlier the mountain had released its snow, tragically taking my boyfriend Marc-André Leclerc and climber Ryan Johnson with it. (*See pages 165 and 354–357.*)

View to the southwest over the vast Juneau Icefield from the summit of Devils Paw. *Brette Harrington*

I looked beyond the towers to where the sun was setting. The great pyramid of Mt. Fairweather was silhouetted on the horizon, one of the last views Marc had seen from the summit of the Main Tower on March 5, 2018. Seeing Fairweather now reminded me of when Marc took me to meet Fips Broda, who recounted the story of the second ascent of this mountain, in 1958, at his home in West Vancouver. Marc would have been thinking of Fips when he looked across at the peak. It was clear to me, now, that Marc had led me to the icecap. This was where I needed to be.

All that spring I eased my grief-stricken mind by dreaming of climbing mountains on the Juneau Icefield. The Devils Paw was the largest and most intriguing. I studied photos online to learn more about the mountain—it looked steep and wild. Of the Devils Paw's four summits, the two northernmost looked to have the greatest vertical relief, so this is where I focused my search. The northern summit had been climbed by Roger Schäli and Simon Gietl in 2015 by the northwest ridge. The second and highest summit had been reached from the east in 1949 by Andrew Griscom, David Michael, and William L. Putnam, via complex glaciers and icefalls. An old aerial photograph from a northwestern vantage showed a massive jagged fin splitting the west face, as well as hidden gully systems. I became fixated on finding a route up the unclimbed 1,000-meter west face.

My motivation to return to the Juneau Icefield was enmeshed with the hope of making a recovery of Marc and Ryan's bodies. I knew this was like chasing an illusion. They were already gone, and finding their lifeless bodies wouldn't change that. But my heart searched desperately for Marc. At night I had recurring dreams that they would come back from the mountain, safe but exhausted after a long adventure. During my waking life I knew this was not possible.

Either way, I felt I needed to stay in the area to see how the sequence of events would unfold, to see how conditions would change over the season, and to formally acquaint myself with the

Caro North and Brette Harrington ski-toured 20 miles across the icefield in early June to reach Devils Paw, where they skied a steep couloir and assessed rock quality for a later climb. *Brette Harrington*

icefield. Not only this, but also I needed to reflect on my life with Marc-André. Together our lives had revolved around mountains, and we had many plans. In October 2017, Marc had kite-skied out onto the Patagonian icecap to climb the Cordón Mariano Moreno—a one-day, 58-kilometer round trip from his camp at the edge of the icefield. He and I had been preparing for a similar trip together to explore the mountains and icecaps of northern British Columbia. Though Marc could no longer fulfill this dream, I felt he was still showing me the way. I collected potential climbing ideas as a skeletal plan, but I allowed inspiration to lead me.

On June 1, I flew onto the Juneau Icefield with my friend and climbing partner Caro North. She and I spent two weeks climbing and skiing various peaks, first climbing a new route on South Duke Tower, then ski-touring 20 miles across glaciers to Devils Paw. (The lack of wind made us resort to traditional ski touring instead of using kite power.) We climbed and skied the southeast couloir, and I checked out the quality of the rock and condition of Devils Paw for a later date. Despite icy layers of frost, I saw spidering cracks that shattered the rock surface and would make for protectable climbing. The mountain seemed compact and relatively sturdy, in contrast to the crumbling reputation I'd gathered from previous reports.

When Caro left in mid-June, I teamed up with Gabe Hayden, a friend and climbing partner of Ryan Johnson. In two trips we made three first ascents on the Taku Towers and the south side of the Fourth Mendenhall Tower. [*See sidebar on page 48 and map on page 53.*]

I left Alaska in mid-July to attend to a few obligations but was set on returning as soon as possible. The month of August was warm and wet in Juneau, so I stayed in British Columbia to rock climb and wait for the skies to clear over the icecap. As September approached I simply could not wait any longer. I booked a flight back to Alaska, knowing that I might end up spending the month under a rain cloud.

Upon my arrival in Juneau, the first part of September showed nine full days of sunshine in the forecast. This was unheard of for late summer. All the climbers were making plans to head into the mountains, but my mind was occupied. The extended search to recover Marc and Ryan had ended. There was no more path to follow, it simply ended. It was then that I realized perhaps they were not meant to be found. Perhaps they should return to the earth, as I feel Marc would have wanted. Even so, the air felt heavy. I believe everyone who had been involved in the search, and both the families of Marc and Ryan, felt it too. But I remembered Marc telling me the previous October that if anything were to happen to him, he wanted me to be strong and independent, to keep going

Harrington below Devils Paw in September. *Gabe Hayden*

and keep climbing. This weather window was an opportune moment to celebrate Marc by attempting my biggest project, the Devils Paw.

Gabe and I hired a helicopter to fly up to the icefield once more. As we traced the vast Taku Glacier, my mind was drawn away from the anguish I'd felt from the search and into the present moment. We were attempting to climb a massive mountain, and it required our full attention. Dustin, our pilot, dropped us off in the cirque between Devils Paw and Michaels Sword. The dark granite walls encircled us like a fortress. The west face of the Paw looked icy and uninviting—a fresh layer of frost coated the rock and a biting wind blew. Gabe and I packed our bags to spend one night on the route. When the sun hit the face around noon we started up. I pressed my feet firmly on the rock and heaved my weight over them. The backpack was dragging me down, making 5.8 moves feel more like weight lifting than climbing. I stopped after 60 meters to belay Gabe. We decided to bail, return to camp, and prepare for a single-push mission the following day.

The alarm woke us at 4:30 a.m. Two hours later, we started up the mountain. Despite having removed the bivy gear and stove, our packs still felt heavy. We carried two 60-meter ropes, crampons, ice tools, climbing rack (including a bunch of pitons), food, water, jackets, and rappel cord. We simul-climbed the first 200 meters of 5.8 terrain, then the mountain steepened into 5.10, and we began belaying and hauling up the bags. The first crux was finding protection on a vertical face. The rock was so blank we even contemplated the time-consuming task of hand-drilling a bolt. But soon Gabe found an incut flake, behind which he hammered in a knifeblade piton. He committed to the moves over run-out terrain at around 5.11a. I followed carefully behind.

By noon we had pulled over the lip of the lower headwall and entered the gigantic heart-shaped bowl in the center of the west face. Like a hollow that once held a less resilient rock, it is here I imagined would be the heart of the mountain. The angle eased into 4th-class terrain, so we stashed the ropes in our packs and scrambled another hundred or so meters. The upper mountain consisted of three steep tiers of cliff bands. The rock here was more compact, which meant

Ice Pilgrimage: Inside the Juneau Icefield Research Project — see page 52.

FIVE NEW ROUTES

FIRST ASCENTS IN THE DUKES, TAKU TOWER, AND MENDENHALL TOWERS

BRETTE HARRINGTON MADE two trips to the Juneau Icefield in June 2018, first with Caro North and then Gabe Hayden. The following is a summary of their new routes and some climbing history on each formation.

SOUTH DUKE, NORTHEAST FACE. Harrington and North climbed the first route up this face on June 2 (500m, 5.10b M5+ 85°; see photo at left). Mixed terrain with difficult protection and loose blocks gained a steep snow couloir angling left to a headwall with two rock pitches (5.10b).

This formation was first climbed, presumably via the easier southeast side, in a solo ascent in 1965 by Edward Jack Miller. In 2014, John Kelley and Kris Williams climbed Bo Duke-It (1,300', IV WI5 M6+) on the west face of the north summit. Kelley soloed a new route (5.9 WI3) on the south face in 2017. Kelley also climbed North Duke twice in 2014 (possibly the first ascent of the formation), by the north ridge and the south ridge.

NORTH TAKU TOWER, SOUTH FACE. Harrington and North climbed a five-pitch route (5.10+) on the left side of this face (route 1 in the photo) in early June. Harrington returned with Hayden and did two longer routes up buttresses farther right: Solarsphere (route 2, 360m, 5.12a) and Sweet & Spicy (route 3, 360m, 5.11c).

This formation was first climbed in 1949 (Forbes-Merritt-Schoeblen) by the west ridge (1,200', 5.5), the ridgeline above these climbs. Earlier ascents on the south face of the west ridge of North Taku include Dancing Bear (6 pitches, 6b) by Christoph Hainz and Roger Schäli, climbed in 2008, and attempts by an American pair on two routes in 2014, one going up the major break between the Harrington-North and Solarsphere and one farther left. In 2000, Stefan Ricci and Michael Wolf climbed the Magic Line (IV 5.9 A1) up the south face.

FOURTH TOWER, MENDENHALL TOWERS, SOUTH FACE. Harrington and Hayden climbed a new route on the right side of the southern prow, starting with slabs to reach a prominent corner system and finishing with 150m of steep crack climbing (5.11b). The first ascent of the Fourth Tower was in 1972 (Benedict-Greenough-Greenough-McKibbon) by a winding route on the south face. In 2009, Blake Herrington and Jason Nelson climbed the south-facing prow leading directly to the summit: Resignation Arête (12 pitches, 5.11+).

Harrington starting up the west face of Devils Paw. A reconnaissance had revealed that, "The mountain seemed compact and relatively sturdy, in contrast to the crumbling reputation I'd gathered from previous reports." *Gabe Hayden*

less protection. I pulled over small protrusions and rooflets, placing wires and cams wherever I could find them. We alternated between simul-climbing on terraces and pitching out the steeper sections. Finally we had made it through the third and final tier. Once again we put away the ropes and soloed the final 150 meters of 5.8 to the top.

A frosted white snowfield led us to the summit, revealing our first views of British Columbia. Deep, dark valleys were filled with color: The green of trees and the browns of soil contrasted beautifully with the bright white of the icefield behind us. Looking back toward Juneau, all was white, but the sun was low in the sky, painting the snow with bands of warmth. In all of my travels and years of climbing, I have not stood on a more magnificent and peaceful summit. Not a gust of wind disturbed the air.

We traversed the summit snowfield and set up our first rappel by digging out a small boulder to sling with a cord. I watched the cordelette attentively as Gabe weighted the anchor, making sure it did not roll off the boulder. The cord held, and I followed Gabe down, but the low-angle rappel caused our ropes to catch when we pulled them, so I carefully climbed up the snow-covered slabs to free them, then downclimbed back to Gabe. Our second rappel was a full and free-hanging 60 meters into a rime-covered gully. I descended slowly in space, absorbing everything around me. The sunset cast an orange and purple glow across the evening sky.

[Above] **The line of Shaa Téix'i (ca 1,000m, 5.11a), the first route up the west face of Devils Paw's main summit. Although it appears taller from this angle, the northwest (left) top is lower.** *Brette Harrington* [Right] Rappelling into the sunset. *Gabe Hayden*

As the black of night wrapped itself over the land and a scape of stars painted the sky, far in the distance I spotted a tiny yellow glow from the lights of a cruise ship. It looked beautiful, sailing away into the night. I was for a moment distracted by the warmth of the lights of town sparkling across the Taku Inlet, reminding me of the comforts of modern society.

Soon, I thought, *the storms will return to the icefield, blanketing the glaciers under deep and intolerable cold. And yet, even the lifelessness of this place is mortal—ever-diminishing under the onslaught of climate change and the shortening of winter. How much time will pass before all of the ice melts away? Perhaps someday this land of ice will be replaced by a green valley, spark a settlement, and foster life.*

I looked down to a land submerged in darkness. Marc's pitons rattled on my harness, and I selected each one decisively. I recalled the many lessons I had taken from Marc during all of the years we had climbed together: hammering bird beaks into incipient seams high on Great Sail Peak in Baffin Island, or the horizontal cracks that held our angle pitons on the Chinese Puzzle Wall in British Columbia. I imagined he was with me, overseeing the descent, and I knew he would be proud.

Around 3 a.m., the light of my headlamp became noticeably dimmer. I strained my eyes in search of piton placements in the compact rock. On a small, sloping ledge, Gabe and I decided to curl up for a moment to relax and recharge our minds. After about half an hour, the chill of the night set in and I knew it was time to start moving again.

Rejuvenated, I felt fully absorbed in the task at hand: taking our time, building trusty anchors from pitons, nuts, and slings, pulling our ropes carefully. We made more than 20 rappels. Eventually, I lost track of the number. We arrived back at the base of the mountain at 9:30 a.m., 27 hours after our climb had started.

Gabe and I staggered back to the tent and fell asleep. To our dismay, a heavy rainstorm blew in unexpectedly and engulfed us in a dense cloud of water. We spent hours wiping the walls of the tent. The following day, strong winds blew the rain clouds out, but we worried that our frail single-wall tent might fail. It was as though the mountain had enticed us with the prospect of a nine-day weather window, and then, as soon as we completed our ascent, the weather returned to its natural pattern of fury and chaos. This climb was a gift from the mountain.

SUMMARY: First ascent of the west face of Devils Paw (ca 2,600m) by Brette Harrington and Gabe Hayden, September 5–6, 2018. The route is called Shaa Téix'i ("Heart of the Mountain" in the Tlingit language, ca 1,000m, 5.11a). This was likely the second ascent of the main summit.

ABOUT THE AUTHOR: *Brette Harrington, born in 1992, is an alpine climber and rock climber based out of British Columbia. She spoke about this climb in an extensive interview in episode 12 of the Cutting Edge podcast.*

ICE PILGRIMAGE

MORE THAN 70 YEARS OF STUDYING THE JUNEAU ICEFIELD

DREW HIGGINS

When considering the world's great pilgrimages, perhaps you think of Mecca's Hajj, Japan's Kumano Kodō, or Spain's Camino de Santiago. I think of a pilgrimage across ice, of dozens of scientists, staff, and students skiing and slogging 80 miles over plains of sun-warped snow and between the dark peaks of Alaska's Coast Mountains. It's a kind of annual homage to a mysterious ice world we're trying to understand, even as it's shifting beneath us.

The Juneau Icefield Research Program (JIRP), founded in 1946, is one of the oldest glacial monitoring programs in the world, second only to the Swedish research station Tarfala. Every summer, researchers and undergraduate and graduate students spend eight weeks studying the phenomena of these glacial systems, beginning in Juneau in June and traversing north across the icefield into Canada by August. The expedition bunks at permanent sheet-metal camps along the way, while collecting GPS, isotope, radar, mass balance, and other data—measurements that track how these maritime glaciers are functioning and fluxing.

And they are fluxing—in fact, they're shrinking, and by a lot. By some measures, Alaska's glaciers are losing mass faster than any other polar region, contributing significantly to sea level rise (Gardner et al. 2013). Studying glaciers allows us to reconstruct past climatic situations, but also to predict changes that will disrupt human and biological communities. In southeast Alaska, glaciers support the tourism industry, from cruises to dog sledding tours, as well its fisheries, since cold-loving, stream-spawning species like salmon rely on their meltwater and nutrient inputs.

JIRP's long-term data reveal sobering realities of how these glaciers have morphed in mass and elevation over decades. The Lemon Creek Glacier, on the more temperate and maritime-influenced western edge of the icefield above Juneau, retreated by 1,200 meters between 1948 and 2011, or about three-fourths of a mile (M.Pelto et al. 2013). The other glacier for which there is robust historical data, the Taku, is the thickest glacier in Alaska, with a sprawling accumulation

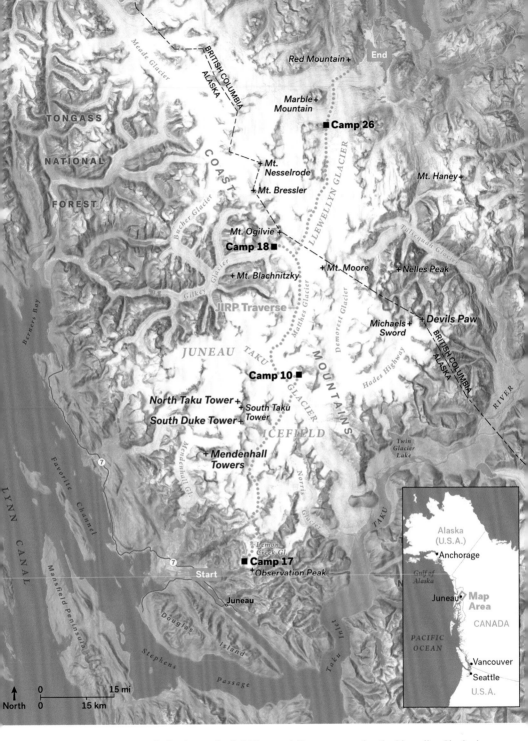

Map labels:
- Meade Glacier
- TONGASS
- NATIONAL
- FOREST
- BRITISH COLUMBIA
- ALASKA
- Red Mountain +
- **End**
- Marble + Mountain
- ■ **Camp 26**
- + Mt. Nesselrode
- Mt. Haney +
- + Mt. Bressler
- LLEWELLYN GLACIER
- Bucher Glacier
- Mt. Ogilvie +
- **Camp 18** ■
- Tulsequah Glacier
- + Mt. Moore
- + Nelles Peak
- + Mt. Blachnitzky
- Gilkey Glacier
- Glacier
- JIRP Traverse
- Matthes Glacier
- Demorest Glacier
- Michaels + Sword
- + Devils Paw
- JUNEAU
- TAKU
- MOUNTAINS
- Hades Highway
- BRITISH COLUMBIA ALASKA
- **Camp 10** ■
- GLACIER
- North Taku Tower +
- + South Taku Tower
- South Duke Tower +
- ICEFIELD
- RIVER
- Twin Glacier Lake
- + Mendenhall Towers
- Berners Bay
- Mendenhall Gl.
- Norris Glacier
- TAKU
- Favorite Channel
- 7
- LYNN
- CANAL
- Mansfield Peninsula
- Lemon Creek Gl.
- 7
- ■ **Camp 17**
- **Start**
- + Observation Peak
- Juneau
- Douglas Island
- Taku Inlet
- Stephens
- Passage

Inset map:
- Alaska (U.S.A.)
- • Anchorage
- Gulf of Alaska
- Juneau • **Map Area**
- CANADA
- PACIFIC OCEAN
- • Vancouver
- • Seattle
- U.S.A.

Scale:
- 0   15 mi
- North   0   15 km

[Photo opposite] Participants in the Juneau Icefield Research Program crossing the Llewellyn Glacier in Canada, the last section of the program's six-week traverse over the icefield. The 80-mile route is shown above in orange. *Andrew Opila* [Map] Peaks and glaciers of the Juneau Icefield; the mountains described in Brette Harrington's article (previous pages) are highlighted in red. The camps are private research facilities, never open to the public. *Marty Schnure | Maps For Good*

[Top] **Camp 10**, one of the permanent bases the program uses throughout the field season, above the Gilkey Trench. Though inviting, these camps are not open to the public. [Bottom left] **Tori Kennedy**, 2018 student researcher, practices ascending out of a crevasse. [Bottom right] **Seth Campbell**, director of academics and research, reviews ground-penetrating radar data with students. *Andrew Opila (all photos)*

zone. JIRP's survey program has focused primarily on the Taku system, which includes several branches, measuring and monitoring its surface velocity and elevation. For most of the 20th century, the Taku was advancing and increased in thickness and therefore mass. But in 1993, it reached its maximum thickness. It has thinned ever year since.

The length of JIRP's records allows researchers to tell complex stories and to ask compelling questions in new arenas. In 2018, researchers established a multi-week tent camp at the Matthes-Llewellyn Glacier divide, a point of low glacial flow ideal for radar imaging and core drilling. With multiple radar systems, they imaged the stratigraphy of the ice, monitored flow, and measured snow densification. They determined the deepest ice was around 900 meters, or over half a mile, thick. With shallow radar and ice cores, they discovered previously unknown liquid aquifers in the ice, which raised a host of questions: How do these aquifers form? Do they happen every year? Are they seasonal or long term? How might they contribute to mass loss?

From its inception until 2010, JIRP was under the tutelage and leadership of Dr. Maynard Miller. A beloved though sometimes polarizing figure, Miller served in the Navy in World War II and as the chief geologist for the first U.S. expedition to Everest, and was an early scholar of human-induced climate change. He began as a field assistant to the pioneer glaciologist William O. Field, who later recounted that JIRP grew out of conversations with Miller wherein the pair contemplated what factors controlled glacial systems. Glaciologists at the time only studied the termini of glaciers. But Miller and Field speculated that the "health of a glacier is found in its upper source region, not at the terminus." Curiosity piqued, their first reconnaissance of Juneau's "high ice" began with aerial surveys in 1946, and the annual traverse launched in 1949.

Despite having serious scientific goals, the program was never solely an academic pursuit. Miller was a passionate educator and always had students with him on the ice, performing field-work as well as learning and playing in the landscape. This legacy continues today, as JIRP in many ways serves as a educational institution, training early-career scientists in field methodology and glaciology before they venture into other regions of the cryosphere such as Greenland and Antarctica. The expedition teaches mountaineering and glacier travel skills to all participating students and scientists—how to navigate the palaces of ice and snow, to travel in the shadows of and on top of mountains.

The program's storied mountaineering history began with Dr. Miller, who accomplished an impressive tick list. While president of the Harvard Mountaineering Club, Miller made the first American ascent of Mt. Saint Elias, in 1946, with William Latady, Dee Molenaar, and William Putnam. It was after that ascent in August that he first explored the Juneau Icefield, funded in part by the American Alpine Club (AAC). Miller's other notable climbing feats included the first ascent of Mt. Bertha in the Fairweather Range in 1940, with Bradford Washburn and Lowell Thomas Jr., and various peaks in the Boundary Ranges, rising above the Juneau Icefield. Miller also chaired the AAC's safety committee and helped launch the annual publication *Accidents in North American Mountaineering* in 1948.

The program has both attracted accomplished adventurers and made them. Geologist and climber Art Gilkey, for which the Gilkey glacier and trench are named, and Ome Daiber of "SnoSeal" fame, were both expedition leaders. In 1971, students and mountaineers Eric Reynolds and Dave Huntley started the "Marmot Club" during a JIRP season (to become a "Marmot," one had to climb a peak with an existing member of the club). That summer, the two made prototypes of down clothing and equipment that would later be the genesis of the Marmot outdoor gear company. Mountaineer and glaciologist Alison Criscitiello, who led the first all-female ascent of Lingsarmo (Pinnacle Peak) in India, was a JIRP student in 2003. Canadian explorer and writer Kate Harris was a student in 2004, and later served on the JIRP board of directors. Groundbreaking avalanche researcher Ed LaChapelle was a JIRP field leader in the 1950s. These are the types of characters who are pulled into the Juneau Icefield's gravitational field time and time again.

Studying and exploring this landscape feel inextricably linked, connected by a love of the place, even as we sit in a place of knowing its doomed fate. As Aldo Leopold wrote, "One of the penalties of an ecological education is that one lives alone in a world of wounds." The 2018 season was characterized by gloriously sunny weather and low snow. But every year feels like it's a low snow year, at least anecdotally. Blue ice appears earlier, our snow pits are shallower, and the snowline creeps up faster. Such changes complicate the traverse, our migration that has followed the same timeline for decades. Last summer, we abandoned our second base camp two weeks earlier than usual because spreading blue ice threatened to trap us in the center of the icefield.

These abrupt shifts dictate the nature of our fieldwork and travel. Journeys off the nunatak—that is, any time we leave rock outcrops to travel on snow and ice—are increasingly precarious. Expedition members now where helmets and harnesses at all times while on glacier. We are frequently roped up in areas we've previously not been. The sketchy conditions remind us all of the dismaying truth that the Juneau Icefield is anticipated to be entirely gone by 2200 (Zeiman et al. 2016). The wasting process will continue for centuries, and these snowfields will transform into fjords of epic proportions. Until then, the pilgrimage continues.

About the Author: *Drew Higgins, 25, is a freelance science writer and environmental educator based in midcoast Maine. The 2018 field season was her second on the ice with JIRP.*

SLOVAK DIRECT

CLIMBING A LEGENDARY ROUTE ON DENALI

ANNE GILBERT CHASE

It was June 1, and Chantel Astorga and I were making our way up the East Fork of the Kahiltna Glacier under clear skies. The expansive south face of Denali emerged as we rounded a corner, and the mighty Slovak Direct, rising nearly 9,000 feet to the highest point in North America, just to the right of the Cassin Ridge, came into view. Just over one year earlier, we had stood in this same spot, ready to attempt the Slovak. After a day and a half of climbing, 4,000 feet up the wall, a huge storm rolled in. We retreated to a safe bivy in a bergschrund at 14,500 feet, still about 3,000 feet above the foot of the face, and waited out the storm for 24 hours, until a small break in the weather allowed us to continue our descent.

Once back on firm ground, Chantel and I sat on our packs, rehydrating and chatting about what we had just experienced. We both felt relieved to have escaped the storm but bummed to have been shut down by weather. We knew we had the ability to climb this route, and the fire inside was burning strong. We made a pact right then to return the following year and finish what we'd started.

Chantel and I met in 2010, when we were both guiding on Denali, but it wasn't until the spring of 2016 that we started making plans to climb together. Chantel was interested in Mt. Foraker's Infinite Spur, and I was interested in the Slovak Direct. After some deliberation, we decided to try the Slovak the following year. This route was first climbed in May 1984 by Blažej Adam, František Korl, and Tono Križo of Slovakia. The team placed 150 rock pitons during their 11-day ascent and descended the South Buttress. The route they created is considered one of the most difficult on Denali (20,310 feet). By 2016, 32 years after the first ascent, only half a dozen more teams had succeeded.

After our first attempt on the Slovak, Chantel and I came back even more mentally and physically prepared. In October 2017, the two of us and my husband, Jason Thompson, had topped out on the previously unclimbed southwest face of Nilkantha (6,596m) in the Garhwal region of India. We named our route Obscured Perception (1,400m, VI WI5 M6 A0 70°). Succeeding on such a big route in the Himalaya gave Chantel and me the needed familiarity and confidence to head back to Alaska together.

We flew onto the Kahiltna on May 13, giving ourselves six weeks on Denali to acclimatize and wait for a good weather window. We had timed our departure just right, as a recent 10-day storm had dropped up to 12 feet of snow in certain areas of the Alaska Range, and we arrived soon after this mega-storm cleared. However, unsettled weather still hung over the range, and it took us longer than expected to make our way to the

[Photo] **Chantel Astorga leads steep mixed on day one of the Slovak Direct.** *Anne Gilbert Chase*

[Above] **The Slovak Direct (Adam-Korl-Križo, 1984) ascends about 2,700 meters, finishing on the Cassin Ridge.** *Andy Houseman* [Opposite page, numbered photos are keyed to locations shown above] **(1) The first steep crux on day one; see photo on previous page. (2) Anne Gilbert Chase leads the difficult rock pitch above the first bivouac, the climbers' high point during their 2017 attempt.** *Chantel Astorga* **(3) The elegant icy corners in the heart of the wall.** *Anne Gilbert Chase* **(4) Starting the third day of the climb, high over the East Fork of the Kahiltna Glacier. The second bivouac was in the small, snowy saddle in front of the rock point just below the climber.** *Anne Gilbert Chase* **(5) Astorga leading the A2 rock pitch at 15,100 feet, the key to the upper slopes of the south face.** *Anne Gilbert Chase* **(6) Heading for the summit (20,310 feet), which the two reached at 6 p.m. on their third day of the climb.** *Anne Gilbert Chase*

14,000-foot camp on the West Buttress of Denali. Knowing that we'd given ourselves plenty of time, we appreciated the slow pace up the mountain, enjoying powder skiing and spending time with friends along the way.

Once we made it to 14,000 feet and established our base camp for the coming weeks, we started the process of acclimatizing by climbing and skiing on the West Buttress and West Rib. I made it to the summit once during this process and also skied multiple days from 17,000 feet. At the end of May, we got word that a high-pressure system was moving over the mountain. We felt acclimatized and strong. We rested two days before skiing down to the base of Ski Hill, where we'd left a cache of gear. The next day, under cold, clear skies, we started the long walk up the East Fork of the Kahiltna, spirits high for the good weather and our chance for redemption.

At 4 a.m. on June 2, we awoke to clear, calm skies and got the final word from Chantel's boyfriend to "Go like Valentino"—a reference to Valentino Rossi, an Italian motorcycle racer. By 6 a.m. we were crossing the bergschrund and moving together, motoring up the first 1,000 feet of low-angle snow climbing. I felt the cold air filling my lungs and sensed the strength in my legs as we climbed toward the first crux—I had anticipated these sensations nearly every day since we'd bailed the year before.

We uncoiled our single rope at the start of a tricky rightward traverse. Depending upon the year and snow level, this featureless slab of granite can be both difficult to climb and to protect. But the hardest stretch, about 80 feet long, was in good shape for us, with supportable snow and ice over the rock, even giving us a few cam placements to protect the follower. Chantel delicately made her way across the traverse and brought me over, and then we simul-climbed the rest of the 700-foot traverse to the base of a granite wall, where the route reared upward. The WI6 ice pitch above is another crux of the first day on this route, with anything from steep water ice to choss and unconsolidated sn'ice. Unfortunately, we had the latter. Chantel left her pack to haul once she'd finished the steep terrain, and she carefully navigated the bad protection, loose rock, and rotten ice to complete the pitch.

This year was different. Racking up below the intimidating pitch, I felt a strong sense of confidence. With a very patient belay from Chantel, I carefully made it through.

I took the lead for a few more difficult mixed pitches, and then 1,000 feet of snow wallowing brought us to the bivy site at 14,500 feet in a bergschrund. We set up our tent and made some water before lying down. We'd been told this would be the only comfortable bivy on the route, and we were happy to have a few hours to rest and relax.

We awoke early the next morning to heavy spindrift falling down the nearly 6,000 feet of slope still above us. Once the sun hit the upper mountain, however, the spindrift subsided. Moderate ice and mixed terrain got us to the steep and intimidating rock pitch that had been our high point the year before. I felt nervous standing at the base. During the previous attempt, the spindrift had been so intense on this pitch that Chantel's lower body was buried with snow as she belayed. I had to put my head down and brace myself from the fire hose of snow. It was pretty disappointing to feel that I wasn't strong enough to lead that pitch, in those conditions, but in the end we made the right decision to turn around.

This year was different. Racking up below the intimidating pitch, I felt a strong sense of confidence. With a very patient belay from Chantel, I carefully made it through and found a good belay a full rope length above. Once Chantel arrived at my stance, we realized that we were off route and needed to be more to the right. Luckily we were able to trend right on the next pitch to gain the correct corner system and not lose any elevation.

Soon we arrived at the base of the impressive dihedral system we had seen in so many pictures, with a massive granite wall on the left and a small climber tackling a steep pitch of perfect water ice in the back of the corner. It was those photos that had first attracted me to the Slovak years before. The sun had left us and the temperature was dropping. I led us up amazing and strenuous water ice for a few rope lengths as Chantel shivered at the belays below. Finally, around four in the morning, we topped out the corner system and chopped a ledge just big enough for us to sit in our shared sleeping bag for a few hours. No sleep was had, but a little rest, water, and a few laughs went a long way.

The warm sun encouraged us out of our bag. Just above was the final rock crux, a steep A2 pitch at 15,100 feet that climbs directly up rock to the right of the 5.9 X "Ramp Pitch" followed by early parties up the Slovak. Chantel has a strong background in El Cap speed climbing, so this moderate aid pitch went quickly and smoothly for her. After one more difficult mixed pitch, we were through the majority of the technical climbing on the route.

Our weather forecast had predicted that we would encounter a strong pulse of weather that day, but until that point the day had been sunny and calm, and we started to think the forecast might be wrong. Unfortunately, as we made our way up moderate mixed terrain, the visibility started to deteriorate, the snow started to come down, and the temperatures dropped well below zero Fahrenheit.

Astorga (left) and Chase back at Kahiltna base camp after their descent from the summit. *Colin Haley*

As the storm reached full throttle, we were in a total whiteout, climbing low-angle terrain right next to the giant active serac band called Big Bertha. We couldn't see Bertha, but we could hear her creaking and cracking, and our hearts beat faster, hoping we were far out of the line of fire. Cold, wet, and exhausted, we fought our way up the final technical pitch sometime around midnight. Although we were psyched, we knew we had to keep going to find any sort of protection from this storm. Under strong winds and blowing snow, we coiled the rope and put our heads down, plodding up knee-deep snow for an hour or so until we found a protected flat spot near the Cassin Ridge around 3 a.m. We quickly set up the tent, tossed our stuff inside, and jumped in. After being on the go for 33 hours, with very little food and water, exhaustion and relief lulled us to sleep.

We awoke a few hours later to the sun hitting our tent. All we had left was 3,500 feet of snow walking to the summit of Denali. With our gear littering our little bivy platform, we brewed water and ate the last of our quality food, savoring this moment of relaxation and calm, the intensity of the previous days slowing letting go.

At 6 p.m. on June 5, Chantel and I stood on the summit of Denali, a place we had both been many times before, but this time feeling the sense of accomplishment and peace we'd earned after making the ninth known ascent of the Slovak Direct and the first female ascent of the route. Filled with new energy, we ran and laughed our way back to 14,000-foot camp in just four hours, reaching our tent there at 10:30 p.m. We each lay in our own sleeping bag on big inflatable pads, talking and giggling like two little girls having a sleepover, until our eyelids grew heavier and we found ourselves overtaken by sleep.

SUMMARY: Ascent of the Slovak Direct on Denali (ca 2,700m, Alaska Grade 6 and approximately WI6 M6+ A2 by the line followed), June 2–5, 2018, by Chantel Astorga and Anne Gilbert Chase (both USA). This was the first female ascent of the route and perhaps the most difficult Alaska Range ascent yet by an all-female team. Chase spoke at length about this climb in an interview for episode nine of the *AAJ's* Cutting Edge podcast.

ABOUT THE AUTHOR: *Anne Gilbert Chase, 34, is a professional alpinist and registered nurse finding balance between a life in the mountains and a life at home in Bozeman, Montana, where she lives with her husband, Jason Thompson, and cat, Nili.*

CHAMONIX STYLE ON THE KAHILTNA

THREE SEASONS OF SPORT-ALPINISM IN THE CENTRAL ALASKA RANGE

COLIN HALEY

In June 2007 my friend Mark Westman and I climbed the southwest face of Denali via the Denali Diamond. It was the fifth ascent of one of the hardest, most technical routes the mountain has to offer. We climbed the entire steep lower wall in one day, made one bivouac on the snow slopes above, and then slogged up the upper Cassin Ridge. To me it seemed obvious immediately afterward that we should have left behind the tent, sleeping pads, double sleeping bag, and extra food that the bivouac required—and that without that extra weight we could have simply climbed the route in one long day. It would have been somewhat more physically challenging, but I think a lot more fun.

That ascent of the Denali Diamond was the last time I've bivouacked on a climbing route in Alaska, but since then I've climbed the south side of Denali twice, the south side of Sultana (Mt. Foraker) three times, and the north side of Begguya (Mt. Hunter) twice. In the 1970s these faces were hard enough that to simply get up them in traditional alpine style was at the cutting edge, but modern equipment and techniques have dramatically reduced the difficulty of ascending steep alpine terrain. Following trends that began in the Alps decades ago, I have been playing different games on these big Alaskan routes, climbing them alone, for speed, or both. I call this style of climbing sport-alpinism.

Sport-alpinism is essentially the art of creatively inventing new challenges when the most natural challenge—simply ascending the face of a mountain—is no longer difficult enough to truly inspire a climber or demand all of his or her skill. Climbing solo, climbing fast, traversing multiple peaks, enchaining multiple routes, climbing everything free, avoiding the use of ascenders, or climbing in winter are all dimensions of sport-alpinism. These invented challenges are neither the new future of alpinism to which we should all aspire, nor is sport-alpinism an abomination of traditional ethics that is eroding the purity of the alpine experience. It is simply an evolution, especially in mountain ranges that already have seen a lot of traffic, where the majority of the most natural and compelling lines already have been climbed.

The actual definition of "traditional alpinism" is fairly nebulous, but perhaps the most central element is climbing virgin terrain, as opposed to repeating earlier climbs. To the most traditional of alpinists, first ascents seem to be the only climbs of significance. However, sport-alpinism has been practiced for decades and by many of the most elite alpinists, creating some of the most memorable ascents of each era. In 1952, Hermann Buhl bicycled from his home in Austria to the north face of

Ready, set, go! Colin Haley at the bergschrund on the Japanese Couloir start to the Cassin Ridge, psyched to start charging toward the summit of Denali. *Colin Haley*

Piz Badile in Switzerland and soloed the Cassin Route on the northeast face in under five hours. Reinhold Messner, one of the most vocal proponents for adventurous alpinism, was also an elite practitioner of sport-alpinism, with many incredible repeats of previously climbed faces: the north face of Les Droites solo in 8.5 hours (1969), the north face of the Eiger in 10 hours with Peter Habeler (1974), and the south col route on Chomolongma without oxygen with Peter Habeler (1978).

More recently, some types of climbing have been distilled into activities that involve much less adventure but a much higher level of athleticism. Indoor competition climbing is at the farthest end of the spectrum, demanding an extremely high level of athleticism but with essentially zero adventure. However, not all sport-centric versions of climbing are based on finger strength; the type of alpine climbing practiced by Kilian Jornet—mind-blowingly fast ascents of mostly well-traveled routes—also involves relatively little adventure but an incredible level of athleticism. (Of course, ascents that involve a high level of adventure *and* athleticism are extremely impressive, but I think it is important to recognize there is an inherent trade-off between adventure and athletic achievement. A climber at 6,700 meters with a rack of traditional protection and haul rope hanging from the harness, climbing 10 meters above the last piece of protection, will never climb moves even remotely as difficult as the climber on a boulder problem 6,700 meters lower, with ten pads below. Likewise, speed records on mountains like Chomolongma would not be nearly as fast if not for fixed ropes and other climbers' tracks in the snow.)

Although sport-alpinism is far from new, I think it's time more climbers recognized its existence, its differences from traditional alpinism, and its inevitable future application in more and more mountain ranges around the world. It's also time to acknowledge that, just as most rock climbers have now accepted that both traditional rock climbing and sport climbing have their place and can happily coexist, sport-alpinism is neither better nor worse than traditional alpinism, simply different.

GROWING UP IN Seattle, the central Alaska Range was the semi-local version of Himalayan-scale climbing that my mentors often talked about. By the time I made my first trip to the Kahiltna Glacier, in 2003, nearly all the biggest faces had been climbed, and had been climbed by multiple routes. During a total of 10 trips to the Kahiltna Glacier so far, only one unclimbed line has really called to me: a wall on the southeast face of Sultana that became Dracula (Årtun-Haley, 2010). To me, repeating the three mythic routes on the three steepest faces (north buttress of Begguya, Infinite Spur on Sultana, and Cassin Ridge on Denali) seemed more inspiring than making readily available first ascents of smaller, less serious routes on the lower peaks. The question I eventually asked myself was how to create the most fun, challenging, and exciting experiences on routes that were already described in guidebooks.

Most of my recent trips to the Central Alaska Range in May and June have been preceded by a period of "training" in Chamonix. This mostly just means racking up a lot of mileage climbing and skiing in alpine terrain, day in, day out. The style of alpine climbing I practice in Chamonix is focused on fun: Nearly every day starts and ends in the comfort of town, never carrying heavy backpacks or making bivouacs. I certainly do have fond memories from some incredible bivouacs over the years, but mostly I enjoy fluid movement over mountains, while sleeping/shivering on ledges laboriously chopped from ice is, for me, usually more of a detraction from the experience than a perk. More significantly, I've never been very physically strong, and I enjoy climbing with a small backpack drastically more than with a big, heavy one. Regardless of speed records, I've realized that the most enjoyable, rewarding form of alpinism to me is climbing without bivouacs. My dream is to take the fast, fun, and bivouac-less version of alpinism that I practice in the relatively tame environment of Chamonix and export it to bigger, wilder mountain ranges. To me that is the magic mix of challenge, fun, sport, and adventure. Thus, climbing fast has become a dimension of sport-alpinism that I practice often.

Another dimension of sport alpinism that has captured me is solo climbing. I can't justify this fascination in the name of fun, because usually solo climbing involves less pure fun than climbing with a good friend. But to me there is a great draw to soloing, perhaps in part due to the maniacal purity of having to overcome every obstacle without assistance from anyone else. I enjoy having complete control over my interaction with the mountain and knowing that all successes and all failures are my own, without ever an afterthought of, "I wonder how I would have done leading that block," or "I still think we should have gone up the dihedral to the right."

As my experience and confidence in the Central Alaska Range grew, so did my vision of how to interact with the landscape, without a doubt influenced by the generation before me. When I started climbing in Alaska, sport-alpinism was already gaining momentum, with fast repeats of the Slovak Route on Denali (60 hours, Backes-House-Twight, 2000) and the Infinite Spur on Sultana (25 hours, Garibotti-House, 2001). That trend had begun in 1976 when the visionary Charlie Porter made the first solo of the Cassin Ridge in 36 hours. I started with dreams of simply repeating the Kahiltna's mythic routes in traditional alpine style, like my mentors had done, but slowly realized that what I most wanted to do in the Central Alaska Range was make fast, solo ascents of the "Big Three."

During the past three years I have completed that dream, one climb per season: soloing the Infinite Spur on Sultana in 12:29 bergschrund-to-summit (June 1, 2016), the north buttress of Begguya in 7:46 bergschrund-to-summit (May 12, 2017), and the Cassin Ridge in 8:07 bergschrund-to-summit (June 5, 2018). Each of these ascents was the speed record for the feature—by a large margin—and in the case of the Infinite Spur and the north buttress of Begguya, it was the first solo ascent of the feature. [*Detailed reports of the Sultana and Begguya ascents can be found at the AAJ website (AAJ 2017 and 2018), and more detail on all three climbs is at www.colinhaley.com.*]

The Cassin Ridge is the most famous route among the Big Three and thus the speed record that garnered the most media attention. However, it is without any doubt the least significant of these three ascents. Technically, the Cassin Ridge is by far the easiest among the three, and for that reason the one that had been climbed solo several times previously. Additionally, the descent of Denali is many times easier than of Begguya or Sultana, so the whole outing is much less serious and committing.

When starting up the Cassin Ridge I was amped to try to set an impressively fast time, but I felt none of the trepidation that hard alpine soloing usually entails—I was essentially certain that I would succeed in climbing the route, and even that it would feel pretty easy. My solo was significant because of the fast time in which I accomplished it, but for no other reason. By contrast, the north buttress of Begguya and the Infinite Spur are very serious routes to climb solo, regardless of speed. I would be very proud of those two solo ascents even if each had taken me five days.

In each of these three cases I had previously climbed nearly the entirety of the route during earlier attempts or ascents, so it should not be overlooked that I had a very clear idea of what difficulties awaited me, and thus could prepare my equipment, strategy, and mentality for maximum efficiency. It's clear that in terms of adventure, these ascents would have been greater if I weren't already familiar with the terrain, and greater yet if the same terrain had never been climbed before. However, there is only so much adventure that can be removed from a humongous, technical route in a high-altitude, semi-arctic environment.

In fact, the pursuit of sport-alpinism sometimes creates a much greater level of adventure. Being alone on a nearly 3,000-meter route, without a rope, a partner, communication equipment, or bivouac

Looking down from the Black Band of the Infinite Spur on Sultana (top) and the crux rock band on the north buttress of Begguya. *Colin Haley (both photos)*

Haley heading into a crux passage during his record-setting run up the Cassin Ridge, notably wearing only a daypack, single boots, and no harness. *Nicholas Gantz*

equipment, makes for an extremely committing situation, even if you're already familiar with the route. My descent off Sultana after soloing the Infinite Spur, during which I was hit by a bad storm that arrived earlier than forecast, was the biggest epic of my life. My ascent a few days earlier, with Rob Smith, was much less adventurous, even though we set a new speed record and at the time I wasn't yet familiar with the terrain. The difference in adventure between different climbing tactics, such as climbing solo versus with a partner or climbing nonstop versus with bivouacs, is usually far greater than the difference in adventure between an alpine "onsight" and "redpoint."

REGARDLESS OF HOW one feels about sport-alpinism, I think it is objectively true that athleticism is the only dimension of alpinism in which the current and future generations can improve upon past accomplishments. In the adventure dimension, no one today can outdo what was done a hundred years ago—or even 40 years ago. In fact, I personally would go so far as to say that no climb today is even *equal* in the adventure realm to what was done in the past. Satellite imagery and satellite communication are available essentially everywhere on Earth. Venturing into even the most difficult-to-reach, remote, and unexplored valleys today does not compare to the unknowns faced by people like George Lowe and Voytek Kurtyka, let alone Shackleton and Mallory.

Of course adventure is not dead. There are still thousands of mountain faces on which a small, lightly equipped team can have the adventure of a lifetime climbing virgin terrain. Nonetheless I think it is undeniable that slowly, slowly the adventure aspect of alpinism is diminishing and only in the sport dimension will tomorrow's alpinists go beyond past accomplishments, whether on new routes or established climbs.

This shouldn't make you feel that you were born too late, however. For those with creativity, the mountains will always provide all the mind-blowing, ego-destroying experiences that anyone desires, no matter how few unclimbed mountains and faces are left. With the equipment and knowledge that modern alpinists enjoy, pushing the limits of the sport dimension is ever more appealing. Sixty years ago, the leading alpinists began to realize that expedition-style climbing provided too certain an outcome of success. Now that most alpine climbing equipment is half the weight that it was in the 1960s and 1970s, and far more functional, will climbers begin to decide that on many mountains the classic alpine-style formula (two climbers, two ropes, one rack, one tent, several days of food and fuel) also provides too much certainty of a successful outcome?

For a few decades already, the most inspiring and impressive climbing accomplishments in the Alps have not been the routes that were climbed, but instead the creative *ways* in which they were climbed, whether solo, fast, in winter, all free, or part of an enormous enchainment. Likewise, during the past decade the most impressive climbing in Yosemite Valley and the Bugaboos has been in the sport dimension (first free ascents, speed ascents), rather than the conquest of virgin terrain.

I think the mountains of Chaltén in Patagonia are in the midst of this transition. I've dedicated the past decade of my life mostly to climbing there, and have climbed more than a dozen first ascents involving virgin terrain, but my *top ten* personally proudest climbing achievements in Patagonia involved no virgin terrain—they were instead solo ascents and traverses.

I suspect this same evolution will gain momentum before long in higher and more "exotic" mountains like the Trango group, the Gangotri, and the Khumbu—places where there are already many established routes and a wealth of information. The Khumbu now has more infrastructure, rescue services, and communication (including wi-fi and mobile phone networks) than any mountains in Canada or Alaska, and it would be dishonest to pretend that it is a big adventure to climb there. However, the mountain faces are as humongous and steep, and the altitude as extreme, as they ever were, and it is a ripe playground for the next generation of high-altitude sport-alpinism. Messner, Loretan, Troillet, and others saw this decades ago, and it's no secret that the Chomolongma-Lhotse-Nuptse traverse was the last objective of Ueli Steck, sport-alpinism's recent star.

As for me, I feel that I have learned well how to climb the mountains of Patagonia and Alaska in the fast, bivouac-less style that I most enjoy. I'm not sure exactly which mountains will captivate me in coming years, but I am curious if I can apply the carefree, in-a-day, Chamonix-style tactics to mountain ranges not yet stuffed with previously climbed routes. Perhaps I'll realize the extent of my naïveté and succumb to carrying a heavy backpack full of supplies for several days of traditional alpinism, or perhaps I'll have incredible experiences dashing up and down faces that have never been approached this way before.

NOTES ON 2018 CASSIN RIDGE SOLO: On June 5, Colin Haley soloed the Cassin Ridge on Denali in 8 hours 7 minutes from bergschrund to summit. Cassin ascents have been timed in various ways, but this was at least 6.5 hours faster than any previous record. Haley climbed the mountain twice during acclimatization. He then approached the south face via the East Fork of the Kahiltna Glacier, bivouacked, and began climbing with the original 1961 start to the Cassin Ridge. At the crest of the ridge, he downclimbed and traversed to below the bergschrund of the Japanese Couloir, from which previous speed records have been timed, and started his clock at 7:40 a.m. Haley climbed in single boots and carried no stove, protection, harness, or rope—tactics made reasonable, he said, because of extensive acclimatization, prior experience on the route, and years of experience in the Central Alaska Range. Haley discusses this climb in episode 10 of the Cutting Edge podcast.

ABOUT THE AUTHOR: *Colin Haley was born in Seattle in 1984 and makes a meager living as a sponsored alpinist. He recently purchased a tiny apartment in Chamonix and looks forward to having big mountains outside his door to practice carefree alpinism—and perhaps to prepare himself for bigger mountains elsewhere.*

WELCOME TO THE THUNDERDOME

A MOTHER LODE OF ICE AND ALPINE ROUTES IN MONTANA'S CABINET MOUNTAINS

SCOTT COLDIRON

• **MARCH 2018** •

Our skis etch crisp lines in a crystalline mat of snow, broken only where we'd paused to gawk at the deep icy couloirs and jagged buttresses of A Peak's north face, towering 4,000 feet above. From our camp on the north shore of Granite Lake, the Thunderdome had looked like nothing but a bump under A Peak (8,634 feet), the second highest point in Montana's Cabinet Mountains. But as we traverse the lake, the 1,800-foot Thunderdome slowly rises up until it blocks A Peak entirely, and we can see the immensity of the icy veins coursing down its walls.

We gain the south shore and set a skin track up the snow gully before us. On our left, three tiers of quartzite cliff bands rim the lake. Cloaked in turquoise-tinged frozen cascades, it is a virtual playground of ice climbing. But our attention is drawn the other way as Matt Cornell, my climbing partner for this trip, gets his first up-close look at the Thunderdome. A broad river of blue ice spills off the tall buttress to the right. Hemmed in by slate-gray rock walls, the gully chokes down until just a white thread is visible, snaking to the summit. A few minute later we can see another stunning climb: burnished stone sheathed in ice so thin it shows the opaque tint of rock underneath, and dead vertical at its upper headwall. Two hundred yards upslope is a climb I'd done with Christian Thompson in 2014—Blackwell Falls (900' WI5). It features a stunning 300-foot crux pillar, but we had been turned back by a dark, dripping chimney above, and the route had never been finished to the top of the wall. Today I think I see a glimmer of ice in the back of the chimney. Matt is no stranger to big ice climbs, but he looks awe-struck by the trio of huge ice formations above us. We decide on the middle line—the sheer headwall covered in thin ice will be our first big test in the morning.

The Thunderdome (center) and A Peak (8,634 feet) rising above Granite Lake in the Cabinet Mountains of northwest Montana, as seen in February 2018. *Marlin Thorman*

In the far northwest corner of Montana, the Cabinet Mountains rise from the banks of the Kootenai River and cut 35 miles south to the Clark Fork. Approaches here are typified by long, steep-sided valleys teeming with old-growth forests of western red cedar and hemlock trees. In fact, the Cabinets hold one of the world's few inland rainforests—some of the ancient cedars have been dated at over 1,000 years old. In addition to the animals one might expect to see in a Montana wilderness—grizzly, elk, moose, bighorn sheep, and plentiful deer—the Cabinets are also home to Canada lynx, wolves, and wolverines.

I first visited the Cabinet Mountains to climb in 2012 after hearing rumors of big ice formations at nearby Leigh Lake. We found a half-dozen 500-foot ice climbs above the lake, and over the next two seasons I climbed there many times. But these routes lie at the bottom of Snowshoe Peak's 3,800-foot north face. As I found out the hard way, this aspect holds an ungodly amount of snow, which it sheds with alarming vigor and regularity.

After two close calls with serious avalanches, I began searching out other likely terrain in the range, and I didn't have to look far. Just over the ridgeline, a semicircle of cliffs above Granite Lake stood out immediately on Google Earth. I scoured the Internet, but I couldn't find any record of winter climbing there, or even a single photo of the area in winter. Finally, in April 2014, my buddy Jonah Job and I made the 10-mile hike to Granite Lake to find the most impressive concentration of ice climbing either of us had ever seen.

Scott Coldiron leading the last pitch of Mad Max (1,200', WI5+). *Marlin Thorman*

In a stroke of geologic luck, the cliffs at the north end of Granite Lake form a natural amphitheater. Just above them lies the Blackwell Glacier, the last remaining glacier in the Cabinet Mountains. This bowl catches runoff from the massive flanks of both A Peak and neighboring Snowshoe Peak, creating an astounding amount of ice and giving the area an otherworldly feel. We began calling it the Thunderdome in reference to the apocalyptic battle arena from the 1985 movie *Mad Max Beyond Thunderdome*. In another happy coincidence for ice climbers, the Thunderdome stands proud of A Peak, diverting any avalanches that come off its north face.

We made a couple of trips in 2015, climbing a few smaller flows, but stormy weather and short days kept us off the big climbs. Finally, in March, I teamed up with Christian to climb the fantastic pillar of Blackwell Falls. The next month I returned with Jonah, Beau Carrillo, and Ben Erdmann. Our goal was the central couloir on A Peak's north face, a deep gash that splits the tallest part of the face. The entry into the couloir, 500 feet of steep rock, had been scoured smooth by centuries of falling debris. This section appeared to be beyond our abilities and we decided to move on, but for me the hook was set—I vowed to be good enough to climb the couloir the next time I stood in this spot. We traversed along the base and found a moderate couloir with easier access. A day of ridiculously fun alpine climbing culminated in a steep rock and ice finish as we bagged the first ascent of Unprotected Fourplay (1,900', AI4 M5).

The next couple of seasons saw little progress, as I spent the following winter in Patagonia and the year after broke my leg in an early-season ice climbing fall. By January 2018, I had fully recovered and I was champing at the bit to attempt the Thunderdome's three biggest lines, but I was having a hard time finding partners. Perhaps with Bozeman and Canmore offering world-class ice climbing just off the road, skiing deep into the backcountry for first ascents held little appeal.

I had grown frustrated and was working the nerve up to climb solo in the Cabinets when I got a phone call from an old friend. Brian White wasn't calling about climbing but reaching out to a buddy in the midst of a devastating divorce. Despite the fact that Brian had only climbed ice a handful of times, I convinced him that a trip to the Cabinets would be the best medicine for his grief. By the end of the week, he had led his first pitch of ice: 150 feet of steep WI4—and a first ascent at that. We then made an attempt on the Thunderdome's central couloir, but we just couldn't move fast enough to finish the big route on a short January day.

Now I'd had a taste of a Thunderdome king line, and my desire to climb it was at a fever pitch. I went back in with Marlin Thorman a couple of weeks later, and we bagged a solid handful of multi-pitch first ascents. But without an adequate weather window, the big three still evaded me.

My luck changed when Conrad Anker visited Spokane and a chance meeting through a mutual friend led to us climb together at our local dry-tooling crag. At last, someone's excitement about the climbing potential in the Cabinet Mountains matched my own—Conrad and I began planning a trip. When events beyond his control forced him to cancel, Conrad thoughtfully found a replacement, introducing me to a young protégé from Bozeman, 23-year-old Matt Cornell. Matt hitchhiked to Spokane, and we immediately packed our gear and six days of food, and drove to

Coldiron climbing out of the People Eater (one pitch, WI5) on the first ascent. *Brian White*

The Thunderdome in the foreground with A Peak behind. Marked are the three "king lines" of the Thunderdome: (1) Road Warrior (1,100', WI5 M5), (2) Mad Max (1,200', WI5+), and (3) Master Blaster (1,500', WI4 M5). Other routes not shown. On A Peak, (4) is the general location of Unprotected Foreplay (1,950', AI4+ M6 R) and (2) shows the central gash of Canmore Wedding Party (2,500', AI5 M7). *Marlin Thorman*

the trailhead outside of Libby, Montana.

After the long ski in, I messaged a friend on my inReach device to report on our progress.

– At camp with Matt, climbing tomorrow.

– Hey, I think Matt is the kid who lives in a closet under the stairs at my ex-boyfriend's house in Bozeman.

"Hey, Matt, do you live in a closet under the stairs?" I asked.

"Yup. It's a pretty good-sized closet though."

In fact, most of the year Matt is on the road—three months in Patagonia, a month and a half in Alaska, four months in Yosemite. His parents lent him the old family Subaru when he left home at 18 to pursue the climbing lifestyle. Three years ago, he deemed automotive costs to be holding him back, and he's been without a car ever since. Each spring he rides his bike from Bozeman to Yosemite, and each fall he rides back. In short, Matt is one of the last dirtbag soul climbers.

Over the next five days, Matt and I climbed all three of the Thunderdome's king lines: Mad Max (1,200', WI5+), Road Warrior (1,100', WI5 M5), and Master Blaster (1,500', WI4 M5). At sunset on our last day, we topped out Master Blaster and stood on the summit of the Thunderdome. The gaping blackness of A Peak's massive central couloir loomed overhead.

"I call it Devil's Ass-Crack Couloir, what do you think?" I asked.

"Looks like a death trap right now. I think it's an early season route—before the cornices are big and the avy danger is out of control."

"Will you come back at the start of winter and give it a try with me?"

"Hell yes!" Matt replied.

· **NOVEMBER 2018** ·

In the predawn blackness, Matt and I are climbing, sliding, and crawling through a steep tangle of slide alder. I feel a stalk of devil's club smack into my softshell pants— then the sting of thorns in my thigh.

"Sonuvabitch!"

Ducking under a snarl of slide alder, I clamber up out of the thicket. I feel a sudden tug from behind—a branch has caught on my pack—and I'm sprawling backward and belly-up into the thorny patch of devil's club.

"This is bullshit!"

"Hah-hah, yeah," Matt shouts back to me. "But it'll be worth it if the couloir is in good shape."

Matt Cornell (left) and the author preparing to attempt their new route on A Peak. *Scott Coldiron*

After three hours of arduous scrambling, we're standing at the base of A Peak. The entry to the couloir is still more than 400 feet above us, barred by steep, polished rock. Hiking along the face, we finally spot a weakness—a hidden chimney that slashes across the face in the direction of the couloir. The slot provides a few pitches of gymnastic but fairly easy climbing, and then I find a vertical smear of blue ice leading directly to the couloir. A cloud of spindrift spills over the edge, and soon it's a deluge, forcing me off the direct ice line. Traversing right, I find a snowy ledge that diagonals into the couloir and suddenly we're at the bottom of the abyss. Ramparts of gun-metal stone shoot overhead for hundreds of feet on either side.

Matt and I climb at a furious tempo, thighs burning on steep snow slopes interspersed with rocky steps. The mixed climbing demands funky, physical movement, but we forge on through showers of spindrift up the unrelenting narrow slot. The sun is low in the sky as I plow up another steep snow slope to a house-size chockstone, then flop over the edge to discover a flat snow ledge, big enough to hold the tent we didn't bring. Matt fires up the stove to melt snow as I stack the ropes and sort gear. Ramen noodles are the first real food we've had all day, and we watch the last amber rays of sunlight play across the walls overhead. A cornice overhangs the top of the wall, gleaming white in the sun. It doesn't look far off.

Following a brief rest we continue up, and after a couple of pitches we've come up under a big roof—a conglomeration of huge boulders and choss. I belay under a constant shower of spindrift as Matt pushes on, determined to solve the puzzle overhead. Darkness falls and I see Matt's outline dimly, my headlamp barely piercing the spindrift to illuminate Matt's ghostly form. Light snow is falling, and soon pounding waves of spindrift funnel down the throat of the couloir.

Matt tries every option, methodically testing every possible move. He has been on lead for 90 minutes when I notice that I'm shaking uncontrollably. A storm is forecasted to hit in the morning, and our only ways out are over the top or all the way back down a 2,000-foot vertical bowling alley. If the storm hits while we're in the couloir, we're screwed. Wet, cold, and afraid, I am done, and at last I tell Matt I think we should bail. He agrees and we start our retreat.

After our first rappel, we pull the ropes but they won't budge. We try every rope trick to no avail, so Matt clips in and jugs up the rope. A half-hour later, he reappears and the ropes pull free. The next rappel lands us back under the huge chocktone. I grab a rope and pull—it moves, barely.

Matt Cornell in the lower chimney of what would become Canmore Wedding Party. *Scott Coldiron*

I pull again and the rope is stuck. It's my turn to ascend, but Matt is already wrapping a prusik on and clipping in. It's 3 a.m. when he returns and we're finally able to pull the rope. The rope lands at our feet, and my heart sinks when I see it. A four-foot section looks like someone has run it across a cheese grater, and the sheath is cut all the way through. We're too close to making a fatal mistake, and we agree to wait for first light.

In a bid for style and speed, we've brought no bivy gear. Our down jackets are matted and lifeless. During the long night, we both solemnly swear that we'll never return to this godforsaken place. The tight slot catches every bit of snow or rock that falls down the mountain, and it doesn't seem worth the risk.

We begin rappelling again as dawn lights up the horizon, and six and a half hours later we're making the last rappel out of the couloir as the full storm hits. The first of many avalanches rips down the couloir as we pull the ropes for the last time. We stumble down to the lake and collapse in our sleeping bags.

The next day, a Thursday, I'm dead tired at the wheel, eyelids heavy, but I'm due back in town for a 48-hour shift at my job as a fire lieutenant in downtown Spokane. I leave Matt on the side of I-90—he'll hitch back to Bozeman just in time to make a Zion climbing trip.

It's a busy shift—we're up all Friday night on a three-alarm commercial structure fire. On Saturday, in between calls, I pull up the weather forecast: A beautiful window in the Cabinets is two days out. With Matt gone to the desert, I call my buddy Jess Roskelley just as he's stepping off the plane from a climbing trip. Jess is stoked, so the plan is made. After a shift change on Sunday morning, I repack my bag, and by nightfall Jess and I are once again setting up camp at Granite Lake.

It's midmorning on Monday as I lead the steep blue ice that accesses the couloir—no spindrift this time. The sky is cobalt blue overhead and we make good time up the couloir, secure in the knowledge that we'll have 2,000 feet of pre-rigged rap stations if we need to bail. This time we've packed a tent, and we pitch it under the big chockstone, sipping hot tea in our sleeping bags where Matt and I had shivered the night away just a few days before.

Jess Roskelley just above the bivy boulder on A Peak. At right, Roskelley (left) and the author on the summit. *Coldiron Collection*

The next morning I'm warmed up by the time we reach the belay under the big roof, and Jess graciously gives me first shot at the crux lead—I'm determined not to let him down, and I feel a duty to Matt to finish the crux. I pull up onto the roof, clipping gear Matt had left. Then it's on, and I power through the crux and pull the lip on solid hooks.

Just three pitches later, I'm belaying Jess as he navigates the final step. A steep wall with tricky climbing on loose blocks makes for a nice finish to a stellar climb. He flops over the edge and lets out a whoop. Jess and I stand on top of A Peak in the afternoon sun, laughing about my solemn promise from four days earlier.

Back at camp the next day, Jess pours us each a cup of Canadian whiskey, and we toast to Matt's gutsy crux lead. His efforts at the end of a 22-hour push—climbing to the last hard move of the big roof, pulling on shifting cobbles in the pitch black, only to be shut down by pounding spindrift—had set us up for a relatively straightforward redpoint burn of Canmore Wedding Party (2,500', AI5 M7).

SUMMARY: As of late winter 2019, there were nearly 20 single-pitch ice climbs, eight multi-pitch ice and mixed routes, and two big alpine lines in the Thunderdome and the A-Peak cirque of the Cabinet Mountains. A mini-guide to the area is available to download at the AAJ website.

ABOUT THE AUTHOR: *A native of western Montana, Scott Coldiron spent his teens planting trees in the foothills of the Cabinet Mountains. When he's not exploring the mountains or writing about them, he works at a busy fire station in Spokane, Washington. An interview with the author about the discovery of the Thunderdome ice arena is featured in episode 16 of the AAJ's Cutting Edge podcast.*

ALPINE ROULETTE

THE IMPERMANENCE OF ALPINE PERMAFROST AND HOW THIS CHANGES EVERYTHING

JOHN HARLIN III

In my memory's eye, I can easily see the mistake. As I scampered up a granite wall on the Swiss side of the Aiguilles Rouges du Mont Dolent, I'd noted with mild curiosity that water was dripping from under the two-meter-tall block of rock I was about to climb over. But the granite face felt so solid after the choss of the last several pitches that I paid no mind to this wet patch. Then I touched the top of the block. Suddenly both the block and I were airborne. I flipped over and ground down the wall headfirst, thinking over and over, "I will not let this kill me, I will not let this kill me…" as rocks tumbled beside me and I waited for the rope to catch my fall.

Fifteen meters later, it did, having snagged on a flake that cut it halfway through. I was indeed still alive, but my feet had broken, as X-rays later revealed. A helicopter came to whisk me off to the hospital, then returned to pick up my partner.

In hindsight, it's obvious the dripping came from ice that had been holding the rock in place. The block would have fallen anyway that summer of 2010, whether or not I'd been there to catalyze its erosion.

I have no beef with erosion. After all, without erosion the Aiguilles would be an uplifted plateau that horses could walk over, not a spiny ridge attractive to climbers. I just don't want to be there when erosion happens. And it's happening hard and fast in the Alps these days. My particular nemesis-stone was a meaningless brick in a large mountain. But in the Alps it's becoming increasingly difficult to recognize which brick of rock is solidly attached to the underlying structure, and which is held in place by frozen water—permafrost—at some unknown depth within.

Like most climbers, I knew that years of repeated melt-thaw cycle would pry rocks from the surface of cliffs. What few Alpine climbers previously understood is just how *much* of the mountain we climb isn't monolithic. An awful lot of it is instead frozen in place. Heat up the wall and ice turns to water, which transforms glue into grease. Rarely do we actually see the dripping evidence of that bond weakening, the evidence I foolishly ignored that June afternoon.

ACCORDING TO Dr. Michael Krautblatter, lead author of 2018's *Geographische Rundschau* article "Permafrost in the Alps: features, geographic spread, and future development," permafrost is a sort of "hidden glaciation." The European Alps, he writes, hold approximately 6,200 square kilometers of permafrost—roughly three times more surface area than what's covered by glaciers.

The ice-draped faces of the Mont Blanc massif have lured alpinists for generations. But as ice melts, scientists are detecting great instability in formations like the Tour Ronde and Kuffner Arête (foreground center and right), changing the formula for some classic climbs and eliminating others entirely. *"The Brenva Face, Mont Blanc," 1998, by Julian Cooper; collection Reinhold Messner*

The melting of this permafrost has a huge impact on climbers in the Alps, including when and where they go. July and August used to be known as the climbing months in the Alps, when (unless it was a particularly rainy summer) dry, warm conditions offered the most enjoyable climbing, spiced by occasional thunderstorms. Alas, the Alps are warming roughly twice as fast as the globe as a whole, and the problem with "dry" is that it removes the insulating blanket of surface icefields, which leads to rapid warming of the rock substrate that used to be sheltered. The rock itself contains a remarkable amount of ice filling deep cracks and weak layers—ice that is now liquifying.

A leading authority on the melting of the Alps is Ludovic Ravanel, a geomorphologist based out of the Université Savoie Mont Blanc. A generations-long native of Chamonix, a former mountain hut guardian, and a member of the Compagnie des Guides de Chamonix, he's an expert from every angle. At the Sustainable Summits conference in Chamonix last June (2018), Ravanel noted that mountain permafrost degradation already has been studied for a long time, perhaps most extensively by the Swiss professor Wilfred Haeberli, who has been publishing in the field for half a century.

Ravanel explained the basic process of rock degradation like this: Each time the ground unfreezes, the rock shifts. Each time it refreezes, it locks up again. It also expands. Repeat this cycle enough times and the rock degrades, especially since more and longer unfrozen periods yield ever-greater movement. There's now tremendous movement of rock on the Aiguille du Tacul and the normal route on the Tour Ronde, as researched examples. This process is taking place earlier in the summer, too. In 2018, their recorded internal movement started in June. But what's changing fastest, said Ravanel, is that the massif's arêtes are losing their ice: "The blocks that make up these arêtes are no longer cemented." Blocks like the one that nearly killed me on the jagged arête of the nearby Aiguilles Rouges du Mont Dolent.

"Mont Blanc is my laboratory," Ravenel likes to say. He delights that "permafrost in granite is much less understood than in some other rock types," which gives him as a scientist the chance to explore new territory at an opportune time. As a climber, though, he worries.

The most shocking illustration of the dangers of lubricating meltwater penetrating deep inside Alpine walls came from the collapse of the Bonatti Pillar on the west face of the Petit Dru, high above Chamonix. In 1965 my father, John Harlin II, put up a big-wall route on this face with Royal Robbins; at the time it was considered the hardest aid route in the Alps. It wasn't really an "Alpine" route, as its sheer granite face was more Yosemite-like than classic mixed Alpine fare. Seemingly, the wall was utterly dry, solid, monolithic. In 2005, however, Dad and Royal's 500-meter route fell to the ground along with the entire Bonatti Pillar next door—some 265,000 cubic meters of rock, the equivalent of 1,600 railroad boxcars. At first no one knew why. But in 2011, after another 43,000 cubic meters fell from the face, researchers discovered newly exposed ice that had been hidden deep inside the cliff. Rising temperatures had evidently softened the ice that had glued together this behemoth.

Last fall's massive collapse of the Petit Grépillon in Switzerland's Val Ferret was caught on an impressive video, and a large rockfall on the flanks of Mont Blanc's Taconnaz Glacier woke sleepers in the Chamonix valley far below. But, according to Ravanel in an interview with TVmountain.com, the emblematic event of the year for this range was the collapse of a huge section of the Trident du Tacul, destroying classic routes on its south face. Such collapses are happening all over the Alps. In Switzerland many of the biggest rock failures took place in the heat wave of 2015, including the west flank of Piz Cambrena in Graubuenden and the western flank of the Grande Dent de Veisivi in Valais. Ravanel said more than 850 such collapses have been catalogued since 2007 just in the Mont Blanc Massif, with degradation of the permafrost being the major factor behind most. The ice that's being revealed can be thousands of years old. After a rockfall near the Frendo Spur of the Aiguille du Midi in 2017, the newly exposed ice was dated at 4,000 years old.

Historically, the greatest ungluing has been on south faces, which have always been exposed to the most sun and thus freeze-thawed and deep-melted for ages. What alpinists are finding now, though, is that north is the new south. As heat waves pile up and extend longer, that heat has time to penetrate the shadowed sides of the highest Alpine summits.

DURING THE SUMMER of 2003, some 10,000 people died in France from unusual heat. The Alps lost more ice than ever in one season. The standard route up Mont Blanc—the Goûter—was closed due to rockfall. The Hörnli Ridge on the Matterhorn started collapsing, too; helicopters rescued over 70 climbers trapped on its crumbling ridge.

Meanwhile, Mark Jenkins and I shouldered massive packs in the heat of Courmayeur, under the Italian side of Mont Blanc, intent on putting up a new route on either the Freney or Brouillard faces. These walls mattered to me because my father had established new routes on each of them in the 1960s, one with Tom Frost and the other with Chris Bonington. Since I'd newly rekindled my desire for Alpine "roots climbing," retracing some of Dad's famous first ascents, I wanted to put up my own new route here. (After this, Mark and I intended to move on to the Eiger, where Dad died in 1966 on yet another new route.) But when we arrived at the Eccles bivouac shelters on the ridge that divides the Freney and Brouillard faces, our jaws dropped. The scene was of utter devastation. The glaciers under both faces were brown with the detritus of freight-car size layers of rock. As we watched, more blocks peeled from the walls and shattered onto the glaciers below. It would have been pure suicide to venture onto either face.

In Dad's day (the 1960s), the Eiger's north face was climbed in the summer. The problem with climbing it in winter was that the bitter cold and strong wind would sublimate autumn's wet ice so there wasn't much left to climb during winter. But in the 21st century, summer rockfall on the Eiger is too intense for just about anyone's taste. Meanwhile, winters have become so mild that the new favorite Eiger season is early spring. Also popular is late September, when storms plaster the face with thick, sticky ice that holds the surface in place. When I climbed the north face in late September 2005, it was covered in fresh snow and ice and we witnessed just one fall-ing rock during three days on the face. Football sized, it arced through the sky before plunging into the Spider, where it stuck in the glue of fresh snow. Autumn's thick, soft ice now tends to stay put through the winter without sublimating, and new storms add layer upon layer of wet, sticky snow.

A massive rockfall from the Cosmiques Arête, just below the Aiguille du Midi tram station, on August 22, 2018. *Michel Piola*

Surprisingly, this deep winter snow/ice can lead to even faster melting of perma-frost. Snow acts as a blanket insulating the mountain from cold, high-altitude winter air. So the previous summer's heat buildup becomes trapped under this "feather quilt," to quote Dr. Marcia Phillips of the Swiss Institute for Snow and Avalanche Research (SLF). "The more snow there is on the ground, the warmer the soil remains, as the heat of the summer cannot escape." Then, as the snow melts in a hot summer, ground that was never deeply frozen the previous winter is even more easily pene-trable by meltwater, which compounds the internal thawing in a vicious cycle.

Alpine climbing and skiing has always been known for its "objective" danger—things outside a climber's control, like storms, rockfall, and avalanches. These days, improved weather forecast-ing and the phone apps we view them on make storms much more foreseeable. But there's no app to warn of imminent rockfall. SLF does offer a web app where new events can be reported, but that's post facto. Nothing tells you ahead of time when an unknown subsurface ice bond on your climb or ski tour has decided to liquify.

Did I say "ski tour"? Isn't a mountain frozen solid during winter? Alas, no. On March 18, 2019, part of eastern Switzerland's Fluela Wisshorn collapsed. The rockfall triggered a snow avalanche that swept over a classic Davos ski tour. "Luckily it happened at midnight and nobody was injured or killed," writes Phillips. She cited other large midwinter rock avalanches on the Pizzo Cengalo in December 2011 and Piz Kesch in February 2014. Ravanel explained the coun-

The Eiger's north face, once climbed almost exclusively in summer, is now desiccated and dangerous in the warmer months. *"The White Spider," 2004, by Julian Cooper, collection Reinhold Messner*

ter-intuitive timing like this: "The heart of the mountain continues to warm through December and into January" as summer's absorbed heat slowly migrates inward. "For this reason, the most significant permafrost de-icing occurs in late November and December."

More and more research on Alpine permafrost is being done. For example, the PermaSense project, an interdisciplinary effort between geo-scientists and engineers that started in 2006 with the goal of "maximizing technological advances," monitors the Matterhorn's Hornli Ridge at the 3,500-meter elevation level. This is just one of the project's 29 distinct sensor locations.

Elsewhere in Switzerland, Dr. Phillips reports the SLF has some "30 drill holes at 26 locations equipped with instruments that measure temperature and slope movements every two hours." Many of these data flow into PERMOS, the Swiss permafrost monitoring network, which is available online. Phillips says the SLF's 32-year effort is "the longest measurement series in Switzerland." In Austria, Matthias Rode is part of a team studying permafrost distribution on the headwalls of two receding glaciers in the Dachstein Massif. Their article for the scientific journal *The Cryosphere* (the "cryosphere" is the frozen part of the world) was published online in January 2019. It reports that they're mainly finding permafrost on cold, northerly aspects. They declared permafrost distribution "an important factor for rock slope failure and rockwall retreat" and confirmed widespread findings that north slopes are in increasing danger as their permafrost thaws.

None of this will help you very much when you're climbing. Sure, you'll find that access trails to huts such as l'Envers des Aiguilles, Conscrits, and Charpoua have been rerouted due to rockfall, lowered glaciers, and/or missing snowfields. You can find out that some climbs, such as Dad's route (with Tom Frost and others) up the south face of the Fou in 1963, are now rarely done, in that case because the access couloir has become too dangerous. You can talk with hut keepers and keep an eye on climbing blogs for recent activity, especially if you know the local language. In some regions, like Chamonix, you can find excellent conditions reports in English. But there's no Alps-wide central bank of conditions reports yet. You can still be taken by complete surprise even on the most classic of routes.

WITH ITS EASE of access and egress via the Aiguille du Midi gondola, the Arête des Cosmiques was one of the most popular alpine climbs in the world. On August 21, 2018, climbers were belaying on a ledge when a guide climbed by, remarking in passing, "C'est bizarre, yesterday this ledge was a meter to the left." The next day, this ledge and everything around it fell off.

Caroline George, a mountain guide who lives in Switzerland, recalled, "I remember guiding one day up in Chamonix last summer (2018) when I felt sick to my stomach and just depressed by the sight of dry glaciers at 3,700 meters and all the mountains looking like they were suffering. I have been seeing this evolution for the past 15 years. I wonder what our job as guides will be like in the future. We are facing treacherous objective hazards now that didn't exist before."

But she continues to guide, as that's both her passion and how she makes her living. "Guides adapt and climb what's possible based on conditions and weather, as per usual," she explained. "We don't climb the Tour Ronde once it's dry, we don't climb the north face of the Droites in the summer like people did 20 years ago, the Frendo is collapsing. You see rockfall and you don't go. The mountains show signs, and we need to respect and adapt to them every day, all the time. That's what guides do for a living."

Meanwhile the ice keeps melting. When I was seven years old and living in a campground in Chamonix, Dad took me up the Mer de Glace and on to the Refuge de l'Envers des Aiguilles. The sight and sound of blue ice crunching under my crampons is one of my all-time happiest memories. At the time we could almost walk directly onto the glacier from the Montenvers cog-railway station. Now you take a gondola down. And then a series of stairways, each bolted onto the last as the glacier shrinks ever further. Dates are painted onto the rock to indicate when the glacier was last at that height. In a few years there will be no glacier at the bottom of these stairs. Each year we'll have to hike further upstream just to touch ice.

It's the same story everywhere in the Alps. Researchers like Haeberli are modelling the ground under the glaciers so they know where new lakes will appear. In a few decades most of the valley glaciers will be gone, just as they have vanished from Colorado's Rockies, California's Sierra, and even Austria's Eastern Alps. (In all these ranges, small remnant glaciers still cling to a few north-facing pockets, but these are fading fast, too.) It will be a new kind of landscape, with rivers of ice restricted to nostalgic photos from our time.

But now we know that glaciers are just one facet of the ice story. The ice that used to be known as permafrost, because it was thought to be permanent—this "hidden glaciation" inside the world's mountains—is vanishing, too. And for a climber, what's unseen can still very much kill you. How much of the rock we climb is a veneer held in place by the last vestiges of ancient cold? How much are we willing to trust that it's not drip-dripping somewhere inside? How much will we adapt our vacation schedule and climbing taste to the relatively frozen seasons?

We'll all make our personal risk assessments, as usual—alpine climbing has always featured risk as a kind of virtue. It's just that when you can't trust a mountain's skin to stay in place, and the weakening may (or may not) be taking place at some unknowable depth, we're in a whole new phase of alpine roulette.

ABOUT THE AUTHOR: *John Harlin III, seen at right at age seven high above the Mer de Glace, lived in or near the Alps as a child when his father was one of the leading alpinists of the 1960s. In 2014, "Young John" returned to work in his childhood village as the director of the Alpine Institute at the Leysin American School in Switzerland. He served as editor of the American Alpine Journal from 2002 to 2012.*

[Top] View south from the Tibetan Plateau to the frontier with Nepal, from Dolpo (left) to Chandi Himal. *Julian Freeman-Attwood*. [Right] Reaching the top of Sunkala Topi in the Kanti Himal. *Christof Nettekoven* [Above] Above the Koji La, looking south toward Koji Kang (left) and Kaqur Kangri. *Julian Freeman-Attwood*.

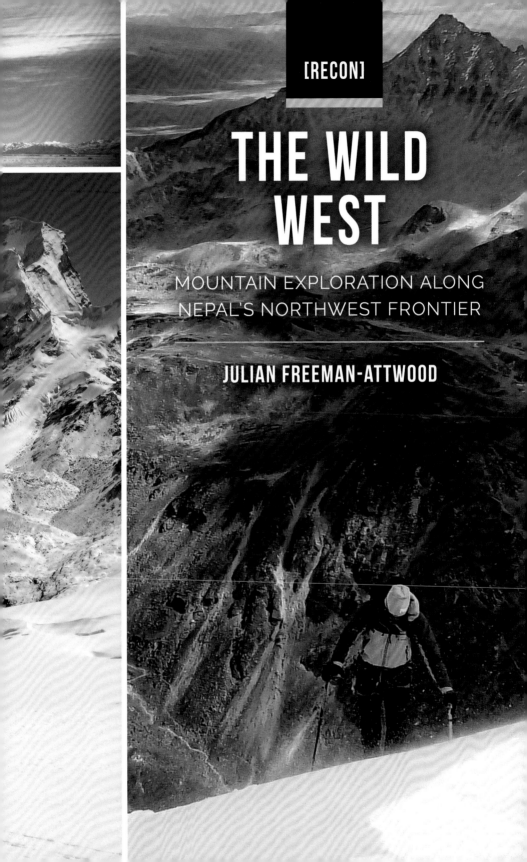

THE WILD WEST

MOUNTAIN EXPLORATION ALONG NEPAL'S NORTHWEST FRONTIER

JULIAN FREEMAN-ATTWOOD

A mule train en route to peaks in the far west of Nepal. *Julian Freeman-Attwood*

Far northwestern Nepal has, until recently, been the area of the country—and indeed of the Himalaya in general—least explored by mountaineers, with the exception of parts of Bhutan and of Arunachal Pradesh (Assam Himalaya) in India. From the western fringes of the Dolpo region westward to the village of Hilsa, south of Gurla Mandhata (7,694 meters), the Nepal-Tibet frontier runs about 225 kilometers. Along or close to this border are approximately 93 peaks over 6,000 meters, of which, as of early 2019, 36 had been climbed and 57 remained unclimbed. The peaks between 5,750 meters and 6,000 meters (many of which are extremely interesting and more technical than the higher mountains) are so numerous that I have not tried to count them.

The overview that follows reflects my experience from researching and undertaking 12 expeditions and travels in Nepal's wild west, from my first trip in 2007 to Kanti Himal, at the east end of this zone, to an expedition to the Takphu Himal in the far northwest in 2018. The area covered is confined to the border mountains of Nepal's Karnali Pradesh province, and specifically to the northern districts of Mugu and Humla. With a few exceptions, most of these peaks lie on the frontier with Tibet.

This article does not include Dolpo, which lies to the east of Mugu, nor Jumla further south, in which lies Kanjiroba and which had been visited in the 1960s by prolific explorer John Tyson and others. Nor does it cover Dharchula, further west, which was visited by Tyson and Bill Murray, and in which lie the 7,000-meter Api and Saipal peaks, both climbed in the 1960s. Much more has been written of these areas than the frontier mountains 50 kilometers or so farther north.

The initial Western exploration of this region involved various parties in the mid-1800s and early 1900s searching for the source of the Brahmaputra River (Yarlung Tsangpo), which rises in Humla and flows north and then east and south some 2,900 kilometers through Tibet, India, and Bangladesh. (See Section 5 below.) Afterward, very few visitors arrived, even after Nepal was opened to mountaineering in the early 1950s. The region was very hard to reach, and without any 8,000-meter peaks and few 7,000ers to attempt, mountaineers focused elsewhere throughout the 1950s, '60s, and '70s.

The first climbing expedition to the region was in 1983, when a Japanese women's team approached Kubi Kangri from Tibet. Nepal opened more peaks to foreign climbers in the 1990s and early 2000s, but only a few teams from Japan responded, as described below. The Maoist

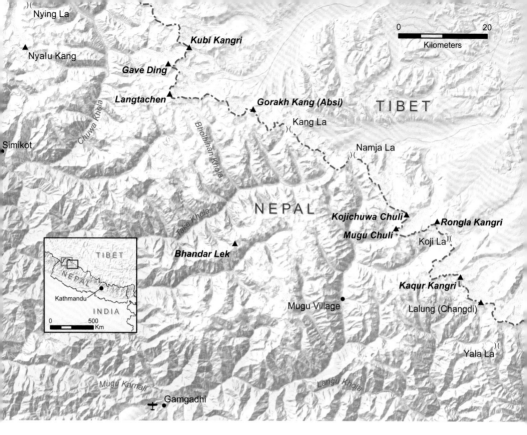

This map covers the areas of Sections 1 through 5 in this article. Access to the eastern areas is through Gamgadhi and Mugu. Access to areas in the west is through Simikot. *Anna Riling*

insurgency from 1996 to 2006 kept most foreigners out of the area. In 2007, I made my first of many trips. Nepal opened 104 new peaks to climbing in 2014, about a third of which were in the west, bringing more climbers to this area, though the numbers are still paltry compared with the well-known mountains farther east.

All of the mountains mentioned below are, at present, completely closed for climbing from the Tibetan (north) side. They only can be accessed from Nepal. A list of open peaks is available from the Nepal Ministry of Culture, Tourism and Civil Aviation ("the ministry"); permits are required to attempt mountains over 5,800 meters.

Access to these mountains starts with getting to either Simikot or Gamgadhi. The jump-off point for the first three sections below is the township of Gamgadhi, which now can be reached by road, at least when not blocked by landslides, or by air in a Twin Otter plane flying from Nepalgunj, on the India border, to Rara Lake (a.k.a. Talcha). Travelers then proceed on foot toward Mugu, three and a half days away, following the Mugu Karnali Nadi east and then north, passing the confluence with the Namlang Nadi flowing westward from the Dolpo. For sections 4 through 8 below, approaches begin with a flight to Simikot.

The sections in this article are arranged from southeast to northwest along the frontier. All heights for permitted peaks are quoted from the Nepal ministry's list; other elevations are from the official HGM-Finn 1:50,000 map series. With some exceptions, I have confined the climbs described here to first ascents or first attempts. I have used the Tibetan word "La" for mountain passes. "Khola" in Nepal is the word for valley or river. "Lek" is the common name given to subranges between the high Himalaya and middle hills in Nepal.

Seen from Peak 6,419m: Kaqur Kangri (6,859m) is the high peak in center; Myung Thang Kang (6,449m, unclimbed and on the permit list) is left and in front of Kaqur; and Lalung is right of center. *Bruce Normand*

SECTION 1: YALA LA TO KOJI LA
KANTI HIMAL (a.k.a. RONGLA RANGE IN TIBET)

29KM ALONG THE BORDER; **3 CLIMBED** 6,000M PEAKS; **14 UNCLIMBED** 6,000M PEAKS

THIS SECTOR IS attainable from Mugu (from the west) by mule trail over the Chyargo La. The traveller should head east some six kilometers south of Mugu village, into the Chham Khola and over the Chyargo La (5,150m). This is a particularly wild area that can only be accessed over the Chyargo La post-monsoon—or indeed during the monsoon. A longer journey would be from Shey Gompa to the southeast; this certainly would not be possible in early spring. Both sides of the Yala La are within Shey Phoksundo National Park.

Just north of Yala La (5,414m) is unclimbed Yara Chuli (6,236m, 29°41'22"N, 82°49'44"E), now an open peak on the Tibet frontier. (The Tibetan name is Sur Lung Kangri.) The ministry lists it as being in the "Palchung Hamga Himal" of Dolpo and suggests a caravan route from Shey, but such ministry approach routes largely should be disregarded.

Westward two kilometers from Yara Chuli is an unclimbed 6,293m peak on the true left bank of a major icefall descending from Tibet into Nepal's Chyandi Khola. On the true right bank of that glacier, at 29°43'09"N, 82°47'55"E, is unclimbed Changdi (6,623m, Tibetan name Lalung; the Finn map marks this peak as Chandi without a "g"). This peak should not to be confused with the Chandi Himal, 100 kilometers farther west. To access Changdi, an open peak, from the south, a formidable icefall must be overcome. Routes on the south face look uninviting but possible. Otherwise, the east ridge from the Tibet border, above the icefall, would certainly be feasible if you could

[Left] Seen from the northwest, Kaqur Kangri is high and behind, with Peak 6,095m in the center foreground. Off camera to the right is Peak 6,030m. *Luke Hughes* [Top right] Seen from above Yala La, to the southeast, are Lalung (left), Peak 6,293m (center), and Yara Chuli. *Julian Freeman-Attwood* [Bottom right] Pack animals headed north past Mugu village. *Julian Freeman-Attwood*

get there. Lalung (Changdi) was first photographed from the Tibet side in 1997 by a Japanese expedition making a reconnaissance of the highest peak in the Rongla Range, known as Kaqur Kangri (6,859m) to Tibetans.

But before we get to Kaqur Kangri, which lies four kilometers to the northwest of Lalung, there is another unclimbed border peak on the Nepal open list, close to the west of Lalung, named Kaipuchonam (6,329m, 29°43'32"N, 82°47'00"E). The Kaipuchonam Khola running up to it from the Chyandi Khola seems unexplored. A further two unclimbed 6,000-meter peaks (6,093m and 6,218m) form the border just east of Kaqur Kangri.

In October 2002, a Japanese expedition led by Toyoji Wada approached from Tibet and made the first ascent of Kaqur Kangri (6,859m) via its east ridge. This peak is also known as Zazi Kangri (Chinese) or Kanti Himal (Nepalese). Kanti Himal is an open peak in Nepal, although quite technical and threatened by serac hazard, and it is unclimbed as yet from the Nepal (south) side. A reconnaissance was done by Sadao Yoshinaga's expedition in autumn 1998, but no safe route could be ascertained on the 1,800-meter south face. (Note: On Google Earth, Kaqur Kangri is incorrectly labeled Kubi Kangri, which is a peak far to the west in the Changla Himla; it is also incorrectly stated as such on Wikipedia.)

A kilometer to the northwest of Kaqur Kangri is another unclimbed peak now on Nepal's open list named Myung Thang Kang (6,449m). This peak is hard to attain from the Mayonithan Khola, to the immediate south of Kaqur Kangri, and is probably best approached from

[Top] **Looking southwest from Rongla Kangri over the top of Kanti East (6,516m, snow dome in right foreground), with fluted Peak 6,273m in the center and Takla Kang (6,276m) in the distance to the left of Peak 6,273m.** *Bruce Normand* [Bottom left] **The south face of unclimbed Peak 6,273m.** [Bottom right] **Koji Kang North (6,275m, left center) from the Koji La.** *Julian Freeman-Attwood (two photos)*

the Koji Khola, leading up to the Koji La, farther west.

Onward to the west are three not particularly prominent unclimbed 6,000-meter peaks, the most interesting of which is a 6,014-meter peak on a promontory just a kilometer from Kaqur Kangri's 1,300-meter west face. The next permitted peak westward is Takla Kang (6,276m, 29°45'40"N, 82°41'43"E). Again, the caravan route suggested by the Nepal ministry to access this peak, via the Takla Khola, is incorrect or at least a convoluted and long way around. It is easier from the Koji Khola.

The border now runs a little north and northeast toward the Koji La (5,495m, 29°49'35"N, 82°42'52"E). There is another prominent unclimbed 6,273-meter peak and then a further two unnamed peaks (6,030m and 6,095m). We then arrive at Koji Kang North (6,275m and on the open list) and Koji South (6,159m). These lie on either side of the Koji La and were both climbed in 1997 by the Japanese, led by Yoshinaga, in pursuit of a route to Kaqur Kangri, prior to its first ascent in 2002. The routes taken were the obvious ones running up from the pass in opposite directions.

The Koji La was an important trade route in old times between Mugu and the Changtang ("north country") of Tibet. It is now infrequently used except, we were told, by smugglers. I led a trip to Mugu and the Koji Khola in 2007 with Nick Colton, Luke Hughes, and Phil Wickens, trying to find a route to Rongla Kangri (see more on this peak below). We climbed a peak just under 6,000 meters near the pass leading to Tibet's upper Rongla Glacier, which had never been visited before.

The south face of Kanti East (6,516m, the south summit of Rongla Kangri) is on the left, with Koji Kang South (6,159m) on the right. *Julian Freeman-Attwood*

SECTION 2: KOJI LA TO NAMJA LA
KANTI HIMAL (a.k.a. RONGLA RANGE IN TIBET)

31KM ALONG THE BORDER; **9 CLIMBED** 6,000M PEAKS; **3 UNCLIMBED** 6,000M PEAKS

THE NAMJA KHOLA is the main valley route that runs north from Mugu village and serves all the peaks of the Koji Khola, the Kojichuwa (Kojichwa) Khola, and on up to the border at the Namja La (4,907m). All the main summits lie to the east of this khola, though to the immediate west, at 29°44'46"N, 82°28'20"E, is a natural rock arch that was first photographed by Ed Douglas on a trip with me in 2009. In 2018 a team led by Anna Torretta attempted to climb the arch but without success (*see p.309*).

From the Koji La (5,495m), the Tibet frontier runs northwest, then west, and then back north. The major peak on the border close to the Koji La is Rongla Kangri (6,647m). This peak gives its name to the whole range, from a Tibetan's point of view, and its main summit lies completely within Tibet. Rongla Kangri's south summit lies on the Nepal border and is itself a permitted peak in Nepal now named Kanti East (6,516m). The first ascent of both Rongla peaks was made by Bruce Normand, solo, in November 2018 by the northeast face of Kanti East and thus by the linking ridge from the south summit to the main summit of Rongla Kangri (*see p.310*).

The next 6,000-meter peak that forms the border, Peak 6,275m, also was climbed by Normand. Immediately west again is a smaller, unclimbed summit (6,272m), followed by another summit soloed by Normand in 2018: Churau (6,419m, 29°50'06"N, 82°38'25"E). This mountain is incorrectly named Kanti on the HGM-Finn map.

Any traveller who remained in the main Namja Khola north of the entrance to the Koji Khola would arrive in only three kilometers at the entrance of Kojichuwa Khola, a remarkable valley with some serious objectives. In 2008, Spanish climbers reconnoitered Kojichuwa Chuli via the Koji-

chuwa La (5,550m), and the next spring two of them and several others returned to attempt Mugu Chuli, which they found too threatened by seracs and avalanches.

I had done a recce here with Ed Douglas and Nick Colton in spring 2009, just after the second Spanish visit, and climbed a sub-6,000m peak on the khola's true right bank. Also on the true right bank, at 29°49'10"N, 82°36'59"E, is spectacular unclimbed Peak 6,047m and another peak about a kilometer northeast at 6,137 meters.

After this trip, we shared with British mountaineer Mick Fowler a safe technical line we had seen on the west face of Mugu Chuli (previously called Gojung, but Mugu Chuli is preferred). This is the 6,310-meter peak some three kilometers further north again from Peak 6,137m. Mick and Dave Turnbull climbed the 1,100-meter face in 2011, descending to the north over a peak called Kojichuwa South (6,264m) and thus making a second first ascent. (This is now a permitted peak.)

North again is another inspiring and unnamed mountain (Peak 6,259m), also unclimbed. Finally comes the permitted but unclimbed Kojichuwa Chuli (6,439m), which lies a kilometer north again. This was attempted via the northwest ridge by a team led by the prolific explorer Tamotsu Ohnishi in 2009 and then by another Japanese team in 2010; the latter reached a northern foresummit but did not continue along the corniced ridge to the main top.

Between here and the Namja La the frontier ridge is of no great interest, more or less part of the Tibet plateau, with no peaks attaining the 6,000-meter mark. The nearest thing to it, six kilometers south of the pass along the frontier, is a mountain called Kaptang (5,965m). This is a permitted peak first climbed in 2009 by Ohnishi and two others, via the north face.

The Namja La (4,907m) is a route much used by Bhotia (Tibetan) traders, probably the busiest pass until you reach the Lapche La far to the west. The author saw 80 laden yaks arriving into Mugu in a single day in 2007. Some 13 kilometers into Tibet was an area that trucks could reach and where transhipment onto pack animals occurred. Now vehicles can get as far as the pass and some way down into Nepal, but not all the way down to Mugu. At Mugu itself, being at just 3,000 meters altitude, yaks go no lower and mules, horses, and sheep take over as pack animals. This 3,000-meter line is approximately as low as yaks tend to go all along northern Nepal and therefore as far as most Tibetan traders go. Thus the "Bhotia line."

[Top] Unnamed and unclimbed Peak 6,047m rising above the Kojichuwa Khola. *Julian Freeman-Attwood* [Middle] The west face of Mugu Chuli (6,310m), climbed by Mick Fowler and Dave Turnbull in 2011. They descended to the left over Kojichuwa South, making its first ascent as well. *Mick Fowler* [Bottom] Another unclimbed rock peak (6,259m) in the Kojichuwa Khola. *Julian Freeman-Attwood*

[Left] Kangla Kang (6,129m) from Kang La. This peak was called Pratibandhit Lek by the German team that made the first ascent in 2017. [Right] The north face of Bhandar Lek (6,024m), climbed solo by Jack Bynum in December 2016, in less snowy condition. *Julian Freeman-Attwood (both photos)*

SECTION 3: NAMJA LA TO KANG LA
KANGLA HIMAL

17KM ALONG THE BORDER; **2 CLIMBED** 6,000M PEAKS

THE KANGLA HIMAL boasts just two 6,000-meter peaks (counting one away from the actual border.) It is a wild area of the Tibet frontier oriented mostly west-east. The first reconnaissance was Sadao Yoshinaga's trip in 1998 following his team's recce of Kanti Himal's south face. North of Mugu, they passed northwest into the Take (Takya) Khola and over a col at 5,100 meters into the Gorakh watershed. They continued to the Kang La itself but not further into Gorakh Himal except a little way up the Kangla Khola. They descended past the grazing grounds of Bholbihan and to Nepka, the only significant village in the Take Khola. It seems they were the first foreigners into the village. Here the Take Khola becomes the Loti Karnali Nadi, and two days down from here it joins the main mule trail from Jumla to Simikot.

In the area just north of the 5,100-meter col mentioned above are two sub-6,000-meter peaks that were climbed by a German expedition (Nettekoven, et al) in October 2017. These were called Sunkala Topi (5,865m, unofficial name) and Lek Fett (5,767m).

The sole 6,000-meter peak on the frontier in this sector is Kangla Kang (6,130m, called Pratibandhit Lek by the German expedition), which lies at 30°00'17N, 82°25'15"E. I had attempted to get to this peak in spring 2015, along with Phil Bartlett, Nick Colton, Ed Douglas, Crag Jones, and Skip Novak, but encountered the worst spring snow for at least a decade and could not get farther than the Bholbihan Khola (see Section 4 below). In late May 2017, I returned and set up an ABC on the Kang La (5,358m, 30°00'49"N, 82°24'19"E) and attempted the northwest ridge to 5,700 meters but was defeated by endless poor weather, snow, and wind. That fall the German expedition completed our route.

An impressive nearby peak in this sector is Bhandar Lek (6,024m, 29°49'26"N, 82°17'50"E), east of the Loti Karnali Nadi. Bhandar Lek is an unofficial name that appears on Google Earth and is unlikely to be the local name.

In December 2016, American climber Jack Bynum walked solo from Simikot without porter assistance via the Margor La to Nepka (the same route taken by the author in 2013; see below) and on to a base camp near the foot of the mountain's north-northeast spur. From here to the summit was about 2,500 vertical meters. Bynum soloed the peak, often exposed and quite technical, in three days and traversed the mountain by rappelling nearly 1,500 meters down the southwest face, landing back in the Loti Karnali Nadi, the last two days without water due to lack of fuel. This was a very notable ascent.

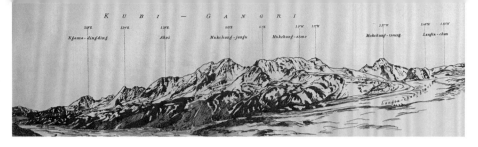

DataBasin, DIVA-GIS, MapCruzin, ChinaMap, Nepal Survey Department, OpenStreetMap, ESRI

SECTION 4: KANG LA TO BHOLBIHAN ICEFALL
GORAKH HIMAL

18KM ALONG THE BORDER; **0 CLIMBED** 6,000M PEAKS; **5 UNCLIMBED** 6,000M PEAKS

THIS IS THE least accessible of the northwestern Himals. There are two access points. One is via the Kangla Khola, which would bring the traveller to only one of the main summits, Gorakh Kang, and is unlikely to yield a safe route on that peak in any event. The other is via the Bholbihan Khola (see below).

Starting at the Kang La (5,358m), the next border peak two kilometers west is Ngomoding-ding (6,133m). It is unclimbed, not on the permitted list, and with a reasonable route only from the Tibet side. This has been referred to as Kangla II, but that is incorrect. The mountain's name is Tibetan and was referred to by Swedish geographer Sven Hedin during his travels in Tibet from 1906 to 1908. (*Hedin's 1906 sketch map of the range, seen from Tibet, is reproduced above.*)

Some four kilometers further west is Gorakh Kang (6,254m), unclimbed and on the permit list. Although it gives its name to the range, it is by a short margin *not* the highest peak in the Gorakh Himal; that honor goes to Asajya Tuppa (see below). Gorakh Kang's Tibetan name is Absi, again mentioned by Hedin. As this peak is not accessible from Tibet, it would have to be tackled via the icefall at the head of the Kangla Khola and then up the west face, or else via the same face from the Bholbihan Khola.

All other peaks in the Gorakh Himal can only be accessed by way of the Bholbihan Khola. The author and others made the first reconnaissance into this khola in 2013. The route to this and all points west of here is via Simikot and its airstrip, which is reached from Nepalgunj by Twin Otter plane. From Simikot, the Karnali River is followed and thus into the Loti Karnali Nadi to Nepka village. We were the second foreign party to visit Nepka, after Yoshinaga in 1998, and thus the first Westerners there. This is an extremely poor region with few porters available; the men that may be hired likely will be very badly equipped.

From Simikot to the mouth of the Bholbihan with mules is an eight-day trek through, at times, some fine primary forest (although it should be said that deforestation is a real problem in Nepal, whether in or out of a national park). The Bholbihan itself is impossible to access with mules, and even with a few porters from Nepka the going in 2013 was extremely taxing over boulders covered in lichen and roots and through thick thorn bushes. Once through these difficulties, the valley opens into fairly easy going, and after 14 kilometers you reach the snout of the Bholbihan Glacier.

At this base camp, a cwm emanates from the northeast and a view can be had of the wide south face of the next 6,000-meter peak (and highest of the range): Asajya Tuppa (6,265m). This is unclimbed and on the permitted list. Its Tibetan name is Muchung-Jungu. There is a col at about 5,400 meters at the base of the mountain's southeast ridge, giving rise to a glacial basin within Tibet; this basin links with the col to the east marking the head of the Kangla Khola, mentioned above. From these border cols, Asajya and Gorakh could possibly be climbed.

Asajya has a west peak (unnamed) at 6,055 meters, and two kilometers on again is a peak at 6,088 meters (HGM-Finn map height) that I unofficially named "False Gorakh" because it has been called Gorakh incorrectly on some maps. Its Tibetan name is Muchung-Tseung. This brings us to the Bholbihan icefall and the west end of the Gorakh Himal and thus to the east end of the Changla Himal.

[Top] This map covers the places described in Sections 5 through 8 of this article. Approaches to all of these areas begin with a flight to Simikot, followed by approach treks of up to 100 kilometers. Until 1961, the Nepal-Tibet border in this area was about 18 kilometers further south than it is today (see section 7). More details and many more photos from these areas can be found with this article at the AAJ website. *Anna Riling* [Middle left] The east faces of Gorakh Kang (6,254m, a.k.a. Absi) on the left and Ngomodingding (6,133m) in center. *Christof Nettekoven* [Middle right] Ancient oak forest in the Take Khola. [Bottom left] Unclimbed Asajya Tuppa (a.k.a. Muchung-Jungu, 6,265m) from the south. [Bottom right] Muchung Tseung ("False Gorakh"), 6,088 meters, from the east. The main summit is far back. *Julian Freeman-Attwood (three photos)*

Langtachen (6,284m, left) and Peak 6,198m from the Laruppya Khola. *Julian Freeman-Attwood*

SECTION 5: BHOLBIHAN ICEFALL TO CHANG LA
CHANGLA HIMAL

38KM ALONG THE BORDER; **4 CLIMBED** 6,000M PEAKS; **15 UNCLIMBED** 6,000M PEAKS

THE TWO PEAKS immediately west of the Bholbihan icefall are firstly the unnamed Peak 6,198m and then Langtachen (6,284m). Neither is on the permitted list, and both are unclimbed. It would be a convoluted but possible journey to reach Langtachen's north face, which is in Tibet, via the Bholbihan icefall. In the post-monsoon of 2012, the author, along with Phil Bartlett, Nick Colton, and Ed Douglas, tried to get to the west face of this peak via the Luruppya Khola. This was reached from Simikot via the lower Dojam Khola, from where the rest of the Changla range is accessed. The Luruppya was probably the most beautiful valley we had ever visited in Nepal, heavily forested with great oaks, wild and magical. After some days this brought us to Langtachen's west face, on which we were disappointed to find no reasonably safe route.

The whole of this section along the Changla Himal and the Chandi Himal further west comprise the headwaters of the Yarlung Tsangpo (which becomes the Brahmaputra as it flows into India). Discovering the exact source for this mighty river impelled various foreign expeditions to roam southwestern Tibet as early as the mid-1800s, and the approximate source was known by 1900.

In 1906, Sven Hedin accomplished possibly the most scientific study of the source by measuring flows at the Kubi Tsangpo's confluence with the Chemayungdung Chu, some 12 kilometers northwest of present-day Laru township. Hedin found the largest flow was from the Kubi Tsangpo, originating from the Changla Himal (Kubi Kangri), and he named this as the source of the Yarlung Tsangpo. Nevertheless, the Chemayungdung Chu (river) is a longer stream by some 30 kilometers, originating in the Chandi Himal (Angsi Glacier) and is backed up by Tibetan tradition as the source, which the Kubi Kangri glaciers are not. Therefore, despite its lesser flow, the longer Chemayungdung Chu is now the accepted source of the Yarlung Tsangpo, being the furthest point upstream from the estuary in the Bay of Bengal. (The most concise work on this whole matter, discussing whether a river's source is defined by length, flow, or tradition, was written by the Indian ascetic and explorer Swami Pranavananda as a result of extensive travels in the region in 1936 and '37.)

But we diverge from our border travels. The range now bends north from Langtachen with the border passing over three unnamed and unclimbed peaks (6,202m, 6,122m, and 6,223m) before landing on Gave Ding (6,521m, 30°07'32"N, 82°09'56"E). Hedin gave the name Gave Ting to a nearby peak, but this lies four kilometers to the east and entirely in Tibet.

In 2011, along with Nick Colton and Ed Douglas, I attempted Gave Ding after making the first recce into the south fork of the Lachama Khola (off the Chuwa Khola, the main drag to the Chang La and thus into Tibet). This south fork took us into the unknown country to the south of Gave Ding and then to the Luruppya La (5,200m), linking to the Luruppya Khola, mentioned above, which we subsequently explored. We attempted Gave Ding's south ridge via a steep couloir gaining the ridge but were forced back by bad weather at around 6,000 meters.

The first ascent of Gave Ding was by Mick Fowler and Paul Ramsden in 2015 by the north face. This is probably the most impressive climb attained in the whole area to date—more technical than either Jack Bynum's route up Bhandar Lek or indeed Fowler's fine route on Mugu Chuli. There was some 1,500 meters of climbing over five days on very steep mixed ground, followed by a day of rappelling. They rightly received a Piolet d'Or for this climb. Another quite distinct 6,045-meter unclimbed peak forms part of the long west ridge of Gave Ding.

Kubi Kangri (6,721m, Nepali name Lachama Chuli and Chinese name Kubi Dongdong) is the next peak to the north and the second-highest covered in this article, after Kaqur Kangri. This was the goal of the 1983 all-women's Japanese expedition who were the earliest visitors to the Lachama Khola and the north side of Gave Ding. At that time, this peak was misidentified, due to earlier maps, as Changla peak, which is in fact up near the Chang La itself. The Japanese were unsuccessful, and it has to be said to their credit that the Nepal side of the range hereabouts is unrelentingly steep with no obvious good routes.

[Top] Gave Ding's east summit and Peak 6,223m just beyond from Gave Ding's summit, with "Gave Ting" in center across the glacial basin. [Middle] Gave Ding (6,521m) from the north. [Bottom] Paul Ramsden climbing Gave Ding in 2015. Behind is the northern Changla Himal. *Mick Fowler (three photos)*

Kubi Kangri (a.k.a. Lachama Chuli, 6,721m) on the left, with Gave Ding high on the right, seen from the Lachama Khola. *Julian Freeman-Attwood*

Kubi Kangri's only ascent was made in 2007, from the Tibet side, by a Japanese expedition led by Atsushi Senda and Toyoshi Wada. (This is the trip that also made a reconnaissance of Langtachen and an attempt on Gorakh Kang/Absi). The Kubi Kangri ascent was by a straightforward route up the southeast face and east ridge. The peak is now on Nepal's permitted list along with its northern summit, Lachama North (6,628m), which is still unclimbed.

The border carries on north for another kilometer to a prominent unnamed and unlisted peak at 6,581 meters. From here to the important trading pass of Chang La, the peaks are all unclimbed and difficult of access on the Nepal side, easier on the Tibet side. The border first heads west then northwest, with some seven unnamed 6,000-meter peaks: Peak 6,233m and then a significant peak of 6,506m, followed by 6,391m, 6,122m, 6210m, and 6,133m, this latter at 30°13'29"N, 82°07'39E. The border range is then uninteresting for about five kilometers before passing over Peak 6,222m and landing on Changla (6,563m, a.k.a. Chema Yungdung) and finally onto Changla's distinct west summit at 6,162 meters.

Changla was also explored by the Japanese women's expedition of 1983 and then visited in autumn 1998 by Tomatsu Ohnishi. His six-man team made the first ascent of Changla's west summit via the north ridge and west ridge. In late September 2010, Changla's main summit was climbed by another Japanese team, led by Hirofumi Kabayashi, from the north.

SECTION 6: CHUWA KHOLA TO LIMI VALLEY
NYALU LEK (HIMAL)

40KM SPAN; **6 CLIMBED** 6,000M PEAKS; **9 UNCLIMBED** 6,000M PEAKS

WE NOW MOMENTARILY diverge form the Tibet frontier to look at the Nyalu Lek, a large group of mountains about halfway between Simikot, to the south, and the border to the north, along with associated peaks to the west, all the way to Ardang (a.k.a. Chyoro Ri) on the south bank of the Limi Valley. Geographically, rather than politically, this is the main Himalayan divide. It is truly arid, and anywhere to the north of the Nyalu La (30°09'48"N, 81°42'26"E) is Trans-Himalayan in nature.

The closest 6000er to the west of the Chuwa Khola, approached by the Lor Khola, is a peak called Chhamsacka (6,246m), which lies just 16 kilometers north of Simikot and was photographed from the east by the author in 2011 from Gave Ding. I then did a recce of it from the west (via the Hepka Khola) in 2015. The first ascent was in autumn 2016 by Becky Coles and Simon Verspeak via a fine route on the east ridge. Some fixed rope and tent platforms were found by them from an unknown previous attempt. (They heard another name for the peak, Lasarmu La,

[Top] Peaks 6,098m (left) and 6,010m (center right), looking up the Limi Glacier from the north. [Bottom] Nyalu Kang (6,265m) on the left and Nying Himal (6,140m) from the Nying Glacier. *Paulo Grobel (both photos)*

which sounds rather more like the pass to the north of the mountain, running into the Thanmuche Khola on the Hepka side.) Immediately west is fine unclimbed Peak 6,028m. The Hepka Khola is the next south-to-north valley west of Simikot, and it is surprising to me that no climbers seemed to have travelled farther up this valley than Hepka village prior to 2015, when I did my reconnaissance. This khola would give access to Peak 6,028m and to the south side of Nyalu Lek itself.

The north side of the Nyalu Lek, which is much more glaciated than the south and has better potential climbing routes, can be accessed either via the Nying La (5,448m, 30°13'29"N, 81°53'07"E), again off the Chuwa Khola, thus going counter-clockwise from Simikot, or over the Nyalu La, thus going clockwise. Both approaches end up at the snout of the Nyalu Glacier in the upper Nyalu Khola.

Looking south from above the Nying La, you can see Peak 6,065m, which a French team climbed by the south face in autumn 2018 and unofficially named Phasang (*see p.308*). South from there are two peaks: 6,084m and 6,022m. In September 2017 a Japanese team climbed Peak 6,022m from the west. The east end of the main Nyalu ridge is Peak 6,150m and then Nyalu Lek itself (6,265m), the

Nearing the summit of Aichyn (6,055m) in 2015, with the Nying Valley below and the mountains of the Takphu Himal in the distance. *Paulo Grobel*

highest of the range. Some two kilometers westward, fine Nying Himal (6,140m) sits at the far west end of the group. All these are unclimbed and unlisted.

There are three more unclimbed 6,000ers to the west of the Nyalu (Nying) Glacier: Peaks 6,098m, 6,010m, and 6,053m. Also in this area, Peak 6,194m was climbed by the French team in 2018 via the southwest face and west ridge, and was unofficially named Limi Koti.

The last two peaks accessed from here have both been climbed; both are just north of the Nyalu Khola. The first is Aichyn (a.k.a. Ashvin, 6,055m), which was climbed by a Japanese team in very early September 2015. French guide Paulo Grobel, who had got to know the area well, and his party were en route to do just the same thing and met the Japanese returning. Disappointed, they made the second ascent of the mountain (also via the west ridge) three weeks later. The day before, they made the first ascent of Aichyn North (6,025m), only just south of the Chandi Himal (Section 7).

There is one 6,000-meter peak to the west of the Nyalu La, and this is Ardang (6,034m), which is on the permitted list and as yet unclimbed. Paulo Grobel had designs on this peak in 2013. His group made a reconnaissance of the Phupharka peaks, just west of the Nyalu La, and had wanted to climb Aichyn that year but were thwarted by heavy spring snow. Instead they headed across the Phupharka country and over into the Limi Valley to Halji monastery and back. They hoped to climb Ardang during the return leg of this interesting journey, but bad weather persisted.

In autumn 2017, Mark Bielby and Emily Ward attempted Ardang without success, but did climb a nearby peak below 6,000 meters.

The north side of beautiful Ardang (6,034m) from the upper Limi Valley. *Paulo Grobel*

SECTION 7: CHANG LA TO LAPCHE LA
CHANDI HIMAL (GANGLUNG IN TIBET)

40KM ALONG THE BORDER; **2 CLIMBED** 6,000M PEAKS; **9 UNCLIMBED** 6,000M PEAKS

WE ARE BACK now on the Tibet frontier. This region is very dry and windy—in essence the traveller is on the Tibetan Plateau, at only a little less than 5,000 meters, anywhere west of the Chang La or north of the Nyalu La.

In fact, this Tibetan-feeling area of Nepal once officially lay in Tibet. Maps of the Survey of India in 1930 show the border from Changla to Nalakankar drawn some 18 kilometers farther south than today's frontier (where the Nyalu Lek range lies). Early maps gave the name Changla to the mountain in the position of today's Kubi Kangri (that is, south of today's Changla), and Nalakankar to a peak within the Takphu Himal, south of present-day Nalakankar (Section 8). In 1961, the border demarcation agreed between China and Nepal drew the line farther north, and eventually the Nepalese opened two peaks to climbers along the new frontier, using the new names Changla (Section 5) and Nalakankar, thus reinforcing that they controlled access to this area and not the Chinese.

But let us continue westward along today's frontier. Just west of the Chang La are two unclimbed, unnamed peaks of 6,030 meters and 6,254 meters. The next peak is the highest in the Chandi Himal—not Chandi itself but Kananu Pukari (6,256m, Tibetan name Ganglung Kangri). Less than a kilometer

[Top] Kananu Pukari (6,256m, left) and Changla (6,563m, far right). *Paulo Grobel* [Bottom] From the slopes of Peak 6,024m: (A) Changwatang (6,130m). (B) Peak 5,988m. (C) Peak 6,022m. (D) Peak 6,040m). (E) Chandi Himal (6,069m). *Guy Wilson*

south of it is another unnamed peak (6,171m). Then, four kilometers west on the border, is Chandi itself (6,142m). This unclimbed peak is on the permit list and lies north of the Nin Khola, which runs parallel to the border. If we continue along the frontier, there is an unnamed 6,022-meter peak, and then a 6,024-meter peak, and finally Peaks 6,069m and 6,025m, which are the last 6,000ers, as the border runs, for the next 45 kilometers. In 2013, Guy Wilson and other climbers from the U.K. climbed Peak 6,204m and attempted Peak 6,069m unsuccessfully.

Just south of the border here, and south of the Nin Khola, is Changwatang (6,130m), which is on the permit list. This peak lies only four kilometers north of "Aichyn North," climbed from Nyalu side by Paulo Grobel's team in 2015, as mentioned above. Changwatang was first climbed by Tamotsu Ohnishi and party in late June 2000, and it was also climbed in 2008 and 2011.

There is an unnamed 6,076-meter peak three kilometers west of Changwatang which is unclimbed. From here to the Lapche La is 25 kilometers.

SECTION 8: LAPCHE LA TO HILSA
NALAKANKAR HIMAL (INCORPORATING TAKPHU HIMAL)

50KM ALONG THE BORDER; **10 CLIMBED** 6,000M PEAKS; **2 UNCLIMBED** 6,000M PEAKS

Til Kang (6,369m, left) and Takphu Himal (6,395m) from the east. *Julian Freeman-Attwood*

THE LAPCHE LA (5,018m) has a motorable track running over from the Tibet side and then south through the upper Limi Valley and over the Nyalu La, and which may soon link with Simikot. One day roads may in turn link with Gamgadhi. Whatever the pros and cons of roads, this will inevitably spell the end of any ancient forest on the Nepal side of the Nyalu mountains.

From the Lapche La west to the Nalakankar La, just 12 kilometers south of Lake Manasarovar in Tibet, in the most northwestern point of Nepal, is a distance of 25 kilometers. The border to this point undulates in typical Tibetan high plains fashion at between 5,000 and 5,700 meters. After the Nalakankar La, the border bends more or less due south, and eight kilometers on is the peak on the permit list called Nalakankar (6,062m), climbed by Ohnishi in 2000 from the south; they also ascended the east face of Nalakankar South, a kilometer south, at 6,024 meters. To the southeast are two peaks, 6,042 meters and 6,055 meters, the latter climbed in 2018 (*see p.102*).

The final group of this overview is the Takphu Himal, overall a part of the Nalakankar Range, straddling the east and west sides of the border. If you count peaks in this group that lie entirely in Tibet, there are nine mountains over 6,000 meters in the Takphu Himal. Takphu North (6,142m) is the northernmost and is on the Nepal permit list. This was climbed in October 2016 by a German Alpine Club (DAV) expedition.

The next 6,000er is unnamed Peak 6,153m at the far back of the glacier leading to Takphu North, climbed in 2016, just prior to the German expedition, by a Japanese team led by Tetsuji Otsue.

The next peak to the south in the main range is Takphu Himal (6,395m and on the permit list), which was climbed in October 2018 during an expedition that I led. In all, our team of five climbed seven peaks in this area, six of them first ascents—many of them solo by Bruce Normand. (*See the expedition report beginning on next page for details.*) Among them was Til Kang (6,369m), which shows itself from Til village, dominating the head of the valley. South of the peaks we climbed is Kandumbu (6,219m), which remains unclimbed. Finally there is one more unclimbed peak (ca 6,180m) within Tibet, to the west of Kandumbu.

The border now runs for 10 kilometers southwest and inexorably downhill to Hilsa village at 3,640 meters on the Karnali River, one of the gateways for devotees to Mt. Kailash in Tibet.

ABOUT THE AUTHOR: *Julian Freeman-Attwood lives on the edge of Snowdonia, North Wales. He has led or participated in some 35 mountaineering expeditions, usually to attempt unclimbed 6,000-meter peaks. The author would like to apologize to any persons or expeditions inadvertently omitted from this overview.*

"Peak 3" (6,422m) and "Peak 1" (6,613m) from Til Kang to the north, taken during the first ascent of Til Kang in October 2018. *Ed Douglas*

TAKPHU 2018

BRITISH EXPEDITION CLIMBS SEVEN PEAKS

JULIAN FREEMAN-ATTWOOD

The Takphu Himal in Nepal's extreme far west is only 15 kilometers south of Gurla Mandhata (7,694 meters), which towers over holy Lake Manasarovar in Tibet, with the holy of holies Mt. Kailash just a little further north. Takphu is best approached via the Nyalu La, a 5,001-meter pass, which we reached in late September after four days of walking from Simikot with a mule train. It would have been three days except for the disappearance of our mules in the Chungsa Khola. Until mules have crossed a divide like the Nyalu La, their thoughts are of home. Our mule drivers gave chase and eventually found 14 of the 16 animals, which meant the others each would carry an extra 10 kilograms. They were not going to be happy with the shirkers who had bolted.

My companions on this journey were Ed Douglas, editor of the *Alpine Journal*; Nick Colton, the deputy CEO of the British Mountaineering Council; Christof Nettekoven, a great mountain chronicler and climber from Germany; and last, but by no means least, the Scottish climber Bruce Normand. Bruce has possibly made more first ascents of 6,000-meter peaks than anyone alive, and after this postmonsoon period on Takphu and beyond, that is even more likely to be true, as will be seen.

From Nyalu La, our route dropped into the Talun Valley, at the top end of the fabled Limi Valley with its ancient monasteries at Halji, founded in the 11th century by Richen Zangpo, and another at Til. Our plan was to approach Takphu via the plateau above the Limi Valley, rather than from Til or Halji down below. Previous expeditions in this area, in 2008 and 2016, had been prevented by villagers from entering the mountains or fined upon their return. Our route thus took us past the grazing grounds of Traktse and up onto plateau proper. Wild ass and Tibetan antelope were seen. On October 6, some 100 kilometers out from Simikot, we established base camp at 4,982 meters in front of a glacial lake near the termination of the Sakya Glacier. The Tibetan herders had already abandoned summer grazing and gone down to their villages in the Limi Valley.

The frontier at Takphu is oriented north-south, and this Himal is part of the longer Nalakan-

Mule train taking a break en route to base camp. *Bruce Normand*

kar ranges that run up to the Lapche La in the north and down to the township of Hilsa on the Karnali River in the south, the entry point for pilgrims, mostly Indians, to Mt. Kailash. Until 2015, most devotees had crossed into Tibet east of Kathmandu and then driven west to Kailash, but the earthquake that year flattened the area around that border crossing. At this point, the only way to Kailash was via air to Simikot and then a five-day walk to the Hilsa border crossing, but since most Hindu pilgrims from India weren't about to walk five days there and back, a fleet of helicopters has ferried the faithful between Simikot and Hilsa in recent years.

Our arrival at base was greeted with snow and some wind. I had a filthy hacking cough that never left me on this trip. Straight in front of base camp was unclimbed Takphu Himal (6,395m) on the right and Til Kang (6,369m), for which we had the climbing permit, on the left. It seemed there was no safe way onto Til Kang, as there was a band of seracs across the whole east side above the true left bank of the Sakya Glacier, and even the east ridge could not easily be attained. It looked like it needed to be tackled from the unseen Tibetan side, starting from a glacial basin that we knew to exist there. As for Takphu Himal, that could be attained up the Sakya Glacier and then up right (true left bank) into what I called the Takphu North Glacier. This glacier had been ascended twice before, first by a Japanese expedition in 2016 that climbed a peak of 6,153 meters at the far back of the glacier, followed a month later by a German team that made the first ascent of Takphu North (6,142m) from a col linking that peak with Peak 6,153m.

On October 8, Bruce, Ed, and Christoph did a recce up the Takphu North Glacier, and in the process Bruce made the second ascent of Peak 6,153m and scouted a route up Takphu Himal from a col linking that to another mountain we called P2, a high peak in Tibet of 6,521 meters. We needed to give these peaks easy identification numbers as there were at least three unnamed mountains in the group.

The weather was not at all the settled affair you might expect post-monsoon, with the mainly westerly airstream often punctuated with a less settled southwesterly flow. It also was abnormally cold. While the others were on the Takphu North Glacier, Nick and I, with me coughing and spluttering, headed north to recce a remote pair of peaks and dump a tent and gear at about 5,400 meters by a small moraine lake. After a day back at base camp, Bruce, Ed, and Christoph headed back up the Takphu North Glacier on October 10, putting a tent in at around 5,750 meters. Meanwhile, Nick and I returned to and occupied our tent by the lake.

The 11th was a cold, blustery, cloud-scudding day with visibility coming and going. One of those days that's too good to renege on a plan but certainly too cold with the wind chill to have hands out of gloves for more then a very short moment. Nick and I had a fairly ruthless trudge of a climb, not technical at all but on one section surmounting some hideous scree and boulders, to get onto the south ridge of Peak 6,055m (30°20'12"N, 81°26'54"E). There was no protection from a continuous southwest wind of perhaps 35 knots. We gained the rounded top in early afternoon and quickly headed down. Nick had slightly frost-nipped toes with his single-layer boots.

The others, meantime, had a hard slog from their tent in soft snow, taking some three hours to ascend the 330 meters to the col at 6,130 meters below Takphu Himal. This brought them to the easy-angled west ridge, which they ascended in bad visibility, near whiteout at times. The top was reached about noon, and with no inclination to stay long they descended with some route-finding difficulty into their glacial basin and spent the night there, returning to base next day. Christoph also had some frost damage to some toes.

After a rest day, Ed and Bruce started off for Til Kang on October 14. The plan was that they would climb this mountain together and then Bruce might go on and solo what he could of the nearby Tibetan peaks. To reach the Tibetan glacial basin at the far (west) side of Til Kang, they crossed the pass at the head of the Sakya Glacier and went over into the upper Sayogan Khola. They kept as much height as they could, traversing west across some tricky ground, to reach the Tibet border col at 5,700 meters; this separates Til Kang, north of the col, from Peak 3 to the south of it. (P3 was the 6,422-meter peak once called Nalakankar before the Nepal frontier was moved to the north and the name Nalakankar applied to another summit by the new border—see p.99.) Bruce and Ed camped at this border col.

On the 15th they headed to the west spur of Til Kang, climbing a little to the right of some potentially problematic seracs. The route was serious rather than technical, mostly 45–55°, and they reached the top at 1:30 p.m. The retreat required a good deal of careful downclimbing. The weather remained very cold, and now it was Ed's turn to sustain some frost damage. They both spent the night back at the col after a great effort.

Ed returned to base in early evening of the next day by the same route as the outward journey. Bruce remained alone in the Tibetan glacial basin, and that morning he headed south from the col to P1, the highest peak in the range (6,613m), some two kilometers away. He climbed the peak by the north face, with some difficulties toward the top of the route. Views in the western distance included Nanda Devi.

He returned to the tent on the col that night and then, on the 17th, headed south to P3 (6,422m), which he climbed from the col between it and P1, essentially via the mountain's west ridge. (This mountain historically has been called Takphu's highest peak, but it is the highest only if you are counting peaks on the frontier ridge rather than the group as a whole, including the Tibetan mountains.)

As if these climbs had not been enough for the supremely energetic Bruce, on October 18 he continued to mop up the range by heading northwest from his tent to climb P2 (6,521m) by its southeast face. Rather than retreat the same way, he traversed over and down to the P2–Takphu Himal col, and then went back up Takphu Himal's west ridge (thus making the mountain's second ascent, a week after the first) before descending its untrod south ridge back to the col tent.

Bruce returned to base camp the next day, October 19, via the same pass linking the head of the Sayogan Khola and Sakya Glacier. We had begun to get concerned. This had been a seriously fine effort by any standard—away for six days and really out on a limb, alone in very wild, high country. The mules arrived the same day. We left for Simikot on October 20, carrying all our garbage—nothing was left at base camp or on the mountains. 📷

The expedition members would like to thank the Mount Everest Foundation and the Montane Alpine Club Climbing Fund for their kind grant assistance.

[Top] "Peak 2" (6,521m) from Takphu Himal. [Middle] "Peak 1," showing the first ascent by the north face. *Bruce Normand (two photos)* [Bottom] The "supremely energetic" Normand on Til Kang, with Gurla Mandhata (7,694m) far back. *Ed Douglas*

CLIMBS & EXPEDITIONS

CLIMBS & EXPEDITIONS reports generally are arranged geographically, from north to south, and from west to east, within a country or region. Unless noted, all reports are from 2018. The complete *AAJ* database, from 1929 to present, can be searched at *publications.americanalpineclub.org*. Online reports frequently contain additional text, photos, maps, and topos—look for these symbols indicating additional online resources:

FULL-LENGTH REPORT	ADDITIONAL PHOTOS	MAPS OR TOPOS	VIDEO OR MULTIMEDIA

Alex Huber partway up the 56-pitch south ridge of Suma Brakk, above the Choktoi Glacier in Pakistan (see p.285). *Fabian Buhl*

UNITED STATES

Kyle Willis following a pitch on the chossy northwest ridge of Boston Peak, near the end of a four-day traverse. Sharkfin Tower is below and left; Forbidden Peak is the rock pyramid in center; and Eldorado Peak, near the start of the traverse and surrounded by glaciers, is high on the left. *Sam Boyce*

WASHINGTON / NORTH CASCADES

BOSTON BASIN, BOSTON MARATHON

SOMETIME IN THE summer of 2017, Kyle Willis told me about his idea to do a technical circum-navigation of Boston Basin in the North Cascades. That August, we packed for a couple of days and prepared for a lot of scrambling. But after climbing Sahale Mountain and seeing what we were getting into, we realized we had grossly underestimated the endeavor and ran back to the car.

Come July 2018, the stoke was high. We packed for four days out and planned to start at the Hidden Lake Trailhead and traverse the ridge clockwise (from west to east), the opposite direction we originally intended, tagging all the major peaks to Sahale.

On day one we busted up the Hidden Lake Trail, taking the turn-off for Sibley Pass. Once on the main ridge, there is a faint climber's trail generally used to access Marble Creek Basin. Our first objective, however, was the Triad. With the limited published information on the Triad, it was unclear if anyone had done a complete west to east traverse of the mountain. Much of this terrain was serious and exposed 4th-class and low 5th-class scrambling. The west face of Middle Triad provides both the best rock and the crux of the Triad Traverse (5.6 R).

After tagging these three summits, we dropped off the ridge and made our way across snow slopes toward Eldorado Peak (8,868'). A quick jaunt up the glacier brought us to a low point in the south ridge. While not described in any guide, this ridge (5.6) provided some of the best climbing on the traverse, with a handful of legitimate classic pitches along the knife-edge ridge. Rambling down Eldorado's east ridge, we realized the sun was setting, so we took advantage of a super-cush camp at the base of this ridge.

On day two, we quickly made our way across glaciers and scenic climber's paths to the Torment col. In trying to keep the traverse as pure as possible, we opted to climb the obscure northwest ridge of Mt. Torment (8,120', 5.8). From the summit we headed east onto the classic Torment-Forbidden Traverse (V 5.6). Wet rock and seasonal snow made things slightly spicy at times, but the generally easy terrain was welcome. We arrived at the Forbidden col at the same time as a storm and fought the wind to get the tarp pitched. It rained for a solid 16 hours.

We awoke soaking wet in whiteout fog, waited out the rain, and then started up the west ridge of Forbidden Peak (8,815', 5.6) in the early afternoon. Visibility was still very limited, and after a quick celebration on top, we continued down the east ledges in dense fog. At the east shoulder of the mountain, we realized we couldn't figure out where we needed to go, so we set up camp.

Day four brought sunshine and our first good view of the likely unclimbed northwest ridge of Boston Peak (8,894'), but getting there via Sharkfin Tower was quite involved. Scrambling southeast directly toward Sharkfin revealed incredibly poor rock. Short of driving a steel pike into the ground, there appeared to be no reasonable way to rappel and stay true to the ridge. So we backtracked a few minutes and located a narrow, steep, and incredibly chossy couloir. A handful of rappels and sketchy downclimbing brought us to the northern edge of the Quien Sabe Glacier. Fighting the clock a bit, we opted to skip the unnamed subpeak west of Sharkfin Tower and traverse a steep hanging snow slope directly to the base of the tower's west face.

We headed up some variation of the undocumented west face and the southwest ridge of Sharkfin (5.8). After a bit of rappelling and traversing, we found ourselves deep in virgin choss on the northwest ridge of Boston Peak (5.5 X). The most memorable part of this ridge was a two-pitch *à cheval* across rock the consistency of feta cheese. Another 1,000' of climbing that's best forgotten led us to the summit of Boston.

A relatively casual jaunt brought us over to the summit of Sahale and down to the Sahale Glacier and Sahale Arm. Originally we'd hoped to continue over Johannesberg, but out of food and out of time, we decided to leave that for another day. We arrived at the Cascade Pass Trailhead haggard and hungry—and bummed to remember a road closure would mean a few more miles of walking. When we finally arrived back at our vehicle at the Eldorado Creek Trailhead, our GPS fittingly read 26.2 miles. With 26 pitches up to 5.8 R, 26 rappels, and over 20,000' of technical terrain (mostly soloed), the Boston Marathon is a proper Cascades adventure. 📷 🔍

– SAM BOYCE

SNOQUALMIE MOUNTAIN, NORTHWEST FACE, TURF TESTAMENT

ON MARCH 31, Mark Bunker and I climbed a previously undocumented line on the northwest face of Snoqualmie Mountain (6,278') that we called the Turf Testament. We did not see evidence of past ascents but would not be surprised to learn the route has been climbed previously.

Turf Testament begins in the large right-facing dihedral a few hundred feet uphill of the Slot Couloir's exit. We found two full pitches of rock, turf, and thin ice in the initial dihedral. Two shorter pitches of connecting dihedrals led to the ridge between the Slot and Crooked couloirs. (Future parties may want to explore steeper variations directly above our second and third pitches.) After a short walk up the ridge, a final chockstone gully led to an exit just left of the summit cornice. Based on conditions (both the climb and our own), we found the route comparable in difficulty to the nearby Pineapple Express, New York Gully, and all of their variations. [*Editor's note: These routes are in the 5.8 WI3 M5/6 range.*] 📷

– ROLF LARSON

The line of Three Little Monkeys (1,100', WI4+ M5 R) on the Black Spider, between the Fric-Amos Route to the left and Elder-Russell summer route to the right (not shown). *Wayne Wallace*

OREGON / MT. HOOD

EAST FACE, THE BLACK SPIDER, THREE LITTLE MONKEYS

WAYNE WALLACE HAD mentioned there was unclimbed potential on the left side of the Black Spider, a rock wall that spans the last 1,000' feet of Mt. Hood's eastern aspect, left of the classic Cooper Spur. A quick scouting mission showed a beautiful vein of ice between the Fric-Amos Route and the Elder-Russell summer line, and Walter Burkhardt and I decided to give it a go.

High cloud cover on March 31 promised to keep the sun off the concave wall. We crossed the bergschrund at 8:15 a.m. and started right in on what we thought would be the crux pitch (WI4+). A few vertical mixed moves brought me to a hanging, detached ice dagger. I was able to carefully scratch my way up it and some mixed climbing above to establish a belay on a shelf. I brought Walter up and tried to connect to another hanging dagger directly above, but huge, unsupported snow mushrooms guarded it. After sending one of these down on Walter, I decided to try to the right. This proved to be the psychological crux of the route (M5 R), with rotten snow over near-vertical mud followed by two vertical mud chimneys.

Heading back left, we found a narrow passage that held sound rock and water ice that took good screws. On the next pitch, I hoped to veer left and finish on the Fric-Amos, but this quick exit was guarded by about 50' of unprotectable downclimbing. I veered right instead and thankfully found a path through wild, gold-colored gendarmes that rose like turrets over the upper face. After a couple of hundred feet of simul-climbing, we popped into the sun and knew we were home free. We called the line Three Little Monkeys (1,100', WI4+ M5 R).

It's worth mentioning that the Black Spider was pretty dry when we climbed it. I think that when this face is fat with ice, our line would be a very reasonable outing. I was lucky to share this experience with Walter. He was a great mentor when I first started going to the mountains, and I owe him a good deal of credit for keeping me safe and motivated over the years. 🖥 📷

— MICHAEL GETLIN

CALIFORNIA / NORTHERN SIERRA – HOOVER WILDERNESS

FORSYTH PEAK, TORRE DEL CABALLO SALVAJE

IN EARLY SEPTEMBER, Matt Cornell, Ryan Evans, and Dylan Thomas horse-packed about 20 miles from Kennedy Meadows to Dorothy Lake, aiming to climb a prominent rock tower along the north-northeast-facing ridgeline of Forsyth Peak (11,091'). Their route followed cracks and corners, with a crux passage of face climbing to bypass a wide crack: Torre del Caballo Salvaje (600', 5.9). Cornell's entertaining account is at the *AAJ* website. 🖥 📷 🔍

— *INFORMATION FROM* MATT CORNELL

Kevin Jorgeson leading the key fourth pitch of Blue Collar (IV 5.13+), the free version of the original northwest face of Higher Cathedral Spire. *Jeff Rueppel*

YOSEMITE VALLEY ANNUAL SUMMARY

EL CAPITAN CONTINUED to produce firsts and speed records in 2018, and a handful of significant new aid and free lines went up elsewhere in the Valley.

In addition to the sub-two-hour run up the Nose by Tommy Caldwell and Alex Honnold in June (*see next page*), several other notable speed records went down on the walls of the Captain. Brandon Adams and Roger Putnam climbed the Shield in 8 hours, 55 minutes on May 5; Josie McKee and Diana Wendt set an all-female Salathé Wall record at 16:24 on June 1; Dave Allfrey soloed the Zodiac in 10:52:50 on June 2; and Alexa Flower, Jane Jackson, and Gena Wood set an all-female record for Zodiac, at 16:20, on June 15.

Two free climbing milestones occurred on the Nose (VI 5.14a). From November 14–18, Keita Kurakami of Japan became the first person to rope-solo the route as a free climb. Kurakami had redpointed all of the pitches on the route the previous year with a partner, but decided he was not satisfied with his style, as he didn't free the route in a continuous push from the ground. The free ascent in November was his first time rope-soloing a big wall. In nearly the same period, from November 16–19, 15-year-old Connor Herson became the youngest person to free the route, leading every pitch with his father, Jim, belaying and cleaning. Just a few days before Connor was born, in 2003, Jim became the eighth person to free the Salathé Wall (VI 5.13b).

Brandon Adams and Kristoffer Wickstom spent 10 days in the spring putting up a new aid line that parallels the Nose, which they named Ephemeron (VI 5.10 A4, *see next page*). In May, Jim Beyer soloed a new route of the left side of El Cap he named Ready to Go (VI A6). The 16-pitch route begins right of Lurking Fear (5.7 C2), shares several pitches in the middle of the wall with Mirage (5.9 A4), and finishes on the West Buttress (5.9 A3). He placed around 35 Zamak rivets, but the new route features no bolts other than those already in place on Mirage and the West Buttress.

On November 19, Canadian Sonnie Trotter, belayed by Tommy Caldwell, did a one-day ascent of an all-free variation to the North America Wall and El Niño that he named Pineapple Express (5.13b). Trotter added three new pitches to avoid the "human-powered rappel" on El Niño.

Elsewhere in the Valley, in October, Shaun Reed and Mark Westerberg completed the first free ascent of Jericho Wall (1,100', IV 5.12a), east of Glacier Point Apron. The free line adds multiple variations to the original 5.8 A2+ put up by Steve Bosque and Josh Mucci in 2013. A month later, Kevin DeWeese and Tyler Poston began work on a new aid route that begins 10' to the right of Jericho Wall. They completed Epidemia de Opiaceos (1,200', V 5.7 A3-) just before the new year.

On Higher Cathedral Spire, Kevin Jorgeson made the first free ascent of the Northwest Face route, calling it Blue Collar (12 pitches, IV 5.13+), with some variations to the original Frost-Robbins aid line (1961), including the 5.13 seventh pitch, first bolted and attempted by Scott Cosgrove and Bob Gaines in the 1980s. Jorgeson spent two seasons working the route before his one-day send in October.

Two of the Valley's most difficult single pitches saw repeats in November. Carlo Traversi made the second ascent of Beth Rodden's traditional testpiece Meltdown (5.14c), nearly 11 years after the first ascent, and Lonnie Kauk made the first redpoint of Magic Line (5.14c R) while placing all the gear on lead. His father, Ron Kauk, first climbed Magic Line in December 1996 on preplaced gear, and Lonnie had repeated the route in that style in 2016.

— ANDY ANDERSON, *WITH INFORMATION FROM ERIC BISSELL, MOUNTAIN PROJECT, AND ALPINIST*

EL CAPITAN, EPHEMERON

IN APRIL, KRISTOFFER Wickstrom and I established Ephemeron (VI 5.10 A4), a 22-pitch line up the center of El Capitan, with roughly two-thirds independent terrain. Kristoffer and I spent one day fixing pitches and nine days committed to the wall to complete the project. It mainly climbs thin seams, primarily through the use of beaks. There are seven pitches of A4 and seven others rated A3. We were pleasantly surprised with how well most of the features linked naturally.

Ephemeron tackles an independent start several hundred feet to the right of the Nose (VI 5.9 C2). After roughly 500' of climbing, it joins Central Scrutinizer (VI 5.11c A4+) for two pitches. It then climbs up the face of Dolt Tower and tackles more new terrain until it intersects with the Nose at the Jardine Traverse. More new pitches were established leading to Camp IV and around the Great Roof to Camp V. A particularly good beak seam to the right of the Pancake Flake was christened Beak'n and Eggs. Ephemeron leaves the Nose for good just above Camp V, following Mediterraneo (VI 5.11 A4) and new terrain to the summit. We placed about 35 bolts on the route and used existing anchors when possible to keep the hole count down.

Scoping the line took several years. While climbing the Nose or surrounding routes, I would spy systems that I thought would make for good climbing. I spent many hours staring up at the wall through telescopes. Many systems were only visible in certain light. Eventually I realized there was a line hidden among the other routes, prime for an ascent. It was an amazing experience to establish a modern route on El Capitan, a cliff largely assumed to be tapped out. Kristoffer and I worked hard to establish a climb that parties looking for a hard aid voyage can enjoy and appreciate. An ephemeron is an insect with a lifespan of only a few days. All things we have done and will ever do are meaningless in the grand scheme, and yet are of immense meaning within our personal spheres. I like to imagine a small insect screaming up at a vastly infinite and timeless cosmic reality. I sometimes feel like that insect. 🔳

— BRANDON ADAMS

Alex Honnold in the lead, with the rope short-fixed to an anchor below and Tommy Caldwell jugging behind, during the final speed ascent before their 1:58:07 ascent of the Nose on El Capitan. *Austin Siadak*

THE NOSE UNDER TWO HOURS
AN ASTONISHING SPEED RECORD—AND A LOOK AHEAD

BY TOMMY CALDWELL, *WITH ALEX HONNOLD*

On June 6, Alex Honnold and I managed to climb the Nose in under two hours—1:58:07—after 11 previous attempts. We had toyed with the idea of attempting a speed record the previous fall but only climbed the route together once, which was enough to whet our appetites and get us psyched for the spring season.

Both Alex and I have extensive experience on the Nose. Alex had previously set the Nose speed record with Hans Florine in June 2012, a record that stood until the fall of 2017, when Brad Gobright and Jim Reynolds climbed the route in 2:19:44 after 15 or so attempts. Alex also holds various other speed records involving the Nose, including the solo, solo link-up with Half Dome and Mt. Watkins, and undoubtedly others. I had previously free climbed the route wall-style, then in one day, then once more with the Freerider in a day. We've both climbed the Nose with many different friends over the years.

From the beginning, I questioned Alex's choice in me as a partner. I was far from being in top shape, due the demands of life, and I had bad elbow tendonitis. My schedule would require me to fly off for various events a few days each week during our window of attempts. The question of risk also held a bit of a cloud over the project. The season before, Quinn Brett, a friend and all-around inspiring person from my hometown of Estes Park, Colorado, had taken a terrible fall while speed climbing on the Nose, which resulted in spinal paralysis. As a father, I feel a strong responsibility to maintain a solid margin of safety. I had never been all that interested in speed climbing, because I thought going that fast would require too many safety compromises.

We approached the project with a relaxed attitude of taking a few slow laps to feel it out, test the systems, and analyze the fall potential. From the start we made a lot of compromises in pure speed in order to make the climb safer. For example, the pitch ending atop Boot Flake is normally soloed during a speed attempt so the second can go right across the King Swing without having to clean

[Top] Tommy Caldwell in high gear on the bolt ladder above Texas Flake during a practice run. *Austin Siadak* [Bottom] The climbers (and photographer) at the King Swing off Boot Flake. *Eliza Earle*

any gear. This pitch was the end of my lead block, and I preferred to place a piece midway up the Boot, partially because this was the location of Quinn's accident. Alex was kind enough not to criticize my decision, though it clearly was slower. Also, since we simul-climbed my entire lead block, I had to place a large amount of trust in Alex that he would not fall and pull me off. On his lead block, he short-fixed some of the steeper and more physical pitches, making it safer for me as the second.

These compromises made the risk acceptable to me as a father, and despite them our "slow casual" laps ended up being pretty fast—usually between 3 and 4.5 hours. Surprisingly, daily laps on the Nose seemed to completely cure my tendonitis.

Our success in going sub-two hours came down to a constant refinement of technique and strategy between attempts. While that might sound obvious, it's surprisingly difficult to talk through the whole route over and over, and it takes a strong partnership to frankly evaluate each other's strengths and weaknesses after each attempt, even more so when you involve the questions of inherent risk. (This is the same process that has made Hans Florine so successful on the Nose over the years.) Alex and I would talk through strategy ahead of each try (generally on a rest day or while eating meals), then do the climb, and then spend the rest of the day debriefing and trying to learn from our efforts.

We improved physically over the course of the month that we

were trying the route, but fundamentally, at this point, the Nose speed record is more about climbing efficiently and not making mistakes than it is about flying up the wall. We continually deleted pieces from our rack to minimize weight. In the end we had just seven cams, 16 draws, 15 free carabiners, one cam hook, one ascender, one Micro Traxion, and one Grigri. I climbed my entire block with just this rack; Alex recovered a bit of the rack about halfway through his block by soloing a pitch and then tagging up some gear while short-fixing. Our only clothing was running shorts, and we carried no water but were able to take a quick drink from some abandoned bottles behind Texas Flake. We broke the previous speed record after eight attempts, climbing the route in 2:10:14. We then focused on going under two hours, which was always the primary goal.

I never felt scared while climbing. The logistics were fascinating, and days with Alex always seem to make me a better climber. We would start each morning at sunrise and be back in El Cap Meadow well before lunch, with plenty of time to lounge with family and

Caldwell displays the paltry rack for a sub-two-hour ascent of the Nose. *Austin Siadak*

friends. The whole experience was way more fun that I ever thought it would be.

But there were some heavy moments. On our first "race pace" lap, I unexpectedly slipped and fell about 100 feet. Then Alex slipped while short-fixing up high but managed to grab his own rope, significantly shortening his fall but tearing a large flap of skin off his finger. After that we vowed not to redline, letting our improvements come from increased fitness and logistical innovations. On June 2, Tim Klein and Jason Wells fell to their deaths while using speed-climbing tactics on the Salathé Wall of El Capitan. We nearly abandoned our attempts after this accident but instead decided to take yet another "slow lap" and reanalyze everything. To us, it felt reasonable to continue our efforts. Four days after their accident, we went under two hours.

One last note about the future of speed climbing on the Nose: a World Cup speed climber travels 15m in around 6 seconds. We climbed a 900m wall in 1:58:07, which is roughly 1/19 the pace of competition speed climbers. Yes, it's a much bigger wall, with more complexities than a competition course, so naturally the pacing will be different. But if you compare the relative speeds of 100-meter sprinters to marathon runners, you see that sprinters are moving at roughly double the speed of marathoners (approximately 10 m/s vs 5.9 m/s)—an order of magnitude closer than our relative climbing speeds. All that is to say: Humans are physiologically capable of much more. There remains much room for improvement. But it probably won't come from Alex or me—I think we're satisfied with our foray into speed climbing.

Tommy Caldwell and Alex Honnold describe the Nose speed record in great depth in episode 8 of the AAJ's Cutting Edge podcast.

BEDAYAN MINARET, EAST RIDGE

ON JULY 10, Giselle Field and I made the first known ascent of the east ridge of Bedayan Minaret (12,080'). This feature is one of the largest in the Minarets, rising nearly 1,000' out of the fleeting icefield below. We started about 100 yards left of the toe with a steep, blackened stem box (5.10a) that presented the most difficult and sustained climbing on the route. Above this a diagonal dihedral/ramp led to the true east ridge, which we followed for eight more pitches as it tapered to the narrow summit crest.

The east-facing aspects of Rice, Bedayan, and Dawson minarets, showing the 2018 route up Bedayan (1,600' of climbing, III 5.10a). *Derek Field*

The difficulty was mostly 4th class, yet almost every pitch had at least one section of 5.6 to 5.8. By our rope, the total length climbed was just over 1,600'. We anticipated a long battle with putrid choss but instead found nice cracks and fantastic ridge climbing on mostly solid stone. We downclimbed the north ridge (4th class) to the east couloir and made four 100' rappels down the couloir to get back to the snow.

— DEREK FIELD, *CANADA*

WHEELER CREST, NEW ROUTES

RICHARD SHORE AND partners climbed a number of new routes along the Wheeler Crest, an area he has explored extensively in recent years. They include the first ascent of the Black Obelisk via its east arête (950', III/IV 5.10); three new routes on Haystack Needle, where Shore and Vitaliy Musiyenko did the first climbing route the previous November (*AAJ 2018*); a new route up Sheepoopi Spire's western shoulder (Cordero al Palo, 800', III 5.10d R); and the first ascent of Poseidon Pinnacle, a sunny and enjoyable pillar of clean, orange rock about one-quarter mile north of Neptune Tower (Deep Sea Fishing, 700', III 5.10). Shore's story about these climbs, along with numerous photos, is at the AAJ website.

— *INFORMATION FROM* RICHARD SHORE

THIRD RECESS PEAK, DIRECT NORTHEAST BUTTRESS

THE DAY AFTER a climb on the Ruby Wall in September, Maxim Belyakov and I decided to check out Third Recess Peak (12,520'). We hadn't done much research and were surprised by the approach—about eight miles (including a 12,000' pass) from our campsite by Ruby Lake. As we got closer, the aesthetic northeast buttress (IV 5.10, Strassman-Wilkinson, 1994, *AAJ 2000*) came into the view. We soon realized the Strassman-Wilkinson starts several hundred feet to the left of the toe of the buttress and does not hit the crest until the upper, lower-angle terrain. "But we came to climb the buttress!" I thought, and I proposed the idea of a direct start to Max.

A nice splitter in a shallow corner and some easier climbing on the second pitch brought us to a steep prow with multiple flaring cracks and occasional roofs. Two pitches of 5.10d climbing on the prow, followed by a few easier pitches (5.9ish) got us to a thin-finger splitter with an overhang that seemed like it might require aid, yet it went at 5.10d/11a and was a lot of fun. Somewhere on the next pitch, we joined the original northeast buttress route and simul-climbed to the top. The Direct Northeast Buttress (1,500', IV 5.10d) features approximately 1,000' of new terrain with fairly good climbing, and I'd recommend it to others searching for a long, varied backcountry adventure.

– VITALIY MUSIYENKO

FOUR GABLES, NEW ROUTES

IN EARLY JUNE, Josie McKee and I climbed a new route on the east face of Four Gables (12,720'), just west of Bishop. Inspired by an article by Dave Nettle (*AAJ 2014*), we decided to check out the face for ourselves. [*In addition to the Nettle-Reed route, there a low fifth-class route somewhere on the far left side of the east face and the Neale-Rowell (III 5.8), which may share some terrain with the Nettle-Reed; see AAJ 1973).*] A six-hour hike from the Horton Lakes Trailhead brought us to the base of the peak. We picked a line on the right side of the face (right of the other known routes), which looked like it would lead to a beautiful golden dihedral toward the top. After a couple of hundred feet of moderate snow, we climbed two long pitches of crack and face, up to 5.10-, until a thin section in the dihedral forced us to traverse right along a series of face holds into another system. Two more 60m pitches led us to a final squeeze chimney and onto the summit plateau: Hashtag Training (1,000', IV 5.10-)

[*Editor's Note: In early September, Jack Cramer and McKenzie Long climbed a similar line, believing they were on unclimbed terrain, and finished directly up the golden dihedral where Clark and McKee went right. They called this the Golden Section (5.9).*]

Five days later, I returned with Tad McCrea and we put up a very good route a few hundred feet left of Josie and my route (but still right of previous lines). Tad had just flown in from Alaska the night before and drove through the night to make it. Our line connected steep crack systems straight up the middle of the east face and ended in an open book dihedral.

After a classic late start and a couple of hundred feet of steep snow, we began climbing at 4 p.m. The first pitch started with some sporty climbing through overlaps and led into a beautiful finger crack through a roof. We trended right to gain an obvious crack system halfway up the face, which led to an open book corner, the "Anti-Face-Book," leading directly to the summit. We climbed seven pitches, most of which were steep and sustained at 5.9 to 5.10, with

The east face of Four Gables. (1) Nettle-Reed Direct (10 pitches, 5.10+, 2012). The 1972 Rowell-Neale Route likely branches right from this line about halfway up. (2) Stevia Mama (1,000', IV 5.10+, 2018). (3) The Golden Section (5.9, 2018). (4) Hashtag Training (1,000', IV 5.10-, 2018). *Dave Nettle*

some trickier 5.10+ here and there in the upper pitches. We topped out around 1 a.m. and shiver-bivied on top until there was enough light for the long descent.

The route has rock with amazing sections of black knobs and fins on the face—a joy to climb. We named the route Stevia Mama (1,000', IV 5.10+) because I got to lead all the pitches. 📷

– WHITNEY CLARK

Joel Kauffman following a mixed step during the first ascent of the North Couloir (1,200', III AI2 M3 R) on an unnamed top nicknamed the Central Tower of Pine. This buttress lies along the north ridge of Peak 12,388' at the head of Pine Creek Canyon near Bishop. *Richard Shore*

ICE COULOIRS ABOVE BISHOP

OVER TWO SEASONS, in the winter and fall of 2018, several partners and I did probable first ascents of three ice couloirs in the eastern Sierra.

The "Central Tower of Pine" (11,670') is a minor bump along the sinuous north ridge of unnamed Peak 12,388', visible to the southwest in the Tungstar Bowl above the head of Pine Creek Canyon. Joel Kauffman and I made the three-hour trudge to the buttress below this bump on January 5, intent on climbing the steep cleft on the left side of the north face. The approach started easily on the dry, drought-stricken Pine Creek Pass Trail. After leaving the trail at the Brownstone Mine, however, our pace slowed dramatically as we struggled through unconsolidated powder snow, falling between the large boulders lurking beneath. As the angle steepened we were fortunate to find a firm, supportable crust. A few hundred feet of moderate snow climbing, with some short mixed steps, gave way to the narrows—a deep *goulotte* averaging only 10' wide and comprised of loose, shattered granite.

We fixed a piton at a somewhat protected belay stance, and loose rock rained down around me while Joel delicately danced up the crux M4+ R pitch. A steep snow ramp followed on the next pitch, and then an intimidating house-size chockstone appeared to block passage. With the low snow level, we were able to worm beneath, behind, then over and around the improbable congestion (M3/4). The angle lessened above and we simul-climbed the long exit gully to the summit. Our route, the North Couloir (1,200', III AI2 M3 R), is only the second known route on the buttress. An unreported rock route, Up the Creek (III 5.10R ?), is rumored to have been climbed by Brian Ketron and Mike Melkonian in the late 1990s or early 2000s.

On November 8, Chad Cochran, Tad McCrea, and I approached the north face of Mt. Emerson (13,210') from a rugged dirt road in the Bishop Bowl. Approximately a half-mile northwest of the Clyde Couloir on Emerson lies a steeper line that leads to a deep notch between the lower, western summit of Emerson and an unnamed subpeak (Peak 12,880'+) along its west-northwest ridge.

The three of us team-soloed the first 700' of 60° névé and alpine ice to reach a constriction high in the couloir where the old remnant glacier dies out. A narrow runnel of water ice continued above for a full rope length to the notch. From there we headed right up the knife-edge south ridge of Peak 12,900' (4th class) for an additional 300'. There was no register, cairn, or any sign of passage on this prominent subsummit. While there is no record of this couloir being climbed as an ice route, we acknowledge that it may have been descended by some extreme skier, due to its visibility from town and proximity to other popular backcountry ski descents. We tentatively named our line the Camel Tail Couloir (1,200', III AI3 4th class).

A few days later, on November 12, I hiked up the trail from North Lake to an icy, inverted Y-shaped couloir that I had spotted from the top of Emerson. This couloir is approximately a half-mile northwest of the popular North Couloir of Mt. Lamarck (13,417') but is completely hidden from any hiking trail. After taking a tumble in the endless glacial moraine above Upper Lamarck Lake and breaking my nose, I staggered up the remainder of the approach and switched into boots and crampons. The left fork of the couloir featured perfect frontpointing up 55° Styrofoam and alpine ice for 800', which led to a notch in the long ridgeline between the Keyhole Plateau and Peak 13,464'. I chose to follow the ridge south toward Peak 13,464', finding some 4th- and easy 5th-class rock scrambling along the way, to reach the familiar and easy descent down from Lamarck Col. The name of the new climb seemed obvious, given its shape and proximity to the lake of the same name below—the Wishbone Couloir (800', III AI2+ easy 5th). 📷

– RICHARD SHORE

CHECKERED DEMON, NORTHEAST ARÊTE, DANCING WITH THE DEVIL

MANY HUNDREDS HAVE passed by the Checkered Demon (13,121') while descending from the adjacent and popular East Arête of Mt. Humphreys. The north side of Checkered Demon features one of the most stunning arêtes in the High Sierra, and the peak is unlike any other in composition and structure. Its psychedelic swirls and multicolored complexion are derived from its 300 million-year-old metamorphic rock—mostly marble with some less desirable quartzite, hornfels, and schist mixed in—which is some of the oldest rock in the range and likely some of the loosest.

Over a couple of trips in June and August, Myles Moser and I established a wild 12-pitch climb up the narrow north arête, clawing off loads of loose rock along the way. North wall–style hammers were indispensable for clearing

The alluring yet dangerous Checkered Demon (13,121'), near Mt. Humphreys. Dancing with the Devil (1,800', V 5.9+ X) reached the decomposing north ridge from the left and continued straight up the arête. *Richard Shore* [Inset] Richard Shore following the knife-edge ridge on pitch seven. *Myles Moser*

the path, and extreme care was taken to belay in protected spots away from the fall line. The soft rock drilled with exceptional ease, and we took some comfort in knowing the belay anchors were solid when nothing else on the mountain was. Most belays consisted of one bolt and a piton, and a few dozen pins were fixed for climbing protection. In some places the rock was so soft we drove pitons straight into it like nails into wood. We grossly underestimated the size of the wall on our first attempt, and retreating by rappel was more dangerous than the climbing.

During our final push on August 5 we reached the knife-edge arête on the upper third on the peak. This was the point of no return—bailing from above pitch seven would be nearly impossible, and attaining the summit would be only way off the peak. The final five pitches were like riding the lip of an Alaskan cornice of shattered rock, and we were unsure if the entire formation would collapse under our body weight. Teetering blocks fell away with ease on either side of the arête, exploding like gunfire in the couloirs more than 1,500' below.

The nearly flat scree slope of a summit was a welcome reprieve, and we lay on top in total exhaustion in the fading evening light. Dancing with the Devil (1,800', V 5.9+ X) had forced us to take great risks, and we nearly sacrificed our souls to achieve this wild collective desire.

– RICHARD SHORE

MORE CHECKERED DEMON CLIMBS: In summer 2018, Derek and Giselle Field completed two short new routes on the west face of Checkered Demon's south ridge. Chex Mix (300', 5.7) and the Devil Wears Plaid (450', 5.10-) climb prominent towers along the ridge and reportedly feature excellent granite. More information is at Mountain Project.

MT. HUMPHREYS, NORTH PILLAR OF EAST FACE

ON JULY 28, Dave Spies, Steven Stosky, and I climbed what we believe to be a new route up the east face of Mt. Humphreys (13,986'), just west of Bishop. Our route ascends the center of the very prominent pillar on the far right (north) side of the highly dissected 1,200' wall.

In his report about the first route up this aspect of the mountain, Galen Rowell described it as the southeast face, but the wall faces only a few degrees south of east. The only other known route is the South Pillar (1,200', III 5.8, Jensen-Rowell, *AAJ 1976*) on the far left side.

We climbed directly up the northern pillar, aiming for a string of conspicuous splitter cracks high on the face. The lower half's mixed bag of rock gradually increased in quality until we found ourselves joyfully jamming those perfect hand cracks. Our eighth pitch brought us to the top of the pillar. We called our route Humphrey Dumphrey (1,200', III 5.8).

– DEREK FIELD

SAWMILL CANYON, SAWMILL SPIRE

ON OCTOBER 20, Myles Moser, Amy Ness, and I hiked into rugged Sawmill Canyon, about nine miles northwest of the town of Independence. This narrow, brush-choked canyon has thwarted many explorers from reaching the intriguing granite fins visible from Highway 395. We navigated around the nastiest bits by climbing a pitch of 5th-class rock over the basalt cliffs in the lower reaches, which gave us access to sandy game trails high above the canyon floor. A fully intact, three-inch-long obsidian spear point lay on a game trail, indicating this was also the preferred approach route of our ancestors.

About a mile and a half up canyon, an 800' needle-like spire shoots skyward from the sagebrush at about 6,200'. Two warm-up pitches led to the base of the sharp northeast arête, along which four pitches of sustained and varied 5.10 and 5.11 led to the airy summit: Sawmill Spire (800', III 5.11).

From the top, a mildly attractive ridge continues upward for another 1,000' or more, but it appears to become increasingly brushy and loose. This Grade V ridge-to-nowhere awaits someone with a penchant for extreme suffering and on-route first-aid skills. We opted to keep it classy and end the first known route in Sawmill Canyon atop the spire, descending to the northwest with single-rope rappels. 📷

– RICHARD SHORE

SHAW SPIRE, EAST FACE, DESAYHUMO

FREESTANDING PINNACLES ARE a rarity in the High Sierra, where it's more common to top out on a flat plateau and surf down scree to descend. But in late August, Jon Griffin, Tad McCrea, and I found a new route up Shaw Spire, a tower below the east peak of Mt. Barnard (13,680'), first climbed by Galen Rowell and Jerry Gregg in 1971 (III 5.8, *AAJ 1972*) by the southeast arête. We approached via George Creek, a notoriously burly and bushy hike, and spied an incredible line straight up the longest and steepest part of the east face. Another team had attempted a similar line a few years earlier but had escaped out left after encountering loose rock, joining the Gregg-Rowell route after four new pitches. Our climb followed an independent line to the right of earlier climbs or attempts.

Morning alpenglow on the east face of Shaw Spire, a freestanding pinnacle below the east peak of Mt. Barnard (13,680'). The 2018 route starts in the center of the face and moves toward the southeast arête, independent of earlier climbs until the finish. *Tad McCrea*

We began with two pitches of mediocre rock up to a left-leaning ramp and a good belay ledge below a wide crack. Jon went straight up the 5.10+ R offwidth for 30m, finishing with a fun chimney to a ledge belay. (Two number 5 Camalots and a number 6 would be more comfortable to protect this pitch.) After a hair-raising 60m 5.10 R corner with friable rock, the rock quality began to improve as we headed up moderate cracks and face near the southeast arête. Darkness fell, causing our pace to slow. A few more sections of short, steep 5.8 to 5.10 climbing led us to a final 5.9 splitter, about 30m east of the original Rowell line. We climbed 12 pitches to the ridge and then linked in to the original line, which traverses left for 100m to the summit.

We reached the top around 2 a.m. and decided it best to wait until morning to find our way down. Although smoke from the summer's forest fires enhanced the sunrise glow on nearby Mt. Barnard, it felt like we were eating smoke for our morning meal, and we called our route Desayhumo ("breakfast smoke," more or less; 1,300', IV 5.10+). We downclimbed and rappelled the southeast arête to descend. According to the summit register, ours was the sixth ascent of Shaw Spire. 📷

– WHITNEY CLARK

Jon Griffin and Whitney Clark approaching the northwest face of Mt. Russell (14,086'). The new alpine route Land of Milk and Honey reaches the remnant glacier on the right side, climbs this and some ice above, and then angles left up rock to the ridge. *Tad McCrea*

MT. RUSSELL, NORTHWEST FACE, LAND OF MILK AND HONEY

IN OCTOBER, Jon Griffin, Tad McCrea, and I climbed a likely new route in mixed conditions on the northwest face of Mt. Russell (14,086'). We spied the line while scoping another objective and returned with our ice and mixed kit a few days later, hiking over the Russell-Carillon col to camp at Tulainyo Lake. From there, it was a casual 30-minute hike around the toe of the north ridge to the base of the face.

Our route began with moderate but run-out snowy slabs and crack systems for three pitches, with amazing moss and turf sticks, to reach the remains of an old hanging glacier a third of the way up the face. (This seeping glacial remnant is the reason for such well-developed patches of moss in the corners and cracks below.) We climbed one 60m pitch of 65° ice up the glacier, traversing left near its top to a belay. After another 25m of ice angling up and left, the terrain steepened and we entered a mixed corner leading to the upper face. A long pitch of stellar 5.8 cracks brought us to the shoulder that butts up to the west face.

By this time, darkness had fallen and the bitter cold wind had picked up significantly. We opted to take 4th-class ledges toward the east summit rather then tackle the overhanging headwall that leads directly to Russell's main top. [*Mt. Russell's original northwest face route (3rd/4th class, Czock-Czock-Luck, 1935) begins on the left (east) side of the face and trends toward the middle to climb directly to the ridge between the two summits. The 2018 climb may share some terrain with the 1935 route near the top.*] By the time we reached the slightly lower east peak, we were all shivering. We descended Russell's classic east ridge to reach the Russell-Carillon col and eventually our camp at Tulainyo Lake, arriving around 2:30 a.m.

Land of Milk and Honey (1,000', IV 5.8+ M3 R 65°) is a quality route and something rare for the Sierra Nevada, but with warming temperatures the hanging ice won't last forever. 📷

— **WHITNEY CLARK**

THE CLEAVER, DOT THE T'S AND DREAMLINER

IN LATE MAY and June, Vitaliy Musiyenko and Shaun Reed climbed two new routes toward the left side of the southeast face of the Cleaver (13,382'), northeast of Mt. Carillon and Mt. Russell: Dot the T's (III 5.11a) and Dreamliner (III/IV 5.11c). Details are at the AAJ website. 📄 📷

— *INFORMATION FROM* VITALIY MUSIYENKO

MT. WHITNEY AREA, UPPER BOY SCOUT LAKE, THE MAGIC MUSHROOM

IN JULY, I backpacked to Upper Boy Scout Lake with Steve Yamamoto and my wife, Giselle Field. Earlier in the summer, my interest had been piqued by a spectacular granite formation with an 800' east face rising above the inlet of the lake. I was told the formation was called Sorcerer Needle and had been climbed by Fred Beckey more than 45 years earlier (*AAJ 1975*). A gear-shop manager in Lone Pine had even copied the sparse words of the *AAJ* report into the store copy of the Secor guide to the Sierra, including an arrow pointing to the spire in a photo—the summit directly above Upper Boy Scout Lake. But the Beckey report seemed vague, and I didn't see any conclusive evidence connecting it to that particular spire.

The breakthrough came shortly thereafter when I was able to positively identify the route Beckey described as the climb called Pinhead (5.10d, or 5.7 A2 in Beckey's day) on the Sorcerer formation in the well-known Needles group, farther south in the Sierra Nevada. The route descriptions match perfectly.

On July 23, Steve, Giselle, and I climbed a striking line on the highest (east) aspect of the Boy Scout Lake spire. After a spicy face climbing start (5.8), we followed a long, right-trending ramp—the most obvious weakness on the face—with five pitches of mostly 4th-class and isolated sections up to 5.8. This brought us to a steep arête split by a slightly overhung, 1.5-inch splitter crack (5.10+), culminating in a short but wild traverse into a chimney. We climbed the final two pitches of discontinuous cracks (5.9) in a violent hailstorm.

We're pretty sure Beckey didn't climb this formation, but someone might have. As far as I can determine, though, there's no record of any prior ascent or name. We called it the Magic Mushroom (800', III 5.10+).

– DEREK FIELD

LONE PINE PEAK, NEW ROUTE AND FIRST FREE ASCENTS

EVER SINCE ROGER Putnam and I started to work on a complete guide to the High Sierra, I became increasingly interested in finding obscure gems around the range. Lone Pine Peak is an often-overlooked giant that has a huge south face and countless buttresses. In May and June, I had an opportunity to make three trips to check out the climbing.

On the first visit, Jeremy Ross and I were able to make the first free ascent of Pathways Through to Space in a day. [*Pathways is a long direct start into Windhorse (V 5.11, freed in 2012).*] We found a variety of nice, mostly wide cracks, which slowed progress, including the roof traverse on pitch five of Pathways that we freed at 5.11a. The wall was as big as advertised, too, with close to 3,000' of rock climbing. I believe this was the first time either Pathways or the original Windhorse had been climbed in a day.

Vitaliy Musiyenko chimneys up and away from the belay during the first free ascent of Streets of the Mountains (IV 5.11a) on the south face of Lone Pine Peak. *Derek Field*

A few weeks later, I returned with Chaz Langlier to have a crack at a prominent arête on the east flank of Lone Pine. Located immediately north of the Three Arrows (*AAJ 1977*), this ridgeline is obvious from Lone Pine, and I expected to find some proof of previous passage and discover a gem from the past. However, Chaz and I found neither.

The route had plenty of spicy climbing, with several long runouts on crunchy rock. Because we did not bring a drill, we did not place any bolts, although they would be appropriate in multiple places. There were several great pitches, yet I do not see this one becoming very popular—the Arrowhead (ca 2,000', IV/V 5.11b/c).

In early June, Derek Field and I checked out Streets of the Mountains (IV 5.10 A1), which takes a large corner system on the south face, just up the hill from Windhorse. We were able to free this line by staying in the main corner system for the whole climb. Wide fist jams to ring locks through a prominent overhang at the top of the corner system was the free crux (5.10d/ 5.11a). The wide pitch below the crux had decomposing rock and really took away from the experience. There are likely better variations around the corner to the right. [o]

— VITALIY MUSIYENKO

Space Force (1,000', 5.11b) on a south-facing wall by the western aspect of Mt. Le Conte. *Vitaliy Musiyenko*

MT. LE CONTE, SPACE FORCE

WHILE APPROACHING CRABTREE Lakes in early July, Roger Putnam and I were stopped short of our destination by a raging thunderstorm. I knew of an intriguing south-facing wall nearby, on the western aspect of Mt. Le Conte (ca 13,960'), and proposed we climb it the next day before continuing the journey. It was only about 30 minutes from our camp at Sky Blue Lake.

Hoping to beat more bad weather, we got to the base soon after sunrise, having chosen a crack system on the approach. I have seen Roger hike 5.12 in the past, so when I saw him hesitating on the first pitch, I knew it was no gimme. The thin layback to a large overhang felt at least 11a. My lead was much more moderate, but wide. Roger then swung into another difficult pitch, with a solid 5.11 finger crack through a bulge.

By the time I was midway up the following pitch, a perfect corner crack, clouds had rolled over the summit and covered the sky, and it started to hail. Roger ran up the next mid-5.10 pitch in no time, and since he still had nearly the whole rack, he started right up the last pitch of the route. At this point we were in a full-on hailstorm. Because we were so high up, it seemed safer to climb over the summit than attempt to rap with a single 60m. After a near miss with a lightning strike and a scary fall (*see the online report for details*), we finished the climb and scrambled to the summit (which felt like its own formation)—Space Force (1,000', 5.11b). [≡] [o]

— VITALIY MUSIYENKO

LUBKEN CREEK CANYON, RUSTY TRINKETS

AN ATTRACTIVE AND sheer granitic wall juts out of the North Fork of Lubken Creek Canyon, south of Tuttle Creek near Lone Pine. This 1,000'-plus cliff is plainly visible from town and many areas in the nearby Alabama Hills, but our research revealed no previous climbs.

Myles Moser and I decided to take a closer look and hiked into the rugged, brushy canyon on the afternoon of March 31, establishing a bivouac at the base of the wall. The cliff lies at about 8,900' and was still holding snow in many of the northeast-facing crack systems, so we chose the seemingly dry "King Line" and started up an arête at the very toe of the cliff.

Myles Moser engaging the crux roof during the first ascent of Rusty Trinkets (1,300', IV 5.12a), the first known route on a prominent granite wall in the North Fork of Lubken Creek Canyon, near Lone Pine. *Richard Shore*

Armed with 18 quarter-inch bolts and ultralight, homemade bed-frame hangers, we managed to stance-drill our way up a line of high resistance, weaving back and forth across lichenous, feldspar-studded granite. Four pitches of varied, run-out 5.10 and 5.11 face climbing led to the most ominous feature on the wall: a stepped 20-foot roof that is visible from town in Lone Pine. Myles executed the crux pitch onsight, with a bold lead out the gymnastic 5.12a roof. I seconded the pitch cleanly, a difficult task given the weight of the follower's backpack.

Above, three pitches of gradually easing 5.9 cracks led to the top of the wall, a rather insignificant summit on a shrubby ridgeline. We descended the snowy gully to the left of the wall with some rappels off trees.

During our hike in and out of the canyon, we found remnants of a very old mining camp, including metal dishware, food tins, and a late-1800s Oliver Ames Co. shovel. We named our route after the antique treasures and the "interesting" fixed hardware we left on the cliff: Rusty Trinkets (1,300', IV 5.12a). ▣

– RICHARD SHORE

CRYSTAL GEYSER CRAG, NEW ROUTES

IN JANUARY 2018, Reuben Shelton and Brandon Thau completed Windchester (7 pitches, 5.11a A0), on the left side of the Crystal Geyser Crag, above the town of Cartago. [*See AAJ 2018 for more information on this area.*] The high-quality route climbs the left side of the crag via hand cracks, a splitter finger crack, and a wild traverse under a roof to steeper face climbing. Shelton and Thau had nearly completed this route in 2017 but had to retreat due to high wind. Almost a year later, the night before their climb, high winds struck again and broke their tent.

In March, Chris Koppl, Vitaliy Musiyenko, and Richard Shore also battled the wind while establishing a six-pitch route on the right side of the cliff. During the descent, Shore pulled a three-inch-diameter tree out of the wall to avoid rope tangles, only to have it ripped from his hands and thrown across the desert by a gust, giving rise to the route name—Tumbleweed (1,300', III 5.11a). ▤ ▣

– ANDY ANDERSON, *WITH INFORMATION FROM* BRANDON THAU *AND* RICHARD SHORE

The southeast face of Langille Peak. (1) Area climbed by East Buttress route (Beckey-Jones, 1970). (2) Three Quarters of a Man (IV 5.11c, Musiyenko-Prince, 2018). (3) Route climbed by Jamie Ervin and Damien Nicodemi in September 2018. It's likely this is also the line of the East Buttress Direct (IV 5.10b, Rowell-Wilson, *AAJ 1989*). These routes finish on Langille's southeastern summit. The true summit of Langille is out view. *Vitaliy Musiyenko*

LANGILLE PEAK, SOUTHEAST FACE, THREE QUARTERS OF A MAN AND HISTORICAL CLARIFICATION

In September, Vitaliy Musiyenko and Brian Prince climbed a new route on the southeast face of Langille Peak's southeast summit that they called Three Quarters of a Man (IV 5.11c). The two followed slabby cracks to the base of the main wall, where they began climbing about 100–200' to the right of the large corner system that forms the wall's left shoulder. Every pitch was long and at least 5.10, with several pitches of 5.11. Prince led the crux up an overhanging crack that shut closed for a body length. Higher up, the cracks they were aiming to climb were filled with vegetation and so they headed left into the East Buttress (5.7, Beckey-Jones, 1970; *AAJ 1972*). They finished their climb on the southeast summit. [*It is possible this route shares some terrain with an unreported 5.8 route on the lower portion of the face.*]

Musiyenko and Prince also attempted to repeat the East Buttress Direct (IV 5.10b, Rowell-Wilson, *see AAJ 1989*) using an overlay provided by David Wilson, similar to the route line shown in the Secor guidebook to the High Sierra, but they were shut down by blank rock five pitches up.

In September, Jamie Ervin and Damien Nicodemi began climbing a line to the left of where Musiyenko and Prince began their attempt, believing they were on new terrain. At the top of Ervin and Nicodemi's first and second pitches in this neighboring chimney system, they found tattered webbing around chockstones. Six or so pitches past those anchors they found a fixed hex. They continued the line to the southeastern summit, believing their route shared the upper pitches with the Rowell-Wilson route.

After their own attempt, Musiyenko spoke with David Wilson, who said that he and Rowell never encountered any blank sections on their route and acknowledged that they probably followed the more natural line to the left. Thus it's fairly likely the prominent chimney system that Ervin and Nicodemi climbed is the original Rowell-Wilson line. 📷

— ANDY ANDERSON, *WITH INFORMATION FROM VITALIY MUSIYENKO, DAMIEN NICODEMI, AND SUPERTOPO*

BUBBS CREEK WALL, PANDA EXPRESS

During the summer of 2017, Adam Sheppard, Daniel Jeffcoach, and I went out to Bubbs Creek Wall and attempted a line left of the Samurai Warrior/Ronin (V 5.12a) and Crystal Bonzai (VI 5.11 A3). We climbed up to a dihedral below a huge, guillotine-like flake/overhang nearly halfway up the wall. This flake was sharp, the size of a small car, and was jammed in the overhang above in a way that made its presence on the wall a small miracle. Daylight ran out when I was still 40' below the scary object and we had a great reason to bail. For the next year, we wondered how to deal with this obstacle.

In May of 2018, Daniel and I returned to find answers. On the first day we approached from Road's End and climbed two pitches to a large ledge. On day two we climbed to our previous high point, where I clipped the retreat gear I had left in 2017 and continued up the nice crack for another 15' before making a wild face traverse to the arête left of the dihedral. I continued up cool face features and flakes, which allowed protection and passage to a ledge above the guillotine flake, all free and on natural gear. We continued free climbing up the crux 5.11 finger crack above and into another corner system, which we followed to a huge ledge where we bivied again.

Unfortunately, we needed to use aid for about 20' off the bivy ledge—the only aid required on this 2,000' climb. We topped out in the afternoon on the third day; I believe future ascents could be done in a long day or maybe two shorter days. In keeping with the other route names on this wall (Samurai Warrior, the Emperor, and the Sensei), we dubbed it the Panda Express (VI 5.11 A1). ⊡

— VITALIY MUSIYENKO

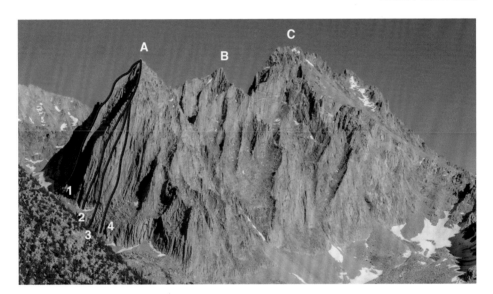

The Ericsson massif from the northwest. (A) Ericsson Crag 3, showing approximate lines of (1) Northwest Arête (Belyakov-Musiyenko, 2016), (2) Vinland (Bartlett-Beckey, 1987), (3) King of the North (Langlier-Musiyenko, 2018), and (4) Mud Falcon (Clark-McCrea, 2018). Reed Cundiff and Fred Beckey climbed the shaded face left of Vinland in 1972 at 5.7. Brujo Dihedral (Neff-Wilson, 1980) is to the right of the other routes. (B) Ericsson Crag 2. (C) Mt. Ericsson (13,589'). Ericsson's north face, climbed in 2018, is hidden behind the ridgeline. *Vitaliy Musiyenko*

MT. ERICSSON AREA, NEW ROUTES

IN MID-MAY, CHAZ Langlier and I made a trip to East Lake, south of the Bubbs Creek drainage, a beautiful base camp for three days and three nights. During our trip we climbed three routes that were likely first ascents.

Trips with Chaz are always cardio workouts, and instead of relaxing after the 16-mile approach, he was keen to start climbing. We chose an attractive dome that I had spotted a few years back, prominent above East Lake to the northwest. The dome had amazing Tuolumne-like rock, and the path we found up its south face (700', III 5.10), with a mix of corners, cracks, and face climbing,

Whitney Clark leading the long lichen-covered dihedral midway up Mud Falcon (1,400', IV 5.11- C1) on Ericsson Crag 3. *Tad McCrea*

would surely be one of the most popular climbs in the Meadows if it were there. I haven't found any information about this formation having been climbed or named—we called it Wild Iris Dome (ca 11,200').

The following day we approached the main objective of the trip: the impressive north face of Mt. Ericsson (13,589'), which I'd seen a few years back from Ericsson Crag 3 and during a winter flight over the Sierra. It stood out as one of the last large unclimbed faces in the range.

After four long pitches of decent climbing, we rappelled from a prominent tower into a loose gully separating us from the rest of the face that towered above us. Above here the climbing was run-out, loose, and dangerous. One pitch involved chimneying between an overhanging ice dagger and a steep rock pillar, onto which I was able to transition and do a few moves of 5.10, with potential for decking from 30'. Chaz led another 60m pitch up flakes and blocks that were total garbage, and before I began my next lead he apologized for what I was about to encounter. It's hard to comprehend how chunks of rock bigger than me could balance on rocks the size of a Nalgene battle, yet they were. It was no harder than 5.10, but with A5 consequences. From the top, we descended the ridgeline east to a loose gully that dropped us to a snow slope below the face. I would not recommend that anyone repeat our route (1,600', IV 5.10 R/X).

Although we returned to camp at midnight, we woke up early enough the next day to try something new on Ericsson Crag 3. [*Musiyenko and Maxim Belyakov climbed the prominent northwest arête on Ericsson Crag 3 in 2015; see AAJ 2016.*] We started with a nice 5.10c/d splitter a few hundred feet right of Vinland (IV 5.9, Bartlett-Beckey, *AAJ 1988*). This led to a huge roof (5.11a) to start the second pitch, with a perfect hand crack cutting the face toward two scary flakes, which were bypassed by wild face climbing out left. Two pitches up the major right-facing dihedral, with continuing difficulties of 5.10d or 5.11a, took us to easier ground right of the prow.

After six pitches we found the big ledge Beckey had described on Vinland and the nice crack Vinland must take from there. Instead of joining that route, we found steeper cracks (5.10) to the right of an obvious arête, and after a couple more pitches the route joined the ridge with an incredible hand crack over a huge roof, with perfect Red Rock–ish holds that allowed a 5.12-looking overhang to go at 5.10a. We scrambled up from there, completing King of the North (1,400', IV 5.11a). Ericsson Crag 3 continues to surprise me with its interesting rock features and the beauty of its setting. 🖹 🔘

– VITALIY MUSIYENKO

ERICSSON CRAG 3, MUD FALCON: In August, Whitney Clark and Tad McCrea climbed a new route on the north face of Ericsson Crag 3 called Mud Falcon (1,400', IV 5.11- C1). They began on the lowest part of the wall and to the right of the Northwest Arête and Vinland, following moderate cracks and face climbing for seven pitches to a massive corner system two-thirds of the way up. The right side of the corner was covered with incredible yellow-green lichen and gave way to excellent stemming and 5.10+ crack climbing for two 60m pitches. In the fading light, Clark aided a thin, broken seam to reach easier ground. One more crux remained: a one-inch, Indian Creek–style splitter (0.75 Camalots) in a corner, capped by a roof (5.11-). They bivied 100m below the top and finished the route in the morning. Clark's full report is at the AAJ website. 📄 📷

SKY PILOT, EAST FACE, CERTIFIED TANTRIC SHAMAN

In July, Tad McCrea and I made the long trek up the East Lake Trail, aiming for the east face of Sky Pilot (ca 12,960'), just south of Longley Pass. After hiking 17 miles from Road's End, we camped at Lake Reflection. The next morning we followed a seldom-used trail and occasional cairns for three miles to reach a talus field below Sky Pilot.

We began at the lowest point on the face and climbed a moderate slab to reach cracks. On the second pitch, after pulling a 5.11-bulge, a loose flake caked in grass convinced me to retreat. The following day we hiked a bit farther up and right along the east face to access a left-leaning ramp that brought us to just above my high point from the day before.

The east face of Sky Pilot (ca 12,960'), just south of Longley Pass, showing Certified Tantric Shaman (1,000', IV 5.10+). The left line at the start marks the first attempt, ending at a loose flake 1.5 pitches up. The route was completed the next day, starting on a ramp farther right. *Tad McCrea*

We climbed an obvious right-facing corner system for two pitches and continued up cracks and other features on the face for five more pitches. Overall the rock was really high quality: Certified Tantric Shaman (1,000', IV 5.10+). Cleaning and completing our original start would make for the most logical and direct line and would be an incredible addition to the climb. 📄 📷

– WHITNEY CLARK

SEQUOIA NATIONAL PARK

NORTH FORK OF GRANITE CREEK, NEW ROUTES

I met Pete Cutler in Patagonia during the winter of 2017. Since he lives in Des Moines, Iowa, and has a professional career, his climbing time is precious, and when he does take a short climbing vacation, he does things like the Salathé Wall in a day or a slew of 5.12 cracks in Indian Creek in a weekend.

We booked some time to climb together in the Sierra, where we were psyched to explore the south faces of some attractive rock spires in the North Fork of Granite Creek. After 16 miles of hiking, it seemed like a sin to walk past Angel Wings, yet we continued over the neighboring ridgeline to the south and set up camp by Eagle Scout Creek, two and a half hours from Hamilton Lake. Our target climbs were on the other side of the divide between Eagle Scout Creek and Granite Creek, but the former has better camping, with less vegetation, a great water source, and a lake for scenic fishing and swimming.

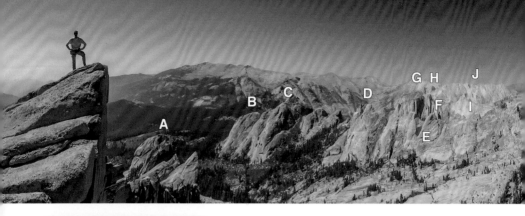

[Above] Pete Cutler on Eaglette Pinnacle after the first ascent of its south face. In the last five years, Vitaliy Musiyenko and partners have done new routes on nearly every formation in this photo. (A) Eagle Scout Creek Dome. (B) Beau-Te Cache Dome. (C) Hamilton Dome. (D) Rowell Tower. (E) Serpent's Tooth. (F) Angel Wings. (G) The Red Rocket. (H) The Globe. (I) Cherubim Dome. (J) Mt. Stewart. [Left] Side profile of the enormous (six pitches!) pillar at the start of Long Dong Wall. *Vitaliy Musiyenko (both photos)*

The following day we warmed up on the south face of Eaglette Pinnacle, doing the likely first ascent of a five-pitch climb: Nothin' But A Good Time (750', III 5.10a).

We still had most of the day, so we descended to the base of the southwest side of Periscope Dome. Our second route started with a 5.10 boulder problem off a ledge and into a nice splitter, then traversed left on quality face. An arch, dikes, flakes, more cracks—the route kept going. We ended up climbing six mostly 60m pitches to the top of Periscope Dome, did a pitch of downclimbing to the notch, a traverse to the base of a steep headwall, and on our ninth pitch climbed 5.10 face to the exposed summit of Wallace Stegner Spire. We got down the east ridge with one 60m rap—Sweet Corn and Steak (1,600' of climbing, IV 5.10).

The following day we approached a large unnamed wall east of Wallace Stegner Spire. Here we found an enormous detached pinnacle leaning against the main dome with a 3m roof about 40m up, and what looked like a hand-size splitter through it. After an interesting 5.10 approach pitch, I watched Pete send the roof first go. He was as excited as a little kid and reported it went at low 5.11. We continued up good cracks (with two bolts to protect a 5.11a bulge), and on the sixth pitch Pete reached the top of the detached pillar.

It looked too blank to climb above, but I wanted to at least try. We moved the belay and I was able to piece together 5.10 face climbing with a few natural gear placements and two bolts for protection. Three easier pitches and a long simul block up easy terrain took us to large trees, where we unroped and continued to a nice summit. We named the formation the Long Dong Wall, and the complete route Sick Gnarski Pillar (1,800' of climbing, IV 5.11a).

The Granite Creek drainages are remote, beautiful, and have some of the best backcountry granite I have climbed, with plenty of other plums to pick. ▤ ▣

— VITALIY MUSIYENKO

TAMARACK LAKE–AREA CLIMBS: In August, Jake Smith and Vitaliy Musiyenko camped at Tamarack Lake in the Lone Pine Creek drainage, below Mt. Stewart (12,205'), and completed three new routes. These included the Antichrist Dihedral (1,600', 5.11b) on the northwest face of Mt. Stewart and Cool Beans (750', III 5.12b) on a south-facing dome left of the Globe (*AAJ 2016*), along the ridgeline north of the lake, which they called the Red Rocket. They also did a new route called Lightning Bolt Cracks (1,000', 5.9) on a large southwest-facing wall called the Shield, on which their friends Betty and Ney Grant had just done the first known ascent: Stonehenge (1,000', 5.10a). Musiyenko's full report and photos are at the *AAJ* website.

The northwest face of Mt. Stewart (12,205'), showing the line of the Antichrist Dihedral (1,600', IV 5.11b). *Vitaliy Musiyenko*

MT. CHAMBERLIN, UNTIL THE WHEELS FALL OFF

IN EARLY AUGUST, Becca Pilkerton and I approached Mt. Chamberlin (13,175') from Cottonwood Pass. After a day of swimming and staring at potential routes, we climbed a mostly new nine-pitch line on the west buttress of Mt. Chamberlin's northeast face. [*The northeast face of Mt. Chamberlin comprises three prominent buttresses (west, central and east) separated by deep clefts.*]

We began by climbing an amazing 65m 5.11 pitch in a clean corner just to the right of the first pitch of Innominata (Nettle-Shelton, 2010, *see AAJ 2011*) on the far right side of the central buttress. Another pitch led us to a large ledge system in the cleft between the central and west buttresses. We headed up and right to reach a recessed headwall on the west buttress. On the left side of this headwall, we laybacked a wide 5.11 crack and then followed easier terrain up and right to intersect Cracked Pepper (Haden-Pennings, 2016, previously unreported). We quickly exited the large dihedral that defines Cracked Pepper and followed a shallow corner system to the left for three challenging pitches. Easy climbing led to the top of the west buttress, where I enjoyed the last 10 minutes of sunlight while Becca toiled away following in the shade. We aided three short sections, but the route likely would go all free at 5.12. The first aid section, on pitch five, could easily be freed with better route-finding. Becca freed the aid on pitch seven while seconding and believes it could be led free with boldness or a few bolts. The tips laybacking on pitch eight free could be led free if a few dangerous blocks were removed. Our route, Until the Wheels Fall Off (1,100', IV 5.11 C1), was named in honor of my odometer rolling over to 200,000 on the way to the trailhead.

– PATRICK LONGLEY

TOKOPAH VALLEY, NEW ROUTES

IN JULY, NEAL Harder, Brandon Thau, and Sebastian Thau, established a nearly 1,000' route on the east side of Lower Tokapah Dome. 1,000 Piece Meal Deal (5.10d) is to the right of previously established routes, with a plethora of compact chicken heads (a.k.a. nuggets). This was the first backcountry first ascent for Sebastian Thau, age 15, the son of Brandon.

Maxim Belyakov and Vitaliy Musiyenko completed a new route on the left side of neighboring Santa Cruz Dome—Knotfest (III 5.11a). Two pitches in a prominent chimney system (5.10) took them to a steep, left-leaning flare, which led to an overhang (5.11a) and onto incredible knobs and chicken heads. [o]

— *INFORMATION FROM* **BRANDON THAU** *AND* **VITALIY MUSIYENKO**

WESTERN SIERRA

SAN JOAQUIN RIVER GORGE, CONFLUENCE DOME, NEW ROUTES

IN SEPTEMBER, CRISTINA Engel, Neal Harder, and I established the first known technical routes on Confluence Dome, located at the confluence of the south and main forks of the San Joaquin River, downstream from Balloon Dome on the west side of the Sierra.

Confluence of Dreams (7 pitches, 5.10) is on the northwest corner of the formation and starts a few meters from the river's edge. Via a series of cracks and dikes, the route attains a prominent 300' electric-yellow dihedral and follows it to the summit.

The following day, Neal and I returned to establish the King Line (9 pitches, 5.10+). The climb starts where the foot of the dome enters the water and follows hand cracks and dikes. Initially, the fifth pitch was A0, but Neal and I returned in October to climb a free variation at 5.10+. [o]

— **BRANDON THAU**

PATTERSON BLUFFS, THE MONEY SHOT

IN OCTOBER, BRIAN Prince and I completed the Money Shot (9 pitches, 5.11 C1), a spectacularly steep route that climbs the left side of the prominent Sunset Buttress, the first route at Patterson Left. [*This Nose-like buttress was climbed by Richard Leversee and Paul Martzen in 1985 and then freed and renamed the Sun Also Rises (10 pitches, 5.12c; see AAJ 1995) by Leversee, Scott Cosgrove, and Jim Zellers. Prince and Thau made the second known ascent of the Sun Also Rises in May 2018.*] Money Shot has two C1 pitches and a crescendo pitch of splitter hand crack with big exposure. It joins the Sun Also Rises for the final three pitches. Scott Thelen and I had climbed the first two pitches of Money Shot in 2000. [o]

— **BRANDON THAU**

NEVADA / RED ROCK NATIONAL CONSERVATION AREA

MT. WILSON, AEOLIAN WALL, JEDI MIND TRICKS

IN NOVEMBER I climbed a new route on the Aeolian Wall, Jedi Mind Tricks, with my friend Kyle Willis. The first pitch is shared with the Original Route (V 5.9 A3) and Dream of Wild Cheeseburgers (Boyce-Willis, 2016; *see AAJ 2017*), a mossy and run-out 5.9 crack described as an "approach pitch" for the Original Route. Above this we headed left toward a hanging basin. Five hundred feet of 4th class brought us into view of our intended line. Looking up, we realized that it overhung enough that bailing from the upper route would be extremely difficult with the gear we had. So we fixed a line down the approach pitch and headed into town to regroup.

We headed back up the next morning equipped with aid gear, pins, and a Beal Escaper. From the hanging basin, a couple of moderate pitches brought us to the meat of the climb, a 200' overhanging corner feature. The climbing remained reasonable and we only busted out the hammer for a few pin placements. We fixed lines and descended to a super-comfy bivy in the basin. In the morning we jugged to our high point, and the crack above was amazing and splitter, providing easy passage to the headwall. Unfortunately, the seams we had hoped to find up high petered out along with our courage. Four solid pitches of slabby, run-out vision questing brought us to a ramp that linked into the Resolution Arête.

All in all, we climbed 13 pitches for about 2,000' of proper 5th class, with 10 of those pitches (about 1,400') being new terrain. While it would take a fair bit of cleaning, the route would likely go free at around 5.12, with a couple pitches of wickedly overhanging splitter finger cracks. 📄 📷

– SAM BOYCE

Kyle Willis approaching Mt. Wilson before making the first ascent of Jedi Mind Tricks (2,000', V 5.10 A2), which joins the Resolution Arête after about 1,400' of climbing. This was Sam Boyce and Willis' third new route on Mt. Wilson, after Dream of Wild Cheeseburgers and Head of State (*AAJ 2017*). *Sam Boyce*

UTAH

HOUSE RANGE, NOTCH PEAK, SOUTHWEST FACE LEFT

FROM MAY 4–7, Matt Meinzer and I established a new free climb on the southwest face of Notch Peak in Utah's West Desert area. The Southwest Face Left (400m, IV 5.11 R) proved to be a serious and slightly loose affair. We placed a total of 26 stainless-steel bolts, 13 of which were used to equip anchors and 13 to protect the climbing. We completed the route over two climbing days, the second of which was an 11-hour effort from car to summit. We had intended to rappel the face, but the upper portion of the route proved too loose to make this a safe decision. This resulted in a painful walk-off down the backside of the mountain in our free climbing shoes.

The southwestern aspect of Notch Peak in the House Range, showing Southwest Face Left (400m, IV 5.11 R). The aid route Airavata (VI 5.10R A4 PDW, Kvashay-Wickstrom, 2016) ascends the smooth face just to the right. Other routes are on the north face, around the prow to the left. *Nate Brown*

Eighty percent of the new route was 5.9 or less on good dolomite rock. The remaining 20 percent proved to be 5.10 and harder. A strong team of experienced alpinists should find this to be an enjoyable adventure—climbers not accustomed to the loose rock typical of a limestone face of this size would do better to attempt the relatively cleaner classics on the other side of the mountain.

– NATE BROWN

The 2,000-foot-high south face of Abraham in Zion's Court of the Patriarchs, showing the 2018 routes (1) Munkuntuwap and (2) Pangea. Earlier routes, not shown, were in the vicinity of Pangea. *Dave Allfrey*

ZION NATIONAL PARK: WALL ROUTES, FREE ASCENTS, AND VIRGIN PEAKS

In addition to one of the heaviest flash floods in the past hundred years, 2018 brought a steady stream of first ascents within the boundaries of Zion National Park, both free and aid.

In late March, Brandon Adams and Roger Putnam finished Pangea (1,800', VI 5.10 A4), up the obvious buttress on the right side of Abraham where all previous routes on south face of the peak had ascended. Pangea meanders up thin cracks, requiring an impressive 40-beak rack, and shares several pitches with the John Wilkes Booth Memorial Route and the Radiator.

In Kolob, Brandon Gottung and Karl Kvashay established the Abbreviated Passage (IV 5.12 A0) directly up the center of Tucupit Point, just before the spring closures, adding to the many new routes and linkups they have climbed on the formation in the last several years. The route has gone mostly free.

In April, answering the challenge of a photo caption in the Zion *Summit Routes* guidebook, Dan Stih climbed two virgin peaks listed as "unnamed...and unclimbed," naming them the Center Pointe (IV 5.9 A2+) and the North Eye (IV 5.9 A2+]. Both lie near the remote canyoneering entrance to Icebox Canyon.

Brandon Adams returned to Abraham in November with Kristoffer Wickstrom and spent seven days establishing a line up the seemingly blank main south face of the peak, well left of previously established routes. Their route required some bolt ladders but also ascends significant natural features and incipient seams. They encountered evidence of a previous attempt a third of the way up the wall. Their route is named Munkuntuweap (2,000', VI 5.8 A4) after the Paiute name for Zion, meaning "straight up land."

Paul Gagner and Ryan Kempf completed a route up the Angelino Wall in November, naming it Museum Piece (V 5.8 A4), as the route looks down on NPS Human History Museum. Gagner had started the line with Bill Crouse 14 years earlier. The line, which took four days, shares the first two and a half pitches with Drop Zone (VI 5.8 A4+, MacDonald-McNamara, 1996) before breaking out right.

Brent Barghahn and Rob Pizem freed an old obscurity on the southeast buttress of Angels Landing named Jokers and Thieves (V 5.10 A3, Cook-Kirkwood) at IV 5.11+, topping out on the prow of the buttress. Barghahn also established a difficult three-pitch route with Craig Huang in late November that follows a steep corner system on the south buttress of Mt. Majestic. Emerald Corner (5.12+ A0) is an open project—the outrageous last pitch involves bolted face climbing out a leaning corner splitting a double-overhanging prow and is expected to be mid- to upper 5.13.

Dakota Walz and Collin Turbet completed a new route on the south face of Angels Landing, with five pitches of 5.10 crack climbing and another five adventure pitches to the summit. Apollyon (1,300', IV 5.10+) means angel of death or place of destruction in biblical mythology—Walz took a 30-foot ground fall while establishing the first pitch.

Dan Stih climbed three more virgin peaks in the fall in the vicinity of the Court of the Patriarchs, naming them Battleship Rock, Nipple Peak, and Princess Spire, the latter of which had previously been attempted from the north by two different parties. He also rope-soloed a new line on Cable Mountain, succinctly named the North Face Route (III/IV A1+), more than 20 years after his first new route on the face, Hammer and Sickle (VI A3, Raimonde-Stih, *see AAJ 1997*).

— STEFFAN GREGORY *AND* ETHAN NEWMAN

ZION NATIONAL PARK, MOONLIGHT BUTTRESS, MOONSHADOW

IN 1971, THE young and strong team of Jeff Lowe and Mike Weis walked up to the base of "Chimney Tower" and climbed what became the famous Moonlight Buttress. Forty years later, Jeff was crippled by a disease that rendered him incapable of talking or walking, let alone climbing. I told him I wanted to climb Moonlight in the best style—ground-up and onsight. He typed into his iPad and turned it toward me to read: "You can do it. Let me know when you do."

Spoiler alert: I failed on the onsight. But from Moonlight I looked over to the right side of the buttress to study a line I had always wondered about. It appeared quite featured and broken. In August 2018, Jeff died from his health complications. [*See tribute on p.358.*] Shortly thereafter, my buddy Jarod Sickler and I hiked to the base of Moonlight Buttress, 100 feet to the right of the historic line. Lying in the grass was a rusted Leeper bolt hanger, presumably from the first ascent of Moonlight. We took it as a good omen from Jeff and Mike and headed up with it in our pocket.

Intent on finding a moderate free line, we connected dihedrals zigzagging 600' to a midway ledge. From there we entered a massive varnished corner system easily seen from the road. The upper headwall revealed at least five different options of where to go next. After cleaning some dangerous loose blocks from the first half of the line on rappel, we hiked to the top via the West Rim Trail and rappelled in to decide how to connect our high point to a good exit. Eventually we found exactly what we were looking for.

We returned two months later and pushed the route to a dramatic finish, with the crux in the last 50', completing a sustained line of enjoyable, varied cracks—Moonshadow (1,100', IV 5.11b). Hopefully we did Jeff proud by finding a line not only in Moonlight's shadow but also his own. Many thanks to guidebook author Bryan Bird for his wise counsel and to the Bit & Spur Saloon for nightly libations and protein replenishment.

— JEREMY COLLINS

Jeremy Collins enters the crux bulge on pitch 11 of Moonshadow, a new 5.11 route up Moonlight Buttress. *Dan Krauss*

Keiko Tanaka leading the complicated and dicey first-pitch traverse during the first ascent of Ancient Art Simulator on Scarlet Spire. Recent rockfall had made the direct start seem unappealing. *Steve Bartlett*

THE DEEPER MYSTERIES
A NEW STASH OF SPICY TOWERS IN SOUTHEASTERN UTAH

BY STEVE "CRUSHER" BARTLETT

THE DEEPER MYSTERY Towers are a previously untouched area of desert sandstone formations, a mile east of the Mystery Towers, which themselves are just east of the well-known Fisher Towers. The Deeper Mysteries can only be seen from the nearby mesa called Top of the World, and from up there everything below is remote and flattened as if viewed from an airplane.

In 1995, during the first ascent of the Wait of the World (6 pitches, A3+) on the Atlas, on the eastern edge of the Mystery Towers, Chip Wilson and I had spotted an inviting hoodoo along the adjacent steep hillside. Up close it was scrappy, but just around the next corner were more impressive spires. I dubbed the largest the Mysteron. Later, I discovered a side canyon of Onion Creek that burrowed deep into this area, allowing easier access. Even so, the logistics were daunting—we opted for lower hanging fruit elsewhere.

Fast-forward two decades and low-hanging fruit is hard to find. Keiko Tanaka and Joe Shultz, who, with Neil Chelton, had recently climbed Beaking in Tongues (7 pitches, A4, Bartlett-Levine, 1997) in the Fisher Towers, sought me out to tell me they'd enjoyed the route and to ask for suggestions for similar objectives. *Hmmm*, I pondered, *would they be interested in exploring a new area?* I asked and they were enthusiastic. Chip Wilson, whom I phoned to see if he'd like to join us, not so much. In April, Keiko, Joe, and I drove to Onion Creek, shouldered our loads, and set off with provisions for three nights. The Deeper Mysteries are rowdier than the Mystery Towers or just about anywhere else I've visited on the Colorado Plateau. Hoodoos sit hard against cliff bands and buttresses that ascend

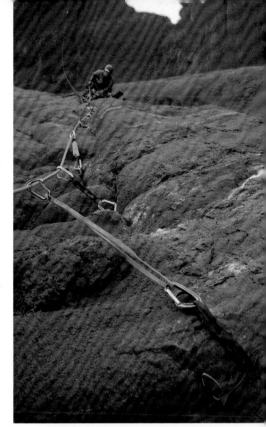

to the Top of the World, 1,000' above. A massive fault cleaves the mesa and has excavated a chaotic zone of boulders, precipices, and ravines, framed by pale, fresh-hewn cliffs. In the other direction, back toward Onion Creek, tortuous gullies hacksaw through raw red ridges. The terrain is overly tilted, and further collapse appears imminent.

The first night, desert winds rattled our sleeping bags and peppered us with gravel. Furious roars reverberated in the dark and kept us awake. The next morning the gale abated. We slept late and circumnavigated the Mysteron, post-holing through dust. Over 200' high, the landform featured a curious summit: a jumble of car-size erratic boulders, fallen or rolled from who knows where. On the more conventional Cutler sandstone flanks below, one seam came within reach. After the approach and sleepless night, I was feeling every one of my 61 years and happy to let someone else lead. Joe—who would have been eight years old when Chip and I were climbing the Atlas—stepped up and got going. He hammered all manner of pitons into what proved to be a continuous, if rotten crack, while I napped and pretended to belay.

Next day, the second pitch was to be my lead. Midway, I took a Screamer-ripping fall—my first fall on a desert aid pitch in nearly 30 years. That pitch ended at the topmost band of solid rock. The third pitch looked awful: a gross flare lined with stacked projectiles, supported by each other or by vestiges of dried mud hiding somewhere in back. Next morning, Keiko carefully "fraid-climbed" (or was it unafraid-climbed?) via stems, laybacks, pitons, and cams to the SUV-size summit block. As Joe and I joined her on this remote, hard-earned summit, we were startled by a yell, the first sign of another human in three days. It was Chip. He merrily jumared our ropes and joined us on top.

Two weeks later, we returned and climbed a

[Top] Looking down at some "interesting" placements on pitch two of the Shadow of Fear on the Mysteron. *Steve Bartlett* [Bottom] Nearing the belay on the third pitch of Sandromeda (350', 5 pitches, 5.8 A3+) on the Pink Squirrel tower. *Joe Shultz*

[Left] Keiko Tanaka leading the fourth pitch of Ancient Art Simulator (5 pitches, 5.7 A3+) on Scarlet Spire. This tower features a boardwalk approach to a corkscrew summit reminiscent of Ancient Art in the nearby Fisher Towers. *Steve Bartlett* [Above] Steve "Crusher" Bartlett at the base of the Mysteron in Utah's Deeper Mystery Towers. Crusher first visited the desert Southwest in 1984 and has been a driving force in exploring new routes on the Colorado Plateau ever since. His book *Desert Towers* is the definitive climbing history of the area. *Joe Shultz*

splendidly isolated spire, reminiscent of the Fisher Towers' Ancient Art, a half-mile south of the Mysteron. Over 300' tall, Scarlet Spire took Keiko, Joe, and me five days to climb. Pitch one, Keiko's lead, featured a traverse close to the ground that lasted into the night in the search for a piece worth rappelling from. Next day, as I cleaned this pitch and jumared the last few feet to join Keiko at the belay, I gently tried to trundle a loose stone—and a mattress-size block dropped off, shoving me aside and causing Joe, at the base, to run for his life. On the third pitch, Joe actually placed a couple drive-in ice screws. As with Ancient Art, the final, corkscrew pitch was accessed by a walk along a narrow, rounded spine we called the Land Bridge—undercut and dropping hundreds of feet on both sides. And the summit? It was a coffee table, barely balanced, a stacked relic from the Stone Age that was nearing its demise.

Behind Scarlet Spire was its twin, minus the skeletal top-knot. In the fall, Neil Chelton joined Keiko, Joe, and me for a five-pitch climb up this formation, which we named the Pink Squirrel. Nearer to the Mysteron, three smaller towers also were climbed. Neil led the 80-foot Mister Ron, and later he soloed the Corkscrew, car-to-car, in a day. Keiko also led a 120' pillar atop a high ridge. We named this the Watchtower for its panoramic views of the Deeper Mysteries, the Mystery Towers, and, beyond, the Titan, far away in time but right here and now in style and vision.

SUMMARY: First known routes in the Deeper Mystery Towers outside Moab, all established in 2018: Shadow of Fear (220', 5.8 R A3) on the Mysteron; Sandromeda (350', 5 pitches, 5.8 A3+) on the Pink Squirrel; Ancient Art Simulator (340', 5 pitches, 5.7 A3+) on Scarlet Spire; Alotta Sandgina (120', 5.7 A2) on the Watchtower; Exfoliation Station (80', A2+) on Mister Ron; In Vino Veritas (100', A3) on the Corkscrew. ⊡

GRAND CANYON NATIONAL PARK, KEYHOLE RIDGE

ON NOVEMBER 24, 2017, I started my fifth trip down the Colorado River through Grand Canyon, putting in at Lee's Ferry with seven people in two boats. Early in the trip, under the auspices of a national park research permit, we mapped unexplored caves, primarily those accessible only via technical climbing. During a three-day layover, Andrew Chandler, our trip leader and a talented cave surveyor, and I opened several pitches (up to 5.9 A2) to access numerous caves, mapping roughly 800' of passage and leaving no fixed gear other than bits of webbing for rappel. The style and setting were exotic, but as the permit bears a non-disclosure agreement, the location of these routes cannot be reported.

A stripped-down Ethan Holt makes the rappel into a large pool below Keyhole Natural Bridge, part of the descent from Keyhole Ridge (ca 1,000', 5.9). *Cole Taylor*

Any river trip through Grand Canyon presents endless climbing possibilities, but downstream logistics often make for limited opportunities. As we continued the float, I bided my time, mindful of keeping the raft upright and waiting for the conditions to align: a willing partner, a reasonable objective, and a layover day. The bow was drawn on December 7, at Keyhole Camp, river mile 140.

At dawn, Ethan Holt and I meandered up the Bright Angel shale on the downstream side of 140 Mile Canyon toward a prominent ridgeline through the limestone layers above. We dodged right around the first band of Muav limestone, then soloed a chimney through the next band to a broad terrace. The bulk of the Muav layer was above us, steep and chunky, and we contoured right until locating a feasible line. We tied in and climbed this layer in two long pitches, up to 5.9, tiptoeing through shattered junk to connect hand cracks and chimneys.

At another terrace, beneath the Redwall limestone, we traversed left, back to the ridgeline, then edged up horizontal chert veins in a zebra-striped chimney. A steep plaque on the next pitch offered the best climbing of the route: a thin crack through Velcro-textured black rock. The climbing rambled from there—loose 4th class with bits of 5.this-and-that. Crimp the occasional fossil. Watch the river below. Mind the rubble. We simul-climbed a long pitch to the rim of the Redwall.

We considered the next layer, but instead packed the gear and hiked south along the Redwall terrace toward a hopeful aperture of descent. Wild burros, long-feral remnants of old miners' stock, have stomped an incredible trail system along this terrace, making for a pleasant stroll to Keyhole Natural Bridge. We slung a block and rappelled into the pit behind Keyhole Bridge. At the edge of the Keyhole, we threaded pockets in the limestone about 15' back from the lip. A hundred feet below was a large murky pool. I stripped to my undies and rapped in. Hugging the side of the pool, chest deep in the water, I felt my way along a sloping mud bank before bouldering out the far side with dry hair. Ethan doesn't wear undies, so he entered the Keyhole naked in his harness. After one more rappel we walked down to the river through dusk, until we were around a campfire with friends serving us cocktails and hot dinner.

After the trip, I learned from the local canyoneering cognoscenti that the Keyhole had seen one known descent, in the mid '90s, when Cecelia Mortenson and friends descended to the river, then returned out their fixed lines. If our climb had been done, we couldn't tell, and we left it as such—Keyhole Ridge (ca 1,000', 5.9).

— COLE TAYLOR

SACAJAWEA PEAK, GRAND CENTRAL COULOIR AND RIGHT VENTRICLE

In 2016, JOE Crane and I ventured into Idaho's Lost River Range to pit ourselves against the unrepeated Broken Wings (400m, WI5, Dickerson-Lords-Mordicai, *AAJ 2006*) on the north face of Sacajewea Peak (11,936'). Due to the fickle nature of mixed climbing in this range, we were not successful until our third attempt. Beautiful smears of ephemeral ice, tight chimneys, and spicy mixed climbing left us hungry for more.

The north face of Sacajawea Peak (11,936') in Idaho's Lost River Range, showing (1) Right Ventricle (220m, WI4 M3, 2018), (2) Grand Central Couloir (440m, WI4+/5-M5, 2017), and (3) Broken Wings (400m, WI5, Dickerson-Lords-Mordecai, 2005). A 13-pitch rock route has been completed on the face to the right of Grand Central Couloir. *Joe Crane*

In June 2017, Joe and I returned with intentions of establishing a new line on the center of the face. As we walked by Gold Digger (250m, WI4 M7, Avenius-Lords, 2008) on the nearby Golden Pillar, our hearts sank when we noticed all the ice had melted and fallen off. We set up camp and murmured about how we might have waited too long. As the sun set we scoped our intended line and saw very little ice, save for a section up high that looked promising.

In hindsight most of the ice was difficult to see because of the deep chimneys on our line. At the start, easy climbing up a snow apron brought us to the base of a narrow slot. Dry-tool moves around a small roof led to steep snow and fresh ice that was pouring over several chockstones. The chimney eventually widened into a steep couloir that provided mellow snow climbing. This ended at the base of a meter-wide chimney that was full of perfect one-swing ice. This dream-like chimney continued for approximately 160m, save for a small snow patch in the middle. The slot then constricted so tight that the leader was forced to turn sideways. Fresh smears of ice lined the walls of the constriction, and rotten snow mushrooms filled the back. One last overhanging mushroom at the top of the constriction greeted the leader, after which the chimney widened into a pleasant couloir that deposited us 20m east of the summit—Grand Central Couloir (440m, WI4+/5- M5).

A year later to the day, Joe and I found ourselves back at the base of Sacajewea's north face, starting up a shorter line on the left side of the face. Mellow snow climbing through a narrow passage led to a large, heart-shaped bowl, where two obvious lines begin.

After noticing signs of rockfall coming out of the left line, we opted to head right. We entered a narrow couloir that offered steep snow and Styrofoam ice, with mellow mixed moves around a series of chockstones. Toward the top, the couloir turned abruptly left and then veered back right before terminating at the base of a narrow chimney that was lined with beautiful ice and wild snow formations. Once again, the chimney was so tight we were forced to turn sideways and apply a mixture of wide-crack technique paired with traditional ice climbing to make upward progress. With one tool and crampon on ice and the others on rock, we slowly worked upward through this lovely chimney system for a pitch and a half before a pleasant snow couloir led to the ridge—Right Ventricle (220m from the top of the Heart, WI4 M3). 📷

— DALLIN CAREY

MT. WILBUR, NORTH FACE, WINTER-CONDITIONS ASCENT

IN LATE OCTOBER, Justin Willis and I headed into Glacier National Park to explore the area's potential for fall alpine mixed climbing. During a warm and clear weather window, we made what we think was the second ascent and first "wintery" ascent of the 2,500' north face of Mt. Wilbur (9,321') in a 23-hour car-to-car push from the Many Glaciers Trailhead.

The first ascent of this face was during the summer season of 1961 by Gil Averill, Tom Choate, and Renn Fenton. Their route was described as an extremely difficult climb involving many overhanging chimney pitches. We experienced good climbing up to M5, on a rather terrifying blend of sedimentary and metamorphic rock, very little of which is held together well. The cruxes were the same chimneys that the first ascent described. Given the poor rock, we feel the climbing is likely far better in winter conditions.

Justin and I are excited to continue exploring the potential of this area, but with caution: Dangerous snow conditions, big remote faces, and bad rock make climbing here very serious.

— GRAHAM ZIMMERMAN

Mt. Wilbur (9,321'), showing the north face route, first climbed in 1961. Justin Willis and Graham Zimmerman made the first known ascent in wintery mixed conditions in October. *Graham Zimmerman*

WOLVERINE PEAK CIRQUE, NEW ROUTES

IN AUGUST, I was invited to join an expedition with Sean Canterbury, Mark Evans, Evan Johnson, Jared Leader, Shingo Ohkawa, Heath Rowland, Oli Shaw, and Greg Troutman—an unruly group of climbers from around the country—for two weeks of exploration in a seldom-visited nook of the Winds. A north- and east-facing cirque centers around Wolverine Peak (12,631') and lies just south of the Wilson Creek Lakes, west of Washakie Park on the east side of the range. According to group research, very few parties have visited the area. The first, being none other than Fred Beckey and James Garrett, visited multiple times, along with several others, and completed a nine-pitch route on the east face of Point 12,612' called the Illness (V 5.10 A3, *AAJ 2000*) and an 1,800' 5.8 on the north ridge of Saddle Mountain.

I was behind the group's schedule and navigated my way to base camp solo. The 10-mile hike was one of the more majestic approaches I can recall, as the landscape resembled something out of a Bob Ross painting, with an abundance of deep blue alpine lakes, wildflowers, and happy trees. By the time I arrived, two days after everyone else, the group had done recon, cached gear, and established two new routes on a formation they dubbed Susser's Spire, a.k.a. Sucks To Be Second Tower.

[Top] The Wolverine Peak cirque in the Wind River Range. Accessed from the St. Lawrence Ranger Station on the east side of the range, this north-northeast-facing cirque lies just south of the Wilson Creek Lakes. Formations from left to right: Saddle Mountain (12,551'), Thunderbolt Spire (ca 12,320'), Lightning Rod Spire (ca 12,280'), Wolverine Peak (center, 12,631'), Point 12,612' (The Shield, the broad east face, was climbed in 1999), East Buttress, Far East Buttress, Front Buttress, Susser's Spire. [Left] Shingo Ohkawa on pitch three of Trundor and Bummus (5.8+) on the Front Buttress. *Mark Evans (both photos)*

The subsequent two weeks were filled with a bit of choss wrangling, some stellar rock climbing, and mediocre-at-best fishing. Rest days included plenty of whiskey, swimming, games, herbal assistance, and herbal assistance naps. The group as a whole managed 12 ground-up first ascents, all on traditional gear, on six of the eight major formations: Lightning Rod Spire, Mt. Wolverine, East Buttress, Susser's Spire, Far East Buttress, and the Front Buttress.

In today's age of many motivated climbers, it seems you have to travel further and further off the beaten path to access the unknown. That extra effort, however, makes the reward that much sweeter. The climbing, beautiful scenery, exceptional weather, and absence of crowds all made it seem too good to be true.

SUMMARY OF ACTIVITY IN WOLVERINE PEAK CIRQUE: Ride The Lightning (310m, 7 pitches, 5.8, Evans-Rothenbush-Troutman) on Lightning Rod Spire; Adamantium (380m, 8 pitches, 5,10-, Leader-Rowland) on Wolverine Peak; Initech (300m, 6 pitches, 5.10 C2, Evans-Rothenbush-Troutman) and Initrode (300m, 6 pitches, 5.11-, Evans-Rothenbush-Troutman) on East Buttress; Front Baggin' (270m, 5 Pitches, 5.10-, Johnson-Leader-Rowland) and Peripheral Vision (250m, 4 Pitches, 5.10+, Canterbury-Shaw) on Far East Buttress; Crocodile Hunter (140m, 5 pitches, 5.10+, Evans-Rowland-Troutman), Umami (100m, 3 pitches, 5.11+, Canterbury-Shaw) and Fun Police (45m, 1 Pitch, 5.5, Canterbury-Ohkawa-Shaw) on Susser's Spire; Eye of the Storm (120m, 3 pitches, 5.11, Evans-Troutman), Choose the Right (120m, 3 pitches, 5.9, Evans-Troutman) and Trundor and Bummus (110m, 3 pitches, 5.8+, Ohkawa-Rowland) on the Front Buttress. 📷

– NICK ROTHENBUSH

CATHEDRAL PEAK, NOBLE BEAST

CATHEDRAL PEAK'S BIG east-facing wall, rising above Cathedral Lake in the eastern Wind Rivers, has a long history, attracting the attention of climbers since at least 1979, when Fred Beckey and Jim Kanzler completed the route they named Orion's Reflection. NOLS courses camp nearby every year, and Wyoming hardmen like Greg Collins and Dave Anderson have passed through the area.

I didn't see the wall until 2015, when the NOLS course I was instructing made a base camp nearby for a week. It was hard to stay focused while teaching camp cooking or rappelling techniques with the headwall looming through the clouds in the background. Later, Internet research and chats with experienced Wind River climbers didn't turn up any beta about the prominent crack system leading to a bizarre, overhanging summit block. Two other routes had been completed since Beckey's route—the South Tower Direct (McNamara-Rowell, 1999) on the left side of the face and the Flight of the Golden Camalot (Hunt-Keith, 2001) on the right—but this central line appeared to be unclimbed.

Three years later, toward the end of July, I finally hiked the seven miles from Dickinson Park to the base with Ben Dueweke. The line looked as good as I remembered, but our attempt was stymied by mild altitude sickness and some ridiculously good fishing, not to mention the challenging steep section with tricky gear at the top of the third pitch. Despite our setback, the rock quality was promising.

A week later I was back with my friend Chris Kalman. We began climbing at 6 a.m. on July 28. Chris quickly dispatched the difficulties and runout at the previous high point and we were in business. Two more 5.11 pitches led us to the massive cleft that splits the upper two-thirds of the mountain into the soaring buttresses from which its name is derived.

[Top] The east-facing wall of Cathedral Peak, above Cathedral Lake in the eastern Wind River Range, showing (1) Approximate line of South Tower Direct (McNamara-Rowell, 1999); (2) Noble Beast (Kalman-Loyka, 2018); (3) Orion's Reflection (Beckey-Kanzler, 1979); and (4) approximate line of Flight of the Golden Camalot (Hunt-Keith, 2001). *Justin Loyka* [Bottom] Justin Loyka making the athletic and airy traverse high on Noble Beast. *Chris Kalman*

Justin Loyka heading up a beautiful thin-hands splitter on the fourth pitch of Noble Beast (1,300', 5.11 C1) on Cathedral Peak. *Chris Kalman*

We moved the belay up to the base of one of several beautiful crack systems accessible from our five-pitch start. Three pitches of sustained but moderate jamming led to a great ledge. All the climbing up until here had been basically free, though Chris fell while leading the first pitch, and I fell repeatedly while leading the fourth. We never considered pulling the ropes to retry these sections, as there was still a ton of unknown terrain above.

The next pitch, with more burly 5.11 layback-ing, started out brilliant before deteriorating into badly exfoliating rock, requiring Chris to pendulum left to maneuver around it. He took an ugly, swinging whipper while attempting to free climb above the pendulum. Unfortunately, the rock remained flakey from here on out. We were feeling pretty whupped by the physical climbing, and so we took to aiding (with no hammer, pins, aiders, or daisies) to finish the four upper pitches.

We exited a 25-foot roof to the right via a wild hand traverse, assisted by a heel-toe cam evolving into horizontal chimneying. Chris then aided a vegetated crack while in the smoky sky a blood-red full moon rose behind us. The cramps I'd been experiencing finally subsided just as Chris was starting to bonk, and I led a final pitch of delicate choss-wrangling as the stars came out.

We clattered down a huge gully to the north and arrived in camp around midnight. We called the route Noble Beast, due to the elegance of the line (noble) and the burliness of the climbing (beastly). It is 1,300' long and was climbed in 12 pitches at 5.11 C1. The occasional exfoliating stone detracts from the overall quality, but I have never done so much sustained crack climbing on a Wind River route. 📷

— JUSTIN LOYKA

THE MONOLITH, DISCOVERY, ALL FREE

IN JULY, SAM Lightner Jr., Mike Lilygren, and Shep Vail returned to the Monolith along with Alex Bridgewater, and the climbers freed the remaining aid on Discovery, a 1,600' route on the northeast face. Rappelling in from the top of the formation, as the team did in 2017 when they completed a three-year effort to establish the route (*AAJ 2018*), Bridgewater redpointed pitch 12 at 5.13a, freeing 25 feet of tips and stemming that had gone at C1 before. The team also created a more direct line through the middle of the route, freeing a new 5.12a pitch in the process. As of late August 2018, Discovery (1,600', 15 pitches, 5.13a) had not yet seen a continuous free ascent. 📷 🔍

— *INFORMATION FROM* SAM LIGHTNER JR.

YELLOW WOLF
A LANDMARK FREE CLIMB IN WYOMING'S ABSAROKA RANGE

BY WHIT MAGRO

JUST OFF THE Chief Joseph Scenic Highway in northwest Wyoming is a section of the Clarks Fork Canyon of the Yellowstone River called the Box, in which there is a 1,000', south-facing granite wall that we've named the Chief. There are 10 routes on the Chief, most of which were quietly established ground-up in the early 2000s by a dedicated and tight-lipped crew of Bozeman climbers. Many of these are hard free routes, but a few remain aid climbs and probably always will.

Yellow Wolf is the most recent free route on the wall and is also the first line on the north rim of the canyon established top down. The idea was to establish a repeatable, high-end free climb, so it seemed appropriate to approach it this way. At the beginning of 2016, I spent some time solo, scouting and establishing a cache of rope and gear at the top of the wall, which is quite hard to access. Once spring had sprung, I invited my friend and Wyoming climber Greg Collins to the Clarks Fork for his first visit. With a substantial amount of rope, we rappelled, bolted anchors, and fixed lines while cleaning all the loose and scary chunks of rock from the wall.

Once the lines were fixed, endless days of working the route began. We were excited for the prospects, but at the beginning I had my doubts that it would ever go free. Later my brother Sam and Brady Johnston joined the effort, helping to work the route and add bolts to the upper pitches. We kept this team dynamic between Greg and Brady's crew and the Bozeman contingent for the next year and a half—whoever had time would head down with whoever they could find to work the route. The names on the topo represent all the people that had a hand in scrubbing, chalking, working, and climbing on the route during its development. It was an amazing team effort.

Toward the end of this two-year project, it was primarily Brady and me going for redpoint burns. At the end of October 2017, winter was knocking. During Brady's first go at the crux fourth pitch, he cut his finger badly due to the very cold conditions. Now it was my turn—the cold temps were helpful for the friction and I managed to send the 40m pitch on my first try. Brady selflessly agreed to let me go for full send, which I managed to do that day. Yellow Wolf (1,000', IV 5.13+/14-) has one pitch of 5.13+ /14-, three pitches of mid-5.13, one 13-/12d, and five pitches at 11+ and below.

Yellow Wolf is named for the famous warrior from the Nez Perce tribe who served under Chief Joseph. As the Nez Perce fled for the Canadian border during the late summer of 1877, they traveled through Clarks Fork Canyon, eluding General Oliver Howard and his troops. Because of this rich and sacred history, we who have been responsible for the climbing development of this canyon have always made an effort to keep the area a place of mystery and intrigue.

Yet so much effort and hardware went into this line that it would be a crime for it to remain a secret. In my opinion, it's hard, sustained granite free climbing at its finest, and I look forward to it being repeated. May you tread lightly and respect the ethos of this special place. 🔍

CRAZY HORSE
THIRTY-TWO YEARS LATER, A SECOND NEW ROUTE ON CLOUD PEAK

BY ARNO ILGNER

The massive east face of Cloud Peak in the Bighorn Mountains of Wyoming, showing the line of In Honor of Crazy Horse (1,200', IV 5.12a). The route took four seasons to complete and was the author's second route on the wall. The first of these, A Shimmering Abstraction (Ilgner-Petro, 1986), as well as Medicine Crow (Gray-Marine, 2016), are to the right of the 2018 route. *Arno Ilgner*

THE BIGHORNS ARE less known to climbers than the more popular Wyoming ranges of the Wind River Mountains and the Tetons. Route activity on Cloud Peak (13,166') reflects this, showing only a few routes. Until 2016, in fact, the large granite east face only had one route on it—the one I did with Steve Petro in 1986: A Shimmering Abstraction. Three decades later, this lack of activity spurred me to investigate the possibility of doing another route on the face. [*In 2016, Spencer Gray and Alex Marine put up Medicine Crow, left of the 1986 route; see AAJ 2017.*]

The process started in 2015. I partnered with Jeff Lodas and we approached the face from the east. It was a 13-mile approach with the last half being very difficult, with no established trail. We camped on a knoll on the east side of Glacier Lake, within a one-hour hike of the face. Jeff and I pushed the route to halfway up the wall, where we hit a blank section. We probed for ways around it but ran out of time and descended. We also were concerned about finding a way around a 30-foot roof that appeared to block the exit to the summit.

In 2016 we decided to approach from the west, starting at the West Tensleep Lake trailhead. This approach is also 13 miles, but with an established hiking route to the summit of Cloud Peak, mostly on trail. We intended to camp near the summit so we could access the wall from the top. Doing this would allow us to examine whether we could find a feasible exit for our line. We rappelled in, cleaned some loose flakes, and indeed found an exit. We then descended to the blank section we'd found the previous year—it looked possible to free climb, but would need some bolts to protect it. We ran out of time and bolts, though, so we climbed out and decided to come back the following year.

In 2017 we had the bright idea of using an ATV for the first half of the eastern approach, where there was a trail and ATVs were allowed. However, several axle bolts came loose and fell off when we were close to Cloud Peak Reservoir, deep into the backcountry. Jeff hiked out to get repair parts and tools, which delayed us two days. We fixed the ATV, continued a short distance, and parked. Then we hiked the difficult last half of the approach to Cloud Peak.

We camped on the south side, below the Merlon formation. The first day, we hiked to the summit, rappelled down our route to the blank section, and added bolts. We worked the pitch on top-rope and were able to figure out the beta and do it free. After a rest day, we approached the wall from the east for a continuous attempt. We freed all the pitches up to the bolted blank section, but couldn't free it this time. The weather was unsettled, and by evening we were caught in a storm two pitches from the summit. We descended. We were out of food and exhausted, so we hiked out, leaving it for the following year.

In 2018, Jeff wasn't interested in returning for another attempt, so I partnered with Taimur Ahmad, a boulderer from the Washington, D.C., area. Taimur's bouldering skills would come in handy for freeing the crux pitch.

We approached from the west in early August and camped literally 30 yards from the top of the route. The weather window was great: sunny skies and little chance of rain. The first day we rappelled to put in a couple more bolts, creating an intermediate belay at the top of the blank crux pitch. Then we spent some time improving our beta and climbed back out.

We rested the next day and then rappelled to the base of the wall, where a fourth-class black-dike ramp meets the start of the technical rock. The lower pitches went quickly, and by midday we were at the crux. This pitch actually has a lower and upper crux, the upper one being more difficult. I led through the lower crux and fell on the upper crux. I worked on it from a no-hands stance in the middle of the pitch, trying several times until I did it free at 5.12a. I rested a short time and then continued up the 5.10 section that would finish the pitch, got pumped, and fell. It seemed I'd focused so much on the 5.12 crux that I didn't pay enough attention to the easier climbing or rest long enough to regain my strength.

I lowered back to the belay so Taimur could lead the crux pitch, which he did quickly. Taimur was pleased because he felt that free climbing this pitch would be his major contribution to our success—and it was! We climbed the rest of the pitches and arrived on top after sundown. It was a long day, but we succeeded.

I'm somewhat disappointed by my mistake but happy that I persevered four years in a row to see the project to completion. Suffice to say that Taimur and I did the first full ascent and Taimur did the first free ascent. I can be happy with that. I named the route In Honor of Crazy Horse (1,200', IV 5.12a) as a tribute to the Lakota Sioux who had struggled to preserve their hunting grounds, the Powder River Basin, that lie to the east of the Bighorn Mountains. Hoka Hey! 📷 🔍

[Top] **Jeff Lodas climbing the last pitch in 2017, his third year of work on the route.** [Middle] **The ill-fated ATV.** [Bottom] **Taimur Ahmad (left) and a very happy post-send** Ilgner. *Arno Ilgner (three photos)*

ALASKA

The upper east face of the east summit of Caliban. (1) Marshall Mathers Memorial Route (17 pitches, IV+ 5.11 R. (2) Calibration (IV 5.8), ending on the northeast ridge. (3) Pillar Arête (V 5.10b, Hokanson-Johnson, 2008). *Ryan Hokanson*

CALIBAN, CALIBRATION AND MARSHALL MATHERS MEMORIAL ROUTE

IN LATE JULY, Lang Van Dommelen, Chris Williams, and I flew into Gates of the Arctic National Park looking for adventure, suffering, and ecstasy on the walls of the Arrigetch Peaks. They did not disappoint. Coyote Air dropped us on a gravel bar in the belly of the Alatna River valley. Shouldering our 120-pound packs, we began the long approach up Arrigetch Creek, beginning with two hours of river crossings, tussocks, and bushwhacking. For the rest of that day and part of the next, we slogged along Arrigetch Creek and eventually made it to a camp on the valley floor, directly below Caliban (7,181'). [*Caliban was first climbed in 1969 by Arthur Bacon, George Ripley, David Roberts, and Robert Waldrop, from the southeast side, during the first climbing expedition into the Arrigetch. See AAJ 1970.*]

The next day, July 25, we warmed up by establishing a long variation start to Pillar Arête (V 5.10b, Hokanson-Johnson, *AAJ 2009*) on the northeast ridge system of Caliban. Calibration (1,500', IV 5.8) follows a shallow ridge system between choss gullies and ends at the base of the first main tower of the Pillar Arête, which the first ascensionists had reached by scrambling from the north side. We climbed 10 roped pitches, interspersed with 4th- and easy 5th-class soloing. After joining the Pillar Arête, we descended by scrambling and rappelling to the east, reaching the ground about 15 hours after we left it.

After two days of rest and exploration, we attempted the shorter but steeper east face of Albatross. After a few approach pitches, several difficult (up to 5.11) and poorly protected pitches led to a dead-end at a stack of precarious flakes. [*Details of this attempt are at the AAJ website.*]

We now felt ready to attempt a major objective, the unclimbed east face of Caliban. [*This face culminates on the east summit (6,994'), a distinct peak about half a mile from the main summit.*] On the far left side of the east face, about 1,000' of low-angle slabs lead to a 1,500' headwall. Like our previous route on Caliban, we used a shallow ridge system to move through the slabs and approach the face. A few roped pitches and a couple of hundred meters of 4th- and easy 5th-class took us to the headwall.

The steeper rock began with two easy pitches (5.7–5.8) on stellar rock, following corners and splitter cracks to a good belay ledge. The next two 50m pitches up the headwall featured superb 5.10 face climbing past good gear and long splitter cracks, which took us to a belay below an obvious right-trending chimney and corner system. Chris got the lead for a terrifying 5.10 R leftward traverse to reach the blunt ridge on the left side of the face. Above, a thin, flaring seam

Chris Williams climbing on the upper pitches of the Marshall Mathers Memorial Route on the east face of Caliban in the Arrigetch Peaks. *Gus Barber*

went through a small roof and into an enticing finger crack. After a stiff tips-crack boulder problem with a mandatory foot cut, 40m of impossibly splitter fingers and tips opened up in front of me, and I just grinned ear to ear while shadowed clouds began to appear over my shoulder. I got to a belay ledge just as it began to rain. Luckily, it was just a squall that stopped about 30 seconds after Lang and Chris reached the belay.

After drying out, we climbed three more pitches of 5.8 to 5.9 climbing on consistently good finger cracks up to a large ledge on the ridge. Faced with stacks of car- to house-size boulders on slabs, we followed a ledge system left off the ridge and into a gully. Three pitches of easy climbing on wet and marginal rock brought us to the east summit of Caliban around 2 a.m. For future parties, the large ledge on the ridge might be a logical descent point for this route, as that's where the good rock really ends. We did not continue west along the summit ridge to the Caliban's highest peak.

To descend, we made two 70m rappels into the gully behind the ridge we climbed. Three more rappels got us into the next gully system over (we believe this is the gully climbed by Norm Larson and Lorna Corson in 1993, see *AAJ 1995*), which took us to the ground.

Midway through our descent, as the sun began to appear again in our valley, Chris swears that he heard an ice cream truck driving through Arrigetch Valley, and Lang and I began to see shapes in the colors of the early sun. To stay awake, we began to recite rap lyrics, mostly Eminem. This trippy episode spawned the route's name, the Marshal Mathers Memorial Route (2,500′, 17 pitches, V 5.11 R). We stumbled into camp 25 hours after we began and collapsed into our tents.

While sitting at one of the final ledges on the M.M.M. and watching the last light of the sunset play across the expanse of granite, I had a feeling of profound appreciation for the opportunity to be there and ecstatic anticipation for where I was going. Although I began my climbing career as a gym and comp climber, I had always seen the act of free climbing big walls in the alpine as the epitome of the sport. While I had realized a dream, I knew this was only the beginning of many more adventures to come. 🗒 📷

– GUS BARBER

SHOT TOWER, FREE ASCENT OF WEST RIDGE, AND OTHER CLIMBS

BROOKS RANGE AVIATION delivered Drew Lovell, Forest McBrian, David Moskowitz, and me to Circle Lake on a warm and sunny afternoon on July 22. Over two days we walked into the valley called Aiyagomahala—the "Gentle Giant" in the creation myth of the Nunamiut people—where arctic sunshine allowed us to climb Shot Tower's stunning west ridge (Roberts-Ward, 1971) on our third day in the range.

The night before, we had entertained the possibility of freeing the west ridge, even though we had no clue what the route's 60′ aid section would involve, beyond reports of tied-off pins in thin cracks. Climbing beta in the Arrigetch remains vague, even on the most popular routes, a phenomenon that is, arguably, one to cherish in this day and age. Bearing this in mind, I hope the value of sharing our observations outweighs any negative effects. At the very least, it may spare interested climbers the burden of carrying aid gear up an otherwise moderate 1,500′ route.

At first sight, the original aid pitch high on the route looked like it would go free, albeit at a difficulty above our team's prowess. Fortunately, a more moderate option appeared feasible along the far left edge of the slightly overhanging golden headwall. We climbed a short system of 5.11a cracks, then moved left around the arête onto a slightly run-out 5.9 slab above a roof, where the northwest face dropped precipitously below. One more short pitch of 5.8 in a corner merged with the original line about a pitch below the summit. It is very possible others have taken this detour, but there were no signs of passage and we left none ourselves. Finding and free climbing a variation of this fantastic route in the wild Arrigetch was a personal benchmark, thanks in no small measure to the unfailing encouragement from the finest partners one could have, along with a dose of good luck with the weather.

Over the following weeks of our 22-day trip, we camped and rambled in the Aquarius and upper Arrigetch valleys, climbing or attempting several routes. Drew and I climbed a remarkable 500' 5.10 dihedral on the lower flanks of the huge, unclimbed eastern buttress of Xanadu, requiring two attempts in the intermittent cold rains of early August. We referred to the right-facing corner as the Virga Dihedral, as we were frequently wondering whether the leaden clouds building over the crest would produce real precipitation. Typically, I forecasted rain while Drew argued it was only virga. We were each right at least once. 📄 📷

Steph Williams prepares to lead the free variation to Shot Tower's classic west ridge. The original aid cracks are visible to her far right. *David Moskowitz*

— STEPH WILLIAMS

NEACOLA MOUNTAINS

PEAK 8,505', SOUTHEAST FACE

On May 3, 2017, Barry Smith and I touched down on the southernmost prong of the Pitchfork Glacier and shuttled loads to a base camp higher on the glacier. During the first break in the weather, we attempted an east-facing couloir on a feature we called the Gnome. We climbed 800' with difficulties up to WI4 before bailing just short of the summit due to poor rock.

Two days later we headed off to attempt Peak 8,505' via its southeast flank. After 2,000' we descended due to unstable snow conditions. We rested in base camp for the remainder of the day and returned the next night to continue to the summit when conditions were more stable (3,000', 55° WI2).

In one final weather window we attempted the Gnome again, this time from its northern side. We were turned around after several loose and unconsolidated mixed pitches on the upper ridgeline. While there is much potential on the southern prong of the Pitchfork Glacier, it seems as though the middle and northern prongs are where the good rock and most aesthetic lines are to be had. 📷

— TESS FERGUSON

[Clockwise from top left] **Tom Livingstone leading difficult-to-protect névé during his and Uisdean Hawthorn's attempt on the north face of Jezebel.** *Uisdean Hawthorn* **The broad chimney at the high point of the 2018 attempt on Jezebel's north face.** *Tom Livingstone* **The unclimbed north face of the east peak of Jezebel (9,620'), showing the 2018 attempt.** *Tom Livingstone* **Approaching the east face of Jezebel's east peak. The lower portion of Fun or Fear (1,200m, M6+ AI6 R 90˚) is shown. The summit is above and left. The 2016 route Hoar of Babylon begins farther right.** *Uisdean Hawthorn* **Livingstone coming up to the east summit of Jezebel after climbing the east face.** *Uisdean Hawthorn*

JEZEBEL, EAST FACE, FUN OR FEAR

UISDEAN HAWTHORN AND I flew into the Revelations on March 23. We landed on the Fish Creek Glacier, almost directly below the east face of Jezebel (2,932m/9,620'). Our main objective was the unclimbed north face of the east peak, an impressively steep 1,200m wall, but we were unable to land below it due to the boulder-strewn glacier. In preparation, we stashed all our climbing kit at the peak's northeast col while waiting to make our attempt.

After a couple of days of mixed weather, during which time we built a ski jump above base camp and made use of the excellent skiing conditions, we received a good forecast. We skied back to the northeast col and descended to the north face. We had scoped the face and concluded there was only one safe line—the rest of the face is threatened by enormous seracs. Though we were slightly concerned about cornices above our line, they didn't look too big.

On March 31 we climbed eight pitches and 350m up our intended line, onsight and all free. Two attempts in 2017 on a nearby line had reported vertical, unprotectable sugar snow, but luckily we found steep névé. Protection was sparse, however, and pitches often involved moving together until a belay was reached. Pitch two was 60m with no gear, and pitch three was 75m until a poor belay.

After our eighth pitch we reached the main feature of the line—a broad chimney, likely several pitches long—but heavy waves of spindrift now washed down the cliff and chimney. The first section was black diorite rock, bizarrely compact yet chossy, and with overhanging steps. After this we could see 60m of overhanging sugar snow. There appeared to be no way to bypass this pitch and no way to tunnel up through the sugary snow. Furthermore, a large snow mushroom sat right at the top of the chimney. We had known about this mushroom from the outset but were now *very* aware of it.

Due to the conditions, we chose to descend from atop our eighth pitch, so we can't be absolutely certain the pitch is "unclimbable." To us, though, it looked unclimbable by fair, safe, or rational means, and we were bitterly disappointed. We rapped back to the glacier, leaving wires as anchors.

After a few days of rest we decided to focus our attention on the east face of Jezebel's east summit, as we didn't think the conditions would improve on our intended north face line. After one false start due to unexpected snowfall on April 5, we launched the next day. We decided to try a line to the left of Hoar of Babylon (Graham-Silvestre, 2015, *see AAJ 2016*).

On April 6 we started with six steep névé and mixed pitches, which maintained interest and just about avoided the sunshine as it came round onto the east face. We climbed in blocks of three leads, following the obvious couloir feature. We then climbed about six more pitches of steep ice and mixed, before following a couloir for 200m to reach the east ridge. We followed this until nightfall, and then flattened out a bivy beneath the large final tower. From the bivy site, we did more ridge traversing to a moderate mixed pitch. We then unroped and climbed 150m to the peak's eastern summit, arriving at 12:30 p.m. This ascent was very satisfying and the technical climbing was thankfully mostly at the start of the route.

We descended our route up the east ridge to a col, then made three rappels on rock gear and downclimbed and walked down easy terrain in the broad, open couloir on the south face. The problem now was how to get back to the east face and the Fish Creek Glacier. From the couloir we had to climb four 60m pitches up the left side of the col between the east and south faces, and then made three rappels, one 60m downclimb on snow, and then a final rap to reach the Fish Creek Glacier and wallow to our skis. We named our route Fun or Fear (1,200m, M6+ AI6 R 90˚). 📷

— TOM LIVINGSTONE, U.K.

SERAPH, NORTHEAST FACE, MAKEMALO; HYDRA, NORTHEAST FACE, FA PA CAOU PER AQUI

AT THE END of March, Thomas Auvaro, Jeremy Fino, Antoine Rolle, and I traveled to the Revelation Glacier. Having read Clint Helander's stories, the "Revs" seemed to be the perfect place to fulfill our dreams of adventure on unclimbed walls.

After days of preparing gear and food, a gorgeous flight with Paul Roderick and a warm welcome from Clint and Andres Marin (who were also heading into the Revs to attempt a new route on Golgotha), we first had to deal with unsettled weather, heavy snowfall, and furious wind. When the first good weather window appeared, our eyes were caught by an obvious gully on the west face of unclimbed Peak 7,963', to the north of Apocalypse and south of Hesperus. At 4 a.m. we were at the base and started climbing. Entering the deep cleft was like a mystical experience, and the pitches offered steep, incredible ice and névé climbing up to WI6 and 90°. However, after 900m and 14 hours of climbing, we were stopped under a 40m roof of black compact rock. A hard aid pitch or loose and contrived mixed climbing could have led us to a pass and the easy final ridge, but that was not the way we wanted to end the route and we chose to rap down. We were back at the base after a 24-hour round trip, so close but so far.

Bad weather then came in once more. Cooking, listening to music, preparing gear, and a bit of skiing around camp was our daily routine. Thankfully, three days of good weather were announced before

[Top] Steep, aesthetic névé climbing during the French attempt on a direct line up the west face of unclimbed Peak 7,963', just north of Apocalypse. They were stopped just short of the ridge by a massive roof that would require aid climbing or detouring off the line to easier terrain, and they chose to descend from that high point. [Bottom] The northeast face of Hydra, showing the line of Fa Pa Caou Per Aqui (600m, M8). A 2014 route (Irwin-Vonk-Welsted) took the obvious gully system on the left, then moved right across a snowfield to the same exit as the French route. *Matthieu Rideau (both photos)*

being our plane returned. Due to frostbitten toes contracted while skiing, I had to let my friends climb and do whatever I could do to support them. After skiing the south face of Sylph, Antoine, Thomas, and Jeremy decided to try a direct gully on the northeast face of Seraph (8,540'). [*Chris Thomas and Rick Vance made the first ascent of Seraph in 2015 via Mandarin Mounty (2,300', 5.10 A2 WI5+) on the east face; see AAJ 2016.*] After 600m of climbing, including some technical mixed pitches at the beginning, they reached the summit. They returned to camp after 14 hours to enjoy a good meal and a small glass of whiskey. They called the route MaKeMaLo (600m, ED-M7). Nice day out!

Last day, last try—the idea was to return to the first unclimbed summit and open an easy route on the south face. But a strong and warm wind caused the guys to change plans to the northeast face of Hydra Peak (7,800'). [*Kris Irwin, Darren Vonk, and Ian Welsted made the first ascent of this aspect in 2014; the French line is to the right of the earlier route and shares the same exit from the face; see AAJ 2015.*] With multiple pitches of delicate mixed climbing along a diagonal ramp, they managed to reach the summit at dawn to complete Fa Pa Caou Per Aqui (600m, ED M8) and enjoy an unforgettable view of the endless Alaskan wilderness. Emotion was obvious on our four faces when we all met after this last beautiful day. Paul picked us up the next morning; it was time to go home. But we were all already talking about when our next trip could be. 📷

– **MATTHIEU RIDEAU**, *FRANCE*

ALASKA RANGE / KICHATNA MOUNTAINS

PEAK 7,984', ATTEMPT; SERENDIPITY SPIRE, CHARLIE ZULU

"WHEN IS THIS storm gonna end?!" a local pilot asked. Speculation erupted from almost every weary patron in Conscious Coffee, Talkeetna's finest (and only) coffee shop. The Alaska Range was in the midst of a historic and unrelenting storm, depositing foot after foot of new snow upon the range's flanks. The days of un-flyable weather were growing to double digits, and I started a mental tally of pilots who told me, "I've never seen it this bad."

Eventually the storm did break, allowing me to undertake two expeditions to the Cathedral Spires of the Kichatnas, both with generally great weather.

On my first trip, from May 26 to June 4, I had the pleasure of climbing with Tad "Poppyseed" McCrea—team name Muffin Wizards. Our expedition was largely a reconnaissance, giving us some great climbing and inspiration for future missions. We flew into the Tatina Glacier and baked up some delicious climbing on the Peak 7,984' massif with an incomplete mixed route stopping one or two pitches below the nearest summit due to poor ice and snow conditions. We climbed roughly 2,500' with difficulties up to M5 and 85° and simul-climbed the majority of the

Serendipity Spire above the Tatina Glacier. Charlie Zulu (1,800', IV 5.10 55°) reached the col at right and continued up near the right skyline. *Zach Lovell*

Chris Robertson follows a quality crack pitch on the headwall of Serendipity Spire's south ridge during the first ascent of Charlie Zulu. *Zach Lovell*

proposed line. Our attempt travels up a couloir that was climbed by Adrian Nelhams and Dean Mounsey in 2010 before busting right at a weakness up more sustained mixed terrain.

A week later, from June 10–14, I had the opportunity to fly right back to the Tatina Glacier with Chris Robertson. We had only a single, small weather window before a large storm arrived, and we set our sights on the south/southwest side of Serendipity Spire (ca 6,800'). This relatively small formation for the Kichatnas was first climbed in 1980 by Andrew Embick and Alan Long via a prominent couloir above the Tatina Glacier that finished with two rock pitches (*AAJ 1981*).

From our camp just west of Mt. Jeffers, we enjoyed a 15-minute approach before climbing up moderate névé that eventually steepened to 55° for the last few hundred feet before hitting rock. Our line favored the west face down low, crossing the south ridge to the east face up high, chasing the most appealing splitter cracks. Charlie Zulu (1,800', IV 5.10 55°) was climbed in 15 pitches. We believe we made the second ascent of the formation, and our route was climbed all free. Serendipity Spire is certainly worth considering for future parties, especially when short weather windows only allow for Lower 48–size objectives. 📷

— ZACH LOVELL

CENTRAL ALASKA RANGE

WEST KAHILTNA PEAK, SOUTHWEST FACE, RIDE THE BULLET

ON APRIL 13, Kurt Ross, Steven Van Sickle, and I flew into Kahiltna International and skied to a point near Camp 1 on Denali's West Buttress route to scope out the southwest face of West Kahiltna Peak (12,835'), between the east fork and northeast forks of the Kahiltna Glacier. We woke early the next morning and made our way to the base of our intended route.

Steven began the first block, climbing two pitches of ice runnels and snow. On the third pitch, unfortunately, he took a bad leader fall as an ice bulge failed and collapsed above him. He was caught by a screw, but we determined he had broken his leg and texted Talkeetna Air Taxi (TAT) and the park service via inReach. A couple of hours later, rescuers were able to long-line him off the face and down to the glacier, and eventually fly him back to Talkeetna.

After a lot of deliberation, Kurt and I decided to go back up the face the next day. We quickly reached our high point, where Steven had fallen. That section of ice proved to be the most rotten and dangerous of the route, and the rest of the pitch ended up being the technical crux, including a few points of aid. We climbed several more pitches of sustained ice and mixed, including an amazing 200-foot-plus steep ice hose, before traversing left to a small snowfield and chopping out a bivy ledge. The next day we climbed three more quite good pitches to the top of the technical climbing, where we unroped for 500' or so of easier climbing to reach a shoulder on the west ridge. From there we roped up for crevasse hazard on the upper snow slopes leading to the summit, reaching the top 36 hours after leaving camp.

We descended eastward toward East Kahiltna Peak and then rappelled and downclimbed the south face to reach a pocket glacier above the east fork of the Kahiltna. Although this descent is quick, I would not recommend it, as it is quite exposed to serac hazard that we hadn't been able to see from the top. A safer but much longer option would be to traverse to the east peak and descend its south ridge. Once on the pocket glacier, we had some trouble finding a way back into the main east fork. Kurt managed to find a sneaky way around an icefall in the dark, which led us back to our camp. Our route follows an amazing system of ice chimneys and runnels, and we feel it could become a very classic hard route in the range, due to its easy access from base camp. We're calling it Ride the Bullet (4,000', AI5+ R M6+ C1). I'd like to thank TAT and its awesome crew of pilots and

The southwest face of West Kahiltna Peak, showing the line of Ride the Bullet (4,000', AI5+ R M6+ C1). Nik Mirhashemi and Kurt Ross completed the route over two days in mid-April. *Nik Mirhashemi*

office staff for their help, as well as the park service and its helicopter crew for a very quick rescue. I never want to have to use search and rescue, but it's nice to know that Denali rangers are rock solid. Also, thanks to Steven for encouraging us to go back—and for being a tough SOB. 🔲

— NIK MIRHASHEMI

WEST KAHILTNA CLIMBING HISTORY: *West Kahiltna Peak was first climbed in May 1967 by a five-man German-American team that ascended an icefall directly from the Kahiltna Glacier to the upper south face, where rock climbing and the "hardest ice we had ever seen" slowed them down. Peter Hennig, Bernhard Segger, and Lowell Smith reached the top around 8 p.m., and the full team endured a sitting bivouac during their all-night descent.*

In 1983, Ned Lewis and Stacy Taniguchi climbed a steeper icefall (the "southwest buttress") to reach a col below the upper south face, then followed the 1967 route to the top.

In 2008, Japanese climbers Yuto Inoue and Tatsuro Yamada climbed West Kahiltna to start their planned enchainment of the two Kahiltna Peaks and the Cassin Ridge on Denali. They disappeared during this climb, and their bodies were identified a year later in an inaccessible location, left of the upper Cassin Ridge, at around 19,800 feet on Denali. The exact line they followed up West Kahiltna remains a mystery. The two Kahiltna peaks previously had been linked by German climbers Bertl Breyer and Udo Knittel who, in 1980, climbed West Kahiltna's north face, directly above the Kahiltna's northeast fork, then traversed over East Kahiltna before descending from Kahiltna Notch at the base of the Cassin.

In 2011, Italian climbers Diego Giovannini and Fabio Meraldi climbed the west ridge of West Kahiltna (Alaska Grade 4, 5.8 75°), bounding the left side of the big southwest face.

LIGHT TRAVELER
A RAPID SECOND ASCENT

BY SAM HENNESSEY

ON JUNE 4 and 5, Michael Gardner and I made the second ascent of Light Traveler (M7), on the southwest face of Denali. [*Editor's note: Light Traveler takes a direct line up the southwest face, between the Denali Diamond and the Cassin Ridge.*] Marko Prezelj and Stephen Koch made the first ascent in June 2001 (*see AAJ 2002*) in a 51-hour continuous push round-trip from the 14,000-foot camp on the West Buttress Route. Our strategy was a bit different—we climbed from Ski Hill Camp at 7,200' on the Kahiltna Glacier to the summit in 36 hours, stopping only for a four-hour soup and foot-drying break at around hour 15. [*Their time from the bergschrund to the summit was 31 hours.*]

We found the climbing to be of the highest quality, with perfect granite providing solid protection for thin strips of ice often only inches wide. The technical cruxes came down low, but the physical crux certainly was breaking trail on the upper Cassin after many hours on the move.

Summarizing nearly 9,000' of climbing in a few words seems futile, but some memorable moments include a snow-mushroom offwidth, laybacking a steep crack with perfect dime edges for crampon points, and wandering aimlessly in a snowstorm on Kahiltna Pass during the descent after being awake over 40 hours. We both highly recommend the route and are still inspired by the style of the first ascensionists, launching into the unknown with no bivy gear.

[*Editor's note: Denali ranger and historian Mark Westman observed in the national park's 2018 Mountaineering Summary that the Gardner-Hennessey ascent was not only the fastest of this route but of any of the four routes generally considered to be most difficult on the mountain's south and southwest faces: Denali Diamond, McCartney-Roberts, Light Traveler, and Slovak Direct.*] 📷

CHUGACH MOUNTAINS

The long, serrated northwest ridge of Mt. Dimond (7,202'), which Taylor Brown and Tim Stephens climbed at the end of March. Hidden behind is the northeast ridge, which Brown and Mat Brunton climbed in September. *Taylor Brown*

THOMPSON PASS, PROBABLE NEW ROUTES

THROUGH THE END of February we had excellent powder skiing in the Chugach, even at sea level, until Dumpsters started blowing across the parking lots in Valdez from a 100 mph wind event that lasted for a week. These winds destroyed the skiing but created ideal alpine climbing conditions with firm snow.

On March 31, Tim Stephens and I climbed the full northwest ridge of Mt. Dimond (7,202'), the largest alpine feature in the Thompson Pass arena. We encountered difficulties up to M4 with 3,000' of climbing over the 1.8-mile ridge traverse, passing multiple large gendarmes. I had attempted this ridge the weekend before with Jason Stuckey and Chad Diesinger, but turned around just shy of the summit under impending darkness, after battling stiff 40–50mph winds all day. Tim and I doubled up on a snow machine and drove it to the base of Mt. Dimond via the snowcat track that is set by Tsaina Lodge for skiing. From the toe of the glacier at 4,200', it took us five hours to summit and another two hours to descend the north face. The ridge required multiple rappels, but the only section where we roped up to climb was a large gendarme on which we did three pitches of M3–M4. The rest of the climb was 4th and easy 5th class, with very good rock for the Chugach. The only documented technical ascent in the area was a Paul Turecki route up the main gendarme back in the 1990s.

On April 15, with no new snow and excellent alpine conditions prevailing, Ryan Sims and I chartered a ski plane from Tok Air Service for a bump to the head of the Worthington Glacier, from which we climbed an unnamed peak (ca 6,600') via the northeast ridge at M3. On June 11, during the last good freeze of the spring, I left the trailhead at 4 a.m., traveled alone up the Worthington Glacier, and took a heavily glaciated pass to drop onto the Hoodoo Glacier and reach the west ridge of Girls Mountain (6,134'). This gained about 1,000' to the summit, from which I was able to ski perfect corn down the standard route on the north side. In late July, Jessica Young and I climbed the northeast ridge of Peak 4,700' in the Mt. Dimond area, with five roped pitches up to 5.7. [*More details and photos of these climbs are at the AAJ website.*]

After a month of straight rain in August, September brought above average temperatures and sun for the entire month. On September 8, Mat Brunton and I made a complete traverse of Sapphire Peak (6,300'), near the head of the Worthington Glacier, going up the west ridge and down the southeast ridge. The west ridge featured good greywacke rock with a few pitches of 5.6. This route is a classic Alaskan alpine climb with its easy roadside access, thoughtful glacier travel, and spectacular climbing and position.

As the sunny weather continued, Mat and I climbed the complete northeast ridge of Mt. Dimond on September 15. From behind the Tsaina Lodge, we took an old trail through the brush to get up into the alpine. We gained the northeast ridge by scrambling up peak 5,132' and then continued along the 1.5-mile ridge, climbing up and over many gendarmes, with technical difficulties up to 5.6. At a few points we donned crampons and climbed sections of 50° alpine ice. We did not use a rope, for it would have just dislodged loose rocks onto the second. Seven hours after leaving the road, we summited in building clouds and light snowfall.

With diminished visibility and wet rock, we decided to descend the 4th- and 5th-class east face, which required us to partially circumnavigate Mt. Dimond and climb back up and over peak 5,132' in order to reach the trail back down to the highway. It was a long day at 12 hours round-trip, with approximately 7,000' of elevation gain and loss.

– TAYLOR BROWN

WRANGELL MOUNTAINS

CHISANA GLACIER, FIRST SKI DESCENTS

AFTER WATCHING A constant barrage of storms strafe south-central Alaska in the late spring of 2018, Mat Brunton and I headed into the Wrangell Mountains hoping to visit a semi-protected area on the drier side of the range. On May 15, Zack Knaebel of Tok Air Service dropped us off at approximately 8,300' on the upper Chisana Glacier, where we set up base camp. This area had been visited on multiple occasions by Danny Kost, who did the first ascents of numerous nearby peaks (*see AAJs 1999, 2000, and 2001*).

Over the next week, we climbed 11 peaks, many of which had been climbed previously by Kost, and skied down 10 of them—likely all first ski descents. Three of our climbs may have been first ascents, including Peak 9,605', northeast of our camp, which we dubbed Megamid Peak. *Details of these ascents and descents, along with a map of the expedition routes, are at the AAJ website.*

– TAYLOR BROWN

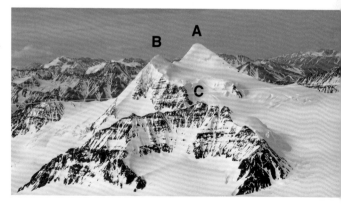

[Top] Mat Brunton climbing the south ridge of Little Deborah (10,522'), a peak first climbed by Danny Kost in 1998 and named for its resemblance to Mt. Deborah in the Alaska Range. Brunton and Taylor Brown likely made the first ski descent, also via the south ridge. [Bottom] (A) Little Deborah seen from Peak 10,630'. (B) Little Debbie. (C) Peak 9,400', also known as Sarah's Peak, is the rocky summit in the foreground. Four other peaks climbed and skied in 2018 are just off picture to the right. *Taylor Brown (both)*

MT. HUXLEY, NORTHEAST RIDGE TO NORTHWEST RIDGE (SUPER-HUX)

IN EARLY JUNE, Andrew Peter, Scott Peters, and I completed the second ascent—and the first complete ascent from base to summit—of Mt. Huxley (12,216') by a new route. Huxley is approximately eight miles west of Mt. St. Elias (18,008').

Paul Claus, who made the first known ascent of Huxley in 1996 after landing his plane on an adjacent snow dome, landed us in his turbine Otter at 8,800' on the Columbus Glacier to the north of Huxley, with a stunning partial panorama of the Bagley Icefield and many sizable peaks in the St. Elias, Chugach, and Wrangell ranges. "Big" does a disservice to the locale. Paul's son, Jay, had suggested Huxley after it became obvious our original objective was not accessible. Good journeys commonly include changes to the original plan, and flying to a completely different range, with very little information about what we'd find, is certainly a "change of plan."

After caching gear and food, we skinned southwest up the glacier until we intersected a set of wolverine tracks—evidence of our straight-line

[Top] Mt. Huxley (12,216') in Wrangell-St. Elias National Park. Super-Hux (3,400', Alaska Grade 3-, AI3+) gained the peak's northeast ridge by the snowy spur on the right, then traversed to the northwest ridge near the top to attain the summit. *Andrew Peter* [Middle] Andrew Peter enjoying a spectacular position just below the summit of Huxley. *Scott Peters* [Bottom] Traversing below a serac on the north face of Huxley, with the Bagley Icefield beyond. *Andrew Peter*

proximity to food sources at Icy Bay and also of wolverines' humbling intrepidity and stamina. We placed what we dubbed Wolverine Camp, and the following morning we continued south, along Huxley's eastern flank, to get eyes on the peak's southeast ridge. Our reconnaissance suggested it would go, but it seemed neither easier nor more appealing than the northeast spur, which we chose for our attempt.

We set off on the morning of June 3. Scott and I had learned from a cold bivouac on the north ridge of University Peak in May 2017 that having one sleeping bag per climber is worth the extra weight, so we each carried a single Z-Rest pad, sleeping bag, snacks for two days, two liters of water, and no stove.

After 30 minutes of booting through shin-deep snow, we hit the base of the spur leading up to the northeast ridge. The spur involved about 2,000 vertical feet of sustained 45–65° snow and ice, up to AI2+ , with solid screw and picket placements. Visibility deteriorated as we ascended, but wind was negligible. We reached the shoulder and found an overhanging rock shelter in virtual ping-pong-ball conditions. After much discussion, we began a long traverse under the summit pyramid's north-facing hanging glacier. Twenty minutes after we'd set off, the clouds opened to almost perfect bluebird skies. Lucky or good, we accepted the weather window with smiles.

The traverse involved some interesting route-finding and led us to the col connecting the northwest ridge of the summit pyramid with the adjacent dome (what we believe was Paul's 1996 Cub landing site). The crux of this ridge was an AI3+ corniced step on fragile sn'ice. A short snow traverse brought us to the tiny, corniced summit; we managed to get all three of us onto it without a collapse, though we had anchored our packs to the traverse to minimize the applied load. We left the summit around 8 p.m. and returned to the col a couple of hours later to settle in for a pretty comfortable bivy: 5° to 10°F and virtually still.

The next morning we began the traverse-in-reverse under bright skies, reaching the top of the spur at around 1 p.m. Five rappels took us to terrain we could downclimb, and we returned to Wolverine Camp in the early evening of June 4. We named our route Super-Hux (3,400', Alaska Grade 3-, AI3+). 📷

— BEN IWREY

CHILKAT RANGE, PEAK 5,805' (ENDICOTT TOWER), FIRST ASCENT

ON JUNE 10, 2016, my father Mike Miller and I set out into the Endicott River Wilderness, located about 50 miles northwest of Juneau in the Chilkat Range. Our objective was to climb one or more unclimbed peaks in the preserve and then pack-raft the 20-mile Endicott River back to the west side of Lynn Canal and get picked up by a boat for the ride back to Juneau.

From Juneau we flew to Gustavus, jumped on a Glacier Bay tourist catamaran, cruised up the east arm of Glacier Bay, and got

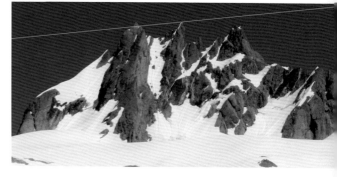

Endicott Tower (Peak 5,805') from the valley below. The first ascent in June 2016 followed snow slopes to the left of the most prominent rock tower, then weaved up the left skyline ridge to the summit (hidden behind). *Dylan Miller*

Sunset from Adams Inlet, northwest of Juneau. Endicott Tower is the left-most of the three prominent summits. Unclimbed Mt. Young is to the right. *Dylan Miller*

dropped off in a sandy cove at the base of Mt. Wright, near Adams Inlet. We inflated our rafts and waited for the incoming tide to suck us into the 14-mile Adams Inlet. We waded and crisscrossed the Goddess River delta, sometimes crossing swift, waist-deep rivers, and made camp for the night. We then hiked a full day through the Endicott Gap (a two-mile-wide flat valley floor) to Endicott Lake, the headwaters for the Endicott River. Here we stashed our water gear and tromped 2,000' up through the Tongass rainforest to a pristine hanging alpine valley, where we made our base camp.

We were now directly below our main objective, the southwest face of Peak 5,805', which we named Endicott Tower and which marks the highest point in the wilderness area. Only a few miles away were Peak 5,280' and Mt. Young (5,700'), both unclimbed.

After several days of rain the weather cleared, so the next day we established a high camp at around 4,000'. We had incredible views of the Fairweather Range—the sunset is still burned into my memory.

The next day we began climbing. Right off the bat we had to get around a 25' bergschrund by climbing a 40' pitch of mixed rock, snow, and ice to gain the main face. From here we swapped leads for 700' of steep snow runnels—60–75° perfect Styrofoam névé to the top of the snow, where the mountain became rockier. The next pitch was mixed: 60' of wet 5.7, which turned to 40' of WI3 and back onto steep snow. Another short pitch through deep and steep unconsolidated snow brought us to the ridge, which we traversed to a rock outcropping. We pounded in some pitons and made a 60' rappel down the other side of the ridge. The multitude of summit spires made it hard to determine which was the true top. We made for the most obvious and easiest looking summit spire, which featured loose, blocky 5.6 that we simul-climbed. To our delight, we found that we were on the true summit.

From the top we looked southeast to Juneau and pointed out our home, which put into perspective how far out there we really were. We retreated off the summit the way we came, reascending the rock wall that we had rappelled, which was awkward and so rotten that we were able to make hand and foot holds by scraping and kicking holds into the chalky limestone corner. From the ridge, a series of rappels from picket anchors led us back to our high camp. The next day we made our way back to the green valley. We took a day to recoup, during which a friend with a Super Cub flew in and retrieved our mountaineering kit.

Picking up our water gear, we floated down the Endicott River, portaging a section where the river dives into a gnarly gorge. Along this portage we climbed another small peak (2,680') and encountered some of the hardest bushwhacking we'd ever experienced, moving at a quarter mile per hour through alder and steep river gorges, packs overflowing with rafts, dry suits, paddles, food, and sleeping gear. We were relived to link back up with the river, where we enjoyed a final seven miles of braided glacial flow, seeing signs of bear, wolves, and moose, and casually reached the west side of Lynn Canal. 📷 🔍

– DYLAN MILLER

COAST MOUNTAINS / BOUNDARY RANGES

SHARK'S TOOTH, FIRST ASCENT BY SOUTHEAST RIDGE

ON SEPTEMBER 2, Matt Callahan and I set out to climb a peak hidden deep in the mountains north of Juneau that we had dubbed the Shark's Tooth (ca 5,700', 58°43'4.45"N, 134°45'32.11"W Google Earth) for its resemblance to a tooth of the ancient megalodon, a prehistoric 40-foot shark.

Approaches in Southeast Alaska are always worthy of note—this one consisted of four miles of nearly continuous bushwhacking through devil's club from the Glacier Highway up the Davies Creek Valley, a small old-growth section of the massive Tongass National Forest. We reached the head of the valley, and from here we climbed to the 4,500' saddle separating the Davies Valley and the

The Shark's Tooth was climbed by the southeast ridge, the prominent right-hand skyline, gaining about 1,800'. *Dylan Miller*

unnamed valley to the east that flows north to the Gilkey River. Reaching the saddle, we exalted in the views of the stunningly prominent Shark's Tooth across the way. We descended into the new valley, traversed to the base of the mountain, and climbed up 2nd- and 3rd-class benches to a campsite on a majestic granite slab with pools of water and boulders all around.

Our intended line was the southeast ridge, which was obviously the easiest way up the mountain, gaining about 1,800' from the saddle. It required a 5.7 intro pitch to gain the ridge, then scrambling, which led to two pitches of memorable 5.6 and 5.7 climbing on great granite. Before we knew it we were standing on top—a dream come true. We reversed our approach and made it to the car at dusk. 📷

— DYLAN MILLER

MENDENHALL TOWERS: FIFTH TOWER, THE FIFTH ELEMENT; SIXTH TOWER, THE SIXTH SENSE

DURING THE EARLY days of March, I received a call telling me that Ryan Johnson and Marc-André Leclerc were overdue from the north side of the Mendenhall Towers. I had known Ryan for almost a decade and we had established numerous first ascents together in the Juneau area.

As the days went on and bad weather made helicopter searches impossible, our fears gave way to the reality that Ryan and Marc would not be coming home. Between friends, we concluded that they now had the most bitchin' headstone in all of Juneau—the Mendenhall Towers. Ryan would have liked it that way.

The following months flew by. I hadn't met Dylan Miller before he picked me up at the

Dylan Miller leads steep cracks on pitch four of the Sixth Sense (1,000', 5.11), southeast face of the Sixth Mendenhall Tower. *Jason Nelson*

Juneau airport near the end of July, but friends had recommended him as a climbing partner, and soon we were loading into the helicopter for a ride to the Mendenhall Towers. With a clear weather window only a couple of days long, we chose what we anticipated to be a reasonable plan of trying to climb the fifth and maybe the sixth or seventh of the Mendenhall Towers. Dylan had previously climbed the Solva Buttress (1,000', IV 5.8, the south buttress on the Fifth Tower) and was familiar with the descent. The helicopter dropped us right at the base of the Solva, where we set up camp and spied some enticing splitter cracks to the right, in the center of the southeast face.

Our route followed a left-leaning crack system on the left side of the pyramid-shaped face. Most of the climbing was in the 5.8–5.9 range. Dylan made for a solid partner and we breezed through the pitches. A crux just above halfway featured a splitter finger crack that petered out, forcing a leap of faith to a jug (maybe 5.10d) and another crack.

This was the first route on the prominent southeast face and the third route on the tower (the other two being the Solva Buttress and the east ridge, first climbed by Clint Helander and Ryan Johnson). From the summit, I could look down and see the crevasses where Marc and Ryan still lay. We downclimbed and rappelled the Solva Buttress and finished back at our camp with lots of light to spare.

We chose the Sixth Tower for our next objective, largely to avoid some crevasses that blocked easy access to the Seventh. The south face mostly appears as broken rock divided by a series of ramps, but the east side steepens into an appealing buttress lined with clean vertical cracks. A glacier-ravished ramp and an excellent steep crack led to grassy slabs that we soloed for about 300' until we encountered a bunch of steep cracks. We chose the leftmost. Two pitches of great 5.10 led us to another ledge. From there, we encountered more steep cracks on the final portion of the buttress, with a crux 5.11 boulder problem off a pillar near the top.

From the summit we could see the coastal inlets were now almost completely obscured by clouds. If we didn't get down fast, we could be stuck for days. We mostly reversed our line of ascent, and about 15 minutes after touching down from the rappels, camp was packed up and the helicopter we had called appeared through a narrow gap in the clouds. Minutes later we were back in Juneau, with almost no transition time to process the climbs or seeing Ryan's final resting place.

We named our routes the Fifth Element (1,200', 5.10d) and the Sixth Sense (1,000', 5.11). Both featured great climbing and deserve to be repeated. 🗎 📷

— JASON NELSON

NORTH FACE OF MAIN TOWER
TRACING THE STEPS OF A FINAL CLIMB IN THE MENDENHALLS

BY CLINT HELANDER

ON MARCH 4, Juneau resident Ryan Johnson and Canadian Marc-André Leclerc started up the unclimbed north face of the Main Tower (6,910') in the Mendenhall Towers massif. In the early afternoon of the next day, Leclerc posted a photo from the narrow summit. Johnson sent a short video to a friend, spinning in a slow circle to show the view from the top. Johnson had completed numerous first ascents on these formidable granite spires, but the north face of the Main Tower was undoubtedly his dream line.

The north face of the Main Tower in the Mendenhall Towers (right center), photographed on March 13, 2018, shortly after the disappearance of Ryan Johnson and Marc-André Leclerc. The two likely climbed ice streaks in the center of the face to mid-height on the 2,500-foot wall, then zigzagged up snow bands and ice to the summit. The Fourth Gully descent route is the narrow slot to the left, below the east ridge. At right is the north face of West Mendenhall, first climbed by Johnson and Sam Magro in 2008. *Kieran Brownie*

From the summit the pair headed down the east ridge and then made five or six rappels down the Fourth Gully. Something happened near the bottom of the gully, and they never made it out. The scale of the ensuing rescue and recovery attempt is a tribute to the impact these two men had on communities across the world.

The exact line of their first ascent of the north face will likely forever remain unknown. However, I had the honor of attempting this same face with Ryan in October 2015. We began on the left side on the face and climbed a long, steep apron of snow, eventually roping up and climbing one long pitch up a blank slab covered by a thin veneer of powder. Encountering airy snow and ice that was climbable but not protectable, we decided to bail. As I stared up at the face above, I remember tracing a zigzagging line of thin ice daggers and slanting snow ramps that seemed to offer the most feasible path up the rearing granite wall. I imagine that Ryan and Marc had better conditions than we did in 2015, but there is no doubt the upper half of this 750m wall would have presented an extremely challenging combination of ice and mixed climbing.

I was invited to join Serge Leclerc, Marc-André's father, and friends of Johnson's on a flight into the Mendenhalls days after the pair were declared deceased. Along with the overwhelmingly emotional task of removing our loved ones' base camp cache, we were able to fly incredibly close to the wall. Not only did I observe ample ice, I felt some lingering presence of their passage up the face. Many tears were shed as we traced their week-old footprints leading down the east ridge from the summit. I had no doubt these men had authored the most impressive first ascent in the Mendenhall Towers' history. Beneath the crushing sadness, there was an undeniable sense of awe. 📷

Nearing the summit of Peak 2,845m, with the north side of Mt. Logan in the background, across the Logan Glacier. *Glenn Wilks*

PEAKS SOUTH OF MT. UPTON

JONATHAN WAKEFIELD AND Glenn Wilks (U.K.) flew onto the unnamed glacier that flows toward the Logan Glacier from Mt. Upton, directly north of Mt. Logan, with the aim of ascending unclimbed peaks. We first tried to access this area in 2011, but high winds prevented two attempts to get there.

We were flown from Silver City airstrip on the shore of Kluane Lake by Icefields Discovery, which is run by Sian Williams, daughter of legendary glacier pilot Andy Williams. In our 12 days on the glacier arm to the south of Mt. Upton, from May 8–19, we reached four tops surrounding our camp, at heights of 2,840m, 2,800m, 2,680m, and 2,845m, respectively. The final tottering towers of shattered granite on the second and third peaks, east and southwest of camp, allowed only one person at a time onto the tops. One peak was elusive on two attempts, with unstable snow slopes high up.

Highlights of the trip included skiing the upper glacier bowl to the immediate south of Mt. Upton and the summit of our final peak, which had an incredibly beautiful hanging glacier with views to the north face of Mount Logan.

Mt. Upton stands at just over 3,500m and is believed to have been climbed only once, in 1992, by Barry Blanchard and four others. It was named after one of the original glacier pilots to venture into the Yukon. [*The 1992 team led by Blanchard did two traverses along the eastern rim of this glacial basin, climbing Peak 3,068m and a number of other summits. It is believed they may have traversed over Peak 2,800m, the second summit reached by the 2018 expedition, but the rest of the 2018 climbs were likely first ascents.*]

The area still has many unclimbed peaks. Some of the rockier peaks are steep but look desperately loose, with no obvious lines to the summits. The feeling of adventure in such a remote, uncharted place outweighed not being able to climb these. The climbers give thanks to the Mount Everest Foundation for gracious support of this expedition. 📄 📷 🔍

— GLENN WILKS, *U.K.*

MT. LOGAN, SOLO ASCENT AND RESCUE

In 2017, Canada's 150th anniversary, I tried to reach the summit of Mt. Logan (5,959m) via the King Trench with a partner but had to turn back from the summit plateau. Stimulated by my desire for freedom and strengthened by my experience in 2017, a project to climb my country's highest peak alone took shape.

I was flown in on May 15 and immediately took note of the unique and unexpected situation: I was completely alone at base camp, a big contrast with the previous anniversary year. Before I left, another team of two climbers was dropped off, but I left camp first and broke trail all the way up, mostly on skis.

My climb went well until Camp 2. I had a very diffi-

On top of Mt. Logan, Canada's highest point. *Monique Richard*

cult day while carrying equipment to Camp 3 during acclimatization, and while descending that day I was caught in a whiteout and fell into a crevasse, which I was able to escape with much difficulty. When I finally returned to Camp 2, a six-day storm forced me to barricade myself in my tent and reflect on whether I should continue. I was able to regain my motivation and set out again.

Due to a very limited weather window after the storm, I adopted a "light and fast" strategy, only carrying a simple bivouac tent to Camp 3 at 4,838m. Because of the narrow window, I decided to bypass Camp 4 and carry on to Camp 5 at about 5,100m on the plateau below the summit.

On the morning of May 30, I launched my final push. It was very cold and my feet were frozen. The top of the mountain looked cloudy, but there was no wind, so I decided to continue. At 2:38 p.m., I reached the summit, with no sign of life for kilometers around. During the descent, concentrating on my skiing due to dangerous ice patches, I descended too low and realized that I had to go up a 300m subsummit to find my tracks. Exhausted, I found my tent again around 1:30 a.m., and then had to spend hours melting snow and eating before I could rest.

The next day I climbed back to Prospector Col (ca 5,500m) and decided to stop to recharge the dwindling batteries in my GPS; I then realized the charging cables had broken due to the cold. I decided to spend the night near the col and leave early the next day, but that night the weather worsened. At this point, I realized that the situation was becoming critical and that continuing in the storm with zero visibility, without a GPS, and while exhausted would be reckless. I made the decision to call for help.

The authorities asked the two climbers below, at Camp 3, to come up and help me down to Camp 4, where an evacuation could take place. Once there, a helicopter arrived about 45 minutes later, taking advantage of a brief opening in the weather. I am very grateful to climbers Stéphane Gagnon and his son Guillaume Gagnon, and to the Parks Canada staff who coordinated and carried out the evacuation.

Mt. Logan is an extraordinarily wild, immense, and hostile mountain, and I was able to take the full measure of it during this solo expedition, which was the highlight of my mountaineering life.

— MONIQUE RICHARD, *CANADA*, *TRANSLATED BY GUILLAUME COSSETTE*

EDITOR'S NOTE: *In May 1995, Canadian Derrick Stanbury made the first solo ascent of Mt. Logan, via the King Trench route. Richard's ascent was the first solo to the summit by a woman, though her subsequent rescue leaves the door open for a woman to make a complete solo ascent and descent. In 2017, Natalia Martínez (Argentina) attempted to solo the east ridge of Logan but was evacuated by helicopter from 3,700m after an earthquake rendered the terrain above and below her camp unstable.*

Hunter Lee at an unplanned bivy 20 meters below the top of Mt. Colonel Foster's east face. *Ryan Van Horne*

VANCOUVER ISLAND
SIGNIFICANT ASCENTS FROM 2016 THROUGH EARLY 2019

BY WHITNEY CLARK & LINDSAY ELMS

THE RUGGED MOUNTAINS of Vancouver Island have seen much activity, from new rock routes to major ice lines and first winter ascents. The following is a summary of significant developments in the last few years.

In May 2016, Ryan Van Horne and Marie-Lou Piché visited the southeast face of Kings Peak (2,065m), located in Strathcona Provincial Park, and climbed a new line on one of the many southeast buttresses. Their route was 500m of mostly 4th- to mid-5th-class, with a few sections of 5.9, to where it meets the east couloir shortly after joining the east ridge. The full outing took three days.

Also in May, Danny O'Farrell joined forces with Chris Jensen and established the Owinmitisaht Ha'houlthee Ridge over a period of three days on Mariner Mountain (1,778m). They headed up the Bedwell Trail past Noble Creek and started up the eastern ridge, finding lots of 3rd- and 4th-class terrain with some sections up to 5.6. After 600m of rock, they traversed along the ridge and eventually followed the south face to the summit.

On June 28, Van Horne soloed a new route on Mt. Colonel Foster (2,135m). He set up camp on the mountain's south col and the following day traversed under the west face and completed a new route to the summit ridge. The 400m route was mostly low 5th class with a few short steps of 5.8.

Another notable ascent of Mt. Colonel Foster was made on July 24. After climbing to the north col, Garner Bergeron, Hunter Lee, and Philip Stone traversed around to the mountain's west side and made the first ascent of the northwest arête. After 100m of 4th-class scrambling, they climbed 16 pitches up to 5.9 on mostly excellent rock. They joined the well-established summit traverse and descended by the normal route, making ten rappels down the northeast side.

The following summer, on August 10, 2017, Karsten Klawitter and Hunter Lee climbed a new route to the right of the west ridge of Victoria Peak (2,163m). The first six pitches involved climbing up to 5.10a, and on the seventh pitch they had to aid through an overhang. Once up the face, they crossed the west ridge route (800m, 5.8) and climbed a new finish on the upper headwall. After three pitches up to 5.9, they made an airy traverse and climbed one more section of steep rock before reaching the summit. They named the route Summit or Plummet (600m, 13 pitches, 5.10a A1).

Two weeks later, on August 27, Lee and Van Horne climbed a new route on the east face of Colonel Foster. Their line branches off from Cataract (1,350m, 5.8, Homer-Stone, 1988) after soloing up the low-5th-class approach ramp. Rather than make that route's rappel along the waterfall, they climbed the arête directly above Cataract Falls, left of the original line. After seven pitches up to 5.10a, they found themselves on the upper glacier. They called the route Exposure Arête.

That winter got off to a good start when, on December 22, 2017, Van Horne, Lee, and Mal Nicol climbed a new route on the northeast face of Mt. Harmston (2,009m). This was probably the second winter ascent of Harmston (the first was on December 29, 2014, by Aaron Smythe and John Waters, via the southeast ridge). The 2017 team encountered thin ice on the lower section of the mountain, but once on the upper face conditions improved. To gain the summit ridge they had to "body saw" through a cornice. Once on the ridge they simul-climbed to the top. They called the route Northern Lights (700m, WI3+ M3 TD-).

On March 10, 2018, Chris Jensen, Lee, and Van Horne climbed a new mixed route up the north

[Top] **Summit or Plummet (13 pitches, 5.10 A1)** on Victoria Peak's northwest side. *Hunter Lee* [Middle] The line of **Northern Lights** on the northeast face of Mt. Harmston. *Hunter Lee* [Bottom] Hunter Lee climbing the first pitch of **Threading the Needle (310m, D+ WI4 M3)** on the north face of Elkhorn Mountain. *Chris Jensen*

[Top] Ryan Van Horne finishing the third pitch on the south face of Mt. Grattan. The prominent peak behind is Mt. Alava. *Hunter Lee* [Bottom] The Uber Couloir on Elkhorn Mountain South. *Max Fisher*

face of Elkhorn Mountain (2,166m), taking a direct line to the summit. Their route joined Winter Needle (200m, 5.7 AI4, Pierce-Walker, 1996) toward the summit. They descended the northwest ridge, arriving at their camp 15 hours after setting off. They named the route Threading the Needle (310m, D+ WI4 M3).

On July 17, Lee and Van Horne climbed a new route on the south face of Mt. Grattan (1,550m) in the Alava Bate Sanctuary area. The route consisted of 10 pitches up to 5.9 for 500m. The only other known routes on the peak are on the east and west ridges.

There were a few significant winter ascents at the beginning of 2019. On February 5 and 6, Max Fisher and Mike Ford climbed a prominent couloir on the east face of Elkhorn Mountain South (a.k.a. Mt. Colwell, 1,989m), completing the first winter ascent and second overall ascent of the biggest mountain wall on Vancouver Island. (The first route up the face was Elk Well (1,250m, IV 5.8), climbed in August 2013 by Michael Loch, Mike Morris, Mike Shives, and Ryan Van Horne.) The 2019 line had previously been dubbed the Uber Couloir, and the climbers thought the name should stay. It was climbed in 36 hours car-to-car (1,400m, TD+ AI4+).

During that same weather window on February 5 and 6, Lee and Van Horne climbed another new route up the east face of Mt. Colonel Foster. The route departs from Into the Groove on the lower flank and weaves high onto the shoulder of the northeast peak. Conditions on the lower-angle terrain were good, yet steeper sections were marginal as the ice was heavily aerated and thin. Fortunately the climbing was never too difficult (WI3+). In all, they climbed 14 pitches of ice, sn'ice, and steep snow to reach the upper ridge, only to find themselves on a knife-edge with no bivouac site. Van Horne was forced to downclimb some 20m to the belay, where the two dug a snow cave in the wee hours of the morning and settled in for a few hours. After a stunning sunrise, they reclimbed the 20m to the upper ridge and rappelled to the notch between the northeast and northwest peaks, from which they downclimbed and rappelled the mountain's west side. They named the route Threshold Extension (900m, TD+ V WI3+).

In late February 2019, Will Gadd, Peter Hoang, and Chris Jensen climbed frozen Della Falls in Strathcona Provincial Park for its first ascent. At 440m, it is one of Canada's tallest waterfalls. To access the line, they took a boat to the northwest end of Grand Central Lake and then hiked 14km in snowshoes to the base. They climbed seven pitches up to WI6. 📄 📷

— WITH INFORMATION FROM LINDSAY ELMS, HUNTER LEE, MAX FISHER, AND VARIOUS PUBLISHED SOURCES

Travis Foster finding splitters on pitch eight of the Vercoe-McMahon Memorial Route, a.k.a. Dude Wall (1,020m, VI 5.11 A2) during the first ascent. *Drew Leiterman*

NEW ROUTES IN THE DANIELS RIVER VALLEY AND NEARBY AREAS

IT WAS A busy season in the Coast Mountains outside of the city of Powell River, northwest of Squamish, a burgeoning center for Pacific Northwest big-wall climbing (*see articles in AAJ 2018*).

In the Daniels River Valley, which only saw its first two climbs in 2017, teams succeeded on three new routes. In late June, Travis Foster, Drew Leiterman, John McMahon, and Elliot Vercoe made a valiant effort on the northeast face of the Super Unknown, a few hundred meters left of the only route on the formation, Sacred Stone (1,200m, VI 5.11, Guilbault-Landeck, 2017). June was a drenching month along the South Coast, and the team received rain on four of eight days on the wall and eventually bailed. Vercoe returned to Australia, and McMahon to Cranbrook, and then, in mid-August, Foster and Leiterman returned with better weather to complete the sardonically named Vercoe-McMahon Memorial Route, a.k.a. Dude Wall (1,020m, VI 5.11 A2).

In mid-July, Matt Burbach and Leif Solberg made the first ascent of a formation just east of Super Unknown called the Penguin, via Ego vs. Mosquito (900m, 5.9+ C1). Burbach and Solberg climbed the route in a single push—the Daniels' first Grade IV. They suggested a grade of J10 be added to the difficulties. "So much climbing was in vertical jungle," Solberg explained, "that a rock grade can't really be given for it. Our 'J' rating is similar to that of the Yosemite decimal system—for J10, think 5.10."

Meanwhile, Colin Landeck and Josh Schuh were busy attempting a new route that shares close proximity with the first ten pitches of Sacred Stone before branching left into corner systems on the right side of a large prow. They were stymied by a lack of gear, however, and had to retreat.

After a resupply in town (including quite a few more Metolius blue finger-size cams), Landeck and Schuh returned with Burbach, Mike DeNicola, and Max Merkin. DeNicola joined Landeck and Schuh to finish the aforementioned line—Super Unknown's second complete route—over five days. The Prow (1,200m, VI 5.10 A1) begins roughly 200m left of Sacred Stone (also left of

Landeck and Schuh's first attempt) and takes a plumb line up the buttress dividing Super Unknown's northeast and northwest faces. "Once cleaned," Landeck said, "this will be an incredible route, topping out the amphitheater roofs, perhaps the only 'truly hard' climbing on the whole formation."

It wasn't just the Daniels that saw action. In early August, Zoe Manson and I climbed a 600m alpine dome called the Gem on the southern tip of the relatively popular South Powell Divide ridge hike, which extends for 20km from roughly Amon Rudh in the Eldred Valley southward to the aforementioned dome (and, curiously enough, has nothing to do with the Powell River). The Rob Richards Memorial Route (600m, IV 5.10) follows a plumb line, utilizing a 280m crack system up the middle of the southwest face. Rob Richards, our friend and mentor, died from a sudden heart attack in June at age 55. He was a prominent first ascensionist and historian of rock climbing in the Powell River area.

Further north, Zoe and I made the first ascent of a remote alpine spire we named Rogue Tower via its south face (300m, 5.10 C1), along the seldom-visited Montrose Divide, which rises between Montrose Creek and the Toba River. This cirque of granite towers was unvisited by climbers beforehand. (The only record we could find of any party previously exploring the Montrose Divide was a trip by John Clarke in 1984.) The approach took two days of sailing with friends, followed by 40km of logging roads—fortuitously expedited with the help of our buddy Rob Richards' old logging crew, the only other humans in hundreds of square miles—and finally a 1,500m fourth-class gully to reach base camp.

[Top] Evan Guilbault, Zoe Manson, and Max Merkin below Lady Wall's southwest face. [Bottom] The Rob Richards Memorial Route on the Gem. *Evan Guilbault Collection*

Back around Powell River, Manson, Merkin, and I nabbed the first ascent of a formation I had spotted while out ridge-walking the previous year. The Lady is located in a subalpine valley branching off the southwestern edge of the North Powell Divide, which continues from the Gem dome to Toba Inlet. We summited the southwest face on August 18 via Lady Wall (550m, V 5.10 C3). Every pitch of the route revealed memorable moderate crack climbing, with one crux pitch high up requiring ten hours of delicate aiding on my part. "This is the steepest thing I've jugged since Leaning F$%@ing Tower!" Max gasped after space jugging for 40m. Lady Wall is accessed via a two-day ridge walk beginning on the Amon Rudh climbers' trail in the Eldred River Valley.

For the past 30 years, to talk about Powell River big-wall climbing meant only one thing: the Eldred Valley. Yet here we are at the end of this report, having barely made mention of that easily accessed big-wall paradise. But with many new efforts beginning there last year, it would not surprise me if a whirlwind of new routing occurs on the more accessible walls in 2019. ▣

– EVAN GUILBAULT, CANADA

TANTALUS RANGE, SERRATUS MOUNTAIN, NORTH BUTTRESS

It had all gone wrong. I sat drinking beer in the Edinburgh evening sun, grumpy and frustrated about my flight to Canada the next day. I'd planned a dream trip to see my best friend and old climbing partner in Vancouver, and then, three weeks before I was due to arrive, she broke her leg. Excited as I was to be heading to Canada, I was gutted to have two weeks with no prospect of climbing.

Yet less than a week later, here I was, halfway up a granite buttress in the Tantalus Range, putting up a new route on Serratus Mountain (2,321m) with my hero—and now friend—Jen Olson. I couldn't believe my luck. Canada West Mountain School had linked me with Jen the day I arrived in Vancouver, and after a few days of climbing together we couldn't resist the challenge of an unclimbed north-facing buttress that led to the east ridge of Serratus Mountain.

On July 31, after an early start, we made our way across the moat and zigzagged up ledges on the lower buttress. We were the only people on the mountain. In fact, we were the only people in the entire range. Having only climbed in Scotland and the European Alps, I've never encountered such solitude or such an expanse of unclimbed rock.

Juliet Harris leading the fifth pitch of Planet 50-50, a new route on Serratus Mountain. *Jen Olson*

The route continued to entertain us while never going harder than 5.9. The steep rock came to an end after just over 200m, but there was plenty more adventure ahead. After some scrambling we traversed left across the first snowfield on the face, aiming for a ledge system on other side. A bit more scrambling brought us to 500m of 40° snow to gain the east ridge, leading to the east summit of Serratus. Without continuing to the higher north summit, we descended via the glacier on the north face.

Planet 50-50 (700m, PD 5.9) seemed like an apt name for the route—it's a United Nations campaign that focuses on overcoming challenges that stop women from reaching their potential. The fact that I had "no partner, no plan, no nothing" when I arrived in Canada is what opened up the potential to meet Jen and to have one of the memorable experiences of my life. 📷

— JULIET HARRIS, *SCOTLAND*

NORTH SHORE MOUNTAINS, WEST LION, NORTH COULOIR DIRECT

In February two separate parties climbed the North Couloir of West Lion, just north of Vancouver in the North Shore Mountains, making the first known ascents. Matteo Agnoloni first soloed the route (300m, WI3+) on February 10. He had hoped to link the couloir directly into the peak's northwest ridge but instead opted to chop through the cornice at the top of the gully, rappel 20m down the other side, and climb moderate ice up onto the ridge. Six days later, Ethan Berman and Tim Nielsen climbed the couloir to the notch at the top and then did a short mixed pitch (M5) to reach the ridge, continuing with moderate snow and ice, broken by a short pitch of WI4, to reach the summit. The North Couloir Direct went in 13 hours car-to-car. 📖 📷

— *INFORMATION FROM* ETHAN BERMAN, *CANADA*

Brette Harrington leading the 5.12a/b third pitch of Crouching Tiger on the Chinese Puzzle Wall. *Kieran Brownie*

CHINESE PUZZLE WALL, CROUCHING TIGER

I FIRST CORRESPONDED with Brette Harrington in 2016, asking her to write an article for the *AAJ* about her recent route Hidden Dragon, climbed with Marc-André Leclerc on the Chinese Puzzle Wall (*AAJ 2017*). It was a great honor when Brette and our mutual friend Caro North invited me to join them to attempt another route on the wall just five months after Marc's tragic death. Marc and I had talked about the wall, which rises above Nesakwatch Creek on the west buttress of South Illusion Peak, and he assured me I would flip over the steep face, many roofs, and high-quality rock.

On August 4, after the arduous hike to the foot of the wall, we agreed to try a line Marc and Brette had started two years prior. We quickly passed their high point, a pitch and a half up, and continued on terra incognita. Some serious cleaning was required to make the initial pitches freeable, and some retro-bolting of sections that we aided. (I, embarrassingly, contributed to neither.) The culmination of my two days there was an airy and overhanging 5.11 hand crack on the fifth pitch, one of the finest pitches of untouched stone I've ever had the pleasure to climb.

We all hiked out on Monday morning, and then Brette and Caro returned on Wednesday and basically finished the route. At the eighth pitch, the new line made a natural traverse left into the finish of Brette and Marc's neighboring line, Hidden Dragon, with three more pitches to the top.

The following Monday, I rejoined Brette and Caro, and we hiked back in that evening. We started early the next morning, and Brette made an impressive send of the cruxy 5.12a/b third pitch: a roof-capped tips splitter. A few pitches higher, Caro began to feel ill. She watched as I belayed Brette while she freed the 5.12b crux of the route, sending the pitch on her first try. All the remaining pitches previously had been freed, so at this point Caro bid us adieu and returned to the ground on fixed ropes.

Brette and I team-freed the rest of the route except for the 5.12a eighth pitch, on which I hung on lead following the traverse into Hidden Dragon. Caro had freed this pitch previously, and Brette followed clean, so we felt in our rights giving the route a free grade. That said, the line still awaits a team-free ascent. The new route is called Crouching Tiger (500m, 11 pitches, 5.12b).

As I hiked down steep and beautiful slabs early the next morning, I took a moment to admire nearby Slesse Mountain through the thick smoke from nearby forest fires. I felt very strongly as if I were directly in the presence of Marc-André Leclerc. As if he were no more gone than Slesse was, shrouded in the haze. 📄 📷

— CHRIS KALMAN, *USA*

Chris Wright nearing the top of Macdonald's north face on day three of the climb. *Graham Zimmerman*

THE INDIRECT AMERICAN
A LONG-SOUGHT ROUTE UP THE NORTH FACE OF MT. MACDONALD

BY CHRIS WRIGHT, *USA*

I HADN'T BEEN dreaming of mountains. I was just enjoying my fall, soaking up the sunshine and going rock climbing, but when things align for a seven-year project you can't really say no, so instead Graham and I said yes and we got in the car. Five days later we stepped off a Revelstoke sidewalk covered in fresh snow, wiped the slush from the windshield, and drove home through a storm. In between were three days of the most unlikely good fortune.

If you've ever been to Rogers Pass in the Selkirk Mountains on a clear day you've probably seen it, because it's right above the road and staring you straight in the face: an enormous corner and handsome streak of ice high on the north face of Mt. Macdonald (2,883m), forming the most conspicuous undone line in western Canada. I remember first pulling into Revy one drippy winter night in 2011 on a road trip with a friend as he shopped for a new place to live. A week of incredible skiing convinced him to move there immediately, and me to visit almost every year since. On each of those occasions I'd repeat the experience of looking up at Macdonald's mighty north face. Each season I'd try to convince myself and my friends it was a good idea, but there was always something in the way.

A few things actually. Foremost among them, the bottomless powder that makes Rogers Pass famous for skiing is not generally ideal for climbing, and the avalanches it can produce threaten both the approach and descent. Since the mountain is directly above the Trans-Canada Highway, it's also completely closed to overnight or multi-day climbing during the bulk of the winter to allow highway crews to control the slopes with explosives. It took me a few years to realize that for the route to be viable the collection of factors that had to align would be daunting. First, the ice would need to be there, but it would need to form before the control work and closures started in late November. Second, avalanche hazard had to be low and the weather needed to be clear—both rarities for British Columbia in winter. I owe a great debt to Percy Woods at Parks Canada for helping us navigate these difficulties by sending over fresh photos and conditions reports whenever I asked.

Marked-up photo in *Rogers Pass Alpine Guide* showing the line of the Indirect American. The zag to the left was after the crux on day two. *Chris Wright*

Graham Zimmerman and I both had our annual reminder of "The Rogers Pass Thing" on our calendars again, but I was occupied with projects at home in Bend and was unconvinced we would actually do anything about it. When I finished a new climb at Smith Rock and found my schedule clear, I lazily checked the weather one morning. To my surprise, the forecasts agreed the perfect window was coming. I texted Graham that we should drive north the next day. When we got there we spent a day watching the face, taking pictures, and making guesses. We got the go-ahead from amused park employees, packed, and went to bed early.

On the morning of November 11 we left the car well before dawn, and after a few kilometers of walking on the dark highway we were soon wallowing through steep devil's club, scrambling over cedar limbs, and crossing great rakes of debris in between. We plowed upward via a deep couloir, eventually roping up as we started mixed climbing on snow-covered, compact quartzite. We climbed through the afternoon, and as the short day came to an end we dug a bivy on an enormous snow ledge directly beneath the obvious drip that defined the middle of the route.

At sunrise on the 12th we swung into the white line that had drawn us in, which yielded 90m of excellent climbing on a funky vein of thin ice. Funnily enough, of the climb's 23 pitches, that ice comprised only one and a half of them. As irony would have it, Graham got to lead those pitches too, and then I took over and drew two hard leads on pitches of M6+ and M7, including a rather terrifying traverse across a water groove bereft of both ice and protection.

Above this was the major question mark on the route, a blank section on which we hoped either mixed climbing or aid would allow us to reach another flow of ice higher up. Unfortunately, it was prohibitively steep and lacked climbable cracks, and it led only to more delaminated patches of junk plastered to featureless stone. Instead we traversed hard left, and as darkness fell we climbed into the next rock band, trending toward the existing route up the central rib of the face. [*The upper portion of this rock rib, accessed from the face to the left, was first climbed in August 1963. Two summers later, Fred Beckey and Jerry Fuller climbed a more direct line to gain the rib and followed it to the top.*] After several pitches we reached a snow ledge and dug in for another night, regretting the optimism that had convinced us to pack food for only a day and a half.

Once again starting at sunrise, we traversed back into the primary weakness and climbed four more exciting mixed pitches that led to the east ridge about 50m from the summit. The weather was perfect as we topped out at noon, a hundred miles of wild mountains in every direction and all of them shining. We downclimbed and rappelled the southwest ridge to the top of the Herdman Couloir, descended this to join the Crossover Slidepath, and reached the road around 5 p.m. and town shortly after.

We called our route the Indirect American (1,000m, WI4+ M7), an invitation to someone luckier or stronger than us to straighten it out in the future. We woke in Revelstoke the next morning to wet snow falling, our dream of the north wall already fading into memory, just us and the rocks and the clouds, the ice and the air, a sense of purpose and the sun passing as one more dream was finally made real.

Chris Wright and Graham Zimmerman discuss this climb in episode 15 of the AAJ's Cutting Edge podcast.

PIGEON SPIRE, SOUTH FACE, DRACO

JOSH LAVIGNE AND Craig McGee completed a beautiful new route up the south face of Pigeon Spire in August, with help in earlier seasons from Jesse Bouliane and Marc Piché. Draco (800', 10 pitches, IV 5.12-) follows cracks and corners to the right of the southeast buttress, eventually reaching a headwall with a huge golden dihedral, which was climbed in three long pitches of "meat and potato" jamming. A photo-topo is at the AAJ website.

— *INFORMATION FROM CRAIG MCGEE AND MOUNTAINPROJECT.COM*

PIGEON FEATHERS AND SNOWPATCH SPIRE, THREE NEW ROUTES

I FIRST WENT to explore the west face of Lost Feather Pinnacle in East Creek Basin in 2016 with Lisa Mullaly, climbing only two pitches. In July 2018, I went back with Mike Loch to try the third pitch, and a month later, on August 8, completed the first ascent of Double-Double (180m, 5.11c A1) with Sébastien Tanguay. Pitches one and two were freed on lead, but pitches three and four were only done on top rope or with a few hangs, as the cracks were still quite dirty. I estimate the route will go completely free in 2019 at 5.12+ or 5.13-.

The "pitch you came for"—pitch six (5.11+) of Draco on the south face of Pigeon Spire. *Craig McGee Collection*

Sébastien, Éliel Bureau-Lafontaine, and I then established a nice moderate route on the southwest face of Prince Albert Tower, which we named Fat Albert (150m, 5.9). With five pitches of corners and slabs, the route begins 50m to the left of Solitary Confinement.

On August 15, the three of us completed a new route on the western shoulder of the south face of Snowpatch Spire. Started with our friend Chris K. Willie, this climb is a memorial to him; his piton hammer was engraved and hung at the base of the third pitch by Dylan Cunningham, who also put a lot of effort into the route. Guy Like You (230m, 5.12) starts with the first two pitches of South Saddle Schtickup, a route recently established by Chris Brazeau. After two moderate pitches and a short scramble, the route steepens with a finger crack that widens to an offwidth-squeeze and is very sustained at 5.11+. Pitch four traverses left across the wide, left-facing corner and climbs a 5.12 bolted dike. The final 50m pitch links two shallow left-facing corners and clocks in at 5.12-. The route can be rappelled with two 60m ropes. ⊡

— OLIVIER OUELLETTE, *CANADA*

MORE NEW ROUTES IN THE PIGEON FEATHERS: Jonny Simms climbed two new routes from the East Creek Basin, the first with Marley Hodgson on Lost Friends Pinnacle, right of Fingerberry Tower: Friday the 13th (5 pitches, 5.10-). They also started a new line on the east face of East Pigeon Feather Peak, and Simms returned with Crosby Johnston to finish this route: Nightrain (350m, 5.11). Simms' entertaining account of this climb is at the AAJ website.

The Milkwater (1,250m, V WI4 M4) on the east side of Mt. Temple. Striving for the Moon takes the obvious ice line to the left. *Alik Berg*

THE YEAR IN THE ROCKIES

SOLO CLIMBING SEEMS to be making a resurgence in the Canadian Rockies, including a pair of impressive solo ascents on Mt. Temple (3,544m) toward the end of the year. Finding excellent early season snow conditions in December, Alik Berg climbed a new route up the east side of the mountain, the Milkwater (1,250m, 750m to ridge, V WI4 M4), in a 20-hour round trip from a bivy on the Moraine Lake Road. The route starts 200m right of Striving for the Moon on an obvious ice flow and then trends right and then back left in gully systems to gain the east ridge, just short of the top of the Aemmer Couloir. Berg continued up the east ridge to the summit and descended the regular tourist scramble.

The next day Quentin Lindfield Roberts partially followed Berg's tracks to solo Striving for the Moon (1,250m, WI6) in 21 hours car to car. First climbed in 1992 by Barry Blanchard and Ward Robinson, the route has rarely been repeated.

Backing up to the summer season, Vern Stice (who participated in the first ascent of Jeanette Peak in April; *see report below*) and Jeff Dickson completed the first recorded traverse of Mt. Alexandra and neighboring Queens Peak. In late July, a bike-and-hike approach of at least 16km got Pedro Guerra-Zuniga, Gen Kenny, and Robb Schnell to the north face of Beatrice Peak, beyond the massive east face of Mt. Ball. A 300m climb up a moderate ice slope brought the trio to the summit. In the Fryatt Valley, Craig Hartmetz, Martin Schwangler, and Jordanne Taylor climbed Walk of Shame (600m, AI3 5.7) in late October, following the prominent Y couloir up the north face of Mt. Xerxes.

Plenty of interesting long rock climbs also were established in the mountains. Dave Peabody and Mark Taylor climbed the northeast buttress (250m, 8 pitches, 5.9) of McGillivray Mountain in May. A mix of bolts and gear was used to protect this prominent buttress visible from the Trans-Canada Highway in the Bow Valley. Far to the south in the Crowsnest Pass area, Clay Geddert, Josh Schuh, and Daniel Vanderpyle completed the previously attempted Northeast Arête of Chinook Peak (245m, 5.8 X) in June.

On the imposing Peyto Tower on Mt. Wilson, Niall Hamill first rappelled, cleaned, and installed 14 bolts (including anchors) on a new line, then returned with Grant Stewart to establish Prairie Gold (280m, V 5.11c). The route follows the leftmost major dihedral system up a face that is characterized by bulletproof quartzite in its upper 200m, just to the right of the Prow (5.9). Hamill states that many more free routes are there to be climbed.

In the Banff area, the east-facing Grand Minnewanka (7 pitches, 5.10d A1) by Paul Gardner and Paul Taylor is found after a 7.5km bike ride along the Lake Minnewanka shoreline trail. A few aid moves were required to overcome the huge roof system on pitch four. And in Jasper, the trend toward long bolted face climbs on Ashlar Ridge continued with the addition of Canadian Compressor (11 pitches, 5.11c) by Konstantin Stoletov and a team of eight from Edmonton.

A summertime visit by Adam Ondra (Czech) resulted in the Bow Valley becoming home to two out of three of North America's 5.15b sport climbs. Ondra added a 5.15a at Echo Canyon named Sacrifice before dispatching Disbelief (5.15b) at Acephale. (The first Alberta 5.15b was Alex Megos' Fightclub, put up in Banff in 2016.) This visit is likely to add to the seasonal influx of traveling climbers to Canmore and Banff.

A few quite significant repeats also were done. Sasha DiGiulian (USA) and Mike Doyle, climbing together and with local partners, repeated Sonnie Trotter's "alpine trilogy" of long 5.14 routes near the Bow Valley: War Hammer (15 pitches, 5.14a) on Castle Mountain, the Shining Uncut (13 pitches, 5.14a) on Mt. Louis, and Blue Jeans Direct (8 pitches, 5.14a) on Mt. Yamnuska. DiGiulian managed the Uncut a few days before Doyle and then sent Blue Jeans to complete the second ascent of the trilogy; Doyle completed the last climb and the trilogy a few days later.

Prairie Gold (280m, 5.11c) on Peyto Tower.
Grant Statham

Though this is a worldwide mecca of ice climbing, new ice and mixed first ascents in the Rockies were surprisingly rare. In February, the prolific Raphael Slawinski added Bride of Frankenstein (100m, M8), an unclimbed hanging dagger on Mt. Wilson, above the ice route Skinny Puppy. Dave Rone climbed two difficult new ice routes: Sun Pillar (100m, WI6+), with Scott Backes, in the Icefall Brook area, and Full Cup (170m, WI 6 R), with Jon Jugenheimer, in the Stutfield Glacier cirque.

In November, at the Storm Creek Headwall, Olivier Ouellette and Quentin Lindfield Roberts equipped the Bodhi Tree (M8+ WI5), just to the right of Buddha Nature, though the send (and onsight) fell to Slawinski. Accessed by the 60m first pitch of Buddha Nature, the Bodhi Tree goes in two pitches. Earlier, the author had added a mixed pitch above and right of Buddha Nature.

The most audacious attempt of late 2018 was by Stas Beskin, who climbed the first pitch of the Real Big Drip in the South Ghost area for the first time as a pure ice pillar (normally bolt-protected M8), though he did not complete the full route due to the startling nature of the third-pitch pillar, which perhaps had formed for the first time in the modern ice climbing era.

Back in the high mountains, Jon Walsh scooped the second ascent—and first free ascent—with Quentin Lindfield Roberts of the Owens-Walsh Route on Mt. MOG in October. Originally climbed in 2007 by Rob Owens and Eamonn Walsh at IV+ M6+ A1, the 600m route had ice at the previous aid section during the free ascent. On the same day in October, Peter Hoang and Michelle Kadatz made the much-attempted second ascent of Zeitgeist (530m, IV+ M7 WI5 R) on

Quentin Lindfield Roberts leading wild terrain during the second ascent—and first free ascent—of the 600-meter Rob Owens–Eamonn Walsh Route on Mt. MOG. *Jon Walsh*

the north side of Mt. Bell, also put up in 2007. As a sign of the times, once these climbs were presented on the Internet, both of them received multiple ascents.

In mid-January, coming full circle on the note that began this report, Niall Hamill made a rope-solo ascent of most of Zeitgeist, including the crux, skipping the last two moderate, snow-covered pitches. In summary, a new spirit of contemporary audaciousness is in the air, though it doesn't always follow the old rules of onsight ground-up climbing ending at the summit. [*The online version of this report describes a number of other ice and rock routes in 2018.*]

— IAN WELSTED, *CANADA*

SELWYN RANGE, JEANETTE PEAK, FIRST KNOWN ASCENT

ON APRIL 2, at 5:10 p.m., Canadians Vern Stice of Edmonton, Pascale Marceau of Canmore, and I (from Minnesota) reached the summit of Jeannette Peak, which we believe was previously unclimbed. At 3,089m, it is the highest summit in the Selwyn Range, with a prominence of 1,657m.

Our original idea had been to approach the peak by logging roads extending to the south and west to Kinbasket Lake, but local snowmobile clubs and outfitters said this access was impassable, and in any case the slopes above this approach would be very avalanche-prone. Thus we chose to fly in by helicopter. We opted for a winter-season ascent simply because we prefer snow and ice climbing over rock.

Jeannette's upper ridges form a horseshoe ring holding a significant plateau glacier on the west side. Pascale and I had attempted the north ridge three weeks earlier but were thwarted by a technical rock crux and risky avalanche conditions, a little over 100 vertical meters below the summit. On our second attempt, an early morning flight landed us in the valley west of the peak at about 2,000m. We ascended a snow slope up the northwest shoulder, and by late morning we had reached the glacier plateau and set up camp in a spot relatively free from cornice fall and avalanche runouts; we named it Shark Fin Camp for the obvious feature that towered above us.

Around noon of the same day, with bad weather slated to arrive soon, we set out toward the summit. Soon our path was blocked by an icefall, forcing us to detour to the ridge sooner than originally planned. At every little rock step, we were delighted to find a way around. By late afternoon we had reached the top. Jeannette has two small summit plateaus; unsure which was the actual top, we went to both and determined that the eastern was slightly higher. We rated our ascent up the northwest shoulder and west ridge PD.

— LONNIE DUPRE, *USA*

OPAL RANGE, MT. BLANE, WEST FACE, LIFE COMPASS

ON APRIL 25, in predawn light, Brette Harrington and I crept up the well-trodden path through King Creek Canyon, headed for Mt. Blane (2,993m). Blane's west face is clearly visible from the Kananaskis Trail road, rising 1,000m above the trail, and Brette had been eyeing it for some time.

We traversed the base of the wall to a narrow gully, and by 10 a.m. Brette was leading up sun-affected ice before traversing rightward on rock. I followed as rapidly as I could, but I was slowed by steep terrain, shrinking holds, and loose rock underfoot. I marveled at Brette's delicate touch as I tucked my axes away, pulled off my right glove, and crimped hard. We estimated the climbing on this pitch at 5.10a.

I led the next few rope lengths of 70° to 80° snow slopes, which we simul-climbed to another rock band. Several mixed pitches brought us to the rightmost edge of the upper snow slope. We made a long traverse to the left, beyond a false summit, then

The route line for Brette Harrington and Rose Pearson's Life Compass (980m, TD+ 5.10a M4+ 80°) on the west face of Mt. Blane in the Opal Range. This line is similar to a route climbed in the summer of 1957 by Heinz Kahl and Peter Schotten. Other summer routes climb the face to the left. *Patti Henderson*

quested upward on snow for several more rope lengths before an improbable traverse on ledges brought us to a final hidden snow slope and a clear path to the summit, which we reached at 8 p.m.

We had hoped to downclimb the northwest ridge, but after a hundred meters of roped downclimbing, unconsolidated snow and darkness stymied our progress. After some discussion we decided to abseil the northwest face. An hour of digging provided only fractured rock, and Brette resorted to slinging a low-angled bump on the ridge for the first anchor. Two more rappels took us to snow slopes and a long descent on foot. It would be 4:30 a.m. before we reached the car and began the one-hour drive back to Canmore, each taking turns at the wheel.

We named our climb Life Compass (980m, TD+ 5.10a M4+ 80°) in dedication to Marc-André Leclerc and the dramatic change Brette's life has taken after his disappearance in March. I would like to further dedicate it to all those who are left behind, including Brette, when their loved one is lost in the mountains.

– ROSE PEARSON, *NEW ZEALAND*

EDITOR'S NOTE: *At the time that Harrington and Pearson climbed Mt. Blane, they were unaware that several previous routes had been climbed in summer conditions on this face. (Current guidebooks provide limited information.) Their line was widely reported as a first ascent. However, with information from Raphael Slawinski and David P. Jones (who is working on an updated guidebook for the region), it became apparent that Life Compass followed much of the same line climbed by Heinz Kahl and Peter Schotten in 1957, likely with a more difficult start than the 1957 route and a significant variation to the left near the top.*

[Left] Ice arch on the Kaparoqtalik Glacier. [Right] "Moai Ridge" on Bylot Island. *Grant Dixon (both photos)*

MONTH-LONG SKI EXPEDITION AND VARIOUS ASCENTS

DURING 28 DAYS in May, Grant Dixon, Louise Jarry, Marek Vokac, and I skied a "horseshoe" loop through the Byam Martin Mountains, starting and finishing on the south coast of Bylot Island. (Bylot is just north of Baffin Island.) I had been drawn to this project by the alluringly named Mt. Possession, the only officially named peak in the northeast region of the island.

After shuttling 25km by snowmobile across frozen Eclipse Sound from Pond Inlet to the shore of Bylot, we skied north up the Kaparoqtalik Glacier and then across unnamed glaciers flowing eastward toward Bathurst Bay, climbing several peaks along the way. On May 17, two weeks into the expedition, we climbed Mt. Possession (794m), which turned out to be a hill between glaciers, with far higher neighbors.

With Possession out of my system, we headed west and then south past the high peaks of the island, and finally down the Sermilik Glacier to return to Eclipse Sound. In all, twelve peaks were climbed en route, six of which were probable first ascents, plus two new routes on the previously ascended summits. We skied a total of 264km including side trips. [*Greg Horne and Louise Jarry had made two previous month-long ski touring and climbing expeditions on Bylot Island; see AAJ 2005 and 2007. A full report and table of peaks climbed during the 2018 expedition is available at the AAJ website, along with many superb photos.*]

— **GREG HORNE**, *CANADA*

MT. MENHIR, EAST FACE, AND OTHER ASCENTS

BETWEEN THE 15TH of June and the 15th of September, Enzo Oddo and I established three new routes on the granite walls of the Weasel and Owl valleys. During the ten days we spent climbing Midgard Serpent (1,100m, VI 5.9 A5, Jarrett-Rzeczycki, 1995) on the west face of Mt. Thor, we got good views of Mt. Menhir and its impressive headwall. We spied a logical line with our binoculars and in August established a new route on its unclimbed east face.

It took us one long day to climb eight pitches up easy slabs and haul our gear to the base of the headwall. It rained heavily during the first night, and next morning we waited in our portaledge for the rain to stop and then climbed two free pitches on the headwall. That night on the wall was extremely cold, and we awoke in the morning to all the ropes and gear covered with ice. Once everything thawed, we made a big A4 traverse (plus 7c free moves) to the left on hooks, followed by three pitches of A2 and A3 up big dihedrals. We reached the summit the following day via five pitches of free climbing up to 7a. We named our route Lords of Baffin (900m, 19 pitches, 7c A4).

We also attempted a new route on Breidablik and made one-day repeats of the central pillar on Overlord Peak, the Scott-Hennek Route on Asgard's North Tower, and Arctic Dreams on Asgard's South Tower.

We established two routes on peaks we believed to be previously unclimbed in the Owl River valley, near the June Valley shelter. Each was climbed onsight and in a single day. Pilier Sud du Beroddovas (900m, 7b+ A1) is located on the left side of the east face of what we named Beroddovas Peak. [*This wall is the right "leg" of Ozymandias; see note below.*] The route follows a series of corner systems for six pitches before 400m of scrambling brought us to a large ledge and a final pitch of 6a. We also opened La MA DAI (6 pitches, 7a) on the east face of a small rock formation just to the right of Beroddovas.

The two "legs" of Ozymandias above the Owl River, showing the 1978 Scottish route (left) and approximate 2018 French route (right). Both have about 3,000 feet of climbing. *Gregory Strange Collection*

— CÉDRIC BERVAS, FRANCE

HISTORICAL NOTES ON OZYMANDIAS: *The slabby east-facing pillars above a prominent bend of the Owl River (66°46'13.72"N, 64°44'12.62"W) were named Ozymandias, after the Shelley sonnet's "two vast and trunkless legs of stone," by a British expedition in 1961. In 1978, a Scottish team spent ten days camped below these formations (AAJ 1979). Dave Nichols and Gregory Strange climbed the left "leg" over two days (3,000', 5.8), and other team members climbed routes up the two "arms" on either side of the main formations (not the same as the French route La MA DAI). Jock Moreland and Guy Muhlemann climbed about 300' of a line on the right "leg" that eventually became the French route Pilier Sud; they also found evidence of a prior attempt.*

NEWFOUNDLAND

LA HUNE HEADWALL, DORYMAN PASS BY

ON HIS SECOND visit to La Hune Bay on the south coast of Newfoundland, in August 2017, Randy Baker from Maine rope-soloed the first known route up the La Hune Headwall, a broad, west-facing expanse of steep slabs: Doryman Pass By (900', III 5.9, with a direct finish added after the first ascent). Baker also climbed a 400' route (Blue Door, 5.9) up the east face of a prominent tolt, a solitary rock knob above the bay. The only previous climb known in La Hune Bay was by Peter Fasoldt and Eli Simon (*AAJ 2009*).

— INFORMATION FROM RANDY BAKER, USA

GREENLAND

Unclimbed peaks above the south arm of the Neild Bugt Glacier. *Jim Gregson*

NORTH LIVERPOOL LAND, MANY FIRST ASCENTS

BUILDING ON THE successes of my earlier expeditions to the region (*AAJs 2008, 2015, and 2016*), Ingrid Baber (Germany), Sandy Gregson, Ron Kenyon, Simon Richardson, Mark Robson, and I (all U.K.) visited the Neild Bugt area from mid-April to mid-May, intent on making more first ascents and carrying out ski reconnaissance into new terrain.

Flying into Constable Pynt/Nerlerit Inaat just after a period of storm, we were inserted onto the icecap by the very capable snowmobile team operated by our logistics supplier, Paul Walker of Tangent Expeditions International. Base camp was close to the location used in 2014 and 2015 (approx. 71°21.7'N, 22°07.4'W). This time we noted much greater snow cover on the glaciers and mountains, the latter having a distinctly more wintry appearance than previously seen.

Despite low temperatures throughout the trip, during the first two weeks we completed high-level ridge traverses of the Hulya peaks, linked the ridges of Kuldefjeld and Høngbjerg (a.k.a. Mt. Mighty), and made a technical ascent of the Tower of Silence. On the latter, intense cold meant that a frontal assault on the steep granite of the west face was avoided in favor of an intricate line of icy grooves and chimneys just to the right.

Two new routes were established on the north side of Castle Peak, and a new line climbed on Longridge Peak, reminiscent of Tower Ridge on Ben Nevis. In the Seven Dwarfs Range, following a couple of first ascents during this trip, only one of the summits is now unclimbed. A full traverse of all seven would give an ambitious party a major and committing adventure. Richardson and Robson were particularly active in achieving this roster of successes, but all group members had a share in these achievements.

Intermingling with all this climbing activity, a number of long exploratory ski tours were carried out to the north and east of base camp. There was copious evidence of polar bear presence in the form of numerous fresh tracks, often at some distance from the coastline. This ski exploration revealed many mountaineering objectives in the form of unclimbed Arctic peaks plus opportunities for technical rock climbing on some big exposures of sound-looking granite. Several easier summits were reached.

The trip was subjected to one of the most challenging periods of storm I can recall in all my 19 expeditions to Arctic Greenland. Very persistent low pressure brought high winds from changing directions, and, more unusually for Greenland, prolonged periods with heavy, wet snowfall. This may be linked to climate change, the evidence of which is now sadly rife across the Arctic. The conditions cost us a week of climbing, during which time the deluxe latrine we had carefully constructed completely disappeared under new snow, as did our sun-lounger complex, which had been pressed into service as a replacement. Two tents and the occupants were buried, severely bending—though fortunately not breaking—the poles.

After this period, Baber, Richardson, and Robson made a very

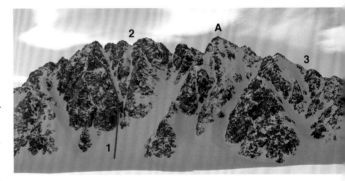

[Top] The Tower of Silence (730m) and the line of the first ascent: Silence is Golden (300m, 7 pitches, TD, Scottish V, Richardson-Robson, 2018). The pair continued to the top of Dwarf 7 (left) and descended via the Gregson route Nanok. [Bottom] The Hulya Peaks from the north. (1) Firepot Couloir to the summit of Hulya V (400m, AD, Scottish III, Richardson-Robson, 2018). (2) Traverse to (A) Hulya I (D+ Scottish III, Richardson-Robson, 2018). (3) Marmotte Ridge (PD, Buisse-Hoare, 2014). *Simon Richardson (both photos)*

cold and bold high-level traverse, linking the summits of Mt. Thistle (first climbed in 2014) with the first ascents of Mt. Reckless and Midnight Peak. They returned to camp looking a little stressed after a brief few hours of bivouac/rest during a wild, windy night.

We arranged our snowmobile pickup via a satellite phone call to Constable Pynt, after which a further burst of heavy snowfall reburied all of our kit. Despite this weather, the snowmobile team duly turned up on time the next day to transport us back to the airstrip. The expedition thanks the Mount Everest Foundation, the Gino Watkins Memorial Fund, and the Austrian Alpine Club (U.K.) for its financial support.

A full report on this expedition, detailing all of the climbs and ski exploration, GPS coordinates, and much other useful information, is available at the AAJ website. 🗎 📷 🔍

— JIM GREGSON, *ALPINE CLUB, U.K.*

MYTHICS CIRQUE, ATAATAP TOWER, NORTHEAST FACE; AURORA TOWER, SOUTHEAST FACE AND NORTHEAST RIDGE

IN JULY AND August, Lionel Daudet, Patrick Wagnon, and I (all French) visited the Mythics Cirque, about 350km north of Kulusuk. We sailed there on Ada 2, a 15m yacht owned by the well-known sailor Isabelle Autissier.

We climbed two new routes. The first, on the northeast face of Ataatap Tower (a.k.a. Father or Daddy's Tower, ca 1,350m), took us 10 days in capsule style. The 1,000m climb, with difficulties of 7a A2, starts to the right of the 2012 Libecki-Pringle route, Built Fjord Tough (1,050m, V 5.12 A2). [*The two routes share about half a dozen pitches on the final headwall.*]

We completed our second route in one long day. Four hundred meters of technical climbing toward the right side of the southeast face of Aurora Tower (1,451m), opposite our route on Ataatap, led to a long summit (northeast) ridge. The crux was an offwidth for which we had no big cams, as we had been trying to travel light. The 600m route was 7a. This was the second ascent of Aurora Tower, the highest in the cirque; it was first climbed in 2016, via the southwest ridge, by a multinational team (*AAJ 2017*).

We also visited an adjacent fjord and climbed a perfect 300m granite slab with small edges. The grade was 6b, and the climbing was difficult to protect. In addition, Patrick and I did a lot of paragliding in the region.

Many thanks to our sailing crew: Isabelle, Olivier Meinier, and Ariane Richasse. Navigating through icebergs is committing and a different game than sailing in the Bahamas, but they always dropped us where we wanted. 📷 ▶

— **PHILIPPE BATOUX**, *FRANCE*

[Top] The southeast face of Aurora Tower from Ataatap Tower, showing the line of the 2018 French route, finishing on the northeast ridge. The 2016 first ascent of this formation began on the opposite side and finished by the left (southwest) skyline ridge. [Bottom] Lionel Daudet climbing on the northeast face of Ataatap Tower. *Philippe Batoux (both)*

Robert Jasper on pitch seven of Stonecircle. All alone in the Fox Jaw Cirque, Jasper managed a GoPro, traditional camera, drone, and solar station by himself, returning with unique and impressive imagery from a solo climb. *Robert Jasper*

STONECIRCLE

SOLO AND BY "FAIR MEANS" IN THE REMOTE FOX JAW CIRQUE

BY DANIELA JASPER, *WITH INFORMATION FROM ROBERT JASPER, GERMANY*

In July and August, Robert Jasper made a "by fair means" solo expedition, sea kayaking to the Fox Jaw Cirque, where he put up a hard new free route on the Molar. He was accompanied by friend and photographer Frank Kretschmann as far as the last Inuit settlement at Kungmit, at which point Kretschmann went home and Jasper paddled alone in a folding kayak up Tasiilaq Fjord. He carried a four-week supply (90kg) of food and equipment. After 12 days of hard paddling and then ferrying equipment, Jasper established base camp below the "teeth" of the Fox Jaw.

After scoping the walls, Jasper decided to try the unclimbed pillar that forms the southwest edge of the Molar, left of the 2009 Italian route El Cavajo dell'angel (420m, 7b, Lanfranchi-Pedeferri). Reaching the rock via the lower section of the snow couloir separating the Molar from the smaller Milk Tooth to the west, Jasper climbed seven pitches in two days, returning to base camp each night due to unstable weather. He left three ropes in place and re-led the other pitches each day.

The climbing proved difficult, as there were no continuous crack lines. However, the rock was good, compact gneiss. Pitch grades were mostly 6a and 6b, with the exception of the sixth-pitch crux, which was 7c. On the third day of the climb, July 31, Jasper decided he should push for the summit despite poor weather. After overcoming a black roof on pitch eight (7b), all was going well until it began to rain 80m below the top. Fortunately the terrain was now easier. Climbing carefully through thick mist, he reached the summit and the clouds dropped away. "I was all alone, no person in sight," he said later. "It was like in heaven!"

Jasper rappelled the route, regaining his tent after an 18-hour day. After 30 days in the wild he returned to Kungmit, closing his personal "stone circle." He said the expedition had pushed him to the limits: "a huge adventure in a magnificent natural setting—an absolute jewel of my life." Jasper roped-soloed Stonecircle (450m, 12 pitches plus scrambling, 7c) in redpoint style over three days, using a Silent Partner belay device. He left 30 bolts and bits of other fixed gear. This is the sixth known route to the summit of the Molar. [*See route line on next page.*] 📷 🔍

The south face of the Molar, showing (1) Stonecircle (7c, 2018), (2) El Cavajo dell'angel (7b, 2009), (3) Ingirumimusnocte (7b+, 2009), and (4/5) Lovin' All the Right Places (5.10 A2+, 1998) and Le Privilege du Renard (7b, 2016). The last two routes appear to climb very similar terrain. Just to the right is the Incisor, with three known routes on this aspect. *Marc Daviet*

FOX JAW CIRQUE, THE MOLAR, LE PRIVILEGE DU RENARD

IN 2016, THE Julbo eyewear maker ran a competition in which the winner would have the opportunity to climb somewhere in the world with mountain guide and technical adviser Christophe Dumarest. An accomplished "amateur," Antoine Rolle (a member of the French national mountaineering excellence group), was selected from 40 candidates, and in August 2016 the two visited the Fox Jaw Cirque.

After a day spent scoping a line on the right side of the Molar, Dumarest and Rolle set off, only to discover a sling partway up pitch two. Had the route been climbed? The large corner above offered no real crack and appeared improbable, and the two decided the previous party had given up at this point. Dumarest finished the pitch, dubbing it the Psycho Corner (7a).

Higher up, their fifth pitch provided a 7b crux. At the top of pitch seven, one rope length below the top, they descended. After a rest day, they reclimbed the route and finished the eighth and last pitch to the top. The 450m climb was named Le Privilege du Renard and graded 7b (7a obl). This route appears to be quite close to the 1998 Briggs-Libecki route Lovin' All the Right Places (465m, IV 5.10 A2+), and it may be the line attempted in 2014 by a British pair who retreated due to wet rock and run-outs they deemed unjustifiable. 🔍

— LINDSAY GRIFFIN, *WITH INFORMATION FROM RODOLPHE POPIER AND MARC DAVIET, FRANCE*

HISTORICAL NOTES ON FOX JAW CIRQUE: *The Fox Jaw Cirque has long been the accepted name for a collection of gneiss spires in the Trillingerne Group, on the east side of the Tasiilaq River Valley. However, back in 1975, when it was visited by Tony Howard and Mick Shaw (U.K.), it was known to Greenlandic people as the Organ Pipes. Howard and Shaw most likely made the first ascent of the Molar, via the couloir separating it from Milk Tooth (a.k.a. Baby Molar), finishing up the north face at around UIAA IV/V.*

ASTA NUNAAT, SOUTH RIDGE, GIOIELLI VIVENTI

ANDREA GHITTI AND I chose to visit East Greenland because we were looking for exploratory mountaineering, a bit like climbers in the Alps during the 18th and 19th centuries. In addition, a great Italian alpinist, Robert Peroni, has lived in Tasiilaq for the last 25 years. He directed us to a beautiful rock peak north of Ikasagtivaq Fjord. Asta Nunaat was first climbed in 2006, via the west face, by Andreas Fichtner, Christoph Hainz, and Roger Schäli at 7b A2 (*AAJ 2007*). We hoped to climb a new route up the south side.

The sharp spire of Asta Nunaat with the lines of (1) Tartartuga (2006) and (2) Gioielli Viventi (2018). *Fabio Olivari*

After a journey of one and a half hours by boat, we walked up to the snout of the Nialigaq Glacier, which flows southwest from the peak, and established base camp 300m above the boat drop-off. On August 8 we waded through 40cm of poor snow on the glacier to reach a campsite below Asta Nunaat. Next morning we awoke to a breathtaking view of fjords full of icebergs and in the distance the infinite ice cap. We left the tent and climbed a 200m snow couloir of 50–60° to reach the start of the south ridge. The first four pitches on the ridge gave us relatively little trouble (V+ maximum). The fifth and sixth pitches took a slightly impending corner, which we free climbed to where a roof blocked our path; we aided past this and then climbed more easily to the belay. Above, we followed a logical line of corners, chimneys, and cracks, past various VI/VI+ sections, to the summit. It was our first new route.

After a difficult rappel descent, during which the rope got stuck twice due to the exceptional friction of the granite and eventually had to be cut, we reached the tent at 1 a.m., spending the last hour in the dark, in the rain, with frozen hands. We left seven pegs and around 10 slings on the descent.

We named the route Gioielli Viventi ("Living Gems," 320m, nine pitches, VI+ A1), a term that Robert Peroni uses to describe the smiling Greenlandic children. 🖹 📷 🔍

— **FABIO OLIVARI**, *ITALY*

SOUTH GREENLAND / TASERMIUT FJORD

HONEY BUTTRESS, SOUTHEAST FACE, HANGING BUS; NALUMASORTOQ, EKSTRA LAGRET, FREE ASCENT

IN JULY AND early August, Dawid Sysak and I visited the Nalumasortoq-Ulamertorsuaq region, where we climbed a new route and made a first free ascent. Afterward, we also made a free ascent of the classic Geneva Diedre/War and Poetry (5.12c/d) on Ulamertorsuaq in a two-day push.

Our new all-free route climbed the central pillar on the southeast face of Honey Buttress, a formation first climbed in 1998 by Ian Parsons and Tony Penning at British E3/E4 5c (5.10d R, with less than ideal rock and hard-won gear). Parsons and Penning were accompanied to base camp by a friend named Bob Honey, for whom the formation was named.

Our climb took 27 hours camp to camp, summiting on July 14. The cracks were clean of vegetation, which allowed us to onsight almost every pitch; two pitches were redpointed. We cleaned most of the big blocks from the line. Our rappel route, using pitons and nuts for anchors, partially

The southeast face of Honey Buttress. (1) Approximate line of the original British route (Parsons-Penning, 1998). (2) Approximate 1998 Swiss route. (3) Hanging Bus (12 pitches, 5.11+, Różecki-Sysak, 2018). *Patryk Różecki*

followed the line of ascent. We named the route Hanging Bus, after a huge granite block on pitch five. The climb was around 400m (12 pitches) following a logical line of cracks and chimneys on very good granite, with good natural protection throughout and difficulties up to 5.11+.

Our second objective was Ekstra Lagret on Nalumasortoq. This line lies just to the right of the original British Route (1995) on the Left Pillar, and was first climbed in 2002 by Chris Chitty, Ari Menitove, and Steve Su at 5.11 A2 (*AAJ 2003*). This team used natural protection throughout, but the following year, sadly, three Danish climbers, thinking they were making a new route, added many bolts to the line. As the first ascensionists thought it might go free, we decided to have a try.

Shallow corners and cracks led to pitch four, where we were shut down by mud and grass. Using some aid, we continued to pitch six, then fixed 100m and rappelled to the ground, realizing the route would need much gardening. Our next push was a two-day cleaning session, with a night on the uncomfortable ledge at the top of pitch six. We used ice axes to remove earth and grass from the cracks, and also worked some of the harder moves.

After a rest at base camp, we headed up one more time, and on July 26 free climbed the line in a single 14-hour push, with steep, superb jamming and laybacking. The crux is pitch five (5.12+): a boulder problem followed by sustained 5.11+ climbing to the anchors. The two 5.12/12+ pitches high on the wall, immediately after merging with the British route—Ekstra Lagret joins the British Route four pitches below the summit—are a little easier. We did not add any fixed gear. The bolts in place are of hardware-store quality; fortunately there is good natural pro next to most of the bolted belays. We rappelled the British Route. 📷 🔍

– PATRYK RÓŻECKI, *POLAND*

HISTORICAL NOTES ON HONEY BUTTRESS: *In 1998, Ian Parsons and Tony Penning (U.K.) hoped to climb the steep north face of Half Dome, but after sitting below this formation for a wet day, they saw the attractive buttress opposite drying out and elected to climb it instead. The line on the photo is the best approximation of their route, given more than 20 years of elapsed time and memory. Toward the top, their line took them well onto the left flank of the buttress, and they finished on the quasi-horizontal arête that connects the top of the pillar to the mountain behind. Parsons and Penning followed this ridge back to the slabs, turned left, and then rappelled these slabs to reach the glacier near the start of the terrace at the base.*

Just after the two British climbers left the area, Denis Burdet, Roger Dubois, and Olivier Schaller (Switzerland) climbed another route on Honey Buttress called Pet Gaz (500m, 13 pitches, 6c A1); see photo above for their route line.

MEXICO

LA POPA, EAST FACE, SUPER BLOOD WOLF

LOOKING NORTHWEST FROM El Potrero Chico, a distant prow of rock called La Popa is visible on clear days. In sharp contrast from busy Potrero Chico, La Popa (a.k.a. El Gavilan) is deserted. On January 21, 2019, Jacob Cook (U.K.) and I made the third known repeat—though not free—of La Popa's first route, El Gavilan (9 pitches, 5.13a). This route is on the east face and was established by Kevin Gallagher and Jeff Jackson in 1997. [*Spanish Harlem (11 pitches, 5.11+ A0, free at 5.13 except for one move), put up by Marcus Garcia, Alvino Pon, and Rodney "Rodman" Blakemore in 1998, is the only other known route on La Popa and is located on the prow itself.*] We deemed a return trip worthy to pick some low-hanging fruit too tempting to pass up.

We slept among the amazing boulders near the bottom of the approach with our friend Savannah Cummins, who would join us and take photos. Our chosen route was a plumb line up a clean-looking corner system with sheer faces on either side, about 200m to the left of El Gavilan. Doing the long, steep, cacti-infested approach a second time would be the cost of entry. We arrived at the base on February 3 with three ropes, a full rack, hooks, 14 bolts, and a power drill ready for action.

Venturing up the first pitch, I drilled three bolts and enjoyed some serious vertical bushwhacking. Jacob took us another pitch higher through some nice slab climbing and a difficult drilling stance. We decided on the masochistic method of fixing our ropes and returning to camp via the cacti-ridden talus, only to hike back up the next day to finish the route.

After six more pitches of wide, loose, bushy, and generally unpleasant climbing, having placed a total of 12 bolts on the route, we topped out at night and vowed to never return, despite having missed the free ascent. We rappelled the severely overhanging El Gavilan, satisfied with a good adventure: Super Blood Wolf (275m, 5.11a A1).

— TONY MCLANE, *CANADA*

[Top] The east face of La Popa, showing (1) Super Blood Wolf (275m, 5.11) and (2) El Gavilan (9 pitches, 5.13a). Spanish Harlem, the other route on the formation, is on the left skyline. [Bottom] Tony McLane makes room for his head in a wide crack on Super Blood Wolf. *Jacob Cook (both photos)*

El Toro, showing approximate lines of (1) El Sendero Luminoso and (2) La Sombra Luminosa. *Drew Marshall*

La Popa, Super Blood Wolf, First Free Ascent: When Jacob and Tony told me about their new route on La Popa, I was skeptical. They said I should go for the first free ascent, but why didn't they want to go themselves? Jacob assured me the rock was not that bad for virgin limestone and probably only about 5.11+, so I roped my friend JP Thomas into going out there.

After a pleasant bivy at the base of the wall, we counted 300 paces between El Gavilan, a neat-looking climb that would be our rappel route, and the start of Super Blood Wolf, the most obvious line of weakness on the cliff. We moved very slowly up the climb, on account of the choss, resisting the urge to hang on gear and clean up the crux pitches. Instead, we subjected each other to showers of loose rock as we freed the line at 5.11.

From the top, we walked 300 paces to the right along the edge, looking for a bolt that marked our rappel line down El Gavilan. As it started to get dark, we tried calling Jacob for help, and eventually JP spotted a gray bolt hanger next to a fallen cairn. It took us three hours to do the overhanging rappels in the dark, and we didn't get to sleep until 3 a.m.

— DREW MARSHALL, *CANADA*

EL POTRERO CHICO, EL TORO, LA SOMBRA LUMINOSA

For me, climbing is all about getting to the top, so when I arrived at El Potrero Chico, the mecca of bolted big walls, and learned that there were no bolted routes to the most prominent summit, all I could think was, "*Someone* should put a route up there!" As my second season in Potrero came to an end, I decided to be that somebody. My goal was to find the longest, straightest, and cleanest line to the top of El Toro on its massive north-facing wall, and to keep it 5.10 and under (at which I failed).

I began work in the 2015–'16 season, developing pitches five through ten and 24 to 26. The lower pitches were accessed using the Paguvi Gully, one of the two seldom-climbed traditional routes from the 1980s and '90s that reaches the summit of El Toro. In the off-season I collected donations of retired ropes, with the plan to fix the entire face. Thus, the 2016–'17 season began with hauling ropes and bolts to the summit via the south-side hiking trail. I had estimated the route would be 24 to 25 pitches. It was then that I met Zachary Dostaler and Matthieu Morin-Robertson, two Quebecois just crazy enough to think working on this project sounded like a good idea.

Considering that all we knew about this route was that it was huge, unexplored, and full of cactus and loose rock, things went pretty smoothly. As it turned out, the mountain was even bigger than expected, and as we descended from the summit we fixed nine ropes. Arriving at pitch ten and a previously stashed rope was quite a relief, because from there we could rappel from previously established anchors. I had been fearful of an epic, but in fact we were drinking margaritas as the sun set, having started at 3 a.m.

It was during this day that much of the line was determined. Specifically, I had been unsure of where pitches 11 to 15 would go. From the ground, I could see an intriguing corner leading to an obvious ledge, but the pitches leading up to it looked really hard. When I arrived at this ledge, I walked out to the edge, took one look

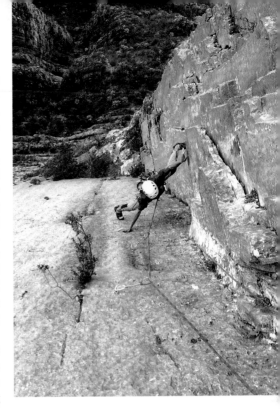

Drew Marshall following the crux stemming corner (5.12c) of La Sombra Luminosa. *Jacob Cook*

down the corner and, wow—it didn't matter how hard it went, this was the line!

In the end, pitch 15 would be the free crux at 5.12c (*see note below*), but I put in a bolt ladder for the route to be climbable at 5.10 A0. The calcite traverse below on pitch 14 that I was worried would be unclimbable went at 5.11-, and the corner pitches 11 to 13, which I thought would be easy, are difficult, technical, and sustained at 5.11, 5.11+, and 5.11. As it turns out, photos taken from a mile away can be misleading.

Over the next few weeks, much of it with Zach's help, pitches 12 to 23 were bolted in rapid order. I also discovered a new start by rappelling straight down from my existing pitches and into the slot canyon known as the Ampitheatre, which I had never thought to explore from below. It was another "Eureka!" moment—another beautiful and hard corner! I returned the next season (2017–'18), finished pitch 11 on rappel, recovered most of the fixed lines, and then bolted the final 5.7 pitch, pleased to find a surprisingly clean line of rock that finishes just a few feet from the otherwise chossy summit.

It was now time to make the first ascent. I made an attempt shortly thereafter with two friends, but we moved slowly and bailed after pitch 12. Finally, toward the end of the season, I met Seth Williams. We started in the evening, camped on top of pitch six, and began climbing the next day at 6 a.m. There were still fixed ropes on pitches 11 to 15, and holding no illusions about making a free ascent, I pulled on them a few times. As a result, we moved smoothly up until pitch 20, which turned out to be the final crux, at 5.11+. With that behind us, the rest of the climb proceeded pretty smoothly and we topped out a little after dark.

I held off on publicizing the route until I came back in the 2018–'19 season and added a few bolts as well as some cairns to better mark the descent. The route is named La Sombra Luminosa

("The Shining Shade"), a play on the route's famous neighbor to the left, Sendero Luminoso, whose physical shade and metaphorical shadow my route will always be in. It also carries a mystical undertone that felt appropriate to this otherworldly adventure. 🗏 📷 🔍

— ERIC WERFEL, *USA*

LA SOMBRA LUMINOSA FIRST FREE ASCENT: *In February 2019, Jacob Cook (U.K.) and Drew Marshall (Canada) freed this route in one long day, grading the crux corner 5.12c. Marshall's entertaining account is at the AAJ website.*

EL SALTO, LA GARGANTA

IN DECEMBER 2017, Pete Fasoldt (USA) established and freed La Garganta (6 pitches, 5.12+), up-canyon from La Boca. Fasoldt climbed the route ground-up and solo, in about a week of effort, and then freed the climb in one day, belayed by Sara Violett. 📷

— *INFORMATION FROM* PETE FASOLDT

EL SALTO, SAMADHI, ONSIGHT FREE ASCENT

SASHA DIGIULIAN, ACCOMPANIED by Molly Mitchell (both USA), onsighted Samadhi (450m, 5.13a) in February 2019 for the third known free ascent. The pair spent 14 hours on the route, which is sustained at 5.12 or harder on the top five pitches. Samadhi was established in 2006 and free climbed in 2009 by Alex Honnold and Chris Weidner; Urs Moosmüller (USA) made the second free ascent.

— *INFORMATION FROM* SASHA DIGIULIAN

SAN ISIDRO CANYON, ALAS DE ÁNGEL

IN NOVEMBER I paid a visit to the nonprofit youth development organization Escalando Fronteras in Monterrey, and in addition to the days I spent observing and collaborating in their activities—integrating and educating disfavored youth through climbing—I often took time to explore the known and lesser-known climbing areas around the city. Originally I hoped to find some interesting multi-pitch trad climbs, but when I saw the huge potential for high-end multi-pitch sport climbs in the area, I shifted my focus. In the up and coming sport climbing paradise of El Salto, south of Monterrey, I met with local route developers Joel Guadarrama, Carlos Mac, and half-local Mark Grundon. Mark was keen to show me some walls he had in mind for a multi-pitch, ground-up bolting adventure.

We chose the tallest and most solid-looking wall for our attempt, located in San Isidro Canyon, just west of El Salto. The Mexican sun can burn a Belgian's skin in less than 15 minutes, but although the wall faces southeast, thankfully our line was protected from the sun by a ridge on the left. The base of the climb is in the shade from 10 a.m., perfect for lazy climbers.

After establishing the first two pitches, we continued in capsule style with a portaledge, reaching the summit in two days. Topping out the cruxy sixth pitch, I had the pleasure to meet the *Opuntia microdasys*, a cactus also called Alas de Ángel. Pulling onto the ledge system, I tried to push aside the cacti with my hammer, but those smart, flexible bastards catapulted a million itchy hairs in my face and all over my body. But it wasn't over: I still had to haul two bags and a portaledge through the hairy cactus field while Mark jumared behind it, ready to get a load of itchy hairs all over him, too. It was a bad night in the portaledge.

Pitch eight is the real beauty of the climb: perfect crimps on a dark brown headwall, sustained and exposed. Sadly, there is a single boulder move at the start that might raise the route's free grade to 8a; the rest of our eight-pitch route Alas de Ángel is sustained in the mid-7 range. We didn't free the full route because of lack of time, but I will definitely come back soon to finish cleaning the route and try to free it. [*Editor's note: The complete version of this report, available online, contains interesting reflections on the value of ground-up bolting on long routes.*]

— SIEBE VANHEE, *BELGIUM*

CHIHUAHUA / PARQUE NACIONAL CASCADA DE BASASEACHI

LA CATEDRAL, THE FIRST LUCKY STRIKE

AT THE END of January, Christian Fascendini, Matěj Svojtka, and I arrived in Basaseachi National Park with one goal: to open a new line. Our plan was to establish a line on the wall named La Cascada, which already has a few routes, but local officials do not allow first ascents here anymore, due to the possibility of rocks falling onto the tourist trail. We decided to go deeper into Candameña Canyon, as it boasts huge walls everywhere (including the famous big wall El Gigante) and spans more than 10km.

After hiking two hours downstream from the waterfall, we found a southeast-facing wall that to our knowledge was completely unclimbed. We estimated it to be about 250m but realized later that it rose about 500m.

The walls in the canyon are composed of rhyolite, and although some of it was solid, the rock we found was mostly loose and required some cleaning. We spent four days and one night on the wall, climbing ground up. Our route is protected by bolts, drilled from hooks, and whenever possible by natural protection. Unfortunately, we didn't have time to redpoint the route; we reckon the crux pitch will be around 7c. Belays are two-bolt anchors, making it possible to descend by rappelling the route: The First Lucky Strike (500m, proposed 7c).

We named this wall La Catedral. There are many other possibilities for amazing new lines in

Approximate line of the First Lucky Strike (500m, proposed 7c), deep in Candameña Canyon. The lowest pitches are obscured by trees. *Ondřej Beneš Collection*

this area. Our base camp in the canyon below La Catedral had drinkable water from a small waterfall, but this is likely nonexistent in dry conditions. The water from the river is not drinkable.

— ONDŘEJ BENEŠ, *CZECH REPUBLIC*

ECUADOR

Kari Torre, one of several tall, crack-covered cliffs situated at around 4,400 meters, about 20 kilometers northwest of Chimborazo. The first routes in this area were climbed in late 2018 and early 2019. *Edgar Aulestia*

THE TOWERS OF SIMIATUG

FROM DECEMBER 5–9, a crew from Fondo Acceso Andino (the Ecuadorian analog to the Access Fund in the U.S.) explored a new area: the Towers of Simiatug. For rock climbing in Ecuador, this is the discovery of the decade.

In 2015, friends of ours began researching landscapes on Google Earth and then did reconnaissance of this area on foot. The primarily Ecuadorian team who put up the first routes in December included Javier Arizaga, Edgar Aulestia, Keith Brett (USA), Fernando Davila, Juan Carlos Merlo, Santiago Perez, Jorge Proaño, and myself.

Simiatug is a region in the Bolivar province, just northwest of Chimborazo (6,263m), and is home to the Kichwa people, who are ethnic descendants of the Incans; the local population is 99 percent indigenous. Simiatug means the "mouth of the wolf" in the local Kichwa language. For logistics, the indigenous community of Cocha Colorada are welcoming and can provide a meal as well mules and llamas to shuttle gear to the towers; it's a two-hour hike to reach the boulder field base camp (1°20'46.52"S, 78°57'45"W).

This is a high-elevation climbing area, with a base camp at 4,200m amid rocky, short-grass tundra typical of Ecuador's páramo zones. The rock formations consist of andesite and basalt towers with walls up to 150–200m that are mostly north- to east-facing. This is a perfect scenario for multi-pitch traditional climbing at altitude. There is also significant potential for single-pitch crack climbs and very aesthetic highball bouldering near the base camp. The best season is probably September–January.

Over three days, our group established five new routes in ground-up style. Three of these routes reached the summit of the northwestern and most prominent tower in the group, Warmi Torre (Warmi means "woman" in Kichwa). The longest of these routes is Warmi Torre Direct (4 pitches, 5.10+) up the northeast aspect; a two-pitch variation beginning midway up this route climbs the adjacent ridge on climber's right to reach the summit (5.7 choss). Our third route on Warmi Torre, Strange and Eternal (3 pitches, 5.10), is located on the east wall. It is likely the most continuous crack system in the country, following an obvious vertical line.

Left of Warmi Torre are the two Apu Machay Towers. On the easternmost of these, we climbed ¡Asi mismo es esto Griffin! (3 pitches, 5.10+). A single-pitch route, Reina de Simiatug (5.10+), ascends the obvious hand crack on Anfiteatro Wall, a columnar wall below and left of the previous route.

There are two other formations across the basin, east of these routes, that locals call Hatun Urku and Kari Torre. We returned over a number of weekends in January 2019 to attempt these formations and other, shorter climbs. On Hatun Urku, we climbed a pair of routes: Inti Ñan ("Sun Path," 3 pitches, 5.11+), on the left side of the main wall, and Llantu Ñan ("Shadow Path," 2 pitches, 5.10+), on the right side. On Kari Torre, we have established four pitches (to 5.11 A2) but are still one pitch shy of the summit.

We left bolts and pitons for anchors on the routes we climbed and also established a common rappel line down Warmi Torre to facilitate an easy descent to base camp. 📷

— **FELIPE PROAÑO**, *ECUADOR*

[Top] **Looking southwest from camp at (A) Anfiteatro Wall, (B) Apu Machay Towers, and (C) Warmi Torre.** Hatun Urku and Kari Torre are farther left. [Bottom] Keith Brett on the first ascent of Warmi Torre Direct (free at 5.10+). *Edgar Aulestia (both)*

PERU

Nevado Huantsán's west summit (6,270m, left) and main summit (6,395m), as seen from the south summit. The steep rock and mixed wall between the two tops had deterred previous parties. *Ben Gustave*

CORDILLERA BLANCA

NEVADO HUANTSÁN, SOUTH RIDGE TO MAIN SUMMIT

An Italian team that included Casimiro Ferrari reached Nevado Huantsán's western summit from the south in 1972 (*AAJ 1973*). At 6,270m, this top is only about 125m lower than the main summit, but the gap proved too difficult to cross for the Italians and subsequent teams. Since then, other climbers have reached the west summit without continuing to Huantsán's main top, including Spanish (*AAJ 1978*), Polish (*AAJ 1981*), Americans (*AAJ 1985*), and French (*AAJ 1990*), along with a few undocumented climbs.

Nathan Heald leading steep mixed below the summit of Huantsán to complete the first known ascent of the main top from the south. *Devin Corboy*

On July 28, Devin Corboy (USA), Macario Crispin (Peru), Arttu Pylkkanen (Finland), Javier Reyes (Chile), Johannes Suikkanen (Finland), and I traveled from Huaraz to Laguna Rajucolta, below the western flank of Huantsán (6,395m). We portered our equipment to a moraine camp next to the glacier at 5,000m the same day.

On the 29th, Macario and I climbed 300m of ice and snow on the west wall (similar to the 1972 Italian route on the west face) and established a high camp at 5,750m, just below the col between the south summit (5,900m) and west summit (6,270m). During the descent, we left fixed ropes on the steeper sections. On the 30th, we re-ascended the west wall to our high camp with the rest of the group.

On the 31st we started climbing the south ridge at 12:30 a.m. and made the west summit (6,270m) by 5 a.m. From there we walked down to the col below the main top and then climbed the 150m west face of the main summit block via steep ice and rock. The summit cornices were unstable and dangerous and required some aid off of a snow stake to overcome; only I touched the highest cornice, while the rest of the team stayed 20m below.

To quicken our descent, we were able to rappel a steeper line instead of retracing our steps down the south ridge and west summit. We arrived back at our high camp at 9:30 p.m. after a 22-hour day. On August 1, we rappelled four times down the west wall, walked the glacier back to the moraine camp, and made it down to Laguna Rajucolta by 3 p.m.

We called our route—the first known linkup of the west and main summits—Apus Circus (1,200m, ED WI4 M5).

— **NATHAN HEALD**, *PERU*

The team approaches the overhanging summit cornices of Nevado Huantsán. *Macario Crispin*

QUEBRADA RUREC UPDATES AND CORRECTIONS

THE 2018 SEASON saw continued interest in the granite walls of Quebrada Rurec in the southern Cordillera Blanca.

In late July, Steve House and Josh Wharton (both USA) made the second free ascent of Qui Io Vado Ancora (585m, 7c+/8a-; *see AAJ 2007 and AAJ 2018*) on Chaupi Huanca (5,179m), with Wharton onsighting the route over two days. The first free ascent, in 2017, also was onsight over two days.

In early August, the Ecuadorian team of Nicolás Dávalos, Fernando Dávila, Juan Carlos Merlo, and Felipe Proaño added a five-pitch extension to the route Pietrorrrago: Vaffanculo! (200m, 6a) on Pumawaqanqa (AAJ 2006), a northwest-facing wall at the start of the valley. Above the initial six-pitch slab climb, the new variation ascends a left-trending crack system under roofs. They called the extension Quien Carajos es Pietro Rago?! (an additional 200m, 6b); it does not top out.

In *AAJ 2006,* Pietrorrrago: Vaffanculo! was noted to be 420m; however, Proaño reports that the upper half of the route, continuing approximately 200m above the main slab, comprises a vegetated, mostly third-class ramp. The formation was also incorrectly spelled Pumhauagangan. "Waqanqa" (or "wakanka") means tears in Quechua, so the spelling should be "Pumawaqanqa" (or "Pumawakanka"); it is also spelled this way in *Huaraz: The Climbing Guide* (Lazo-Timmermans, 2014), which covers rock climbing in the Cordillera Blanca.

Proaño also mentioned there are possibly hundreds of Incan ruins in the valley, some which can only be seen once you're high on the walls. Two items of note include an 8km stone road, which may have led to Chavín de Huantar, and thousands of *tambos* (Incan square house formations). Locals use the latter to herd cattle and sheep; climbers should avoid camping inside them.

— **ERIK RIEGER**, *FROM INFORMATION BY* **FELIPE PROAÑO**, *ECUADOR AND* **JOSH WHARTON**, *USA*

Nevado Huayllaco (5,460m) from the south. The 2018 attempt traversed the glacier plateau from the left and climbed directly up the south face. *Delvaux/Ferreri*

HUAYLLACO, SOUTH FACE, ATTEMPT

NEVADO HUAYLLACO (5,460M, also spelled Huaiyacu) was first ascended in 1963 by Domingo Giobbi (Italy/Brazil) and the brothers Eugenio and Macario Angeles (Peru), who called it Raria Este; they likely ascended the southeast ridge. [*Editor's note: Huayllaco also appears to have been climbed in 1972 from the saddle to the west (see AAJ 1975).*]

On July 25, Marcelo Motta Delvaux (Brazil) and Julieta Ferreri (Argentina) approached the mountain via Quebrada Huayllaco, camping at Laguna Verdecocha (4,650m). From there, they reached the southwest glacier, which provides access to the col between Huayllaco and Nevado Raria (5,576m). They trended right and climbed directly up the south side of Huayllaco, a short, beautiful face (60–70°) that reaches the southeast ridge. Just below the ridge, they encountered a section with powder snow, dangerous cornices, and no protection and finished the climb there. 📷

— MARCELO SCANU, *ARGENTINA*

CORDILLERA HUAYHUASH

JURAU A AND JURAU B, NEW ROUTES (NOT TO SUMMITS)

IN JUNE, JOSÉ MARÍA "Chemari" Andres, Christine Baschinger, Samuel Gómez, Jorge Valle, and I (all Spaniards) climbed new routes on the northeast faces of Jurau A (5,640m) and Jurau B (5,727m), which are the two main peaks on the northeast flank of Siulá Grande (*see disambiguation note below*). We climbed alpine style by logical routes, however did not reach the true summits of either peak.

We reached our base camp at Laguna de Siulácocha (4,290m) on June 13, following acclimatization climbs in the Cordillera Blanca. Chemari and Samuel Gómez teamed up to climb a new route on Jurau A's rocky northeast face. They left base camp on June 18 to make a high camp at around 4,700m above Laguna Quesillococha. The next day they climbed seven pitches, encountering difficult snow climbing, and then bivouacked. On the second day they climbed nine pitches. On day three they made a summit push but were turned back a few meters from the top due to the dangerous state of the snow. [*The two were just below the northwest top; see note below.*] They retreated to their previous bivouac and spent a third night on the wall. On June 22, they completed rappelling the face. They called the route Chanchos y Chacras (1,000m, 6c M4 + 65°); it is characterized mostly by rock climbing, with some stretches of mixed and snow climbing.

Jorge Valle and I teamed up to climb Jurau B. We left base camp on June 19, using the same high camp around 4,700m. On June 20, we began climbing at 4:30 a.m. up a prominent *goulotte* on the northeast side (200m, WI4). We then traversed up and left on obvious terrain for 200m, then up and right for many pitches to reach the northeast rib. After more than 18 hours of climbing, terrible snow conditions and a lack of protection forced us down approximately 20m below the lower northern summit (5,650m). We bivouacked in an ice cave not far below our high point and began our full descent at sunrise, making ten 70m rappels along with downclimbing. The route to our high point was 900m, WI4 + M6 75°. 📷 🔍

— DAVID PÉREZ, *SPAIN*

From the northeast: (A) Siulá Grande (hidden in clouds), (B) Jurau B, and (C) Jurau A, showing the 2018 Spanish routes. Both climbs finished below the highest tops of the peaks. *Tom Dempsey | Photoseek.com*

JURAU A AND JURAU B, DISAMBIGUATION AND NOTES ON 2018 CLIMBS: *The 2018 AAJ perpetuated an error regarding the "Jurau" chain of peaks by noting that a 2017 attempt on the east face of Siulá Grande began on "Siulá Antecima." This should have been described as Jurau B, the modern name for this summit.*

The Nevados Jurau were historically noted to be the chain of peaks extending north to south along the entire eastern flank of Siulá Grande, from Cerro Azulchocha in the north to Nevado Trapecio in the south. This was first documented in a 1939 German cartographic study, and the alphabetical enumerations of the Nevados Jurau were confirmed by the Peruvian government in 1969–1970. Jurau is the Quechua name for a local grass with a purple flower that grows at the base of these peaks.

Subsequently, however, amid a surge of climbing activity on the Siulá Grande massif, ensuing documentation labeled the 5,640m and 5,727m peaks extending from Siulá Grande's northeast flank as Jurau A and Jurau B, northwest of the original Jurau chain. Despite this illogical labeling, it is best to stick with the modern working definition to avoid further confusion. [Sevi Bohorquez has prepared an excellent annotated map and photos, viewable on the AAJ website, to illustrate these discrepancies. Further information can be found at his blog on Andean climbing.]

Therefore, the initial Bernasconi-Bordella attempt in 2017 on the east face of Siulá Grande began on the flanks of Jurau B (5,727m) not, as stated in AAJ 2018, on "Siula Antecima," which is a subsidiary point northeast of the true summit of Jurau A (5,640m) and which was named erroneously by a 2007 Italian expedition.

The 2018 climb by José María Andres and Samuel Gómez on Jurau A ended a few meters below what we could call the northwest summit (ca 5,500m). This minor top is almost 200m away from the true summit, which has just one recorded ascent, by Lindauer and Salger in 1964 (the peak was called "Nevado Bavaria" in AAJ 1965). Likewise, the 2018 climb by José David Pérez and Jorge Valle on Jurau B ended below what would be considered the northern summit (ca 5,650m), which was reached by Pinto, et al, in 2014 (AAJ 2015). The highest top of Jurau B remains unclimbed. 📷 🔍

— **ERIK RIEGER**, *ADAPTED FROM INFORMATION PROVIDED BY* **SEVI BOHORQUEZ**, *PERU*

PUSCANTURPA NORTE, MACONDO

IN JULY, COLOMBIAN climbers Rafa Avila, Diego Cortés, Jhoany Poveda, Luis Ossa, Victor Ortega, and Alex Torres climbed a partially new route on Puscanturpa Norte (5,652m). Their line followed cracks in the columns on the left side of the north-northwest face. On the first pitches, they reported seeing some pitons from the route Macanacota (*AAJ 2001*). [*According to the climbers' topo, the 2018 route ascends mostly to the right of the route Macanacota; however, it is in the same vicinity as the route Barne Sua, and it is unclear the extent to which the 2018 route is new. See AAJ 2004 and 2010.*] On July 27, Avila, Ossa, and Torres climbed the final 200m of the wall proper, and Avila and Torres worked up the final 200m of terrain to the summit. A dangerous cornice stopped the ascent to the very top. The route, Macondo (600m, 7a) awaits a continuous free ascent.

— SERGIO RAMÍREZ CARRASCAL, *PERU, WITH INFORMATION FROM* DIEGO CORTÉS, *COLOMBIA*

The Rajuntay group, showing (1) the solo new route on the northeast face of Rajuntay (5,477m) and (2) the northeast couloir of Rajuntay Norte (ca 5,400m), climbed one month later. *Steve Meder*

CORDILLERA CENTRAL

RAJUNTAY, NORTHEAST FACE; RAJUNTAY NORTE, FIRST ASCENT

THE CORDILLERA DE la Viuda is a subrange of the Cordillera Central (*see Alpine Journal 2000 for more details about the area*). With many 5,000m peaks and moderate climbing, it is an interesting place for exploration and climbing. The highest summit is Rajuntay (5,477m), a beautiful, technical mountain.

On May 1, Steve Meder (France/Peru) and his Peruvian porters Antonio and Jorge Chinchay ascended the Quebrada Uco beneath the slopes of Nevado Uco, at the head of the Rímac river. They camped at 4,930m below the unclimbed northeast face of Rajuntay.

The next day, with doubtful weather, Meder began climbing alone up the northeast face. Near the bottom, at a 5m vertical rock and ice step, he left a piton for his descent. He then continued up steep, rocky terrain to reach a 45° snow couloir. Eventually, he traversed right and ascended another 40–50° snow slope. This brought him to a short rock ridge and the summit. He describes this route as being much easier than the peak's technical west ridge, which he attempted the year prior.

On May 3, Meder attempted an independent, unclimbed summit located along Rajuntay's north ridge called Rajuntay Norte (ca 5,400m, a.k.a. Pequeño Rajuntay). He ascended a 45–55° couloir of hard ice. Around 5,350m, he self-belayed up a steeper section (60° M3) to reach a ridge and what he thought was the summit. However, after later studying the photos, he came to believe another top was higher and he made a plan to return.

In early June, Meder was joined once more by Antonio and Jorge Chinchay for a return to Rajuntay Norte. On June 5, he scouted the route and snow conditions, and the next day he began his climb alone at 5 a.m. and reached the true summit four and a half hours later. The route up the northeast couloir is 350m, D 70° M3.

— MARCELO SCANU, *ARGENTINA*

An overview of the Suiricocha Massif from the west. (A) Nevado Norma. (B) The ca 5,400m peak climbed by Guy Fonck and Beto Pinto in 2018. The ascent followed snow slopes to the col left of the peak, then the north ridge to the top. (C) The ca 5,500m peak climbed by Sophie Denis and Beto Pinto in 2010, which may be called Manon Dos. (D) The ca 5,600m central summit of Suiricocha. (E) The ca 5,450m central-western summit of Suiricocha. (F) The ca 5,425m south-central summit of Suiricocha. (G) The ca 5,450m southern summit of Suiricocha climbed by Sophie Denis and Beto Pinto in 2010. Nevado Vicuñita is out of the frame to the left. *Guy Fonck*

SUIRICOCHA MASSIF, PERU-BELGIUM ARÊTE

In May, Guy Fonck (Belgium) and I climbed an unnamed peak (ca 5,400m, 11°56'5.79"S, 76° 3'18.95"W) in the southern Cordillera Central. It is part of the Suiricocha Massif (sometimes spelled Suerococha) and located just to the north of a peak (ca 5,500m) that may be called Manon Dos, on which I'd previously climbed a new route up the west face with Sophie Denis (*AAJ 2011*). [*See note below about peak names in this group.*]

On May 10 we left San Mateo early to start for Paccha Cocha, shuttled our gear to 4,800m, and then descended and slept at 4,370m. On the 11th, we left at 8 a.m. and shuttled climbing gear to the moraine (4,950m) underneath the snow-covered peak Vicuñita. We began our ascent soon after 1 a.m. on the 12th. There had been a recent avalanche from Vicuñita, so we adapted our initial route, climbing carefully up the first steep snow slope. We reached our mountain's northern ridge by 6 a.m. I hurried up the 260m of snow and mixed climbing above, as I knew the sun's arrival would further weaken the snow. After two hours, I arrived at a false summit—to my shock, we still were 70m short. Finally, we reached the summit just after 10 a.m.

To descend, we used deadman and piton rappel anchors, as well as some downclimbing. The weather changes quickly in the Cordillera Central, and it soon began to snow. By the time we reached the col, the wind had blown snow through every gap in our clothing, and the insides of our boots were like swimming pools. Rather than continue down the way we had climbed, we decided to head northward toward Nevado Norma, to reach a point where one rappel would get us to the glacier. It took us an hour pulling our frozen rope with a Tibloc before we could return to the flat glacier. 🗎 📷

— BETO PINTO TOLEDO, *PERU, TRANSLATED FROM SPANISH BY PAM RANGER ROBERTS*

EDITOR'S NOTE: *The naming of peaks in Peru's central ranges has been somewhat idiosyncratic, and many elevations stated on the IGN map or by climbers appear multiple times or are unconfirmed; this makes it difficult to pinpoint ascents. For example, in 1996, the prolific first ascensionist Evelio Echevarría reported climbs on Vicuñita (5,050m, just north of the peak Rajuntay) and Suerococha (5,312m, just south of the town of San Mateo), a zone over 30km west-northwest of the area covered in this report, generally containing lower peaks, some known by the same names (see AAJ 1997 and the U.K. Alpine Journal 2000). The Suiricocha Massif described here contains at least six prominent summits between 5,400m–5,600m, the tallest of which appears to be the central summit.*

The west face of Jampa II (approximately 5,650m), showing the 2018 route (May 2017 photo). The arrow at the bottom left of the peak shows the entrance to the north couloir, which was used on the 1953 first ascent and all subsequent climbs. Jampa is the peak on the far left. The normal route (left skyline) is the most commonly climbed route in the Cordillera Vilcanota. *Duncan McDaniel*

THE WEST FACE OF JAMPA II
A COMPLEX NEW ROUTE BY AN INTERNATIONAL TEAM

BY DUNCAN MCDANIEL, *USA*

In August, my wife, Vahitiare Beltrami, Simon Schonemann-Poppeliers, and I traveled to the Andean village of Pacchanta, where we met our *compadres*, the Crispin family, to climb some nearby peaks. We spent 10 days in the area, from August 17 to August 26, and attempted three climbs. August usually falls in the middle of the dry season in the Cordillera Vilcanota; this year, the dry season never arrived in Peru, which meant very difficult conditions.

On the 21st we attempted Caracol (5,625m) from a base camp below Jampa but turned around at the Tinki-Caracol col when we encountered chest-deep snow and whiteout conditions. After a rest day, Simon and I made the first known ascent of north ridge of Parcocaya (5,290m) (*see report below*) and returned to Pacchanta.

On the 24th, I returned to the mountains with Luis and Macario Crispin and one pack horse. Our sights were set on the aesthetic pyramid Jampa II (ca 5,650m). Jampa II is the highest summit of the Jampa massif (locals sometimes refer to it as "Juana Sucapana," but I have also seen this name used to describe the rocky summit northeast of Mariposa.) [*These peaks have been called Campa in the past.*] Jampa II was first climbed by its north couloir in 1953 by the German-Austrian team that also made the first ascents of Jampa, Ausangate (standard route from south), Colque Cruz, and Cayangate (northwest icefall to northeast face). Their route was repeated in 1966 by a group of Germans (who also made the first ascent of northwest face of Ausangate), and more recently by locals Lixayda Vasquez and Alfredo Zuniga in 2014, the last known ascent of the peak.

The three of us camped next to a clear glacial lagoon about 1km southwest of the normal Jampa base camp. We awoke at 2 a.m. on August 25 to thunderstorms barraging the jungle to the east. Our day started earnestly, knowing we would be racing those same clouds to the summit.

We approached via the moraine west of camp to gain the glacier and the west face. After a simple glacier ascent, a short rock step led to a 75° ice ramp and, finally, to a fore-summit atop a sharp ridge, which then descends for 50m and bridges the fore-summit to the slopes under the summit headwall. This ridge is hidden when viewing the peak and provided the key passage for our route: an exposed, down-ward traverse over snow and loose rocks.

Once below the main summit, a single pitch on poor rock connected us with the upper snow slopes. At the final headwall, we decided to climb a steep, mixed chim-ney on the right side. This was the best pitch of the climb—sustained, with cool stemming and solid ice (M4). After this, I led an extremely delicate pitch of loose snow plastered over a rock slab (85°) to the summit ridge. The clouds from the jungle had finally caught up with us. At around 12:30 p.m. we took turns climbing the final 5m to the highest point.

We began our descent in a whiteout, making one rappel down the top of the north couloir and then downclimbing and rappelling our route of ascent. On our fifth and final rappel, our rope got caught and we lost about two hours free-ing it. We reached our camp at about 8 p.m.

This was likely the first ascent of the west face of Jampa II (600m, D AI3 M4 85°). Our route was very enjoyable and provided amazing views of the Vilcanota.

It also was special to share this ascent with the Crispin brothers. Luis and Macario grew up herding their alpaca below these mountains, dream-ing of what it would be like to grace their summits. Even though they have only been climbing for about five years, they have amassed an incredible list of difficult summits, including Yeru-paja, Salkantay, Cayangate, Ausangate,

[Top] Luis Crispin (left) and Macario Crispin atop the foresummit on the west face of Jampa II. From here, the climbers had to descend a sharp ridge, hidden from below, to access the headwall looming in the background. The chimney feature and delicate slab that the team climbed are just above Macario's helmet. The Crispin brothers are among Peru's most accomplished alpinists. See also the Huantsán report on p.198. [Bottom] Sunset on the main peak of Jampa (5,500m). *Duncan McDaniel (both photos)*

Huantsán, and Veronica; accordingly, they've been noted in the *AAJ* many times. They are among the most accomplished Peruvian mountaineers in history, but few are familiar with their achievements. 📷

Duncan McDaniel on the north ridge on Parcocaya. *Simon Schonemann-Poppeliers*

CORDILLERA VILCANOTA

NEVADO PARCOCAYA, NORTH RIDGE

IN AUGUST, DUNCAN McDaniel (USA) and I attempted four different routes up four different mountains in southern Peru, and succeeded on one. The latter was Nevado Parcocaya (5,290m), located northeast of Ausangate. The peak appears to have been climbed by its north side, and it was recently climbed by the south face from the glacier. (*There are two recorded ascents; see AAJ 1981 and* 2017.) We focused on an intriguing rock ridge rising from the north side. About 400m of simul-climbing on this ridge (mostly 5.6 with a few moves of 5.8) brought us to the summit ridge, and a short walk across some snow and more rock led to the top. We enjoyed the view of Ausangate's dramatic north face and then scrambled down the east side to a saddle. From here, we downclimbed to reach the valley on the north; no rappels were needed. [*The online report also has good photos from an attempt in the Sirihuani and Nevado Sahuasiray area of the Cordillera Urubamba.*] 📄 📷 🔍

— SIMON SCHONEMANN-POPPELIERS, *USA*

OJE PUNTA, WEST COULOIR DIRECT

ON JULY 9, 2017, I climbed a probable new route on the west aspect of Oje Punta (5,386m), also known as Lliani, in the eastern Cordillera Vilcanota. I left the Ausangate base camp at 5:30 a.m., carrying a pair of rock climbing shoes and a small daypack, and jogged down the valley to the tiny settlement of Huchuy Finaya (4,500m). Crossing to the east side of the Pitumarca drainage, I gained the nearest ridge to the south, scrambled along this rocky crest for half an hour, and

A sweeping view of the Cordillera Vilcanota, looking northeast from Oje Punta (5,386m). (A) Ausangate. (B) Mariposa. (C) Jampa II. (D) Jampacito. (E) Jampa I. (F) Tinqui (commonly spelled Tinki.) (G) Caracol. (H) Concha de Caracol. (I) Puca Punta. (J) Ccapana. (K) Callangate (commonly spelled Cayangate). *Derek Field*

then descended 50m to the east to reach the peak's southwest cirque (ca 5,100m).

My scramble up the central couloir ascended scree and glacier-polished slabs, with the uppermost 100m presenting steeper rock. At the knife-edge summit ridge, I moved northward, passing many precarious gendarmes. I downclimbed my route and made it back to Huchuy Finaya just before noon: West Couloir Direct (250m, PD 5.4).

Despite its proximity to the Ausangate trekking circuit, not much climbing activity has been documented on Oje Punta since its first known ascent (*AAJ 1981*). It is unlikely the rugged west aspect has seen many ascents, if any.

— DEREK FIELD, *CANADA*

Looking southwest from Nevado Tacusiri during the descent. The peaks behind are Cerro Huasacocha (left) and Nevado del Inca. *Supplied by Marcelo Scanu*

NEVADO TACUSIRI, SOUTH FACE TO WEST RIDGE (NO SUMMIT)

ON JUNE 7, Argentine Nehuén Conterno and Peruvians Rodrigo Mendoza and Jorge Sirva drove to the village Alkatauri and hiked one and a half hours to the base of Tacusiri (5,350m), planning to attempt on the south face. Tascuri's first known ascent was from the north in 1980 during a Japanese expedition to Ausangate (6,372m). (Tacusiri lies to the southwest of Ausangate.)

The Argentine-Peruvian trio began climbing at 4,800m, following a couloir on the left side of Tacusiri`s south face, and climbed eight pitches to reach the ridgeline. They encountered a mixture of deep powder snow, some ice, and poor rock. Once on the ridge, they decided against continuing to the summit because of the minimal daylight remaining. They made two 60m rappels down the west face and onto the glacier. From there, they circled around to the south face and back to the car, returning 18 hours after leaving.

They climbers named their incomplete new route Expreso de Medianoche (D+ 65° M4), and they hope to finish the route to the summit with better weather and conditions.

— MARCELO SCANU, *ARGENTINA*

CORDILLERA CARABAYA

CHILPARITI, SOUTHWEST FACE

IN 1967, THE southwest face of Chilpariti (ca 5,550m) was so highly coveted by two visiting expeditions that the British team, led by Roger Whewell, literally bargained for it with the New Zealand Alpine Club in exchange for Trident (ca 5,490m), the only other major unclimbed summit in the Allinccapac massif. Unfortunately, the Brits were unsuccessful on Chilpariti, citing deep snow as their primary opponent. Meanwhile, the New Zealand team, which succeeded on Trident, wrote, "There was much grumbling at Camp IV when we saw what a fine climb the southwest face of Chil-

The southwest face of Chilpariti (ca 5,500m). The 2018 ascent followed the right side of the snow and ice field to the ridge and traversed left to the top. The first ascent (1968) was from the opposite (northeast) side from the col between Chilpariti and the Screwdriver, seen behind and left. *Derek Field*

pariti would have been" (*New Zealand Alpine Journal 1968*).

Whewell and his wife, Elspeth, returned to the Carabaya to attempt Chilpariti in 1968, making the first ascent from the glacier on the northeast side; they first climbed to the high col shared with Screwdriver (5,543m) and then finished on steep rock and ice (*AAJ 1969*). They subsequently bestowed the name Chilpariti (Quechuan for "wedge of snow") on the mountain. To the best of our knowledge, no subsequent attempts have been made.

On August 10, my husband Derek Field and I arrived at the trailhead for Laguna Canocota at dusk. By the time we arrived at our camp by the lake, nestled in herder-made rock walls, a thick fog had turned to a steady rain. The season had been unusually wet, so Derek and I kept our expectations low.

The next morning, our taxi driver from the night before and a new friend, Martin Surco, met us with a school backpack and old soccer cleats. He and his family have herded and fished in the Cordillera Carabaya for generations, and he volunteered to show us part of the way, warning that it would be very difficult to navigate without prior experience. We realized how fortunate we were later that day when Martin split from us at Laguna Añilcocha (ca 4,500m), leaving us to our own devices. We reached a camp that evening at around 4,600m below the northern glacier of Chilpariti.

On the 12th, we began at 5:30 a.m. with four and a half hours of traversing moraine and glacier. We reached the base of the southwest face at 10 a.m. Knee-deep snow up a gradually steepening ramp gave way to more sustained climbing on excellent ice, providing a nearly direct shot to the summit ridge. Eventually, the fog thickened to the point that Derek disappeared, so I just followed his trail of snow pickets and ice screws.

We topped out the southwest face at 1:10 p.m., and, chased by an impending storm, I quickly led us northward along the ridge to the summit, arriving at 1:30. We rappelled back down our ascent line in a blizzard and reached the toe of the glacier again at 5:45 p.m. Our new route up the southwest face is 250m, D 80°, plus over 600m of vertical gain on the glacier below.

– GISELLE FIELD, *USA*

TRIDENT, NORTHWEST FACE AND SOUTHWEST RIDGE (NOT TO SUMMIT); MITÓN, FIRST ASCENT BY EAST RIDGE

IN AUGUST, I led a 10-day traverse across the Cordillera Carabaya between the towns of Macusani (4,300m) and Ollachea (2,800m), including various side trips. We were an entirely self-supported group of four enthusiastic people: Giselle Field, Matthew Scott, Steve Yamamoto, (all USA), and myself. The weather was mostly poor, with nasty snowstorms occurring almost every day.

On August 22, from a high camp on a narrow, snow-covered shelf at 5,000m, Giselle, Steve, and I attempted Trident (5,490m), one of the most difficult major summits in the Allinccapac massif. All of our gear was caked in ice from a snowstorm the previous day, so we were unable to set off until 6 a.m. We started at the toe of the kilometer-long valley glacier on the north side of Trident. We encountered large paw prints at 5,250m, which we took to be puma tracks—the tracks made a one-way path into a large crevasse.

By noon, we reached the northwest-facing ice wall between the southwest and central summits of Trident. We climbed this via a narrow runnel on the far right side, which we called the Honeymoon Chute (AI3, 200m)—it was Giselle and my actual honeymoon. We gained the knife-edge summit ridge at 1 p.m. Moving northeast, two pitches of steep mixed climbing (M4) got us to what we'd thought would be the summit (5,570m GPS). However, we now realized the true summit stood several hundred meters farther along the ridge, on the other side of a deep notch. It appeared to be less than 30m higher than this lesser summit.

We proceeded along the wild ridge-line, climbing up and around terrifying gendarmes (5.9+ R). By 4 p.m. we had reached the notch; the summit stood less than 50m above us but was guarded by a plethora of obstacles. Feeling we'd pushed our luck, we made the decision to retreat by rappelling straight down the west face of the main peak.

A few days later, all four of us headed for the conspicuous, mitten-shaped rock tower crowning the western edge of the range, less than a kilometer northeast of Cerro Esjarane. At 2:30 a.m., we left our camp on the west shore of Laguna Siurococha (4,530m) and scrambled up an improbably steep canyon and tributary to the south shore of Laguna Esjarane (4,870m), the deep blue lake at the base of our objective. Matt stayed here while Steve, Giselle, and I started our ascent with the rising sun.

[Top] The line up the east ridge of Mitón, the first known route up the peak. *Derek Field* [Bottom] Derek Field at the high point before retreating from just below the summit of Trident. "The summit stood less than 50 meters above us, but was guarded by a plethora of obstacles." *Steve Yamamoto*

We chose the east ridge for its aesthetic, direct line to the summit. Getting there proved tedious, but by 8:30 a.m. we had gained the base of the ridge (5,080m). The weather was perfect for rock climbing, and the description for each pitch is mostly, "Follow the ridge—5.7, 50m." The fifth pitch offered the crux: a steep dihedral (5.8) leading into a good crack system. The three of us reached the summit (5,221m GPS) at 12:30 p.m. We named the peak Mitón. Our route up the east ridge, starting from Laguna Esjarane, is 350m, D 5.8 50°.

After soaking in the views, we descended the southwest buttress with three 60m rappels. While rappelling, four condors *swooshed* across the sky in incredibly close proximity. I have had many wonderful experiences with these majestic birds in the Andes, but nothing compared to this. 📷

– DEREK FIELD, *CANADA*

BOLIVIA

CHAUPI ORCO, EAST RIDGE, VARIATION

ON JUNE 26, from a high camp at 5,100m, my wife, Jeanne, and I climbed a possible new variation (AD+) to reach the previously climbed east ridge on Chaupi Orco (6,044m). Our route was necessitated by deep fresh snow on the glacier east of the peak that forced us to find a more expedient path to the ridge. We ascended a southeast aspect, zigzagging past seracs. Deep 55° snow sometimes left us "swimming" and forced to move laterally to find purchase. Toward the top of the face we moved slightly left and climbed a near vertical section of exposed serac to gain the ridge, which we followed to the summit, detouring onto the steep north face to bypass a large crevasse 200m below the top.

A new road completed in the past five years now gives easy access from Pelechuco to this once very remote region of the Apolobamba. We took two days to access the base camp at El Rincon with mules, but it could be reached in one day with a 4x4 vehicle. [*Editor's note: Aaron and Jeanne Zimmerman also made numerous ascents in the Cordillera Real, many of these in the early season of April and May. Find useful details and photos at the AAJ website.*]

— AARON ZIMMERMAN, *USA*

HELICOPTER RESCUE IN THE BOLIVIAN ANDES

IN 2007 AND '08, the Vladostano Alpine Rescue Service, which operates mountain rescue services in Italy's Val d'Aosta, organized training courses for Bolivia's professional mountain guides. Since then, the Bolivian IFMGA guides, operating under the title of Socorro Andino Boliviano (SAB), have made multiple mountain rescues, sometimes saving lives. However, it was obvious that faster and more effective missions could be made with helicopters, as in Europe.

From October 19–28, 16 members of SAB were trained for helicopter rescue under the supervision of European rescue professionals Edy Grange, Sandra Cauchy Leal, and Charly Perritaz. The helicopter operated up to 4,300m, and in May 2019 a second program is expected to take the training further, with practice in long-line techniques up to 5,900m. Landings should be possible up to 5,500m. The flight time for these training projects was financed by Airbus, and SAB is seeking sponsorship for additional activity.

Although the instructors evaluated the Bolivian team as being operational from a technical standpoint, the reliable availability of a helicopter in La Paz remains an issue. However, it seems hopeful that one will be available in La Paz during the 2019 high season for mountaineering, from the start of June until the end of August. To get updates or arrange a donation, contact SAB at socorroandinoboliviano@gmail.com or via its Facebook page.

— ALEXANDER VON UNGERN, *SAB SECRETARY, BOLIVIA*

The Pico Emma Maria–Pico 24 September group from the southeast. (A) Eperon Maria. (B) Pico Emma Maria (5,531m). (C) The Ertl Col, reached by Hans Ertl on an early attempt at Pico 24 September. (D) Pico 24 September (a.k.a. Punta Badile, 5,432m). (E) Punta Cocoyu. (1) Southwest ridge (original route, AD+, Ertl-Hundhammer, 1953). (2) Southeast buttress, approximate line (Hutson Pillar, TD Al4, then 5/5+, Hutson-Mesili, 1983). (3) Humo e Independencia (500m, 6c A0, Brown-Monasterio, 2004). (4) South face (450m, D+/TD-, Hutson-Mesili, 1983, first recorded ascent of Pico 24). (5) Monypenny-McGhie Route (ca 650m, 5.11 and some aid, 2017). (6) Incomplete line by McGhie and Monypenny (2017). (7) Don't Take the Long Way Home (ca 650m, 6b/6b+, Ens-Rauch, 1991). (8) Paititi (160m, four pitches rap bolted from the summit, 7b, Lehmpfuhl-Rauch-Schöffel, 1998; the team approached from the far side via a new route up the west face). (9) Flyvbjerg-Monasterio Route (ca 650m, 6b, 2006). *Erik Monasterio*

PICO 24 SEPTEMBER, MONYPENNY-MCGHIE ROUTE

LATE IN THE climbing season of 2017, Harry McGhie and I (both U.K.) headed to the east side of the Illampu massif, which appeared to have plenty of potential for new routes. We made base camp on a flattish boulder about 400m from the base of Pico 24 September. After an attempt on Illampu cut short by lack of acclimatization and other issues, we decided to look at the unclimbed south-southeast face of Pico Emma Maria (5,531m), which looks a bit like the west face of the Petit Dru. [*Pico Emma Maria and Pico 24 are rocky eastern satellites of Illampu's Pico del Norte.*] I led a hard pitch that required cleaning mossy cracks for every move, and we decided to descend and look for a more expedient alternative. The most attractive was the probably unrepeated Humo e Independencia (500m, 6c A0, Brown-Monasterio, 2004). This turned out to be a great route, like the Papillons Arête on the Aiguille du Peigne but longer and harder. The precariously perched summit block made for a daunting final challenge. Taking a gamble in our light approach shoes (the first ascensionists had rappelled the route), we traversed the main ridge far to the southwest until we could rappel onto the glacier west of the peak and descend this, with one rappel at its base.

We next tried a new route on the southeast face of Pico 24 September (a.k.a. Punta Badile, 5,432m). The steepest part of this face is at the base, and it is also the dirtiest. Harry led the first pitch, then I took over for a steep E4 A1 pitch, that, had it been clean, would have been amazing. After this the angle eased and we picked up the pace, finding a route up cracks and arêtes in slabby terrain. After 450m we were enveloped by storm and decided to descend. [*The first section of this line appears to follow the 1991 Ens-Rauch route Don't Take the Long Way Home.*]

Next day, rather than repeat our previous line, we chose another start farther left. At first this line was also difficult, damp, dirty, and required some aid. Above, we once again were able to climb faster, though every pitch required care and cleaning. Above our previous high point, the face steepened again and the rock became cleaner. We topped out just before sunset and rappelled the route, leaving only slings. We walked out the following day in a snowstorm.

— JAMES MONYPENNY, *U.K.*

NEGRUNI RANGE, PEAK 5,396M, TRAVERSE

IN MARCH, BOLIVIAN resident Davide Vitale and friends traversed Peak 5,396m in the Negruni Range of the central Cordillera Real. As had been done in the past, the Vitale team climbed onto the southwest ridge from the south (AD), but from the summit they then descended the probably virgin east ridge (PD). Peak 5,396m is located in a small hanging valley east-northeast of Laguna Khuna Khota and north of the Palcoco Mine and Alka Khota Valley; it was first climbed in 1969 by a Bavarian team. The Negruni is rarely visited and in the normal climbing season is now probably too dry to warrant much attention. However, at the time of the Vitale ascent, persistent rains had produced nice snow conditions. 📄 📷

— LINDSAY GRIFFIN, *WITH INFORMATION FROM DAVIDE VITALE*

Routes on the east face of Charquini, leading to the eastern summit (ca 5,300m). (1) Juntos al Puma (2017). Jaguar Holocaust (2018) is just to the right of this line but completely independent. (2) Coni's Dream (2018). (3) Felix el Titi (2018). The unclimbed face to the left is exposed to rockfall and not likely to freeze well for mixed climbing.
Alexander von Ungern

CHARQUINI, EAST FACE, NEW ROUTES

AFTER MAKING THE first ascent of the east face of Charquini (5,392m) in 2017 with Sergio Condori (see *AAJ 2018*), I returned several times in 2018 to explore the potential of this small but attractive granite wall.

On May 2, Felix Leger, Jules Tusseau, and I followed an obvious line on the right side of the face in five pitches. This was generally no more than 5 in difficulty, except for a short section where we climbed around a little cave via a slightly overhanging crack before crossing an unprotected slab. I was able to free all this at around 6b. After pitch five, we short-roped up the ridge above and then descended the glaciated south face as night settled, rappelling twice. We named the route Felix el Titi (the "titi" being an Andean wild cat).

On June 28, I returned with Sergio Condori's brother Juvenal, post-holing through unexpected snow on the approach. We followed another obvious line, just to the right (but completely independent) from our 2017 route, Juntos al Puma. The new route is sustained at 6a+, with several small overhangs that were quite "breathtaking" at over 5,000m. After six pitches of good granite, we scrambled and short-pitched to the top. This time we descended the glacier that flows from the col north of the summit, thus avoiding any rappels. We named the route Jaguar Holocaust. (In recent years, as the number of Chinese nationals living and working in Bolivia has grown, the illegal trafficking of jaguar teeth has increased. Although there have been a number of arrests—in February 2018, two Chinese were caught in possession of nearly 200 jaguar fangs—it is reported that successful prosecutions have been slow to follow.)

On July 11, I returned for a third route, this time with two clients, Cornelia and Thomas. We followed a line through the middle of the face (5). This led into the offwidth pitch of Juntos al Puma, which Cornelia and Thomas found quite challenging. Cornelia suggested the route name Coni's Dream, as she had long hoped to climb a new route. 📷

—ALEXANDER VON UNGERN, *ANDEAN ASCENTS, BOLIVIA*

PICACHO PUCUSANI, WEST TO EAST TRAVERSE; PICACHO KASIRI, SOUTH FACE

IN MID-JULY, ROBERTO Gomez (Bolivia) and I decided to check out a prominent formation that every rock climber sees when driving over Cumbre Pass and down toward the Bolivian jungle. Even though local climbers had implied the rock quality was really poor, we figured we should give it a try.

We parked alongside Ruta Nacional 3 approximately 5km after crossing Cumbre Pass and walked northwest for 1.5 hours to a col at 4,850m. This gave access to the west ridge of Picacho Pucusani (as defined by the IMG map 5945-II). Whereas the beginning of this quasi-horizontal ridge indeed had poor rock, we were pleasantly surprised to find good slate as we approached more vertical terrain. The crux of our traverse—two pitches on a slab—featured cracks in excellent rock that took the little protection we had brought (a reduced set of nuts, four Tricams, and four slings). I was delighted to spot a couple of condors as we reached the summit (ca 5,050m).

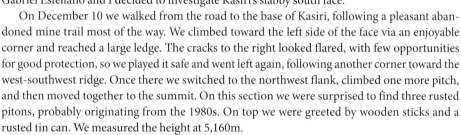

Picacho Kasiri (5,160M) seen from Picacho Pucusani. The 2018 team climbed the steep, shady slabs of the south face (hidden on the right), crossed over the southwest ridge, facing the camera, and followed the upper northwest flank to the top. They descended to the north and then traversed west, past the lake in lower foreground, through the Kasiri-Pucusani col, and back to the road, off-picture to the right. *Alexander von Ungern*

We scrambled down the east ridge to traverse the peak and return to the car, eight hours after leaving. This descent was straightforward, so it is likely the mountain had been climbed in the past, though we have never heard of any ascents.

Looking east from the summit of Pucusani, Roberto and I thought neighboring Picacho Kasiri looked full of promise. With unusually dry conditions and warm temperatures prevailing at the start of December, Juan Gabriel Estellano and I decided to investigate Kasiri's slabby south face.

On December 10 we walked from the road to the base of Kasiri, following a pleasant abandoned mine trail most of the way. We climbed toward the left side of the face via an enjoyable corner and reached a large ledge. The cracks to the right looked flared, with few opportunities for good protection, so we played it safe and went left again, following another corner toward the west-southwest ridge. Once there we switched to the northwest flank, climbed one more pitch, and then moved together to the summit. On this section we were surprised to find three rusted pitons, probably originating from the 1980s. On top we were greeted by wooden sticks and a rusted tin can. We measured the height at 5,160m.

We climbed nine pitches, and although the difficulties never rose above 6a+, the real challenge was the length of the undertaking: The vertical rise from car to summit had been 950m, and we arrived on top at sunset. We decided to call the route Arajpacha, an Aymara word roughly translating as the world from above, the sky, the future, life.

After enjoying a beautiful view, we then had to make an interesting descent over unknown terrain in the dark, first scrambling down a ridge to the north, then making one rappel to the west, and finally a lot of hiking and scrambling down and around the mountain to reach the Kasiri-Pucusani col. From there we descended south to the car, reaching it at midnight, 16 hours after leaving. 📷 🔍

— ALEXANDER VON UNGERN, *ANDEAN ASCENTS, BOLIVIA*

POWER TO THE PROCESS
THREE NEW ROUTES IN THE CORDILLERA REAL

BY ETHAN BERMAN

From mid-June to mid-July, Brian Houle and I visited the Cordillera Real to explore new technical routes. Our main objectives were the southeast face of Cerro Arkhata (5,650m), believed to be unclimbed, and what's traditionally been called the south face of Mururata (5,871m), though it actually faces southwest. Both are accessed from a remote high camp at Laguna Arkhata, a spectacular glacial lake fed by the icefall of Mururata. After acclimatizing with an ascent of Huayna Potosí, we slogged nine days of supplies up to our base camp and immersed ourselves in the vast, towering faces of rock, snow, and ice spilling straight down to the lake.

As with any big mountain expedition, our success was at the mercy of conditions, weather, and health. It was a snowy year in the Real, and upon arriving at the lake we were pleased to see ice on both faces we hoped to climb. There also was a stable forecast for the week to come. Unfortunately, Brian was feeling ill. On July 6, unable to suppress my excitement, I set off solo and climbed the southwest ridge of Cerro Willa Sallaloma (ca 5,588m) in a round trip from camp of about six hours, the first known ascent.

Following shattered ledges from the base, I encountered several steep rock steps until I was forced off to the west side of the ridge. I then traversed a big ledge system to a long snow and ice gully, which I soloed in approach shoes with one ice tool, stemming onto rock where possible. Loose, rocky terrain led to the summit (400m, III 5.5 WI2). I basked in the sunshine, built a small cairn, and, after starting down the ridge toward Mururata, descended loose scree gullies to return to the lake.

Regaining camp, I found Brian feeling better, and we decided to attempt the southeast face of Arkhata the next day. Leaving camp at 2 a.m., we traversed around the lake to the foot of the face and roped up for two pitches of good water ice through the first rock band. We then soloed long snow slopes (and sometimes scree) to a mixed gully. We simul-climbed around three pitches, which had sections of fun stemming between rock and névé or unconsolidated snow. These deposited us below the large snowfield leading to the summit. Brian generously broke trail up waist-deep sugar snow leading to the summit ridge. We traversed onto the west side of the crest (which was in much

Camp at Laguna Arkhata, looking north and showing the 2018 climbs by Ethan Berman and Brian Houle. (1) The Keep (700m, III WI3+ M4) on the southeast face of Cerro Arkhata. (2) Power to the Process (750m, IV WI5 M5) on southwest face of Mururata. (3) Southwest ridge of Cerro Willa Sallaloma. *Brian Houle*

better, icy conditions) and followed it to the top. We were psyched to have realized our first big route in the area: The Keep (700m, III WI3+ M4). We mostly descended our route of ascent but were able to bypass both the mixed gully and ice pitches via easier ground, returning to camp around 11 hours after leaving. [*In 2015, Gustavo Lisi and friends climbed a route on a face well to the left of the Keep. The initial icefalls of the 2018 route may have been climbed before, but local climbers are not clear on this.*]

We then turned our attention to the much steeper southwest face of Mururata. Since arriving at the lake we had been eyeing an aesthetic, unclimbed ice runnel on the left side. Our ascent of Arkhata had not helped with Brian's recovery, so we decided on two days' rest before giving it a go.

On the 10th we left camp at 2 a.m. and climbed what was for me a dream line: a strip of perfect ice giving passage through a massive, daunting face of shattered rock. The approach involved a quick yet hazardous traverse under the band of seracs guarding the majority of the face. From the base of the route, we soloed snow in the initial gully to reach a steep rock band, then belayed two long pitches of mixed terrain, including a rock traverse with limited pro and a thin ice runnel leading to a snow band.

Above, I led a 60m pitch of stellar WI3 ice and set the belay in a small cave on the side of a steep, two-body-width vertical pillar. This proved solid and led to a section of wild stemming on rock with a ribbon of ice in between. I climbed slowly and meticulously, burdened by the thin air well above 5,000m.

Elated to be above the main technical difficulties, I led a long simul block to the top of the face, where Brian took over and broke trail up the glacial plateau to the summit. After a few photos we headed down, rappelling Goulotte Marie on Abalakov anchors. This was a more direct descent to our camp than either our route or the normal route, and it avoided the serac band.

We were thrilled to have climbed Power to the Process (750m, IV WI5 M5) in a 17-hour camp-to-camp push. The name is a reminder of how the digital and social-media era can sometimes indoctrinate us with the fallacy of instant gratification, but what is most important is to stay focused on your passions and embrace the long and sometimes convoluted process that leads to your dreams. We would like to give huge thanks to the American Alpine Club's Live Your Dream grant, the Mazamas, and Alpine Ascents International for their support in making this trip a reality. ◙

ILLIMANI, PICO NORTE (6,403M), SOUTH SPUR, 1989 ASCENT

THE ELEGANT SOUTH spur of the west ridge of Pico Norte, attempted in 2014 and reported to be unclimbed in *AAJ 2015*, was actually climbed in 1989 by Franco Maestrini's Italian expedition. As with the climbers in the 2014 attempt, the 1989 team ascended Illimani's normal route (west ridge) to a point from which they could descend northward to the upper glacier and thus reach the south spur. From the top of the spur, they traversed over Pico Norte and Illimani's main summit to descend the normal route. See historical photos at the AAJ website. 🖸

– ENRICO ROSSO, *ITALY*

CORDILLERA QUIMSA CRUZ

NEVADO ATOROMA, NORTHWEST RIDGE, VARIATION; NEVADO YAYPURI, SOUTH-SOUTHWEST FACE

MY WIFE, JEANNE, and I established a base camp by the moraines below the southern aspects of Atoroma and Yaypuri in the central Quimsa Cruz in early May. After a day spent in reconnaissance, we climbed both peaks on May 5.

On Atoroma (5,580m, 16°54'28.66"S, 67°24'58.54"W), we climbed the southwest flank of the northwest ridge (snow and ice to 55°) to reach the crest above its rocky section, then followed the ridge to the summit (AD). This was possibly a new variation to the previously climbed northwest ridge.

Looking up the Atoroma Valley with Atoroma's southwest face on the right and the rocky south and southeast faces of Yaypuri at left. Visible portions of the 2018 routes are marked; earlier routes not shown. *Aaron Zimmerman*

After descending the northwest ridge to the Atoroma-Yaypuri col, we continued down to the west, traversing under the steep rock walls of Yaypuri's southeastern flanks. We then climbed a possible new route on the 300m south face of Yaypuri (5,610m). A 40° snow slope led to the bergschrund, above which an ever-steepening slope of perfect névé (up to 65°) took us to an easing before the summit block. A short scramble on mixed terrain brought us to the top (AD+). This route is probably only viable early in the Bolivian climbing season, after the snow first consolidates but before the bergschrund becomes extremely difficult to cross. [*In 1994, Dakin Cook and Thomas Miyagawa climbed a route on the southwest face of Yaypuri, but the exact line is unknown.*]

These were both spectacular climbs in a relatively small valley, devoid of any mining activity (a rarity in present-day Quimsa Cruz), and easily accessed with public transportation. Much of the rock in this area was solid granite, and later in the season would probably offer wonderful rock routes. 🗐 🖸

– AARON ZIMMERMAN, *USA*

CORDILLERA OCCIDENTAL

SAJAMA, WEST FACE AND NORTHWEST RIDGE, DAYS TO REMEMBER

MATTHEW WARD FROM Idaho and I made an attempt in mid-July on a gray flow of ice toward the left end of the large, quasi-vertical rock barrier that characterizes the west face of Sajama (6,542m), Bolivia's highest mountain. We bailed on this super-impressive route because the ice was too poorly formed.

With Matthew back home and the weather forecast better for the Cordillera Occidental than the Real—like so many times during 2018—I decided to have another try, this time solo. I took a bus to the start of the approach and then carried a heavy sack up to the standard base camp (4,800m), where I set up my tent in a fierce snowstorm. Next day there were 90 kph winds, the sort of winds for which Sajama is well known. Fortunately, early the following day, August 6, the weather was near perfect, with no wind and a million stars in a clear sky.

Sajama (6,542m) from the west. (1) Northwest ridge (normal route). (2) Days to Remember (2018). (3) West Face—Chilean Route (1,800m from base camp, climbed by Andres Zegers, solo, in just under 7.5 hours, June 2012). (4) Southwest ridge from west-side base camp. (5) Southwest ridge from south-side base camp. All numbered ascents continued to the summit. *Robert Rauch*

I headed up the initial slopes toward the west face, this time opting for a line of black ice farther left than the one Matthew and I had eyed, close to the large icefall in a corner at the left end of the wall. (This broad icefall may have been climbed in the past, but no details are available.) The narrow strip of black ice that I climbed was a little over 100m high: 70m were vertical, and 20m of this was about 3cm thick and delicate to handle. This section I felt to be WI5+, and I took an hour to climb just a few meters—my forearms were as pumped as after a hard sport route.

Above, I continued via a system of gullies, mostly easy but beautiful and logical. These often ended in short (3m to 6m) vertical barriers of blue and white water ice. There was time to recover while climbing the easy sections, but I've never been so tired after an ice climb.

I emerged onto the northwest ridge, Sajama's normal route, and followed this to the summit, arriving at 6 p.m., 13 hours after setting out from base camp. Seventy-three years to the day before my climb, the first atomic bomb in the history of warfare was dropped on Hiroshima, Japan. Because of this, I named my route Days to Remember (WI5+ M4). I had covered 1,750m from base camp to summit. I descended the normal route and was back in base camp at 10 p.m. [*Editor's note: Previously unreported in the AAJ, Chilean climber Andres Zeger soloed a new route in the center of Sajama's west face in June 2012. See photo for the route line.*] 📷

— **ROBERT RAUCH,** *BOLIVIAN TOURS, RAUCHROBERT@HOTMAIL.COM*

Carlitos Torino opening the eighth pitch (6b) of Providencia on Pico Nordenskiöld. *Negro Jerez*

CHAÑI MASSIF, RECENT DEVELOPMENTS

CHAÑI IS A sacred mountain, the highest in Argentina's Jujuy Province at 5,949m (24°03'S, 65°44'W). It was first climbed by the Incas, who sacrificed a little boy on its summit. His body was found in 1905 and his remains deposited in a museum in Buenos Aires. An old Inca route leads to a military refuge below the massif, whose east- and south-facing walls have extensive rock climbing on orange granite.

During two weeks in November 2016, Argentine climbers Negro Jerez, Ignacio Karlen, and Carlitos Torino and Chileans Nicolás and Nicole Valderrama and Papeliyo were active in this area. The two teams made multiple first ascents of smaller spires in the area including Aguja Janajman (5,151m) via Wash 'n' Go (250m, 6b) and Aguja Chilena (5,050m, 100m, 6a+). The next day, the Argentines did the first ascent of Aguja Iñaki Coussirat, named in honor of a friend who had died on Fitz Roy, opening San Percutori (230m, 6b+) with an offwidth as the crux. They then waited out many stormy days, during which the group cleaned and improved the military shelter.

On their 10th day in the area, in unstable weather, the Argentines established a new route on the east face of Pico Nordenskiöld (5,470m). Their line linked three needle-like features interspersed with bits of scrambling. On the first needle, Aguja Julio Altamirano, they climbed five pitches with a crux chimney and an overhang that they rated 7a. They descended to a col and continued by climbing the next needle, Aguja Flor de Pupusa, encountering nice plated rock with 6b cracks for three pitches. From the top of Aguja Flor de Pupusa, they crossed the col to Aguja Intihuasi and climbed three pitches of moderate terrain to its summit. Above here, they took the easiest route due to deteriorating weather, finding sections up to 5+ and 6a. Toward the top, the rock quality decreased and it began to snow, causing them to stop short of the summit of Nordenskiöld. In a violent storm they quickly descended along the ridge to the south and descended a scree gully between Pico Nordenskiöld and Morro Von Rosen. They freed nearly the entire route, which they called Providencia (ca 1,000m, 11 pitches, 7a).

During the same time, the Chileans climbed Morro Von Rosen (5,450m) by a variation of Qhapac Ñan, a line that was established by Matías Cruz and Facundo Juárez Zapiola earlier in 2016. Their route, Variante Antofaya, involved seven pitches up to 6b.

In November 2018, a group of Argentine and French climbers opened various new routes in the Chañi massif. Argentines Martin López Abad and Martin Molina along with French climber Maud Vanpoulle, ascended a needle southeast of Morro Von Rosen, which they thought was virgin but afterwards discovered had been climbed by Martín Altamirano and Martín Castillo in 2011 (see *AAJ 2012*). The group more or less followed the 2011 line on the lower part of the climb but made a significant and more direct 6c variation on the upper section. They named this Bebe Cóndor Vuela (500m, 6c) after the condors that live in the area.

Their next objective was the south pillar of Chañi Chico (5,571m), one of the longest and steepest walls in the area. They followed a system of cracks with difficulties up to 7a. The rock quality was splendid, apart from the top section. To descend, they walked to the west toward the Morro Von Rosen cirque and then made one rappel to a point where they were

[Top] Chañi massif from the east. (A) Nevado Chañi (5,949m). (B) Morro Von Rosen. (C) Pico Nordenskiöld. (D) Chañi Chico. *Google Earth* [Bottom] The south face of Chañi Chico, showing Coca, Hypoxia y Carnavalito (600m, 7a, 2018). Another route was climbed in 2018 just to the left. *Maud Vanpoulle*

able to easily downclimb. They named their route Coca, Hypoxia y Carnavalito (600m, 7a) for the culture of northern Argentina. The next day another group of Argentines (Karlen, Torino, and Pepe de la Cuesta) opened a route slightly to the left of their line and found climbing up to 6c.

Before bad weather put an end to the trip, López Abad teamed up with Vanpoulle and opened two lines of approximately 130m next to the military refuge, grading both around 6b. 📷

— MARCELO SCANU, *ARGENTINA*

CHAÑI MASSIF, PICO NORDENSKIÖLD, ESCUDO DE LA PUNA

INSPIRED BY PHOTOS from my friend Martin López Abad, John Price, Quentin Lindfield Roberts, Will Stanhope, and I visited the Chañi massif in December. We spent 10 days based in a dusty military refugio at 4,700m. Between snowstorms and altitude hilarity, we managed four new routes in the Pico Nordenskiöld amphitheater, an east-facing basin between Chañi Chico (5,571m) and Nevado de Chañi (5,949m).

First up was a cruisy 150m 5.9 on a buttress at the entrance to the cirque, which we named El Viejo after the headwall's appearance. The granite on this climb was typical of what we encountered the rest of the trip: occasional rubble connecting buffed, burnt red stone, featured with holds and splitters.

[Top] **East side of Pico Nordenskiöld, showing approximate locations of (1) Aguja Marco Andrés, (2) Aguja Iñaki Coussirat, (3) Escudo de la Puna, (4) Providencia, and (5) El Viejo. Other routes are not shown.** [Bottom] Quentin Lindfield Roberts on 54-46 Was My Number (5.12+). *Paul McSorley (both photos)*

Our altitude-addled second route climbed a spire just left of Aguja Iñaki Coussirat. Climbed by hospitable locals Negro Jerez, Ignacio Karlen, and Carlitos Torino, that tower honors the vibrant life of Iñaki Coussirat, who died on Fitz Roy in 2015 (*see report above*). Our route on Aguja Marco Andrés remembers our beloved friend Marc-André Leclerc, a kindred spirit that places him in good company with his neighbour. The line followed elegant cracks on the east face, scrambly ridge-work, and a beautiful summit block for 200m (5.11a).

The main event took on the central pillar on the east face of Pico Nordenskiöld (5,470m). Half a dozen pitches through an impressive shield led to easier ground, where we unroped and scrambled 4th- and 5th-class to the peak of Aguja Intihuasi (named by Jerez, Karlen, and Torino, who climbed the adjacent buttress called Providencia (5.11+). We then continued unroped through a choss band that guards the upper slopes of Nordenskiöld. The summit vistas over the Salinas Grandes salt flats to the high volcanoes dotting the western horizon were literally breathtaking. Our line, Escudo de la Puna, is 500m and goes at 5.11a. We descended the ridge to the south and cut down an east-facing gully that took us past Aguja Marco Andrés and into a meadow in the center of the amphitheater.

The last frigid day of the mission was spent watching Will and Quentin exchange laps on a beautiful west-facing crack about 100m east of El Viejo. Will eventually dispatched the pitch and christened it 54-46 Was My Number. This 30m 5.12+ is likely the hardest pitch in the zone.

The Chañi massif has heaps of potential for new rock routes on walls up to 600m and ridges that exceed 900m. With some planning and help from gracious locals, a trip to this unique part of the world will prove unforgettable.

— PAUL MCSORLEY, *CANADA*

RIOJA PROVINCE, TRAVERSE OF NEVADOS DE FAMATINA

IN AUGUST, ARGENTINES Griselda Moreno (leader), Ramiro García, Paula Miranda, and Lelo Saldaña made the first traverse of all the summits of Nevados de Famatina in Argentina's Rioja Province. This traverse was attempted unsuccessfully five times in the 1990s, and it was particularly interesting this time because it was done in the austral winter.

The climbers started the traverse at the north end, at Puesto Tres Piedras, and finished at the ancient gold and silver mine of La Mejicana on August 28 after climbing seven summits of 5,778m to 6,122m in nine days. They had high winds that destroyed a tent and passed by ancient Incan ruins near Negro Overo, the latter being a sacred mountain were deer horn offerings were found decades before. 🔘

– MARCELO SCANU, *ARGENTINA*

MENDOZA PROVINCE, CERRO EL ESCAMPE AND CERRO COPLA BLANCA

FROM OCTOBER 13 to 21, Ramiro Casas and Glauco Muratti explored a *quebrada* (valley) that flows into the Tupungato River south of Punta de Vacas. The pair crossed the Tupongato with difficulty and then walked to the east and southeast along an unnamed creek to reach their first target: an unclimbed mountain they called Cerro El Escampe (4,571m, 32°55'36"S, 69°38'54"W), approximately 12km up the valley. This mountain is west of two big cols that link the unnamed creek with Quebrada Colorada to the north. The two started on the southwest face and then followed the south-southeast ridge before finishing on the upper east face, on the second day of bad weather, finding rotten rock (grade II) and 50° snow.

They then climbed Cerro Copla Blanca (4,630m, 32°55'11"S, 69°42'37"W), the highest summit along the ridge that separates the unnamed creek from Quebrada Negra to its south. Their route on the northeast face had 55° snowy slopes and some rotten rock (grade II), and because of the conditions could not be protected. The overall grade was PD. 🔘

– MARCELO SCANU, *ARGENTINA*

CORDÓN DEL PLATA, CERRO VALLECITOS, RECENT ROUTES

LOCATED WEST OF Mendoza, the Cordón del Plata offers easy access for climbers and a great training ground for nearby Aconcagua. Cerro Vallecitos (5,475m) is one of the highest and most climbed peaks in the range, with an easy ascent via the normal route (south ridge), which was first completed in 1946 by Francisco Ibañez, Ricardo Lopéz Susso, and Luis Vila. The east side is much steeper, and a number of long routes have been established.

In September 2016, Diego Cofone, Matías Hidalgo Nicosia, and Agustín Piccolo opened a line on the east face of Vallecitos, naming it Divina Providencia (1,200m, D+ WI2/3 70°). They made their base camp at El Salto (4,200m) and departed at 11:30 p.m. Their route begins to the right of De Paso Canazo (1,000m, AD WI4 M3, Fiorenza–Pontoriero, 2011) and the Original Route, established in 1953 by Boucher, Memelsdorff, and Waltz.

They began up a couloir, encountering mostly 40° to 50° névé until reaching a short (3m) section of 90° ice. A long rightward traverse brought them to more moderate couloirs and a section of waterfall ice halfway up the face. After a pitch of WI2/3, they continued up mixed terrain, which proved difficult to navigate in the dark. Eight hours after they began climbing, they reached the summit and began their descent via the normal route.

Matías Hidalgo returned the following year with Chicho Fracchia and Matías Sindoni, and in October 2017 they opened a route on the southeast face of Vallecitos, left of previously established climbs, calling it Cascadas del Viento (600m, MD WI5). They left their camp at El Salto around 5 a.m. and crossed the glacier to the base of the face. The crux of the route came in the first few pitches: difficult ice climbing, including a 15m section of 90° to 95° ice. In total, 100m of steep waterfall ice deposited them about halfway up the route. From there, the difficulties eased and they ascended moderate snow couloirs to the south ridge, encountering good névé up to 70°. They reached the summit nine hours after they began climbing. 🖭

— MARCELO SCANU, *ARGENTINA*

CERRO PUNTA YAMAKAWA, SOUTH FACE, SKI DESCENT

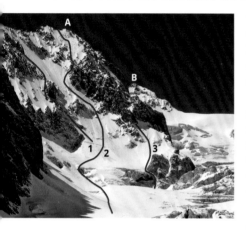

(A) Cerro Punta Yamakawa, showing (1) Morales-Mondragón (2004), (2) the first known ski descent of the south face, mostly along the 1979 Pardo-Peña climbing route, and (3) Ben Dare solo (2011). (B) Cerro Cortaderas. *Billy Haas*

ON OCTOBER 13, Diego Saez Beros, Adam Fabrikant, and I made a ski descent of the south face of Cerro Punta Yamakawa (4,967m) in the mountains just east of Santiago, Chile. This was the first leg of our annual autumn pilgrimage to the central Andes.

We began our trip on October 10, leaving Santiago for Valle de Las Arenas and spending our first night in the climber refuge. The weather was unsettled, and what should have been a single-day approach to a high camp at the base of the Cortaderas Glacier took two days. The second day allowed us to study the south face of Yamakawa, our primary objective.

The idea to ski this face had come from a trip that Adam and Diego did to the area in 2016. (Diego had previously made descents of the Cortaderas Glacier and the tamer northeast side of Yamakawa. Adam had previously made a descent of Cerro Cortaderas on its eastern flank. To our knowledge, there has not yet been a descent of 5,197-meter Cortaderas from the top of its summit pyramid.) The proposed descent of Yamakawa grew in significance for us after our good friend Caleb Ladue tragically passed away in a crevasse fall on the Cortaderas Glacier, directly beneath the south face of Yamakawa, in fall 2017.

On October 13, the four of us left our camp at 3,900m just before sunrise. After an hour of ascending the Cortaderas Glacier, Aaron decided to stay behind; he was feeling a bit sick from the altitude. The rest of us reached the summit before noon and were treated to cloudless blue skies with little wind.

We began our descent directly from the summit and roughly skied down the 1979 Pardo-Peña climbing route. [*There are at least two other technical routes up to M4+ located left and right of this route, climbed by Morales-Mondragón in 2004 and Ben Dare in 2011; see AAJ 2012.*] We found 50cm to 60cm of stable, fresh snow on the face, but hidden rocks kept us cautious. On the upper headwall, we were fortunate to find an improbable yet clean line through fluted rock bands—an incredible experience in downhill route-finding. Once on the middle portion of the face, clean fall-line skiing at around 45° brought us down to the Cortaderas Glacier. The descent was around 900m to the bottom of the face. Afterwards, we remarked at this being the deepest snow we had ever skied in technical terrain. 🖭

— BILLY HAAS, *USA*

Szu-ting Yi paddling across Lago Huahuahue below Cerro Esquinero, on which she and Dave Anderson climbed two new routes in February 2018. The left line is Ice Cream Tempura (490m, 5.10 R C1), and on the right is Rising from the Ashes (880m, 5.11 C1). *Dave Anderson*

CERRO ESQUINERO, NORTHEAST AND NORTHWEST FACES

ON JANUARY 29, 2018, my wife, Szu-ting Yi, and I met Juan Carlos Martinez, a fisherman in Villa La Angostura, Argentina. He warily eyed the two out-of-place foreigners with bulging packs filled with climbing equipment, camping gear, packrafts, and food for 20 days. Eventually, he shook his head and motioned us toward his skiff. Without fluency in a common language, we let the small outboard motor fill the silence as the bow of the boat cleaved Lago Nahuel Huapi in two perfect halves.

Looking for a climbing objective in Patagonia, I had searched "patagonia, cliff" on Google and filtered through the resulting images. Eventually, I saw an image of unique-looking cliff by a lake. The lake was Lago Huahuahue, and I discovered the cliff to be Cerro Esquinero (1,920m). More online sleuthing led to the coordinates of the lake, about 40km northwest of Bariloche. I discovered many trekkers had ascended the low-angled south side to the summit of Cerro Esquinero, but what about the 800m granite walls on the north?

Once onshore, we followed a horse trail for 4.5km and camped next to the Refugio José Diem, a small hut below Cerro Colorado (1,850m). The next morning we started a 20km off-trail journey. In 2011, the nearby Cordon Caulle volcano had erupted, spewing more than 100 million tons of ash into the sky and literally burying the surrounding area. The drifted ash made hiking with our monstrous packs an exercise in patience. We spent the next three days following and losing the tracks of the South American cougar and huemul deer, while Andean condors monitored our progress overhead. The final day of the approach found us thrashing through and then clinging to dense beech shrubs as we descended a near vertical slope to the Huahuahue Valley. Impassable vegetation on the valley floor forced us to slosh through a thigh-deep bog and then wade down a chest-high, slow-moving river. But by nightfall we were camped on the pristine western edge of Lago Huahuahue.

The northeast wall of Cerro Esquinero rises 800m directly above the lake. We paddled across the translucent water on February 4, moored our packrafts to a chockstone at daybreak, and started

Szu-ting Yi at the start of the crux pitch of Rising from the Ashes. *Dave Anderson*

climbing. We followed a slabby, sometimes vegetated crack running with meltwater from the summit snowfields and quickly climbed seven pitches. Then the wall steepened, the temperature neared 80 degrees, and our pace withered. Fishing for a hand jam in a small depression filled with water, I felt something wriggle between my fingers. I yanked my hand back to reveal half a dozen tadpoles. They were happily squirming around in a pool the size of a milk jug 300m above the lake.

Sun, no wind, almost too hot to climb, now tadpoles on the route—was I really climbing a first ascent in Patagonia? The reminder came in the form of a buzzing cloud of vicious tábanos, biting horseflies the size of quarters that were our constant companions. Despite the heat, I pulled my hood over my helmet in an attempt to maintain my sanity against these winged devils.

After tadpoles, tábanos, and pitch after pitch of polished granite, an unstable chockstone the size of a dump truck, oozing with moss and other vegetation, blocked our way just 10m from the top of the wall. Not willing to give up, we rapped 50m to a flat ledge and bivied with nothing but our rain gear to ward off the cold. In the darkness my headlamp caught the reflection of two tiny eyes as a Las Bayas frog hopped away from my beam. The morning light brought warmth but no obvious route-finding solution. After climbing a few dead ends, we began rappelling back to our rafts.

Less than a week later, we were again bivying on a ledge 400m off the ground, this time on the northwest face of Cerro Esquinero, and this time we'd brought our down quilt. The route to this point had been a mix of steep corners and smooth, low-angle slabs. My biggest achievement for the day had been convincing Szu-ting to link a licheny fist crack and a hard, mossy 5.10+ offwidth flare, so I didn't have to lead either one.

Directly above our bivy, a series of spectacular dihedrals split by perfect-looking cracks stretched toward the summit. Some looked like they would require bolts, and all would require cleaning. With little food and a questionable weather window, we opted to traverse 150m to the east next morning and found an easier series of cracks. Szu-ting led up the crux and best pitch of the route, a laser-cut 5.11 C1 finger crack that stretched almost a full rope length. Above, I suffered through a run-out, loose, and wet layback that brought us to a long corner system and the top of the wall. The sun was setting as we scrambled 500m to the summit of Cerro Esquinero. We quickly descended several hundred meters down a low-angled couloir and then made one more bivouac before the bottom.

After resting for a day, we packed up our base camp and paddled 1.5km across Lago Huahuahue on February 14, aiming to return by descending into the Milliquo River drainage to the east. We were unable to find the horse trail, and our descent ended up taking two full days of bushwhacking, river navigating, and slippery slab traversing. As we arrived on the shore of Lago Nahuel Huapi, the wind picked up and sent whitecaps across the lake, as cirrus clouds overhead predicted the end to our amazing stretch of good weather. Tomorrow a boat would shuttle us back to Bariloche. We cooked dinner on the beach and relaxed in the evening glow of our last day in the wilderness of Northern Patagonia.

– DAVE ANDERSON, *USA*

CENTRAL PATAGONIA / AYSÉN REGION

SOUTH AVELLANO TOWER, EAST FACE

FAR FROM THE ever-connected hustle of modern life, deep in the heart of northern Chilean Patagonia, the pristine granite faces and snowy caps of the Avellano Towers rise up from a hidden valley at the head of the Avellano River. They say the best things come to those who wait, which is good, seeing as this was to be my third attempt on a virgin wall among the Avellano Towers.

The legend Jim Donini was good enough to introduce Dave Brown and me to this spectacular area several years ago. On that first trip, back in February 2014 (*see AAJ 2015*), we kicked off the week with a 300m first ascent on the Tooth with Jim. What we saw across from us, however, almost made our jaws hit the ledge. The pristine east face of South Avellano Tower, to our knowledge, had never even been attempted. How big was it? We didn't know, but we had to try.

The first ascent of the east face of South Avellano Tower (900m, E5 6a, Crook-McCune-Sim-Swail), completed in January 2018 after two previous expeditions. *John Crook*

We optimistically scoped a line of continuous-looking grooves leading to the halfway ledges. The glacially polished granite was of El Cap quality but smoother than expected—before long we were lowering to the ground. We attempted to follow another groove but met with the same fate. Our third attempt got us onto the face, but featured a circuitous route in which little altitude was gained, forcing us to abort. The afternoon was spent staring up at the monolith that had repelled us, realizing we were going to need reinforcements.

Dave and I returned in December of that same year with Andy Reeve and Will Harris to attempt a direct line up the center of the face. Our approach was altogether heavier and required us to explore a new approach from the one Jim had shown us. This time we crossed the huge, rough Lago General Carrera in a small, overloaded boat, after which gauchos and their horses took our gear 30km up the beautiful Avellano River valley from the southeast. We then made multiple load carries through glacial rivers, marsh, forest, and moraine. Things started well, but our first attempt was thwarted by a cold storm that left icy ghosts guarding the face.

Returning to collect our gear, we found our first 80m fixed rope was missing! A car-size flake had peeled off from high on the wall, slicing through the rope and leaving blocks strewn all over the ledges. Dave made a heroic lead through a huge roof crack with only half a set of cams and wires to gain the lines above and recover our gear in a torrential downpour. We gave up on any further attempts that year. [*Editor's note: An American expedition in January 2015 also made an attempt on this face, but was turned around after 400m. See AAJ 2016.*]

In January 2018 I returned for a third attempt with John McCune, Will Sim, Paul Swail, and my girlfriend, Ruth Bevan. Jim Donini and his wife Angela's limitless hospitality makes returning to one of the biggest wilderness areas in the world like popping by to see old friends. Following much poor weather in December, conditions gradually improved. Our base camp was idyllic,

Will Sim follows an exposed traverse on the east face of South Avellano Tower, with the Avellano Valley stretching out far below. *Paul Swail*

with running water and plenty of wood nearby. A lean-to made for a sociable shelter, while cooking lessons from Ruth made for excellent eating. By the time camp was fully established, the wall was more or less dry enough to climb.

We made quick progress on my original line, setting ropes to the halfway ledges over the first two days. These pitches follow a soaring line of cracks and grooves through a smooth shield of rock, allowing a spectacular passage of only moderate difficulty. Poor weather threatened to move in by the end of the next day, so we made the decision to go for it immediately.

We gained the top of the fixed ropes by daybreak and attacked the headwall in two pairs. The rock became more varied, with some areas of exfoliating rock. The main weakness centered around a huge corner system, but after a couple of damp pitches, we were forced to quit this. I followed steep and strenuous cracks up the left wall to a ledge, which appeared to be a dead-end. Paul then quested up a steep groove, overcoming increasingly unlikely terrain. After placing a peg in a very awkward position, he made steep moves through a roof on chicken heads, leading to an outrageously exposed traverse back to the top of the corner.

From here I made a long, bold traverse back right over compact black rock to reach a viable groove. An intricate pitch led to some burly laybacking around a roof, and before long we were pulling onto the north face, where easy ground led to a final ramp. We topped out around 5 p.m., with the rising Patagonian winds already threatening to sweep us from the summit. Ruth had traced our progress from base camp and prepared a roaring fire, pumpkin curry, and cheesecake for our return. All pitches were led free by at least one of us. After three trips, the east face of South Avellano Tower (900m, E5 6a/5.11d) was complete.

Our quick ascent left plenty of time for other climbs around the valley, including adventures with Ruth. We climbed three more routes between the five of us, including the Last Gaucho (E5 6B) and a variation to that route on a formation we began calling "Cerro Square Face," northeast of the main towers, and a brilliant easier face, Chicken Run (600m E2), on a formation near Square Face called Aonikenk (*see report below*). 📄 📷

– JOHN CROOK, *U.K.*

AVELLANO TOWERS, SKYLINE TRAVERSE

FROM FEBRUARY 8–26, 2018, Rodrigo Lobo Villarroel (Bolivia) and I climbed in the Avellano Towers, which we reached from Chile Chico up the Avellano Valley—this is the southeast approach, which is the more expensive but "inspiring" option. Starting with a one-day boat ride, we then acquired horse support from a man named Brulio for the final two days to base camp.

Rodrigo and I first climbed the east face of Avellano Tower by the previously established

Avellano pal Verano (360m, TD- 5.10, *AAJ 2006*). Next, we established a possible new route or variation up the central wall of "Cerro Square Face," located just northeast from the main towers, which went at E4 6c+. [*This route appears similar to the Last Gaucho (E5 6b), established one month prior in January 2018; see previous report.*]

Our trip culminated in an epic, three-day, north-to-south link-up of all of the seven major summits via the Skyline Traverse. This was a hell of an adventure, as we endeavored to stick to the real skyline at all times. We encountered pitches up to 5.11+ and soloed about 80 percent of the traverse.

We exited the area to the northeast, which is the "quick" option. This involved a 14km walk to a 4x4 we had arranged to meet. It's approximately 39km total to the main road from the base camp. ▣

– JAMES MONEYPENNY, *U.K.*

AVELLANO TOWERS, THE TOOTH, SOUTH-SOUTHEAST FACE; AONIKENK, AUMKENK AIKE

IN JANUARY 2018, our three-woman team from the U.K., comprised of Michelle O'Loughlin, Freja Shannon, and me, set off to explore the long and wild Avellano Valley. After a hard-going approach from the village of Bahía Murta, beginning January 4, and a few stormy days in base camp, we lucked out as a high-pressure system rolled in on January 10.

From left to right: "Cerro Square Face," climbed by the center of the wall facing the camera; spire attempted by U.K. women's team; and Aonikenk, climbed by two routes. All attempts and ascents were in early 2018. *Sasha Doyle*

The following day we established a new route on the Tooth, where we climbed eight varied pitches (HVS to E2). After some quite easy, loose alpine terrain, we followed a series of traversing crack systems to gain the slabby, south-southeast face in the vicinity of and just right of the route Filo Suroeste (*AAJ 2016*). We call the route Route Canal (250m, E2 5b).

On January 14 we made the first ascent of a tower to the northeast of the main towers. Our route, Aumkenk Aike (400m, 5.10, meaning "travelers stop" in the Mapuche language), ascends the south-southwest face and ridge. We called the peak Aonikenk (GPS 1,721m, 46°25'19"S, 72°28'43"W) after the indigenous people (also known as Tehuelche) of Patagonia. Reaching the peak from our camp required a two-hour approach and a gully scramble. From half-height in this gully, we navigated slabs and 5.6–5.8 territory followed by steeper 5.9–5.10 ground and an awkward corner that ended in a rounded, undercut traverse. Trending rightward, we followed the southwest ridge for another 100m to the top. We descended via the northwest ridge with three abseils and downclimbing to reach the same approach gully.

On January 15, we briefly attempted to climb a spire we had spotted between "Cerro Square Face" and Aonikenk but lacked good weather and energy. After running out of food, and with the weather turning, we began our retreat to the safety of Bahía Murta on January 20. [*See a full trip report PDF at the AAJ website.*]

We were determined to make this an all-female trip to inspire and promote females in the outdoors and feel chuffed to have had a successful expedition. We are just three women that shared a simple, inner drive to go out and do something a bit mad. ▤ ▣

– SASHA DOYLE, *U.K.*

On top of Cerro Don Antonio (1,803m) on the northern Erasmo Icefield. *Besser Collection*

"NO STEREOSCOPIC VISION"
OFF THE MAP ON THE ERASMO ICEFIELD IN CHILEAN PATAGONIA

BY PABLO BESSER

IN THE WINTER of 2006, during a plane flight to San Rafael Lagoon to begin the first north-south winter crossing of the Northern Patagonian Icefield, I saw through the window a huge mass of ice surrounded by impenetrable forests and a glacier that almost touched the ocean. It was the Erasmo Icefield (a.k.a. Erasmus Icefield, approximately 46°9'S, 73°8'W), an ice mass of about 165 square kilometers that is just 7km away from the sea; however, because of its geography, surrounding mountains, and forests, it cannot be seen from the sea. This has helped keep it hidden from visitors.

From the west, you can access the Erasmo from Cupquelan Fjord, an arm of the long Canal Moraleda. From Erasmo Bay, you can follow the Sorpresa River and then a small tributary, El Pájaro, past a series of three lakes, across a mountain pass, and end up at the main tongue of the Erasmo Glacier, flowing down from the larger icefield.

However, what in 2006 was a glacier enclosed by rock walls is today a large lake surrounded by rock walls, with the glacier shrinking into these waters. For our first expedition, the definitive access would be via water, and we would have to carry packrafts to reach the icefield.

· NOVEMBER 2017 ·

TOGETHER WITH TWO Chilean friends, Tomas Torres and Juan Fco. Bustos, we left Santiago for three weeks to explore the access to Erasmo and maybe climb something. On November 1, we rode a speed boat to the end of the Cupquelan Fjord, and from there, over three days, we went up the valley of the Sorpresa River (meaning "Surprise") and then followed the small and narrow but strong stream El Pájaro ("The Bird"). The weather was very nice, even warm.

On the fourth day we reached the system of three small lakes, which we crossed using pack-rafts. Climbing over a mountain pass that we named Paso Rata, we arrived at the lake at the

toe of the Erasmo Glacier—magical, and possibly one of the most spectacular, hidden places in Patagonia. We were the first to set foot there.

The next morning, we assembled our boats and donned dry suits because of the cold water, and we began to navigate between icebergs and granite walls in the lake, colored white by its heavy load of glacial sediments. We reached the other side and climbed onto the glacier, ascending its southern side. At the end of the day, we reached a beautiful small lake overlooking the glacier and Erasmo Lake; we christened it Laguna Canquenes.

Bad weather arrived that afternoon, and it rained for four days in a row, leaving us stranded at the small lake. Running out of time, we decided to head out with two days' worth of food and equipment. We followed the

Areas west and northwest of Lago General Carrera in Chile's vast Aysén region. In the lower left is the northern terminus of the North Patagonian Icefield. (1) Monte San Valentín. (2) Cuerno de Plata, which saw its second known ascent in 2018 (see p.234). Extending to the west-northwest of (P) Puerto Río Tranquilo is the long Exploradores Valley, from which the first ascents of (3) Cerro Pinuer, (4) Cerro Caballo, and (5) Cerro Cheuco were made (see p.232). Above the northern arm of the lake is (B) Bahía Murta, the beginning of one approach to the Avellano Towers (off the map to the east). Also shown is the newly explored Erasmo Icefield, with the 2017 northern approach following the Sorpresa and El Pájaro rivers from Cupquelan Fjord, and the 2018 southern approach climbing up along the Teresa River. The four summits marked are (6) Cerro Mirador del Erasmo, (7) Cerro Teresa, (8) Cerro Don Bigote, and (9) Cerro Don Antonio. *Erik Rieger, base map Google Earth*

valley to its end and accessed the plateau of the icefield by a small, lateral glacier, where we set up camp at 1,150m. That same afternoon we quickly went out to climb a nearby unnamed mountain, which we called Cerro Mirador del Erasmo. This was an easy climb on snow and rock, but it allowed us to see the glacial lakes of Erasmo on a somewhat stormy afternoon.

On November 11 we left very early to reach the main summit of the glacier, a hill 3km south of our camp and approximately 900m higher. We covered that distance by crossing snow slopes and some crevasses, but nothing difficult. However, clouds entered quickly from the Pacific, threatening to leave us in a whiteout and unable to find the summit. Neither GPS nor cartography were of any help because the area is just a white blob on the map labeled "no stereoscopic vision." At the end, we barely beat the clouds in reaching the summit of what would now be Cerro Teresa (1,947m). We descended with equanimity, surrounded by the storm and just following our footsteps.

Short of food and time, we started our return. We chose to go more directly by the south side of the Erasmo Glacier until we reached the lakes. Then we navigated the rivers on our packrafts, covering ground very quickly until the rain came. For the rest of the days, it rained nonstop. This would have been nothing more than an inconvenience had it not been for the passage of the Los Pájaros, which contains a very narrow sector, 3km long, that was too dangerous to raft and required several crossings of the river on foot. To be precise, there were 22 river crossings.

[Clockwise from top left] **Chain of lakes west of the icefield, seen from the Paso Rata; fording the upper Rio el Pájaro in heavy rain; Cerro Teresa (1,947m) from Erasmo Lake; and Pablo Besser crossing the Pájaro.** *Besser Collection*

With rain the crossings became very difficult, with several of them requiring the use of roped belays. After five days of fighting with the river, we finally reached the sea. The next day we were picked up by the same speed boat and returned to civilization after 90km of new ground explored and 19 days of adventures.

· NOVEMBER 2018 ·

ALTHOUGH PATAGONIA IS associated with difficult mountains, technical climbs, and complex meteorology, there is still room for classical mountaineering and exploration. These journeys seek to solve the simple issues of reaching the mountain and overcoming what difficulties the mountain will offer without the help of previous reports or experiences. After our 2017 journey, we felt that Erasmo still offered a lot to explore.

Again, with Tomas Torres, and now Alonso Fuentes, we decided to explore the northeast side of the Erasmo Icefield. We would reach it by the upper valley of the Teresa River.

We flew to Coyhaique and then began our journey toward the icefield from the Exploradores Valley to the south. Going up the Teresa Valley would involve multiple river crossings. These were initially impossible due to the intense rain of the previous days—and it was still pouring—so we waited four days to go up the Teresa.

We traveled with a local muleteer and carried our loads on horses for 22km. The upper valley of the Teresa ends in a wide area of glaciers and rock walls of very poor quality. There was only one potential access point through a large and steep talus ridge, and then across a snow ridge, that might allow us to reach the icefield above. Finally, after two days carrying loads, we reached the ice plateau of Erasmo on the afternoon of November 27. This is a large plain, 5km wide, which to the east leads to the valley of the Murta River and, to the west, toward the Pacific Ocean.

[Clockwise from top] **Cerro Bigote, near the high camp of the 2018 expedition; unclimbed "Cerro Erasmo" (ca 1,900m), located in a very remote setting northeast of the icefield; Chilean explorer Pablo Besser during the 2018 expedition.** *Besser Collection*

The next day, we attempted to reach a hill we could see to the north, possibly the highest in the area. The characteristic bad weather, with low clouds and strong wind increasing rapidly though the morning, prevented us from going very far, and we returned to our camp on the ice. That same afternoon, it cleared up a bit and we set off to climb a small summit near the camp, now called Cerro Don Bigote (1,726m, 46°9'3.28"S, 73°8'.82"W). From the summit, we saw Mt. Teresa, the peak we had ascended the previous year, and the massif of San Valentín to the south, also an old acquaintance. At night, the bad weather reached camp and stayed with us for two days.

On November 30 we went to look for the main peak of the Erasmo Icefield. In four hours we crossed the plateau to the north and started to follow a series of small tops. We were surrounded by clouds, barely orienting ourselves with the GPS and by brief glimpses through the fog. A long slope of ice took us to a small terrace with a very curious rock formation surrounded by ice. After this, we finally accessed the summit ridge and then the peak, which we called Cerro Don Antonio (1,803m, 46°6'33.36"S, 73°6'3.87"W). It was a classic, small, and very airy peak. On one side was the valley of the Murta River, on the other the valley of the Engaño River, and, far away, I thought I could see the sea.

After this ascent, there was no other significant summit to reach in the icefield. However, close by, to the northeast, is a peak the old maps call "Cerro Erasmo." It is not actually within the Erasmo Icefield, but it may be about 1,900m. It appears very difficult to reach this peak. A different approach would be necessary—a very long one—likely up the Murta River, and there would be several lake crossings.

In the final days, the weather did not help us much. There was no time to visit this Cerro Erasmo, and we started back. Our descent was made by following the Teresa River in packrafts, enjoying every row and turn of the river.

These two explorations to a lost place—but, at the same time, very close in Patagonia—exemplify how there are still places for a simpler mountaineering, one that leaves room to enjoy every moment in the mountains as if they were the first. 🖸

[Left] Cerro Pinuer with the route up its north side. [Right] Ross Balharry traversing a snow slope on Cerro Chueco, with a view to the northeast. Cerro Redondo is in the right foreground. *Javier Galleani Calderón*

EXPLORADORES VALLEY: THREE FIRST ASCENTS

After four years of working in the Exploradores Valley, west of Puerto Río Tranquilo, and always looking at these incredible and barely explored mountains, it seemed time to invest some effort to climb some of these peaks. I was sure the views from up high would be amazing.

In May 2018, I met a travelling Scottish fellow, Ross Balharry. He was super-motivated and seemed to be related to the Terminator—like a machine! We first climbed together in the Cordillera Castillo, and I immediately proposed that we try Cerro Chueco (ca 1,900m, 46°29'06"S, 73°00'14"W; see map on p.229) in the Exploradores Valley during the next good weather window.

Good conditions arrived in late May. Our initial idea was to climb a gully called El Dedo ("the finger") to gain access to Cerro Chueco. To get there we had to cross Río Norte, and at first the river was too swollen to cross. Looking at the map, we saw an avalanche path on the mountain's east shoulder that would connect us to the summit, and below this the river was wider and the water was only hip deep. We climbed via the avalanche path—there wasn't enough snow to pose a danger—and made a bivy at its exit. The panorama was incredible, with the north face of San Valentín in all its glory.

At 3 a.m. we left for the summit under a full moon and perfect snow conditions. A giant crevasse cut horizontally across an 80° slope on the mountain's eastern slope; luckily, it was covered by a solid snow bridge. After the crevasse, the slope eased to 60° with steps to 70°, so we decided to continue unroped to the summit, which we reached at full sunrise at 7:30 a.m. In perfect weather, all that remained was to contemplate the 360° view of the mountains. The icefields to the north commanded most of our attention, and we could see many future projects.

In January 2019, with the Exploradores Valley still very much on my mind, and a weather window that could not be missed, I spoke with my friend Luis Torres, who is from Puerto Río Tranquilo, about another climb. We decided on what appears to be the highest peak in the valley at 2,300m (46°36'54"S, 72°56'10"W). We called the unnamed peak Cerro Pinuer, in respect to don Iram Pinuer, who has resided below the peak for the majority of his life.

We ascended from Iram Pinuer's home, 20km into the Exploradores Valley. Upon leaving the forest, we set off in the direction of the north ridge. We made a bivy before the ridge—the plan was to leave at night because of expected warm daytime temperatures, and we wanted to be on the summit at sunrise.

We set off at 3:30 a.m. The first obstacle was an arête of third- and fourth-class rock. Above, the snow was in perfect condition. We followed the slope of the ridge, which was about 60° with steps up to 75°, and arrived at the summit at 7:15 a.m. on another epic windless and cloudless day.

We downclimbed quickly under the warming temperatures, and by 9:30 a.m. we were in a safe area, just in time for the peak to begin sloughing off ice, snow, and rock. We got to our bivouac, threw everything in the packs, and continued on in the direction of the road, happy about a new summit, while the horseflies and the heat followed us all the way.

In the first days of February 2019, another good weather window arrived, our motivation was still intact, and the hills were dry—all ideal for an attempt on Cerro Caballo (ca 1,900m, 46°33'32"S, 72°59'02"W), an unclimbed peak with a few prior attempts. Francisco Croxatto, an explorer of the valley, told me about a route that would get us close to the summit. I invited my friends Nicolas Valderrama and Jenifer Reyes (Colombia) on this project. We began the hike on a cloudy day, ideal for walking, but the forest was brutal, comprised of prickly *taique* and *chaura* shrubs. After five hours we bivouacked just past the boundary of the undergrowth.

Approaching the summit tower on Cerro Caballo, climbed by the north ridge, facing the camera. *Javier Galleani Calderón*

The following morning, we set off at 5 a.m. for the summit. We first had to ascend a stream-fed gully by some rock steps. Above this, a band of snow and 30m of fourth-class rock brought us closer to the north ridge. The main needle stood approximately 120m above. Jenifer led the first fifth-class pitch. We unroped for a section of fourth-class, and then I led another fifth-class pitch. Finally, an easy climb led us to the summit of Cerro Caballo by about 10:30 a.m.

We downclimbed and made two rappels to get to our bivouac, then continued to the road, but not without another hard battle in the forest, which made us question why we even like to journey in the mountains. Yet, the following day saw us happily drinking beers and planning our next peak.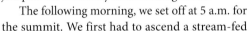

— JAVIER GALLEANI CALDERÓN, *CHILE, TRANSLATED BY PAM RANGER ROBERTS*

HISTORICAL NOTES ON THE EXPLORADORES VALLEY: *Until recently this area was extremely remote. The road connecting Puerto Río Tranquilo west to Bahía Exploradores was not finished until around 2010, and before this the climbs described above would have required two to four days of approach. The teams that managed to access this area were good explorers but lacked the technical skills to tackle difficult climbs.*

In 1938, when access to the Chilean settlements around Lago General Carrera was still extremely difficult, the explorer Augusto Grosse hypothesized that the Erasmo Icefield, north of the valley, was not connected to the main ice plateau to the south. The Exploradores Valley, he reasoned, might offer an ice-free way to connect the Aysén province to the sea. It took Grosse three attempts and several months in the field to complete the crossing and show the feasibility of the route, a feat finally achieved in 1943, just one year before aerial surveys finally revealed the intricate geography of the Patagonian icefields.

After this, the valley wasn't visited by many climbers, perhaps because the high peak of San Valentín captured all their attention, and the best routes to this summit are to the west and south. An attempt via the Exploradores was made by the Chilean team of W. Millar, Sergio Saldivia, Juan Vargas, and Daniel Vidal in 1981, but their expedition ended in tragedy when Vidal died of hypothermia, and their purported ascent from the north is still doubted. The most notable exploration in the area was done by Bill Stephenson (New Zealand) in 1979 and the Gino Buscaini and Silvia Metzeltin (Italy) in 2000. However, these expeditions reached summits with only modest technical difficulties.

The new road through Exploradores Valley gives easy access to some of the most amazing Patagonian landscapes, and this has sparked a boom in tourism. Guides like Javier Galleani, leading tours over the Exploradores Glacier, are in prime position to explore amazing unclimbed peaks.

— CAMILO RADA, *CHILE*

Cerro Cuerno de Plata (center-left) and Monte San Valentin (right) from the northeast. The only known route on Cuerno de Plata is from the south, first completed in 1969 and repeated in 2017. *Pablo Besser*

CERRO CUERNO DE PLATA, SECOND KNOWN ASCENT

In December 2017, Australian climbers Colin Barton, Callum Hawkins, Paul Plank, Geoff Robb, Annette Skirka, Raymond Alfred Smith, Neil Thomas, and mountain guides Sören Kruse, Carlos Vasquez, and Steffen Welsch made the second known ascent of Cerro Cuerno de Plata (3,725m; sometimes called Cuerno del Plata, Tararua, or Silberhorn). The peak is just southeast of Monte San Valentín (4,058m) and is considered the second- or third-highest summit in Patagonia, alongside Valentín and Cerro San Lorenzo (3,706m). It was first ascended by a New Zealand expedition in 1969 from the south (*see AAJ 1971*).

We ascended the south side, passing through a crevasse field, and the maximum steepness was 35°. While the ascent of Cerro Cuerno de Plata is technically straightforward, the landscape on the Northern Patagonian Icefield is just magnificent, and the fact that we had this wilderness all to ourselves was an added bonus. The exposed summit provided a tremendous view of the east face of Monte San Valentín and Lago General Carrera and was a friendly reminder that we have more business there—simply brilliant!

—STEFFEN WELSCH, *GERMANY,* AND SÖREN KRUSE, *DENMARK*

Cerro Aguda's west ridge (right) viewed from the north. The peak was first climbed in 1970 from the south. *Matt Lemke*

CERRO AGUDA (WEST SUMMIT), WEST RIDGE

In February, Itai Cohen, Elaine Kennedy, and I made an ascent of the west ridge of Cerro Aguda (2,641m, also called Cerro Agudo or Aguja Aguda) on the eastern margin of the North Patagonian Icefield. (*See map on p.229.*) The peak had been climbed previously from the south (*AAJ 1971*). This was an all-encompassing adventure in which the journey to reach the mountain was easily the crux.

Cerro Aguda dominates the southern side of Lago Leones, amid dozens of inspiring peaks, with the west ridge plainly visible along the skyline from the lake. Large icefalls flow from the mountains and cascade into the water. After first hitchhiking to the area, we located Phillipe, who owns the Terra Luna Resort, near Puerto Guadal. He provided us with a splendid jetboat approach to the southwest corner of Lago Leones, where our bush bash began. At first we hugged the west side of the outflowing Río San Tadeo. After a quarter-mile, we passed the end of a tiny, rhubarb-infested stream before turning right and entering the bush, through which we thrashed to an upper tarn.

Dreaming of sunshine for what felt like an eternity finally paid off on our sixth day out, when San Valentín showed her beautiful face and allowed us to proceed. We ascended in a south-southeast direction up glacier-polished slabs, which gave us easy access to the broad, flat bench below Cerro Aguda's west ridge.

Fresh snow remained from the previous days' rain, which spiced up the climb. The west ridge offered three steeper steps of climbing separated by wide, flat benches, and there was lot of soloing and scrambling. The crux came up high where I excavated melting snow from a near-vertical 5.7 chimney and hand crack. The day began to fade as we reached the west summit, 1,700m above camp. The true summit is guarded by a 30m-deep notch and gendarme—this will have to wait until my next lifetime or for another crazy seeker of moderate and obscure routes who also doesn't want to wait in El Chaltén for weeks on end. We were content to finish on the west top.

We retraced our route, and it was fully dark by our final rappel. We didn't eat dinner until 1 a.m.

— MATT LEMKE, *USA*

CERRO MANGIAFUOCO, EAST RIDGE

Looking from the Nef Glacier toward Cerro Mangiafuoco, a previously unnamed rock spire halfway between Punta Pantagruel and Cerro Cachet. The first ascent climbed the east ridge (left skyline). *Paolo Marazzi*

PAOLO MARAZZI AND I set off from Italy for the North Patagonian Icecap on December 24. Once at Puerto Bertrand, we waited in vain for a gaucho to help transport our gear up the Rio Soler valley. In order not to waste the first window of good weather, we crossed Lake Bertrand by boat and then continued autonomously on foot up the Rio Soler.

After three days of walking across a maze of crevasses and battling against strong winds, we established camp on the icefield at about 1,600m. From there, we returned to the forest to gather more gear, which a gaucho had brought in the meantime, and to sit out five days of bad weather. By early January, we'd already walked almost 100km. Our lips were so swollen that we couldn't close our mouths, and the skin on our faces was so dry that removing the dead layers became a good pastime for rainy days.

Finally, with a good weather forecast, we set off on January 12 with minimal equipment to climb the east ridge of an unnamed rock spire halfway between Punta Pantagruel and Cerro Cachet (*see AAJ 2018*). After a night in a snow hole on the Nef Glacier, we started climbing at 6 a.m. on January 13. We quickly reached the col where the east ridge begins. From there, we climbed rock and snow, dispatching with the lower section of the climb in just a few hours. The central section, which we believed would be easy, turned out to be somewhat delicate, with difficult route-finding on snow ridges and around gendarmes.

We reached the final section in the early afternoon: two wide cracks running with water, along with a third crack that was narrower but drier. We put on our climbing shoes, and, after an initial runout, we climbed the final cracks in one pitch, reaching the summit at 2 p.m. The day was perfect, with an endless horizon of mountains, snow, and ice. We immediately started the abseils, picked up our bivy gear, and reached our camp before midnight, finally enjoying a peaceful, windless night. On January 14 we began our return to civilization. Despite strong winds and rainfall, we descended the Rio Soler in our packrafts.

By our measure, the mountain is about 2,000m high. We've named it Cerro Mangiafuoco, to be consistent with the other peaks in the area, and our route is called L'appel du Vide (400m, 6c M4).

— LUCA SCHIERA, *ITALY*

Cerro San Lorenzo's seven-kilometer-long, 1,800-meter-high east face, with El Faro (the south pillar) on the far left. The first ascent in 2018 was by the south side (hidden). *Jerôme Sullivan*

EL FARO
CERRO SAN LORENZO'S TOWERING SOUTH PILLAR

BY JERÔME SULLIVAN, *FRANCE*

MARTIN ELIAS, FRANCOIS Poncet (a.k.a. Ponpon), and I approached the east face of Cerro San Lorenzo (3,706m) for the second time in early October. (Martin and I made an attempt in 2017, with Sebastien Corret.) The three of us, longtime friends of many worldly adventures, were accompanied by a spiritual fourth: In Martin's pocket, a card given to him by his mother depicted the Virgen de Lomos de Orios. None of us are believers, yet many mountaineers seem to cling to superstition, and sentimental tokens—a pair of lucky ice axes, an amulet given by a friend—are often brought on a trip to the mountains. So, warmly nestled in Martin's coat pocket, we had our protector.

The path to Cerro San Lorenzo begins at Las Horquetas, a lonely hotel where Quentin Tarentino's *From Dusk Till Dawn* could have been shot. From there, the asphalt turns west and changes into a dusty *estancia* road. Here, for a fist full of dollars, the *estancieros* have bought huge parcels of land for their cattle and wildly endangered the local ecosystems. In the distance, Cerro San Lorenzo stands, as Doug Tompkins said, like an Argentine Everest, because of its shape and gigantic proportions. Thanks to Tompkins Conservation, entering Perito Moreno National Park means leaving the other Argentina behind and joining the thousands of guanoco, rabbit, puma, niandu, cachaña, pichu, and other wildlife that live in this desert sanctuary. Upstream from Lago Belgrano, the flat-bedded glacial valley of Rio Lacteo is carved through colorful volcanic rock. The Puesto San Lorenzo, which sits at the bend of the valley, would be our home for the next weeks.

The majestic throne of San Lorenzo's east face extends like a barrier for 7.4km, 1,800m high at its apex. Absurd drips and curls appear, sculpted by the raging winds or maybe Dalí himself. Immense overhanging cornices and seracs serve as a crown, threatening what would otherwise be a mixed climbing paradise. At the southern terminus lies a huge and attractive 1,200m needle, the Pilar Sur.

In 2017, conditions were poor and our attempt on Cumbre Central, in the middle of the east face, was thwarted by the usual bad weather, leaving us only a 12-hour window. A year later, as a high-pressure system approached, we gave more thought to those cornices and seracs atop the face and ruled it out, agreeing that mountains are many and life is short. Pilar Sur seemed like an attractive option, yet its rock is dangerous (*see AAJ 2016*). We drifted toward the south. Hidden from us until then, a logical line appeared up the cold south face of Pilar Sur, which we had begun calling El Faro ("the lighthouse"). *Sweet virgin, Lomos de Orios, we finally had a plan!*

On October 18 we set out in a fresh blanket of snow brought by a raging four-day depression. Crossing Rio Lacteo proved vivifying in the early hours, and we soon reached the big glacial lake barring access to the east face. Icebergs floating on the lake had all been pushed together by wind, allowing us to hazardously jump from one to the other. Martin remarked, "Guys, we're doing a real shitty move here." Eventually, he broke through a plate of ice and went waist-deep into the water before crawling out. The Virgin was looking after us.

We placed a camp a couple of hours past the lake at the foot of the tremendous east face. The next morning, after a lot of falling in waist-deep holes in the moraine, we reached the slopes below El Faro. It was 10 a.m. when we started climbing. The forecast had proposed a 48-hour window of high pressure, security until the next evening.

After some technical mixed climbing on good rock, we accessed a snow and ice ramp that we had spotted on our scouting trip. We unroped and quickly climbed the 500–600m ramp, which gave access to the steeper part of the face. At the end we roped up again and found poor snow conditions, bad rock, and a lack of ice. Night found us as I started up what turned out to be the crux of the route: 80m of vertical, snow-covered blocks of rock. Fixing rope on the first 30m of difficult dry-tooling, we rappelled down and chopped out some small ledges on an icy slope. At midnight, we were in our sleeping bags.

Cracking my eyelids the next morning, the scenery was stunning: Fitz Roy stood at the distant gates of the Southern Icecap. After a quick game of rock, paper, scissors, Martin got lucky and geared up for the worst pitch of the route—possibly the worst in his life! The rock in this section involved a balanced blend of crumbling sand and oven-size

[Top]"After a quick game of rock, paper, scissors, Martin got lucky and geared up for the worst pitch of the route—possibly the worst in his life!" [Bottom] Francois Poncet on the summit of Pilar Sur with unclimbed Torrecilla in the background. *Jerôme Sullivan (both photos)*

blocks that seemed to fracture at the touch. "*Un asco,*" as the locals say! The three-hour lead brought a constant shower of rocks. At one point, a rock hit our stove, which promptly joined all the other distant, fallen rocks. Without a chance of water, we decided to trust in the Virgin.

More mixed terrain led to the col between the impossible-looking spire called Torrecilla and the south pillar. From here, we transitioned to the north side. Three pitches of rime-covered rock led us to the summit as night fell and clouds engulfed the mountains. The setting sun reflected in my companions' eyes and set alight a flame of folly.

The 12-hour descent lasted all night. Low on the face, Martin noticed something red in the snow. "*Milagro!*" he shouted. The stove, intact after a 400m fall, was restored to us! We reached the foot of the wall at dawn on October 20.

We call our route La Milagrosa (1,200m, 6a M7 A3) and propose the name El Faro for the tower. It was not an especially nice route to climb, but its unique setting in the heart of the giant San Lorenzo and my exceptional companions made this adventure excellent. 🔲 🔍 ▶

CERRO RISO PATRÓN SUR, FIRST ASCENT BY SOUTHWEST FACE

FROM FEBRUARY 9 to March 3, 2018, we spent 22 days in Chile's O'Higgins National Park, hoping to climb Cerro Riso Patrón. This mysterious mountain on the western border of the Southern Patagonian Icefield has seen very few climbers. The central summit (ca 2,550m) was climbed twice: first by Italians in August 1988, via the southeast face, and then in September 2015 by an international team, by the east spur. The south summit (approximately 2,350m) was unclimbed.

Cerro Riso Patrón Sur and the first ascent route on the southwest face. *Matteo Della Bordella*

We planned to reach a base camp in Fiordo Falcón by "fair means," kayaking 100km from Puerto Edén, the closest settlement. Getting permission from the navy, police, and national park turned out to be complicated, and we missed having a lawyer on our team. We finally started on February 10 and were able to finish the kayak approach in three days, thanks to good conditions. Upon arriving at "Fonrouge Bay," we immediately noticed that the usual forest, full of birds, was missing. Instead we found a brown and gray field of broken trees, dead fish, and pieces of ice. The only conclusion was that a huge tsunami must have swept the area just before we arrived, destroying everything within a kilometer or more of the sea.

We immediately started to explore "Comesaña Valley" and potential routes to the peak. [*Fonrouge Bay and the Comesaña Valley were named by the 2015 team after Argentine climbers José Louis Fonrouge and Carlos Comesaña, one of the first teams to explore this region.*] The approach we chose involved crossing a big river exiting the lake above Fonrouge Bay. One of us had to swim across the lake with a rope so we could set up an acrobatic 80m Tyrolean traverse. Rubber boots turned out to be essential gear for wading through the swamps and creeks along the approach.

On the 15th of February, we positioned an advanced base camp about 1.5 hours southwest of the foot of the peak. Everything was now ready—we just needed some good weather! Sitting out a week of storms at ABC, we continuously guessed about strategies and routes. When a small weather window of one and a half days was forecast, it became clear the only reasonable line would be up the southwest face, following mixed ground to an obvious ice ramp that led toward the summit. We stuffed semi-dry gear in our packs and finally started climbing on February 22.

Moderate mixed terrain plus a few harder pitches (including a 25m M7+ wall that took about an hour to climb) brought us to the ice ramp. The ice turned out to be perfect, and we enjoyed pitches up to 90° on blue ice and rime. After 12 hours of climbing, we reached the summit at dusk and enjoyed breathtaking views of the Southern Icefield. However, looking to the north, our dream of traversing to Riso Patrón's central summit evaporated when we saw the obvious difficulties, especially given a short weather window. We decided to be content with the first ascent of this summit; we called our route King Kong (900m, M7+ 90°). After bivying in a cozy cave below the summit, we descended the south ridge and west face.

After another long day extracting all of our gear from advanced base, we started back to civilization in our kayaks, fighting strong gusts for five days of paddling before we could reach Puerto Edén. [*Find episode seven of the AAJ's Cutting Edge podcast for much more on this climb.*] 📄 📷

— **MATTEO DELLA BORDELLA**, *ITALY*, AND **SILVAN SCHÜPBACH**, *SWITZERLAND*

The Cerro Fitz Roy group seen from the west, showing the three routes that Jim Reynolds free soloed in 2019: (1) Complete west ridge of Aguja Rafael Juárez, February 9, downclimbing the Anglo-American Route. (2) Chiaro di Luna on Aguja Saint-Exúpery, February 11, downclimbing the Kearney-Harrington Route. (3) Afanassieff Route on the northwest ridge of Cerro Fitz Roy, which he free soloed up and down on February 21. The other downclimbs are not marked but can be seen from this angle. *Rolando Garibotti*

CHALTÉN MASSIF AND TORRES DEL PAINE: 2018–2019 SEASON SUMMARY

This was the third season in a row with fairly poor weather and conditions. After having anomalously dry seasons in 2012, 2015, and 2016, it has come as a bit of a shock to go back to average Patagonia weather. The only extended windows of good weather were at the start and end of the season, in November and in March.

Other than Martin Elias, Francois Poncet, and Jerôme Sullivan's phenomenal climb in the Cerro San Lorenzo area (*see p.236*), the big news from the Chaltén Massif involved Jim Reynolds (USA), who free soloed up and down Agujas Rafael Juárez and Saint Exúpery and Cerro Fitz Roy. In the early 1900s, Austrian climber Paul Preuss, considered by many "the father of style," preached and practiced free soloing up and down peaks as the "honest, sporting" way to climb (his words). He explained, "If there is someplace you can't go down, you should also not go up." One could have never imagined that Preuss' maxims would one day be applied to a peak like Cerro Fitz Roy. One could conceivably make a stylistic argument that Reynolds' ascents were the first *free* ascents of these formations. If rappels and pendulums are not considered free climbing on a wall such as El Capitan, why should an ascent of a jagged peak be considered free unless the descent is also done free?

On Aguja Rafael Júarez, Reynolds soloed the complete west ridge (1,000m, 5.10) and downclimbed the Anglo-American (350m, 5.10), while on Aguja Saint Exúpery he free soloed Chiaro di Luna (750m, 5.11) and downclimbed the Kearney-Harrington (550m, 5.10c). On neither of these two climbs did he carry a rope or climbing gear. On Cerro Fitz Roy he free soloed the Afanassieff Route on the northwest ridge (1,500m, 5.10c), taking 6 hours 38 minutes to reach the summit

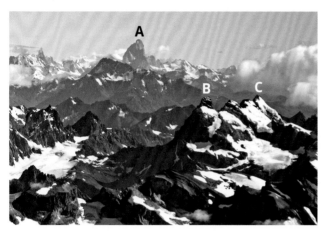

Cerros Nahumaday (B) and Huemules (C) from the south. The first ascent of Nahumaday was by the northwest face, hidden from view. In the distance, Cerro Fitz Roy (A). *Rolando Garibotti*

and 8 hours and 30 minutes to downclimb the same route. He carried a rope and some gear, which he did not use; he also forgot his harness and belay device. All ascents were completed onsight except for a short section of the Anglo-American on Rafael and a prior attempt on the Afanassieff to about one-third height. He described his approach as the "best possible form of the art" he could come up with.

There were a few other noteworthy ascents in the Chaltén Massif. On Aguja Poincenot, Siebe Vanhee (Belgium) completed the first free ascent of Patagonicos Desesperados (500m, 5.12), which was onsighted a week later by Leonardo Gheza (Italy). There were two ascents of the southeast ridge of Cerro Torre, by French and Slovak teams, the seventh and eighth ascents of the route since many of the Maestri bolts were removed.

Elsewhere on Cerro Torre, Jorge Ackermann, Tomas Aguilo (both Argentina), and Korra Pesce (Italy) attempted a difficult line on the left side of the north face, climbing 23 pitches in all, nine of them on the north face and three above Aguilo's 2013 high point on the same line. They reached a small rime mushroom two-thirds of the way up, at the base of the last headwall, which will likely be the crux of the route, before high winds and high temperatures forced them to retreat. They hope to try again next spring.

On the west face of Torre Egger, Alessandro Beltrami, Mirko Povinelli, Giorgio Roat, and Ermanno Salvaterra (all Italy) made a valiant attempt in the center of the west face, climbing two-thirds of the way up a very steep and fairly blank big wall. Over two attempts, they spent 21 days on the wall on portaledges. On the east face of Torre Egger, Brette Harrington (USA) and Quentin Lindfield Roberts (Canada) climbed the first three pitches of Titanic, then climbed nine new pitches on the steep pillar to the left, rejoining Titanic at the obvious snowfield halfway up the wall, where they stopped. They called their line Marc-André's Vision (to 5.12+), as it was the late Marc-André Leclerc who envisioned this line and had hoped to attempt it.

To the southwest of Lago Viedma, and to the east of Cerro Moyano, Daniel Pons (Argentina) and Steffen Welsch (Germany) did the first ascent of the southernmost summit of the chain comprising Cerro Huemules. They started from Estancia Helsingfors, walking along the Moyano fjord, taking a side valley immediately west of Cerro Huemules. They established camp at 1,300m, after walking six hours. The next day, February 2, they walked to the northwest face of the unclimbed peak, started their climb at 2,100m, and did eight short pitches with difficulties to 5.8 and A0, reaching the summit around 3 p.m. They measured the summit at 2,348m (with no GPS) and observed that it is clearly higher than Cerro Huemules itself. They rappelled the line of ascent and reached camp around 10:30 p.m., returning to Helsingfors the next day. They christened the peak Nahumaday.

Torres del Paine

THE TORRES DEL Paine Massif also saw some new routes. In June 2018, Max Didier and Cristobal Señoret (Chile) climbed Estilo Andino, a new route on Cerro Paine Grande's 300m southwest face. Their line is to the far left of existing lines, reaching the heavily rimed west ridge, which it follows to the summit. They found difficulties to 90° and WI4. This was only the fifth ascent of this imposing, beautiful peak, which, at 2,845m, is the highest in the Torres del Paine massif.

Also in August, Nicolás Secul and Cristobal Señoret did the first ski descent of the east face of Almirante Nieto (to 50°), following the line of Genesis, a route put up in 2015. During the summer, Secul and Señoret climbed a new route on the southwest face of Peineta that they called Puro Filete (nine new pitches to 5.11 A1). On the east face of Cuerno Este and on a golden pillar to the right of the route Tchao Pantin, Secul and Leon Riveros climbed seven new pitches, finding difficulties to 5.10+ C1 and stopping some 50m below the shale band, at a point where the cracks petered out.

On the left side of Aleta de Tiburón's east face, Max Barlerin and Kevin Sturmer (USA) climbed the 600 lbs Amoeba, a line that ascends 150m of easy slabs followed by five pitches to 5.12- before joining the classic south ridge.

Peineta, in Torres del Paine, seen from the west. (1) En Cordee Sponsors. (1.1) The variation Duraznos para Don Quijote. (2) Billy the Kid. (3) Puro Filete (2018). *Cristobal Señoret*

South of Torres del Paine National Park, Tomás Marusic, Nicolás Secul, and Cristobal Señoret (Chile) did what is likely the first winter ascent and first ski descent of the seldom-climbed Monte Balmaceda. They approached from the northeast.

Accidents and Rescues

AN UNFORTUNATE DEVELOPMENT this season was the number of accidents that occurred in the Chaltén Massif. Three climbers died on Cerro Fitz Roy, one on Cerro Solo, and there were three other major accidents that required rescues. It is unclear what might have led to this spike. Potentially, it could be related to over-eagerness after so much bad weather. The three deaths on Cerro Fitz Roy were due to exposure, and the two parties involved appear not to have read the forecast carefully enough, as it was clear this was not a day to climb on the high peaks. Neither of the parties had communication devices, which severely hindered the chances of a rescue.

On Aguja Rafael Juárez, a climber fell while simul-rappelling, suffering a severe concussion with displacement of some of the cranial bones. This party also lacked a communication device, and the partner mistakenly thought helicopter rescues were available in the area, so he rappelled down to get help instead of bringing his injured partner down. Fortunately, he ran into two strong parties that proceeded to climb up to the injured person and bring him down.

Another accident occurred on the west face of Cerro Torre, where a climber was hit by rockfall, breaking her leg. There were several parties present, and after calling for help they proceeded to take her down to Circo de los Altares, from which a military helicopter that was secured with some luck was able to fly her out just as a storm was moving in.

Climbing in Patagonia can be quite fun; however, being cavalier in mountains this big can quickly lead to tragedy. Helicopter rescue generally is not an option, and climbers must prepare by choosing objectives well within their skill level, reading multiple forecasts accurately, and making climbing plans based on current conditions—not goals set months before. In addition, climbers should carry an effective communication device and be well-versed and practiced in self-rescue techniques.

The online version of this report, as well as episode 17 of the Cutting Edge podcast (featuring Rolando Garibotti and Kelly Cordes), goes into greater depth on the circumstances of these accidents and on preparing to climb in Patagonia. In addition, the online report details many shorter new routes that could not be included here. 🗎 📷

– ROLANDO GARIBOTTI

The south side of Cerro Almirante Nieto, showing the route Linea de Libertad (approximately 700m of climbing, difficulties to 90°). The climbers continued along the east side of the mountain toward the east summit, descending the normal route from just below the top. *Christian Barra Muñoz*

CERRO ALMIRANTE NIETO, SOUTH FACE, LINEA DE LIBERTAD

WORKING AS TREKKING guide in Torres del Paine for a few years, it was hard to ignore this incredible line on the south side of Cerro Almirante Nieto. I tried the route alone a couple of times, in different times of the year, without success. I realized that to succeed I needed to enjoy this route with someone else. Soon after, I met Felipe Bishara, who had recently become the first Chilean to climb Denali's Cassin Ridge. Just one week after telling him of my project, we got the perfect window in mid-August, right at the end of the austral winter.

[*Editor's note: Cerro Almirante Nieto (a.k.a. Paine Chico) is located on the eastern side of Torres del Paine National Park. It is a large, complex mountain with an east and west summit, both approximately 2,600m—sources differ on which peak is higher. The normal route (AD), first ascended in 1937, is accessed from Camp Torres, below the three Torres del Paine, and climbs the northeast side to the east summit. The steep west side of the massif has seen a number of successful and unsuccessful climbs over the years (see the AAJ online). The route described here ascended the south side of the east peak.*]

We traveled to the park from Punta Arenas and then hiked as fast as we could for about three hours to reach the beginning of our route on the south face. We bivouacked on a small terrace for six hours, sharing one sleeping bag—cozy!

On August 12 we started the real climbing around 2 a.m. The initial *canaleta* (which begins at around 1,300m height) was filled with alpine ice and some snow (75–90°). After 10 hours and 10 pitches of climbing on this ramp (which faces south-southwest), we reached mid-height on the face around 11 a.m.; here we took a small rest on a ledge and analyzed the snow conditions. The wall above faces south-southeast and had a huge amount of snow on its slopes—it was quite intimidating. After some stability tests, we decided to go. Five pitches of really deep, unconsolidated snow and some simul-climbing brought us to the top of the face at around 2,000m.

After 18 hours of uninterrupted climbing, we began crossing a hanging glacier toward the east summit, on the southeast side (ca 2,300m). We spent the next five hours rounding the mountain, trying to connect with the normal route. In darkness, this was the most difficult part of our adventure.

We were low on food and water, and the wind was now blowing 80–110 km/h. When we finally reached the normal route at around 2,400m, we'd lost sensation in our fingers and toes. We made five 60m simul-rappels down the 300m gully on that route and then connected to the trail. We reached Camp Torres around 6 a.m. It was still dark, but we continued three more hours on a nice, smooth trail to reach the road, ending our 31-hour "day."

Our route, Linea de Libertad, is dedicated to the memory of Cristobal Bizzarri, a Chilean climber who passed away while climbing in Peru's Cordillera Blanca. 📷

— CHRISTIAN BARRA MUÑOZ, *CHILE*

CORDILLERA DE DARWIN

CERRO DALLA VEDOVA AND CERRO STOPPANI, FIRST ASCENTS

IN OCTOBER 2018, Chilean mountaineers Harry Brito, Camilo Hornauer, and I made the first ascents of Cerro Dalla Vedova (2,271m) and Cerro Stoppani (2,275m) in the eastern section of the Cordillera de Darwin. Cerro Dalla Vedova is located at the head of the glacier of the same name and is the highest peak of the Cordón Marina. This subrange rises from Kent Pass and Cerro Domo and extends for 25km to the southwest until reaching Hill 1,286m on the margins of the Cuevas Glacier.

Running parallel and to the east of Cordón Marina, beyond the Stoppani and Cuevas glaciers, is another subrange known as Cordón Janlena, whose main summit is Cerro Stoppani. Cerro Stoppani was identified for the first time from the sea in 1913 by the Italian explorer and priest Alberto de Agostini, who is responsible for naming both of the peaks we climbed, the first after the outstanding Italian geographer José Dalla Vedova and the second after the Italian geologist Antonio Stoppani.

At the time of our Unexplored Darwin expedition in October, the summits of the Cordón Marina had no previous ascents. Within the Cordón Janlena, the only reported ascent was of Cerro Ohi (Hillebrandt, 1988). I had previously attempted to climb both Stoppani and Dalla Vedova in October 2017, without success, accessing the mountains from Yendegaia Bay to the east.

On our successful 2018 expedition, we reached the glacial plateau between the two mountains from Cuevas Fjord and by the Cuevas Glacier to the west of the peaks. The lower part of this approach was previously explored by two expeditions (New Zealand in 1970 and University of Magallanes in 1980), and the upper part had been visited by a French expedition (GMHM,

Descending from the first ascent of Cerro Dalla Vedova, looking to the south over seldom-seen peaks of the Cordillera de Darwin. *Cristian Donoso*

2011). From a high camp we climbed Cerro Stoppani first and Cerro Dalla Vedova the next day.

We accessed the Cuevas Glacier by sea kayak, sailing in total autonomy through Almitantazgo Sound and Parry Fjord. The expedition lasted a total of 35 days, with harsh storms in the first days and excellent weather toward the second half of the expedition. *The online report includes many excellent photos of peaks in this area.*

— CRISTIAN DONOSO, *CHILE*

THREE FIRST ASCENTS ABOVE FIORDO FINLANDIA

FROM SEPTEMBER 25 to October 13, the French national women's mountaineering team (ENAF), comprised of Florence Igier, Johanna Marcoz, Marion Pravin, and Maud Vanpoulle, along with two coaches, Gaël Bouquet des Chaux and Antoine Pêcher, completed a successful expedition to the Cordillera de Darwin.

Prior to the trip, the group had identified at least two virgin peaks surrounding Esperanza Pass: Point 1,564m and Point 1,814m on the map produced by Camilo Rada (UNCHARTED project) as well as a possible drop-off point by boat. This zone is adjacent to Glaciar Marinelli and is north-northwest of Monte Shipton, in the north-central part of the Cordillera de Darwin.

On September 25 the group departed from Puerto del Hambre, transported by boatman Fernando Viveros (Chile) for the 100-mile trip across the Strait of Magellan to reach Fiordo Finlandia. The group built a base camp at 54°33'51"S, 69°43'40"W.

On September 30 the climbers ascended two virgin peaks just above the east side of Fiordo Finlandia: Cerro Nylandia (1,114m, 54°32'14"S, 69°42'20"W) and Point 1,044 (1,044m, 54°32'47"S, 69°42'7"W), a peak they suggest renaming "Cerro Fernando," after their ship captain. These summits were reportedly of little technical difficulty but presented a good view to the southeast of the other main objectives, Point 1,564m and Point 1,814m.

From October 3–4, the group set out to attempt Point 1,564m, however were turned back 30m from the summit due to poor weather and other factors. From October 9–10, the group climbed Point 1,814m in better weather. The mountain is reportedly a beautiful, snowy pyramid, with technical difficulties of WI3 and 70° snow. The group chose to rename this summit "Cerro Akila," which means "ice" in the Yagan language spoken by the first inhabitants of Tierra del Fuego. Both routes required lengthy, tedious approaches, bivouacs at the foot of the peaks, and long days of climbing.

The group was picked up on October 12. They experienced an unplanned night out at sea along with 3m seas while recrossing the Strait of Magellan and did not reach Punta Arenas again until the middle of the following day. A full trip report and photos can be viewed at www.ffme.fr.

— *INFORMATION FROM THE* FÉDÉRATION FRANÇAISE DE LA MONTAGNE ET DE L'ESCALADE (FFME)

ANTARCTICA

Looking across Phantom Bay to the Wild Spur Range on Arctowski Peninsula. Divoká is the highest peak a little right of center, with the west face pointing toward the camera. *Michal Sabovčík*

ARCTOWSKI PENINSULA, WILD SPUR RANGE, DIVOKÁ

THE OPPORTUNITY TO visit Antarctica came through Marek Holeček, who told me that he planned to visit the Antarctic Peninsula at the end of 2017 in a small sailboat. There were three spare places. "Why don't you come?" asked Marek. I didn't hesitate—this was a chance not to be missed.

This was also my opportunity to launch an unusual new project. Juraj Koreň is a top Slovak paraglider but something of a beginner when it comes to climbing; I was a paragliding beginner, but Juraj had proposed, "Teach me to climb and I'll teach to you fly." After a couple of seasons of climbing and flying in the Tatra and Alps, we were ready for something more ambitious, and so Seven Virgin Summits was born. We would try to reach an unclimbed summit on each of the seven continents and fly down from each by paraglider. The first part of our project would take place on the Antarctic Peninsula.

We sailed from Ushuaia in late December 2017 on the 17m yacht Altego II. It was the most difficult approach to a mountain that I had ever endured—for six days I lay on the lower deck in seasickness delirium.

We made a short stay at the Chilean Base in Paradise Bay, from which we climbed a 600m hill and made our first flight. Next we sailed west to Port Lockroy on Wienke Island, where we climbed an 850m mountain at the northern end of the Wall Range and flew from its summit. However, during our ascent we found old fixed rope and some pitons, leading us to believe the peak may have been climbed before.

We then sailed northwest to the Errera Channel, between Rongé Island and the Arctowski Peninsula. There, on the mainland, we spotted a fine summit, the highest peak of the Wild Spur Range. We couldn't find a name or altitude, but we were captured by its symmetrical shape and a fine, logical line of ascent. On January 11, 2018, our skipper ferried Juraj and me by small boat to a beach, from which we spent the next hour crossing a glacier to the foot of the west face. We followed a direct line up an icy couloir on the left side of the face, finishing with a snowy overhang. The rocky sections were very broken and offered no real possibility of sound protection. After seven hours we exited the face and followed a short snow ridge back right to the summit, where our GPS registered 1,057m. We named the peak Divoká and the route on the west face Zivot je Life (TD, 90°).

We descended 100m from the summit, launched, and flew down along the face we had just climbed. After landing and making our way to the beach, we called the yacht for a pick-up. Our skipper greeted us with the words, "Guys, I've sailed the world and people say I am insane, but I don't dare think what you are." Half an hour later it was raining. We'd got it just in time. 📑 📷

— **MICHAL SABOVČÍK**, *SLOVAKIA*

ANVERS ISLAND: MT. FRANÇAIS TRAVERSE; MT. NESTOR, WEST RIDGE; MT. ACHILLES, NORTH FACE

AN AUSTRALIAN team—Dave Goldie, Andrew Lock, Liam Silk, and Pat Spiers—visited Anvers Island and made what was probably the first traverse of Mt. Français (2,822m), ascending the Zeus (northwest) Ridge to the summit before descending south across the summit of Mt. Agamemnon (2,577m GPS) and west down the Menelaus Ridge. All but the steepest and iciest sections were skied.

The team also climbed Mt. Nestor (1,302m GPS) via the northwest ridge (a straightforward but steep, exposed snow ascent) and skied up and down Mt. Achilles by the north face. There is no record of ascents of either peak. The four also climbed and skied Mt. Helen (1,278m GPS), first climbed in 1955.

The team's ascents were made over the course of a week, during a traverse south from their landing point on the west of Lapeyrère Bay, with the intention of carrying on to the coast near Biscoe Bay. However with an injury to a member on their waiting yacht and a bad weather forecast, they turned around, unfurled their kites, and headed back around the northwest side of the mountains, kite-sailing from Patroclus Hill (northwest of Mt. Achilles) to northeast of Mt. Nestor in just one hour. A link to an interactive map of their camps and summits is at the AAJ website. 🔍

– DAMIEN GILDEA, *AUSTRALIA*

QUEEN MAUD LAND

HOLTEDAHL PEAKS, VARIOUS ASCENTS

IN JANUARY 2019, on his fifth expedition to Queen Maud Land, veteran polar guide Christoph Höbenreich from Austria led Michael Guggolz (Germany) and Kjetil Kristensen (Norway) to the Holtedahl Peaks. They circumnavigated the range on skis and climbed and named three peaks in the Vinten-Johansenegga massif, two of which were first ascents.

On January 5, the trio made the second ascent of Schneekrone ("snow crown," 2,140m, 71°49'S, 8°59'E). Approaching from the east, the team crossed the Fensterpass ("window pass," 71°48'42.31"S, 8°58'18.97"E), so named because of a rock in the shape of a window, and climbed the triple-crowned Schneekrone by its 50° west face. This peak was first climbed in 2000 by Cestmir Lukes, who called it Elvia Peak, but as this name was never officially submitted or recognized—and it contradicts the guidelines of the Scientific Committee on Antarctic Research (SCAR), which prohibit naming features after sponsors—this year's team renamed the peak Schneekrone, which they have submitted to the relevant authorities.

Würfelturm seen from the north. The first ascent climbed the right side of the broad, rocky ridge facing the camera. *Michael Guggolz*

The next day they climbed Schneeglocke ("snow bell," 2,127m, 71°49.3'S, 8°59'E) via the glaciated east face and a 45° snow ridge to the summit. The following day, the 7th, the three started from base camp on the east side of a third peak, crossed a rocky ridge, and climbed mixed terrain on its northwest face, including a short rock section of UIAA grade III. They named this 2,249m peak Würfelturm ("cube tower," 71°49.9'S, 8°58'E). 📷

– DAMIEN GILDEA, *WITH INFORMATION FROM* CHRISTOPH HÖBENREICH, *AUSTRIA*

NORTH ATLANTIC

Cedar Wright getting a taste of things to come on the first pitch of the route Faroenough, the first climb up the 750-meter-tall Cape Enniberg cliffs. *The North Face | Will Lascelles*

FAR OUT
THE FIRST ASCENT OF A GIGANTIC SEA CLIFF IN THE FAROE ISLANDS

BY JAMES PEARSON

OVER THREE WEEKS in July and August 2017, Yuji Hirayama (Japan), Cedar Wright (USA), and I traveled to the Faroe Islands with hopes of climbing Cape Enniberg. Located at the northern tip of the island of Viðoy, it had one the tallest unclimbed sea cliffs in the world, rising 754m directly out of the ocean.

This area came onto my radar roughly five years earlier. The Faroe archipelago is a self-governing part of the kingdom of Denmark, north of Scotland. Although the Faroese people have been climbing sea cliffs to reach nesting birds for hundreds of years, only recently have climbers been traveling to the islands to establish modern routes. Many of the hiking trails pass through private land, and we secured permission from the owners of Enniberg to approach and climb on the wall. They even offered to sail us out to the base when they next went out to check on the population of nesting puffins at the bottom on the cliff. When would this be? Maybe tomorrow, maybe the next day...

Our plan was to attempt the north face of Cape Enniberg by the line of least resistance, which looked to be a sort of arête between two overhanging faces, leading to some steep grassy slopes and then a ridgeline to the summit. We estimated the line might take somewhere between four and 24 hours to climb, if it was possible at all. Our boat ride departed from the tiny local harbour one evening after 8 p.m. We hoped to be on the summit before a forecast three-day storm arrived at 2 p.m. the following day.

Formed in bands of volcanic and sedimentary rock, the cliffs in the Faroe Islands mix some decent basalt with serious choss—some kind of volcanic ash the consistency of compressed kitty

Looking up at Cape Enniberg, Europe's tallest sea cliff: 750m of choss, grass, and vomiting birds. The 2017 first-ascent route started off-picture at far right to reach the grassy bench, then climbed the 250-meter rock prow in the middle, followed by 400 meters of grassy simul-climbing. *The North Face / Will Lascelles*

litter, impossible to protect or climb without grabbing loosely attached grass hummocks. The rest of the bands sit somewhere between these two extremes, in some unfathomable random order. The Faroe Islands also are home to one of the biggest populations of fulmars in the world. These birds defend their nests by projectile-vomiting partially digested fish. If you climb here, you are going to get puked on—just accept it.

By 10 p.m. we were climbing, a surreal experience with the forever twilight. Cedar, in his element and always thinking about getting to the top as fast as possible, took on the first pitch. He placed one piece of gear two meters off the floor and then basically soloed 50m of decaying grassy slab to the first belay. You know a pitch has been scary when you second in five minutes what took the leader almost an hour to climb. We had barely made it to the beginning of the real rock climbing, and now, looking up toward the expanse of crumbling stone and circling birds, I think we all had a moment of doubt.

Nine hours later, we dragged ourselves onto the soggy grass slopes that signalled the halfway point. The predicted storm had hit 10 hours earlier than expected, and we were cold, soaked to the skin, and covered in vomit. Both Cedar and Yuji had pulled off some audacious and bold choss leads. We were doing it—we just had to keep going up.

The second half of the climb was a series of never-ending grass slopes, interspersed with rock bands of varying height. The original plan had been to simul-climb the obvious ridgeline to the top, following as much continuous rock as possible. However, the ever-increasing rain soon put a stop to that idea, as any more than a body length of rock became nigh on impossible to climb. What would have been 5.9 in dry conditions now would require a long bolt ladder. Instead, we followed the grass upward, weaving left or right until we found a gap, gully, or some other way through. Once on the next level, the process was repeated—for six long hours. I lost count of the number of times we were forced to backtrack, even down past where we had come before. As fatigue and frustration took its toll, simul-climbing became short-roping, which eventually became plain old soloing. Then all of a sudden, we passed another rock band and there were no more. A crew of locals waited for us at the summit. They hugged and congratulated us for the climb, gave us a bottle of gin, and then left to rescue one of their stranded sheep.

Dreams of recovering with a lazy afternoon went out the window as we arrived at the tiny village to find what must have been half the inhabitants waiting for us. Dressed in traditional clothes, Faroese flags flying, we all celebrated the ascent in the most random of fashions: drinking strong spirits out of rams horn cups, a fitting finale to this oh-so-strange route: Faroenough (5.12- X A3).

During our trip, we and Caroline Ciavaldini (France) also established four shorter climbs on the south face of the Trælanípa wall on Vagar Island, which juts 142m out of the sea. The four climbs are mostly bolted and all around 5.12. Recently, a massive section of the wall fell into the sea about 300m to the right of our climbs, but luckily they all were unaffected! 📷 ▶

FOULA, NEBBIFJELD, ULTIMA THULE

FOULA IS THE most remote inhabited island off the coast of Britain, and in Roman times was known as Ultima Thule—the most northern land. Despite being part of the U.K., it takes more time for me to reach it from my home in North Wales than to go to Yosemite or Patagonia. I was there in May with Dave Macleod, one of the best all-round climbers in the world and a purveyor of the delights of Scottish climbing. His down-to-earth nature, as well as his ability to consistently pull hard leads out of the bag when the chips are down, make him a great partner.

Our proposed new line took on the steep central section of the southwest-facing cliff of Nebbifjeld, one of the highest sea cliffs on the island. [*Two easier routes have been climbed along the buttress to the left of the main wall: The Nose (E4 6a, Jones-Turnbull, 2001) and the Lum of Loirafield (E2).*] To scope the exit we used a drone to locate the final corner. From here a 250m rappel, straight down with a few re-belays, brought us to the foot of the route at the top of a series of grassy ledges. While I generally don't mind rappelling, lobbing 300m of static rope down a decomposing, overhanging sea cliff full of vomiting fulmars, sharp edges, and precarious blocks, isn't really my cup of tea, particularly in high winds.

After a few days swinging on our rope and trundling huge blocks, we had found a viable line in the upper half of the cliff. Below this the only way would be via a ground-up approach to link wandering overhanging features. When we eventually went for it, on May 19, we rappelled to the base of the wall and pinned down the end of the static rope with rocks, so it wouldn't blow out of reach in the strong wind. We thought it best to leave an escape route in place, but full gnar points to a team that doesn't!

The rock is sandstone and varies in quality from good to simply sand. The climbing was time-consuming, as we went back and forth, testing holds and placing nests of gear to safeguard progress. Fortunately, we had close to 24 hours of daylight. Dave led the second pitch (British 5c on bubbly soft rock) into a prominent corner, which I led on well-protected solid rock. A hard (6b) pitch then led

Dave Macleod traversing on pitch two (5c), one of the easier leads of Ultima Thule, Nebbifjeld. *Calum Muskett*

Calum Muskett in the final grassy corner system of Ultima Thule. *Dave Macleod (drone photo)*

to ledges, which we followed leftward (walk, crawl, heel-hook, slap, 6a) for nearly 70m to meet our rappel rope, in line with the section of cliff we'd previously inspected.

The wind picked up as we climbed strenuous walls and corners, the next four pitches being 6b. Dave pulled off some smooth leads, though looked surprisingly pumped on the last hard pitch. After the final roof, a grassy corner led more easily (5a) to the top, which we reached with more than a sense of relief. We named the route Ultima Thule (10 pitches, E7 6b). Most pitches are E5 and above, and are quite bold in the mid to upper half of the route. ▣

— CALUM MUSKETT, *U.K.*

THE 24/8 PROJECT: Dave Macleod's Foula climb took place a couple of months after a remarkable effort he completed on March 18–19. Within the space of 18.5 hours, near his home in Fort William, Scotland, he finished the self-created "24/8 Project," which involved climbing an 8a boulder problem (Cameron Stone Arête, 8a+), an E8 traditional route (Misadventure, E8 6c), an 8a sport route (Leopold, having to avoid an icicle on the upper crux!), a grade VIII winter route (Frosty's Vigil, VIII/8), and summiting eight Munros (peaks above 3,000' in altitude).

ULØYTINDEN, EAST FACE, NORDFIT, AND HISTORICAL ASCENTS

IN MARCH, MACIEJ Janczar and Tomasz Klimczak (Poland), based at the Lyngen Outdoor Center, added another winter route to the east face of Uløytinden (1,115m) in the south of Uløya Island. Their 500m line climbs relatively straightforward snow and ice at WI3/4 to the plateau on top. They belayed on rock outcrops using knifeblades. There was also plenty of strenuous digging in unconsolidated snow, leading to the route name NordFit.

This is the third known route on Uløytinden. The second, Starless Spur, to the left of NordFit, was climbed in 2016 by Marcin Chmielinski, Klimczak, and me, but terminated below a huge summit cornice (*AAJ 2017*). I only recently found out about the first route up the east face, a summer climb.

About 15 years ago, Ståle Selnes Bjørkestøl, who lives in Oslo but has family in the Uløya region, set off with a friend for Skjelettinden (also knows as Kua), the 930m rounded summit on the long east ridge of Uløytinden. They reached the top via the south flank above Isvannet Lake. The two continued along Uløytinden's east ridge until it steepened, where they made a long

A pod of orca and the chain of peaks dubbed "Patagonia" on the northeast side of the peninsula north of Oksfjordhamn. It's very possible that no climbs have been done on these mountains in Norway's far north. *Artur Paszczak*

traverse onto the left flank before climbing a depression steeply back right to the summit plateau. Bjørkestøl also found some interesting bouldering on the island.

To the northeast of Uløya lies the island of Kägen. Near the southwest corner, at the back of a southeast-facing cwm, lie large northeast-facing rock walls dubbed Valhalla. These rise as high as 500–550m. Again, I thought these were untouched until Bjørkestøl mentioned he had climbed a couple of routes there, around the time he climbed Uløytinden's east ridge. With typical Norwegian reticence, Bjørkestøl noted that any detailed topos he made are long gone, but remembers the climbs were Norwegian 5 and 6, belay ledges and anchors were easy to find, the views from both the wall and the top were awesome, and that there are definite possibilities for both easier and harder routes in this area.

Farther to the east of Uløya and Kägen, on the peninsula north of Oksfjordhamn, is an impressive toothed ridge that we've dubbed Patagonia. There are no known ascents here either summer or winter (*see photos of "Valhalla" and "Patagonia" in the online report*). 📷

— **ARTUR PASZCZAK**, *POLAND*

NORWAY / LOFOTEN ISLANDS

STORTINDEN AND BRETTVIKTINDEN, NEW ROUTES

THERE ARE MOMENTS in life when one simply knows something special is happening. There's a certain tug at the heartstrings, and a preciousness to each second that reminds us we are lucky to be there. Last winter in Lofoten was filled with those moments. There is a picture of me and Sami on top of Stortinden, smiling like children, a frozen glove I've forgotten still dangling from my mouth. As we climbed out of the wind, I looked up for the first time in ages and there were two glowing green swirls dancing in the sky above the sea, the snow, and the mountain. I pointed my camera and to my surprise it came

[Top] The east and north faces of Stortinden on the island of Flakstadøya, showing (1) All Good Boys Go to Heaven (2018), (2) Line C (2010), and (3) Way Out West (2018). [Bottom] Bad Boys Bring Heaven to You (500m, M7+ 95°) on the northwest face of Brettviktinden. *Chris Wright (both photos)*

out, but I could lose that photo and never forget the image, the moment, or the day.

Over four winters in the Nordland I have never seen conditions so consistently incredible as in early 2018. For weeks each day dawned cold and clear, with every possibility in the islands frozen into perfection. We even started climbing by headlamp after work, knowing we would never get everything done. I also found an exception in having available partners, and with them was able to complete two lines of which I'm quite proud.

The first is Way Out West (600m, M7 A0 95°) on the north face of Stortinden (866m, Flakstadøya island), a route I climbed in late February with my good friend Sami Modenius from Finland. The route is a mostly direct line, taking thinly iced slabs to some typically scrappy mixed climbing and a conspicuous chimney system to the summit. At the crux of the route I went for a ride after tearing a clump of turf out of a seam, and the A0 reflects that I hammered my tools into the crack while resting on my gear, before continuing to free the pitch at M7. Another pitch up high sent me for a second whip as I fell out of a moss-choked offwidth. Sami narrowly avoided airtime himself on a brilliant lead through the chimney to the top, which involved some of the most fantastic and three-dimensional climbing I've ever done. We descended to the west until we dropped into a gully that brought us back past the face to the road.

A few days later, after having raved at them about all my wonderful ideas, I teamed up with Briton Jon Bracey and Slovenian Luka Krajnc. I suggested a line I'd attempted in 2016 on the northwest wall of Brettviktinden (836m) on Austvågøya island. Carl Granlund and I had managed to get through some excellent climbing on the lower face, but a lack of momentum sent us down. I stressed to Jon and Luka that it would be a proper hard route, and it was.

Luka dispatched the lower pitches as we discovered my old anchors and I remembered the way. At my previous high point, Luka repeated my experience on Stortinden by fiddling in a cam just before removing some moss and taking flight. After being stymied in the same section again, he handed the lead to Jon, who made the difficulties look not nearly as difficult as they were. A string of strenuous mixed pitches followed before I took us to the top via a corner system and some interesting climbing along the summit ridge. We topped out to the evening's last glow and a glorious sunset, and descended to the northeast via a few rappels and some downclimbing. We named the route Bad Boys

Bring Heaven to You (500m, M7+ 95°) after Luka's favorite bad pop song of the moment.

A few days later we headed out again for a more casual outing. This time we aimed for a corner left of Trym Atle Saeland and Marko Prezelj's 2010 route, Line C, on the east face of Stortinden. The line yielded enjoyable and mostly moderate climbing to an outstanding view from the summit, a stark contrast to the cold wind and darkness I'd experienced atop Way Out West. We named the route from the same song, calling it All Good Boys Go to Heaven (600m, WI4+ M3).

During the same period, Jon and Luka authored a number of lines throughout the islands, including a proud one in the cleft to the left of Storm Pillar on Vågakallen, while I opened what I believe to be new climbs on the cliffs above Storvatnet lake and below Brettviktinden, on Kallkneet near Kalle, and at Svartfloget near Grunnførfjorden.

If I'd had more time, more partners, and less work, I can only imagine how much more could have been done, but I will have to satisfy myself by remembering we never could have climbed everything, and by being grateful for having been a part of it in the first place. 📷

– CHRIS WRIGHT, *AAC*

GUDVANGEN VALLEY, THE KRAKEN AND OTHER ROUTES

PHILIPPE BATOUX, AYMERIC Clouet, and Michel Coranotte spent 10 days of February in Sognefjord, staying in centrally situated Flam. The conditions were perfect, with lots of ice—all the known lines were in, and some new lines had appeared.

After warming up with various routes in the Gudvangen area [*some possibly new; details are at the AAJ website*], the three repeated the famous Fosslimonster (800m, with 1,000m of climbing, WI6+ M8+), finishing with cramps in their biceps. This was the February 2009 route completed by Robert Jasper and Roger Schaeli (after a previous attempt by Jasper and Markus Stofer), who were then lambasted by the

The huge ice lines of Into the Wild (left) and the Kraken (800m, VI/6+ M6), near Gudvangen. *Philippe Batoux*

Norwegian climbing community for their use of bolts (the two placed 14 bolts on the route; see *AAJ 2009*). Batoux, Clouet, and Coranotte used the bolts in situ on the first M8 pitch, although they think it might be possible to climb without.

The other route climbed by Jasper and Stofer during that 2009 trip was Into the Wild, which was billed as the longest pure icefall climbed to date (900m high but 1,300m of climbing, WI6+ X). Batoux had noticed a thin line to the right, but in five previous visits to the area he had never seen it in climbable condition. The French trio climbed it in a 14-hour day on February 20, adhering to Norwegian ethic of placing no bolts. The ice crux was a 50m freestanding pillar sitting on huge, strange, jellyfish formations above a 20m roof. They named the 800m route the Kraken (VI/6+ M6). 📄 📷 🔍

– *INFORMATION SUPPLIED BY* PHILIPPE BATOUX, *FRANCE*

AFRICA

The incredible 400-meter volcanic tower of Pico Cão Grande. *Jordi Canyigueral*

PICO CÃO GRANDE: LEVE LEVE AND FREE ASCENT OF NUBIVAGANT

THE IDEA CAME up as it often does, after a nice afternoon of climbing and a well-deserved beer. A good friend told us about the spectacular Pico Cão Grande ("Big Dog Peak"), a volcanic plug rising out of the jungle on the island of São Tomé, off the west coast of Africa. We were looking for a climbable volcanic formation to pursue the third stage of a project we call "The 4 Elements," which is about climbing in places that exemplify Water, Air, Fire, and Earth. We started in 2017 with Air in Patagonia, followed by Water in Peru, and now it would be Fire on Cão Grande.

We traveled to São Tomé with Manu Ponce and photographer Jordi Canyigueral. The remote island soon delivered on the promise of adventure: During our 26-day expedition, we received only three days without rain and encountered numerous black cobras. While establishing our new route Leve Leve ("slow slow," the slogan of the country, 450m, 8b+), we climbed many pitches on very wet rock. (Our Fire stage was almost extinguished by rain!) We opened the route in clean style, ground up and without use of aid or removable bolts; we used many cams and nuts. The climbing begins with some impressive overhangs and is very physical and technical at the bottom and more classic at the top. We completed a team redpoint ascent over three days in July; the route awaits a one-day free ascent. All the rappels are bolted.

With a few days left, we attempted a free ascent of the climb just to the left, Nubivagant (455m, Almada-Leah, 2015; 8b A0). This time we had more luck with the weather and were able to free this route in team redpoint style over two days, with the three crux pitches going at 8a+/b, 8a, and 7c+/8a. We also thought the final pitch was harder than originally rated—at least 7b. (Nubivagant and Leve Leve share their final two and a half pitches.) Undoubtedly this is one of the most fun and exotic trips we've made, and we highly recommend a visit to Africa's smallest country. 📷 🔍

— **IKER AND ENEKO POU**, *SPAIN*

AMERICAN EXPEDITION TO PICO CÃO GRANDE: *Shortly after the Spanish climbs, the U.S. team of Sam Daulton, Remy Franklin, Jacob Kupferman, Tyler Rohr, and Mike Swartz, supported in part by AAC Live Your Dream grants, arrived on São Tomé, also hoping to free Nubivagant. During the trip, Daulton and Franklin each freed the four pitches exiting the huge cave at the route's start. (Franklin said they felt the crux second, third, and fourth pitches were 5.13c/d, 5.13a, and 5.12d, respectively.) They onsight free climbed from pitch five to the top on one day, and all team members reached the summit. However, a continuous free ascent was not completed.*

Eneko Pou climbing pitch one (7c) of Leve Leve on Pico Cão Grande. *Jordi Canyigueral*

AKKA'N TAZARTE, NEW ROUTES

BERNARD MARNETTE AND I have visited Taghia several times, aiming to climb classic routes or to open new ones. When we first came in November 2011, Mohamed Amil was a goatkeeper, porter, and hiking guide. After a few years of training, he became one of the best young climbers in Taghia, now able to teach locals and guide foreign climbers; he also runs a local *gite* (guest-house) called Casa Taghia. Together with his friend Mohamed Mesaudi, also a climbing guide, Amil, Marnette, and I have opened various new routes. The first six of these are described in the new edition to Christian Ravier's guidebook to Taghia, published in the spring of 2019.

In 2018, we opened two more routes, in May and October. Both are in Akka'n Tazarte canyon, one and a half to two hours of walking from the village of Taghia. Both lines face southeast, on the right side when walking up the canyon.

Bernard, Mohamed Amil, and I climbed For Radia, named in honor of Mohamed's latest child, over two days. It offers nine pitches (350m) on excellent orange limestone. All belay anchors are equipped for abseil, and a few bolts were placed on the final slabby pitches. Difficulty is moderate in the first half and more sustained above (most pitches having some UIAA VI or VII crux). The route starts and finishes just left of the route Soyez Cool, Mangez des Moules.

La Voix des Bergers ("the shepherds' voice") is an eight-pitch route with difficulties up to VI+, opened by Bernard and Mohamed Amil. The climbing begins with an easy alpine-like ridge (three pitches), then continues with chimneys and gullies (V to VI+). Above the sixth belay, a traverse pitch to the left leads to the final cracks (VI+). The route was not bolted, but some pitons have been left in place. 📷 🔍

— CHRISTIAN FONTAINE, *BELGIAN ALPINE CLUB*

GREAT SPITZKOPPE, NORTHWEST FACE, MAMBA NO. 5

IN EARLY 2016 a friend and mountain guide from South Africa, Neil Margetts, sent me a photograph taken from a small plane of the northwest wall of Great Spitzkoppe. The image showed two long and steep corner and groove systems that appeared to be unclimbed.

Our research led us to conclude that the left corner was an old project named Big Hands (Alard Hufner and Voitek Modrzewski, early 2000s). This attempted to follow a large flake system halfway up the wall and finished on a pedestal of rock below a blank slab. To the best of our knowledge, the right groove system had never been attempted.

Neil and I made our first trip in July 2017. We were joined by a local climber, Richard Ford, a member of the Mountain Club of South Africa (MSCA), Namibia Section. The northwest wall of Great Spitzkoppe is steep, and as the climbing tends not to have continuous crack systems, we decided the best option was to explore the lines from the top down. We approached via the regular route on the northeast side, and then abseiled into the left corner to explore. We concluded the vertical last pitch would likely require a bolt ladder and decided to focus on the right groove.

The right-hand line looked much more promising. The top two pitches would provide hard slab climbing, and the groove feature looked excellent, with good rock, funky trad placements (threads and cams in pockets), and what appeared to be interesting climbing. The entry to the groove looked particularly good.

In September 2018, I returned to Spitzkoppe with a large team: Richard Ford (Namibia), David Barlow, Paul Maine, Lawrence Smoker, Hugh Thomas (all U.K.), and myself. Sadly, Neil could not make this trip. We started working on the Spitzkoppe project on our second day in the area. I recruited some porter assistance from the other chaps, carrying gear and ropes up the scrambling section of the regular route. While they

The 10-pitch Mambo No. 5 on the northwest face of Great Spitzkoppe. Five easier pitches gain the summit. *Robert Powell*

continued up to the summit, I abseiled down the wall to clean and equip the upper pitches. Each of the 10 pitches on the climb has bolt protection, but many also require wires, cams, and threads.

Richard and I returned a couple of days later to attempt a ground-up ascent. The first two pitches follow a flake system up a slab. Above the flake is tenuous slab climbing (5.12-) followed by an easier groove. The fifth pitch, the entry to the main groove system, has excellent varied climbing, with slabs, a steep layback system, and pockets (5.11+).

Two pitches up the groove required back-and-footing, bridging, and spanning with "quarryman" moves (shuffling two hands on one wall and two feet on the other, named after a famous climb in North Wales). This section (5.10 to 5.11b) was nicknamed the Birthing Canal due to the strenuous noises emitted while climbing these pitches.

The next two pitches face climb left of the groove, with pitch nine being a long and difficult bolt-protected slab (5.11+ A0, estimated at 5.12b). We didn't free this pitch on the day because of the heat—it would be better to climb this route earlier in the winter. One more 5.11 pitch leads to an easy gully and the first 5th-class pitch of the regular route, which can be followed in five pitches (5.8) to reach the summit. This is an excellent finish and makes for a big day out.

The team established three further new routes on the trip, from two to five pitches. Details and topos are at the AAJ website. 🖹 📷 🔍

– ROBERT POWELL, *SOUTH AFRICA, WITH DAVID BARLOW, U.K.*

MALAWI / MULANJE MASSIF

CHAMBE, NORTHWEST FACE, PASSION AND PAIN

THE HIGH-QUALITY, COMPACT granite in Malawi is so impressive, it leaves one wondering why it has been largely ignored by climbers. The northwest face of Chambe in the Mulanje Massif looks a bit like two Half Domes stacked on top of each other, with a massive ledge hosting an exotic wooded forest in the middle. [*The entire northwest face of Chambe was first climbed in 1979 by local climbers Ray Baines and Frank Eastwood (Gladiator, 800m, III 5.10 A1).*]

Lucas Alzamora on the new route Mazaroca Ardiente in Mozambique. This granite formation near the village of Liupo was named the Sphinx by the climbers who did the first routes. *Carloncho Guerra*

Richard Ford and I aimed to establish a well-protected, moderately rated climb up the lower Chambe wall that might match the popularity of similar climbs I had put up in Namibia and Madagascar [*see report below.*] In late November, we drilled bolts on lead and were thrilled to establish a fun seven-pitch route: Passion and Pain (450m, 5.9). The route follows a white streak to the right of a large, pointy triangular rock, extending partway up the lower wall. Rappel the route with two 60m ropes. [*The online version of this report includes many helpful recommendations for visiting and climbing in this area.*] 📄 🔍

— JAMES GARRETT, AAC

TWO OTHER RECENT CHAMBE ROUTES: Two difficult, sparsely bolted routes were put up in 2014 by French climbers (names not known) on the lower Chambe wall, left of Passion and Pain, and were recently repeated by a strong South African team: Waiting For Thelma (280m, 6c) and In the Memory of Antoine (650m, 7b A0). Topos are at the Mountain Club of Malawi website.

MOZAMBIQUE

THE SPHINX, MAZAROCA ARDIENTE

ARGENTINE CLIMBERS LUCAS Alzamora, Carloncho Guerra, and Diego Nakamura visited northern Mozambique during September, inspired by photos of the granite domes there. Northern Mozambique has many rock walls, some up to 700m high, however the local culture and religious beliefs make it possible to climb only if local leaders and authorities approve it.

The team's first objective was Lamitihui, a 400m granite tower 15km west from the city of Nampula. The locals approved the climbing, but with distrust. On the second day, after finishing the fourth pitch of their line, the team fixed ropes and descended to the ground, where they were startled by a group of seven or eight lads emerging from the bushes and brandishing AK-47 rifles.

They had no uniforms, wearing only shorts, shirts, and flip-flops. In a tense conversation, the Argentines tried to explain what they were doing. The armed youths marched the team to their barracks and eventually let them go, with the agreement that they would gather their equipment and leave town. The climbers never learned exactly who the armed young men were.

After this frightening episode, the Argentines traveled to a more secure zone near the village of Liupo, 100km southeast from Nampula, where they'd heard of previous climbing activity on a rock just north of the village. They opened a new route over three days, using natural protection and placing a few bolts: Mazaroca Ardiente (230m, 6b+ A0+). [*In 1998, Alard Hüfner and Mark Seuring (South Africa) climbed four routes on this rock, which they called the Sphinx (AAJ 2001). Two of their routes followed corner systems to either side of Mazaroca Ardiente.*] 📷

– MARCELO SCANU, *ARGENTINA*

MADAGASCAR / TSARANORO MASSIF

TSARANORO ATSIMO, BLOOD MOON

IN 2018, I made the long trip to Madagascar from Scotland with my friends Alan Carne and Calum Cunningham. We packed a drill and 200 bolts, which we agreed to place generously, keeping in mind there is no mountain rescue and the nearest hospital is five hours away on bad roads.

Our first foray onto Tsaranoro Atsimo resulted in a three-day ground-up push on a potential line to the left of Mai Più Così (5.13b, Larcher-Svab-Sterni, 1998). Moving into the imposing midsection of the route, we hit a dead end as the wall completely blanked out.

Our second attempt was also on Atsimo, this time weaving between two obvious black streaks on the right of the face. I had previously worried this line would be too close to the recently climbed Fire in the Belly (5.13c, Vanhee-Villanueva, 2015), just to the right. However, it turned out that my perception of scale was vastly skewed—the two lines were not nearly as close as I had imagined.

We climbed the 700m wall over six days, bolting completely ground up, with the intention of free climbing after we finished the gruelling development process. After a couple of days of rest, we returned for the free ascent. However, this did not go to plan as, on the third pitch, Alan took a short but nasty fall, breaking his leg in three places. Calum and I got him down, and after a very stressful 48 hours of travel and medical care, he flew home.

Calum and I returned five days later, mentally drained but with the same burning desire to achieve our goal. At pitch three, where Alan had broken his leg, it was difficult to ignore the thought of what we had witnessed only days earlier. Despite the grades being relatively low in the bottom half of the route (mostly 5.11+ and 5.12 terrain), it is very technical ground and the rock is quite flaky. This had us perpetually on edge.

Pitch nine is the crux of our route. Bolting this pitch was an ordeal that took me five hours and cost me a chunk of my tooth when a skyhook unexpectedly exploded into my face. I was exceedingly happy to free this pitch on my first attempt—and even more so that I'd found the only line of weakness up the imposing blank face. It weighs in at a meaty 5.13c: heady, with a lot of exposure and the crux right at the end.

After three days of effort, Calum and I summited Tsaranoro Atsimo having both freed our new route: Blood Moon (700m, 5.13c). We named it for the rare lunar eclipse we'd all seen earlier in the trip. 📄 📷 🔍

– ROBBIE PHILLIPS, *SCOTLAND*

TRANOKITILY DOME, SWEET AVOCADO

ON THE BIG, mostly crackless walls of Madagascar's Tsaranoro Valley, the few routes easier than 5.12 are very sparsely protected. Many routes have not even been repeated. As Timmy O'Neill and I had done two years earlier in Namibia's Spitzkoppe area (*AAJ 2017*), we aimed to establish a long, intelligently protected easy climb in the "Yosemite of Africa."

Tranokitily Dome sits directly across from the massive Tsaranoro walls, and its featured slabby flanks awaited a first ascent. Timmy, Jeff Rueppel, Sarah Steele, and I put up Sweet Avocado (III 5.8) in April. (The route is named for a delicacy served by Gilles Gautier, the Frenchman who owns

the luxurious yet reasonably priced Tsarasoa Lodge.) Sweet Avocado is well-protected with bolts, requiring only a 60m rope and a quiver of quickdraws for its five rope-stretching pitches. A short scramble to the top leads to an uncomplicated walk-off. This route offers something unique in a magnificent stone paradise that was until now reserved mostly for the hard core. 📷

Sarah Steele on Tranokitily Dome. *Jeff Rueppel*

– JAMES GARRETT, AAC

TSARANORO ATSIMO, SOAVA DIA; CHAMELEON, LES VAZAHAMATEURS

FROM JUNE 5 to 25, a group of six young climbers of the Fédération Française de la Montagne et de l'Escalade (FFME) opened two new routes in the Tsaranoro range. Our team from the "Roc Aventure Programme," with an average age of 20, consisted of Manon Barnier, Tom Durel, Julien Forgue, Tristan Roguiez, Dora Sulinger, and Robin Valet, and was coached by Arnaud Petit and me.

The team first opened Les Vazahamateurs (250m, 6c) on the east face of the Chameleon formation. The route is shady in the afternoon and has a short approach. Next, we focused on our main goal, the Tsaranoro Atsimo, where we established Soava Dia ("bon voyage" in Malagasy; 600m, 7c+), a long effort which we finished bolting the day before most of us had to depart. Both lines are completely bolted, as Tasanaroro's rock faces don't have many cracks.

Soava Dia is to the right of Fire in the Belly and left of Toakagasy, and the routes never cross. Our route can be climbed in a long day, but a good strategy for free climbing is to sleep at the base of the enormous notch splitting the face—it's a five-star bivy! This route is equipped for rappels or it is possible to traverse to Tsaranoro Be and descend that formation's normal route (see below).

Roguiez and Valet stayed for another two weeks to attempt a free ascent of Soava Dia, which they managed, with one bivouac, with Robin climbing all pitches free and Tristan falling once. The route has seven pitches of 7a or harder, with a 7c+ crux pitch.

During our time in the area, expedition photographer Gaël Bouquet des Chaux and some members of the team completed a traverse from Tsaranoro Be to Tsaranoro Atsimo, with two 30m pitches (6a) and two rappels, adding some bolts for anchors and protection. The traverse can be done in either direction. Details are at the AAJ website. 📷 🔍

– JONATHAN CRISON, FRANCE

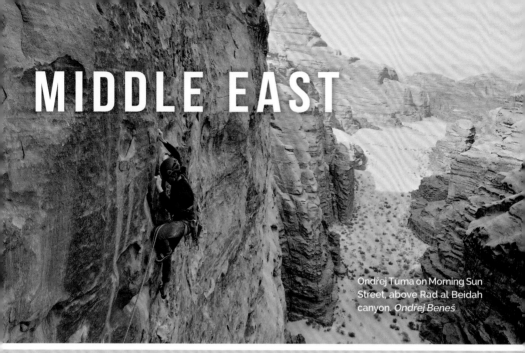

MIDDLE EAST

Ondřej Tůma on Morning Sun Street, above Rad al Beidah canyon. *Ondřej Beneš*

JORDAN

WADI RUM, BARRAH MASSIF, MORNING SUN STREET

AFTER ASKING ARNAUD Petit, a great French climber with experience in Wadi Rum, for various ideas, we arrived in Jordan in January 2019 and drove around to check out the walls that Arnaud had suggested, together with local guide Salim Zalabya. After an evening's debate, we decided on an unclimbed wall accessible from the canyon Rad al Beidah, parallel to the main Barrah canyon. Many questions had arisen upon seeing the wall, regarding its length, steepness, and rock quality, but the line was clear immediately: a black stripe bisecting the impressive east face from top to bottom. We formed two teams—Christian Fascendini and Matěj Svojtka, and myself and Ondřej Tůma—and immediately started to work.

The whole wall looks like waves rippling across the surface of a lake, and for pitch after pitch overhangs followed slabs. The sandstone in Wadi Rum is generally soft, however on our wall the rock was good and no holds broke during the climbing. We established one and a half to two pitches a day, placing bolts from natural stances or hooks. On rest days, it was great to watch the enthusiastic faces of the guys, lit up by their headlamps, as they returned from their daytime shift.

After five days of work and nine pitches climbed, we reached the top of the steepest section and ran out of bolts. Luckily, Israeli climber Elad Omer saved us with a few bolts he had stashed in the village. While Matěj retrieved the bolt cache, Christian, Ondřej, and I began to redpoint the hard pitches. The stress and fear of unstable skyhooks and unknown terrain were replaced by the joy of dancing up these pitches. Compared with other local routes, it was unbelievable how sustained the hard climbing was—our route held nine difficult pitches in a row.

On our last day, January 14, I jumared up the unfinished ninth pitch with Ondřej Tůma while Christian and Matěj redpointed the eighth pitch behind us. Above the ninth pitch the angle of the wall relaxes and we made an easier five-pitch run to the top, finishing at sunset after establishing the first route on this beautiful wall of the Barrah massif. We named the route Morning Sun Street (550m, 15 pitches, 7c+) because it only gets sun in the morning and because of the straight black line running up the center of the wall. 📷

— ONDŘEJ BENEŠ, *CZECH REPUBLIC*

Marcello Sanguineti enjoys Il The nel Deserto on Khanzerya Tower. *Maurizio Oviglia*

WADI SULAM, FIRST ROUTES

In April, a group of 13 climbers led by the Italian Alpine Club (CAI) engaged in an exploratory expedition, organized by the Jordan Tourism Board (JTB), to explore the Wadi Sulam region and establish new rock climbs and canyoneering routes. Wadi Sulam is a wild labyrinth of sandstone canyons about 100km north of well-known Wadi Rum. The wadis of Sulam are situated at about 1,000m above sea level, and the area is reminiscent of a miniature Wadi Rum, with smaller canyons and rock walls up to 200m in height. [*Editor's note: wadi means "canyon" in Arabic.*]

With our guides Ahmad Banihani and Abdulah Al Saheb, we travelled by bus to the village of Showbak, the last inhabited settlement on the road into Wadi Sulam. The next morning we drove to the Showbak plateau in jeeps and established a base camp, then split into teams to explore for rock climbs and canyon routes.

We opened several multi-pitch routes within 20 minutes to an hour of camp, some traditionally protected and some with protection bolts where natural gear was not available. As requested by the JTB, these climbs have bolted belay anchors, and we also equipped one crag with bolted single-pitch climbs at the request of the JTB.

Notable multi-pitch climbs include Il The nel Deserto (200m, 6 pitches, 6b+) on Khanzerya Tower, Via dello Scorpione (100m, 6a) in Black Canyon, and Via Zizzagando (120m, 4 pitches, 6b) on Torre Belluno. Generally, the multi-pitch climbs require a full rack of cams and two ropes to rappel. One day we received an hour of intense rain and hail that flooded the wadis of Sulam, trapping some members of our team against the walls of tight canyons and partially destroying our base camp. [*Photos and route information are at the AAJ website.*] 📷 🔍

— **MARCELLO SANGUINETI,** *CAAI (ITALIAN ACADEMIC ALPINE CLUB)*

TURKEY

RECENT ROCK AND ALPINE ROUTES

Tunç Fındık and partners have developed numerous routes in the mountains of Turkey, with roughly 20 long new rock, ice, and alpine routes from 2016 to 2018. [*See AAJ 2016 for reports on previous Fındık climbs.*] In 2017, in Antalya, Fındık and Cemal Zerepcan made the first ascent of the east face of Çitdibi Tower via Karamursel Sepeti (485m, VI-), with exposed climbing on "sometimes not so forgiving rock." On the east face of Sivridağ, the same two climbed Lost Friends (325m, VI-).

In late October 2017, Fındık and Zerepcan received a military permit to access the Sat Mountains in far southeastern Turkey, a sensitive area near the borders with Iraq and Iran. Here they did the first ascent of the east ridge of Satbaşı Spire (3,475m), an elegant tower with good granite. Their route is called Mudur Yolu (575m, with six pitches of technical climbing up to IV+). Fındık said there are many good climbs waiting to be done in this region.

In the Aladag Mountains, in late August 2018, Fındık, Kemal Doğan, and Burak Gürer climbed the south ridge of Kucuk Demirkazik (3,425m) by the route 1071 (500m, 9 technical pitches, VI-). In November 2018, Fındık, Doğa Ceylan, Bora Maviş, and Serhan Pocan climbed a route up the southwest face of Demirkazık (3,757m): Montaigne (1,300m, with 300m of technical climbing and difficulties to IV+ and M4). In 2017, two other routes were climbed up this face, to the left of Montaigne.

More information and photos of these climbs, plus other recent new routes in Turkey, are at the AAJ website. 📷 🔍

— *INFORMATION FROM* **TUNÇ FINDIK**, *TURKEY*

Satbaşı Spire (far left) in the Sat Mountains. The east ridge is the right skyline. *Tunç Fındık*

OMAN / WESTERN HAJAR

JEBEL KAWR, NORTH FACE, VACANZE (R)OMANE

THIS TRIP TO Oman was like an unexpected gift: It arrived at the last moment, and I had no idea what to expect. I had been planning to realize a dream of climbing the famous Venezuelan tepui; we had a close-knit and motivated team, and we were engaging with a group of reliable locals in a project that would go beyond mere mountaineering, to help the local population and support responsible tourism and resource protection. [*See tepuiproject.org.*] But considering the rapidly changing political and economic situation in Venezuela, we decided to postpone our journey until more stable times.

From the ashes of this project, Simone Pedeferri offered a plan B: Oman. And so we found ourselves as a team of four—myself, Simone, Stefano Caligiore, and my partner Arianna Colliard—driving about the dusty, rough roads of Oman, looking for walls, with 100 bolts, a drill, and a great desire to climb. We soon focused on the north wall of Jebel Kawr, just above the small village of Al Kumeira, and after some searching we found a steep, unclimbed limestone wall about 1.5 hours walk west from the village. [*The north face of Jebel Kawr is 7km to 8km long, with several distinct walls. The Said Wall, directly above Al Kumeira village, has seen at least four routes established over the last decade. The wall described in this report is 3km to 4km west of the Said Wall and has no previously reported climbs.*]

We spent three days equipping the route, emulating the style in Rätikon or Wenden: climbing ground-up, without aid, and drilling only from natural stances or skyhooks. Thus the route is an "alpine sport route": bolted, but with many runouts between. The result is Vacanze (R)omane (450m, 8a). After opening the route, Simone and I both free climbed it, each leading the crux pitches and swapping leads on the easier pitches.

Undoubtedly the moment that impressed me the most was our arrival at the village of Al Kumeira, 12km up a dirt road, with only two houses, four people, and 20 goats. We seemed to have landed in a place completely outside the modern world. An old shepherd of indefinite age welcomed us warmly in his language. He presented us with a giant bag of dates and made us understand, by gestures, that we could camp on his land as long as we wanted. These scenes struck me deeply. How is it possible that these people, who in our eyes have nothing, can share what little they have with complete strangers? And how is it possible that for us (myself included) it is often so difficult to share our riches with those less fortunate than us? 📄 📷

— **MATTEO DELLA BORDELLA**, *ITALY*

GEORGIA

The steep granite headwall of the Grigorenko-Prigoda route on the west face of Ushba, during a 2017 alpine-style ascent and attempted free climb of this 2,300-meter route. *Pawel Karczmarczyk*

The north face of Chatyn-tau. (A) Main summit (4,412m) and (B) west summit (4,310m). (1) East Ridge (5B, 1952). (2) Original finish to Mishliaev Route (6A, 1959). (3) Polish finish in 2016. Other routes on main face not shown. (4) West Ridge (3A, 1903). *Pawel Karczmarczyk*

CHATYN-TAU, NORTH FACE, FIRST FREE ASCENT

FROM JULY 24–27, 2016, Maciej Bedrejczuk, Piotr Sulowski, and I made the first free ascent of the Rhombus, the outstanding north-facing feature on Chatyn-tau (4,412m). Around half a dozen routes climb the 600m-plus rock wall of the Rhombus, and we chose the 1959 Mishliaev Route (6A), which follows a chimney system toward the right side and was used to make the first winter ascent of the north face (*AAJ 2007*).

Sustained difficulties on loose rock with poor protection pushed us to our limits. We climbed alpine-style with two bivouacs (no tent). From the second, below the upper pillar leading directly to the main top, we traversed right and climbed to the col between the west top (4,310m) and main summit. From here we followed the west ridge to the highest point and descended to the Ushba Plateau, where we made our third bivouac. We climbed the 1,160m face at M6+ 6c 70° R. It's worth noting that the north face of Chatyn-tau is isolated from civilization by an approach of two long days up the chaotic and complex Chalati Glacier.

In July 2017, the three of us attempted to make the first free ascent of the 1972 Grigorenko–Prigoda Route (6A) on the west face of Ushba (4,710m); the first alpine-style ascent of the route was not until 2015. We completed an alpine-style ascent with two bivouacs on the face and a third in the col between south and north (4,694m) summits, but wet rock forced us to use aid on four pitches on the headwall. The technical grades of the 2,300m ascent were 6a A2 M5 WI4 70°.

– PAWEL KARCZMARCZYK, *POLAND*

SHKHARA WEST, SOUTHWEST COULOIR (NOT TO SUMMIT) AND SKI DESCENT

In 2008, Americans Jason Thompson, Tyler Jones, and Seth Waterfall visited Georgia's Svaneti region and attempted the first known ascent and descent of a proud couloir dropping from the crest of the 13km-long Bezengi Wall, slightly west of Shkhara West (5,068m). They retreated at about two-thirds height when they encountered ice above a narrow rock choke. Thompson returned in 2015 with Canadians Forrest Coots and Chad Sayers, only to be thwarted by ice filling the line from bottom to top.

Mary McIntyre (USA) and I arrived in May and eventually made a base camp on a relatively flat part of the Xalde (Zalde) Glacier, seemingly the best position to avoid nearby avalanches. We waited eight days there for decent weather. At 2 a.m. on day nine, we dug out the tents and walked up to the couloir. The snow was isothermal garbage, and our ski poles sank nearly to the hand grips. But as we climbed into the couloir, the snow became firmer, and just above the bergschrund, about 500m above camp, we transitioned to crampons. I measured the steepness of the middle of the chute at a reasonable 53°.

The southwest couloir of Shkhara West (5,068m) in center. The summit is the peak to the right. *Brody Leven*

Mary decided to turn around just past the choke at around 4,200m while I continued. My altitude watch read 4,886m at the top of the couloir. I'd had back-of-mind aspirations to continue to the nearby summit of Shkhara West, but the ridgeline appeared too difficult and corniced for soloing. The ski descent was largely anticlimactic. While fully prepared to rappel tricky sections—particularly at the steep crux—I was able to leave my skis on and the rope in my backpack throughout the entire 1,400m descent back to camp. No fixed gear was left on the route. 🖳 📷

– BRODY LEVEN, *AAC*

SHKHARA MAIN, PARTIAL SKI DESCENT (2010)

In the summer of 2010, Boris Avdeev (an American resident) and I went to the Caucasus, where we climbed Shkhara (5,193m) by the Beknu Route on the south pillar (2,200m, 5B 55°). I was then able to make a partial ski descent of this route, from the summit down to a cliff at 4,300m; most of this was skiable—only now and again did I need to take off skis. It was one of my hardest climbs and definitely my most difficult ski descent—arguably the most difficult ski line in the Caucasus. We also did geological work and surveyed the summit by GPS, confirming that Shkhara is Georgia's highest peak. Sadly, it was our last journey together, as in 2012 Boris died in an avalanche on Mt. Dana in California.

– PETER SCHÖN, *AUSTRIA*

More ski descents in the Caucasus: *From 2006 to 2013, Peter Schön and various partners made numerous ski descents in the Caucasus, including the first known descent of Mkinvartsveri (a.k.a. Kazbek, 5,034m), via the southeast face direct, as well as the first descent of the northeast face; a partial ski descent of Janga-Tau (5,058m), first ski descents on Chatyn-Tau West (4,310m), and the first known ski descent of the northeast face of Ortsveri (4,350m).*

KAZAKHSTAN

Kirill Belotserkovskiy starting the ice runnels of the upper part of the December 2018 route on the north face of Ordzhonikidze. *Grigory Schukin*

ORDZHONIKIDZE, NORTH FACE, NEW ROUTES

THE ZAYLIYSKIY ALATAU is the northernmost part of the Tien Shan, and the Tuyuk-Su subrange—the mountains around the Tuyuk-Su valley—are easily accessed from Almaty, Kazakhstan's largest city. It's my home range: I work as a mountain instructor and also climb there for fun. The highest mountain in the valley is Ordzhonikidze (4,410m). In June I soloed a new route on the north face, and then in December I returned with Grigory Schukin and added another route, the hardest to date.

There are no walk-downs from the summit of Ordzhonikidze. The easiest route is Russian 2B or French PD. On the icy north face were three existing routes, the first by Alexander Kolegov's team in 1956. Much later, Vassily Pivtsov and various friends added two more, in 2000 and 2004. All these were 4A or 4B.

I climbed the north face for the first time in 2014, with Pavel Gryaznov, climbing simultaneously and placing one ice screw per rope length. This is totally unacceptable from a safety point of view, especially if you take into account that some of our screws were 10cm stubbies and the ice was pretty soft. Hey, I thought, soloing would be faster and less dangerous, because there would be only one person who could make a mistake.

I had been playing with this idea every since Pavel and I got down off the route, and last summer everything worked in my favor. I had a gap in my work schedule and the weather was, well, not that bad. I started from the Tuyuk-Su mountaineering camp during the afternoon of June 8. I reached the Manshuk Mametova Glacier in thick mist and light snowfall, and decided it would be best to reach the Ordzhonikidze Glacier, which flows beneath the north face, by traversing over Antikainen (4,000m) via the west ridge. For the next couple of hours, I scrambled up the rocky ridge. Upon crossing the summit, the weather cleared slightly and I felt a bit safer descending the snowy slope toward the glacier. Not far from the north face of Ordzhonikidze, I spotted a hollow in the snow below a big boulder. As I had not brought a tent, only a sleeping bag, this seemed a good place to stop for the night.

I set off next morning at 5 a.m., opting to climb a new route on the left side of the face. Fifty meters of steep snow led to a 30m rock band split by an ice gully. After climbing the gully, I raced up snow slopes beneath the seracs. The upper part of the face was covered with a thick layer of loose snow, and in some places I had to dig down a meter to get to ice. Due to this, I spent around four hours climbing the face and reached the northeast ridge totally exhausted. I followed the easy ridge for 200m to the summit, where I called my wife to tell her I was fine. After only a little rest, I headed down the rocky south ridge to Partisan Pass, then descended a snowy couloir to the moraine and walked two hours back to Tuyuk-Su camp.

The total length of the new route is 1,000m at an overall grade of 4B. The steepest ice is around 70°, and there is easy mixed climbing in the lower part.

In December I returned with Grigory Schukin and climbed another route. This time we camped at Ordzhonikidze Pass, and on the morning of the 26th walked down to the base of our proposed line, which started up the 1956 Kolegov Route then climbed more or less directly through the previously untouched mixed rocky area to the left. It took 10 hours to reach the northeast ridge and a further 30 minutes to gain the summit (overall grade of 5A). We descended the northwest ridge toward Ordzhoni-kidze Pass and eventually regained our tent at 7 p.m. The weather during the climb was cold and windy (around -20°C), and when we reached the mixed section at 10 a.m. spindrift avalanches started to affect us. By the time we reached the summit it was a whiteout. 🗎 📷

– KIRILL BELOTSERKOVSKIY, *KAZAKHSTAN*

The north face of Ordzhonikidze (4,410m). (1) Minin (4A, 1956). (2) Belotserkovskiy (4B, solo, 2018). (3) Kolegov (4B, 1956). (4) Belotserkovskiy-Schukin (5A, 2018). (5) Pivtsov (4B, 2000). (6) Pivtsov (4A, 2004). (7) Northwest ridge (3A, Mamontov and team, 1936). *Kirill Belotserkovskiy*

BAYANCOL, SOUTHWEST SPUR AND SOUTHEAST RIDGE

FROM JULY 26 to 28, Murat Otepbayev (leader), Tursunali Aubakirov, Igor Malkin, Maxim Pavlov, and Grigory Schukin from Almaty climbed a new route on the south side of Bayancol (5,841m). Situated directly opposite Khan Tengri above the North Inylchek Glacier, Bayancol was first climbed in 1953, via the north ridge, by Vladimir Sipilov's party (4B). It appears the first route on the south face, above the North Inylchek, was not climbed until 2008, when Almaty mountaineers Gennady Durov and Boris Dedeshko followed the southeast ridge (5A) to the summit, making one bivouac. The lack of attention is easily explained by the fact that more or less everyone visiting Khan Tengri's north-side base camp concentrates on climbing this popular, almost 7,000m peak.

Bayancol's southeast ridge descends from the summit to around 5,600m, where it splits into two arms. The 2008 route climbed the eastern arm, while the 2018 route climbed the western one, a southwest-facing spur. The five Almaty mountaineers climbed 17 pitches up the loose, rocky spur to join the southeast ridge, which they followed

[Top] The south face of Bayancol, seen across the North Inylchek Glacier from Khan Tengri. (A) Pik Odinadtzaty (5,437m). (B) Odinadtzaty Pass (4,850m). (C) Bayancol (5,841m). (D) Pik Kazakhstan (5,761m). (1) The obvious southwest ridge leading directly to the summit does not appear to have had any ascents. (2) Southwest spur to southeast ridge (2018, 5A). (3) Southeast ridge (5A, 2008). *Kirill Belotserkovskiy* [Bottom] Tursunali Aubakirov following Igor Malkin on the upper section of the southeast ridge of Bayancol, with the top section of the unclimbed southwest ridge forming the left skyline. *Murat Otepbayev*

(cornices and a few ice steps) to the summit (5A). After camping on top, they descended northwest to Odinadtzaty Pass (4,850m), from which they continued south down to Khan Tengri base camp. Prior to the climb, they had all summited Khan Tengri from this camp.

In previous times, Bayancol lay on the Kazakhstan-Kyrgyzstan frontier, but a treaty that went into effect in 2008 led to the entire mountain being placed within Kazakhstan. ◙

– KIRILL BELOTSERKOVSKIY, *KAZAKHSTAN*

KYRGYZSTAN

ZOR KUMTOR VALLEY, TWO FIRST ASCENTS

In late September and early October, our Czech-Slovak team made a trip to the Zor Kumtor Valley, which is the last valley flowing north into the long Kichik-Alai Valley before the latter rises to Kichik-Alai Pass (4,082m).

The Kichik-Alai or Little Alai mountains, which lie south of Osh, comprise two ranges that run roughly east-west on either side of the Kichik-Alai River. Thanks to a new gravel road, it was pretty easy in 2018 to reach any of the side valleys above the main Kichik-Alai Valley.

There had been heavy snowfall in mid-September, and above 3,900m there was at least 30cm of fresh snow. We established our

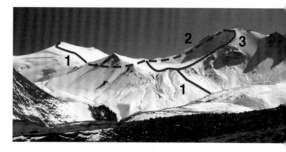

The upper Zor Kumtor Valley. (1) Approach and ascent of the north face of Pik 100 Let Czechoslovakii (4,862m, 2A). (2) East couloir of Zor Kumtor (4,620m). (3) Northeast rib of Zor Kumtor (3A). *Michal Kleslo*

base camp just below the snow line. The Zor Kumtor has two peaks: The higher is more remote and more glaciated, the lower closer to camp but with a short, steep glacier on the north side.

We first climbed the higher peak, which we named Pik 100 Let Czechoslovakii ("100 Years of Czechoslovakia," 39°48'29.67"N, 72°32'44.71"E Google Earth, 4,862m), as Czechs and Slovaks were celebrating this anniversary in October 2018. A direct approach via the main glacier was too complex, so we climbed a steep slope to the right to reach a sort of hanging plateau to the east of the lower peak. From here we continued south across a small glacier to reach the moraines of the main glacier below the higher peak. It was now an easy climb to the top: hard ice covered with a few centimeters of snow rising to 40–45° (in descent we rappelled this section). Just below the top was a broad snow terrace, from which we could easily ascend the last few meters of rock. If the weather permits, from this point you can clearly see Pik Lenin and all the northern Pamir. The overall grade was 2A.

We took a rest day and then climbed the smaller peak, which we named Zor Kumtor (4,620m), as it is visible on the approach up the valley. (The main peak is hidden from most parts of the valley.) J. Smrtka and M.Sranc climbed the right edge of the northeast-facing plateau (three pitches of ice up to 60°), which reached the northwest ridge a little below the summit. They named the route Pelumi (3A). Meanwhile, six of us climbed the east couloir, which rose to 45° below the final cornice, at 1B. Both parties arrived on top at the same time.

The highest summit in this group, which lies a little southeast of the Zor Kumtor in the southern range, is Pik Skobelov (5,051m). These mountains offer much scope for new routes on 4,000m peaks, as they largely have been overlooked due to the proximity of Pik Lenin and its surrounding mountains directly across the border to the south. The climbing season in this region can last as long as from May to October, and no special permit is required for access. 📷 🔍

– MICHAL KLESLO, *PAMIR7000, CZECH REPUBLIC*

View east from the ascent of Pik Vulture to (A) White Lady, (B) Rabbit Ear, (C) Twin Towers, (D) Yellow Tower, and (E) Black Spark. *Mark Aitken*

WESTERN AT BASHI RANGE, MULTIPLE FIRST ASCENTS

THE AT BASHI Range is more than 100km in length and about 30km wide, a beautiful region of snow and rock peaks, many still unclimbed. The highest summit is Pik Rhianydd (4,801m), first climbed in 2017 (*AAJ 2018*), and average peak altitude across the range is around 4,300m. Our expedition was organized by the International School of Mountaineering (ISM), which has done many trips to the At Bashi. The goal was unclimbed summits in the far less explored western sector of the range.

Our team comprised the guides Adrian Nelhams (leader), Max Cole, Tommaso Dusi, and Aleksey Potockiy, along with team members Mark Aitken, Tony Belgrave, Guy Burton, Vincent Gunnarsson, Kamal Kayat, Ruta Mikulenaite, Jason Sheldrake, Harry Wilson, and David Woods.

Arriving in country during August, we approached the At Bashi from the south, which required special permits due to its proximity to the Chinese border. We established base camp (3,762m) at 40°50'50.1"N, 75°36'01.8"E, and later an advanced base at 4,040m farther up valley.

From these camps we were able to summit 13 peaks between 4,152m and 4,768m, of which 11 were previously unclimbed. We were later informed by Vladimir Komissarov (president of the Kyrgyz Alpine Club) that one of our 11 new summits, Pik White Lady (4,768m), the highest and most beautiful peak in this part of the range, had previously been reached during the Soviet era by a survey crew using a helicopter, but no alpine ascent was made before ours. *Descriptions and coordinates of all these climbs can be found at the AAJ website.*

– MARK AITKEN *AND* ADRIAN NELHAMS, *U.K.*

CENTRAL KOKSHAAL-TOO, DJANGART RANGE, MANY FIRST ASCENTS

AT THE END of August, Jorian Bakker (27), Noël Diepens (31), Wout Martens (27), Line van den Berg (26), Rik van Odenhoven (27), and Mats Wentholt (27), with team coaches Court Haegens (47) and Boris Textor (32), traveled to the Djangart Range. This was the last stage of the Royal Dutch Climbing and Mountaineering Federation's two-year training program for young alpinists (NKBV Expeditie Academie). Our team of six had been trained for the last two years by experienced Dutch alpinists and guides.

During the four-week trip, team members climbed nine previously virgin peaks and made 13 first ascents. All-terrain vehicles and horses were used to access a base camp at 41°44'57.4"N, 78°57'3.7"E, and from here various groups climbed in four different valleys. They found generally very solid rock (mostly granite), good snow and ice conditions, and stable weather. Combined with a good team spirit, these ingredients made for a very enjoyable and successful expedition.

On September 3, Haegens, Martens, and van den Berg linked two unclimbed peaks, Pik Vsad-

nik (4,803m) and Pik Pionerov (4,874m), via a 3km ridge that forms the border with China. They named the route No Guts No Glory Ridge (D), encountering sustained difficulties, reaching a maximum of IV+ M4 50°. The outing took 20 hours camp to camp.

On the 9th and 10th, Martens and van den Berg made the first ascent of the north face of Pik Alexandra (5,290m), a summit reached only once before, in 2011, by an Anglo-Danish party (*AAJ 2012*). The striking line leading to the summit was named Dutch Direct (800m, TD+). Martens and van den Berg encountered one pitch of sustained 85°+ ice and about 150m of 80° ice. The angle of the face was never less than 50°, and the ice was of dream quality; only the crux pitch, which had several vertical sections, was thin. At 4,950m the pair sat out a windy night on a small ledge, with no water or cooked food due to a failing gas cylinder. From the summit they descended via a previously unclimbed line on the aesthetically pleasing south side of the mountain.

Also on the 9th, Bakker, Textor, van Odenhoven, and Wentholt climbed Navat Spur (1,000m, D 60°), the aesthetic northeast spur of Pik Buddyness (5,172m). They decided to name the long snow and ice route after the sugary snow they encountered—Navat means "sugar" in Kyrgyz.

On the 17th, Diepens, Haegens, Martens, Textor, van Odenhoven, and Wentholt ascended the provisionally named Pik Ronald Naar (5,014m) by its northeast face (AD+ 50°). This was probably the last unclimbed 5,000m peak in the Djangart, and the team would like to honor Naar for his great inspiration and huge contribution to Dutch mountaineering.

On the north face of Pik Currahee (5,025m), Bakker and van den Berg climbed Line of Decline (450m, TD- 85°) on September 18. Scottish conditions were encountered for most of the day in this mixed/ice gully, and the three crux pitches were steep and thin. They descended to the west via the route of the first ascensionists (D-, Conlon-Davidson, 2013). The route name reflects the quality of ice, which deteriorated as the climbers approached the top. It also indicates the fatigue the pair felt after many weeks in the mountains.

On the 20th, Haegens and Wentholt climbed a direct line on snow and ice up the virgin north face of Pik Emma (4,783m). They named the route Bas van

[Top] **Line of Decline on the north face of Pik Currahee.** *Line van den Berg* [Middle] The Dutch Direct on the north face of Pik Alexandra. *Wout Martens* [Bottom] The Navat Spur on Pik Buddyness. *Boris Textor*

der Smeede Tribute (500m, D+ 80°) in honor of an enthusiastic alpinist and experienced expedition climber—very active within the Dutch climbing community—who died of leukemia in 2017. Pik Emma was first climbed via the north ridge in 2011 (*AAJ 2012*).

Other ascents during this expedition: Pik Andrea (4,566m) and Pik Surok (4,606m) were climbed on September 2 via the west face (PD+); Pik Sutherland (5,080m) on the 3rd by the new route Lost Voice (AD 60°); Eagles View (3,669m, first ascent) on the 8th via the rock route Ragga (150m, 4 pitches, VI+); a new route on Pik 3,920m (Bird Ridge, 420m, 7 pitches, D V+) on the 13th; the first ascents of Lucky (5,172m), Naomi (4,858m), and Catharina (4,840m) via the north ridges (AD- 60° II), also on the 13th; and the first ascent of Pik Ilbirs (4,852m) on the 18th via the west face and north ridge (AD-). A full expedition report should be available in the future at http://expeditieacademie.nl. 🔲

– LINDSAY GRIFFIN, *WITH INFORMATION FROM* WOUT MARTENS, *NETHERLANDS*

USHAT-TOO, PIK USHAT AND OTHER CLIMBS

JAMES BAILIE, ALISTAIR Bell, Vasili Trigas, and I headed into the Ushat-too mountains, south of the town of Inylchek (Engilchek), in mid-August. Research had revealed that the German explorer Gottfried Merzbacher visited the Ushat Range in 1902, but there appears to be no record of anyone ever climbing there.

We traveled to Inylchek by truck and then left town on the 16th, after arranging horses. We followed the Sarydjaz River valley on abandoned Soviet roads until about 2.5km from the entrance to the Taldybulak Valley, which flows west from the Ushat mountains. Here, a cable got us to the other side of the Sarydjaz River, and then we proceeded on foot. In the Taldybulak Valley a small

track is used by locals but requires crossing the river on several occasions, which could make trekking into this valley difficult or dangerous in certain conditions. However, with the proximity of Maida Adyr Base Camp for the Inylchek Glacier, a little east of the town of Inylchek, it should be possible to get an inexpensive helicopter ride into the valley.

After several days of load carrying and exploration we established base camp on grass-covered drumlins at nearly 3,500m (41°54'21.63"N, 79°9'31.65"E). The weather was generally benign throughout our stay—sunny days with only a few periods of sustained rain. Glaciers were dry and allowed easy access to peaks from base camp.

Pik Ushat and the route of ascent on the north face.
Daniel Comber-Todd

We made the first ascent of Pik Ushat (41°55'27.13"N, 79°13'18.71"E GPS), the highest in the range according to the Soviet maps, from the north tributary of the Taldybulak Glacier. We climbed easy snow slopes to the base of the north face, where several pitches of moderate ice led to the of the west ridge, which we simulclimbed to the summit (500m, AD/D). Depending on which Soviet map you use, Ushat is either 5,042m or 5,142m. Our GPS read 5,071m.

We next made an attempt on Pik 4,642m, south of base camp, a picturesque mountain above a high cirque guarded by an icefall. Despite our best efforts, we were turned back by the complex terrain of the icefall, though we feel it should be possible to find a way through.

James and Vasili then made the first ascent of a peak of around 4,600m visible to the north of base camp. Because of its distinct mottled appearance, we nicknamed this mountain "the Beehive." The pair climbed the south face (600m, 5.9 A0) on passable rock interspersed with the occasional steep scree ledge.

The area has plenty of potential. Given the ambiguities of the local maps, unclimbed Pik 5,140m, southwest of Pik Ushat, might be higher than Ushat; when looking at it from the summit of Ushat, we could not be certain which peak was highest. Pik 5,140m's north face offers 500m of steep rock and ice. Also steep, with many lines of varying difficulty, is the north face of Pik 4,775m, west of Ushat. There are also some good lines on the peaks at the head of the north tributary of the Taldybulak Glacier. (*Photos of many peaks in the area are at the AAJ website.*)

Our expedition was supported by a grant from the Expedition Fund of the Australian National University Mountaineering Club. 🖸 🔍

– DANIEL COMBER-TODD, *AUSTRALIA*

PIK POBEDA EAST, FIRST SKI DESCENT (2010)

IN THE SUMMER of 2010, after a ski descent from Shkhara in the Georgian Caucasus (*see p. 265*), Peter Schön traveled to the Tien Shan with Anders Ödman, hoping to make a ski descent of the north face of Pik Pobeda (7,439m). That objective proved too avalanche prone, so the pair opted to ski the more remote Pik Pobeda East (6,762m).

They acclimatized by climbing Khan Tengri (6,995m) by the standard route from the south. Subsequently, their approach up the Zvezdochka Glacier toward Pobeda East took several days, and the pair witnessed frequent avalanches, the proportions of which they had never seen before or would see since. One huge avalanche, probably emanating around 6,500m, powdered them in their tent on the glacier at 4,800m.

After reaching the Chon-Toren (or Teren) Pass at 5,488m, they began a summit push up the 35° to 50°-plus northeast ridge of Pobeda East. Ödman eventually turned

Peter Schön ascending the Zvezdochka Glacier toward Chon-Toren Pass (on the right). To the left and behind the pass is the large bulk of Pik Voenna Topografi (6,873m). The northeast ridge of Pobeda East rises to the right from the pass. *Anders Ödman*

around 200m below the top, wanting to preserve a bit of energy for the descent. Schön continued alone, punching through crusty wind slabs and negotiating tiring unconsolidated snow over rock. Exhausted, he reached the summit at 2:30 p.m. After taking photos, Schön made a lone ski descent of the beautiful ridge: steep, exposed, and above a remote desert of ice and snow. 🖸

– LINDSAY GRIFFIN, *WITH INFORMATION FROM* PETER SCHÖN, *AUSTRIA*

The view north from the Abalakov Route on Pik Pobeda over the Ak-tau Group. (A) Khan Tengri. (B) Pik Pyramida. (C) Ak-tau. (D) Pik Shipilova (6,201m). After climbing Ak-tau, the two Austrians descended the steep glacier between Pyramida and Ak-tau to complete their five-day traverse. *Markus Gschwendt*

AK-TAU TRAVERSE

BETWEEN THE WELL-KNOWN summits of Khan Tengri and Pik Pobeda sleeps a seldom-visited yet interesting group of mountains known as the Ak-tau Group, after its central peak, Ak-tau. [Ak-tau is 6,181m; Pik Shipilova (6,201m) is the highest summit of the group, lying on the long southeast arm of Ak-tau.] In order to acclimatize before an attempt on Pik Pobeda, Simon Taffner and I made a self-supported circular traverse through the range. With little available information, we had to choose our route simply by going and having a look. We most likely climbed no new ground, but the exact track of our journey may never have been completed previously.

In late July, from the standard base camp on the South Inylchek Glacier at just over 4,000m, reached by helicopter, we first traveled east and then headed south along the ridge leading to Majlina (5,285m). Crossing this summit and continuing in the same direction, we reached the upper glacier plateau north of Ak-tau. After a night on the col between Ak-tau and Pik Pyramida (5,876m), we then climbed Ak-tau by its west-northwest ridge.

From there we continued south-southwest down a steep, narrow glacier, near the bottom of which we made our last camp. The following day we reached the Zvezdochka Glacier, below the north face of Pobeda, and returned northward to base camp.

Snow conditions at lower altitudes in this area are generally poor, and often during this journey we had to dig through deep snow—sometimes up to our chests—despite the fact that 2017 and 2018 were known for having relatively little snowfall. Steep faces, narrow ridges with cornices, and heavily crevassed glaciers made the traverse a real adventure. The narrow glacier we descended from Ak-tau could be a real problem in different conditions.

Subsequently, I made an ascent of the Abalakov Route (6A, 1956) on the north face of Pik

Simon Taffner at 5,250m on the knife-edge summit ridge of Majlina (5,285m) during the Ak-tau traverse. *Markus Gschwendt*

Pobeda (7,439m). Snow conditions were good, making this is a far safer line than Pobeda's normal route (the north rib to the west ridge). Simon felt unwell and descended from 7,000m to wait at our high camp at 6,600m while I continued. Late in the day I reached the last rocks on the route. The real summit is either 300m east or west of that point. I believe it is the east top, but suspect that most parties doing the normal route only reach the heavily corniced point to my west. I continued up and to the east until there were only a few meters of snow and ice—and a cornice—above me. At this point I turned back to reach our high camp by dark.

— MARKUS GSCHWENDT, *AUSTRIA*

TAJIKISTAN

PIK KORZHENEVSKAYA, SOUTH FACE, OL'CHA

In January a four-man Kyrgyz-Russian team climbed a new route up the middle of the south face of Korzhenevskaya (7,105m) in the Academy of Sciences Range. The main difficulties of this line are associated with icefalls that in summer often produce huge avalanches, the blast from which will reach the Moskvina Glade Base Camp (4,200m). In the depths of winter it was anticipated the icefalls should be more stable, and in fact only a few small breaks occurred during the ascent, always a safe distance from the group.

Roman Abildaev, Alexey Usatykh (both Russian), Semen Dvornichenko, and team leader Sergey Seliverstov (both Kyrgyzstan) left Moskvina Glade on January 17 and

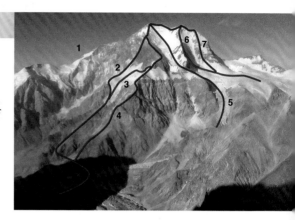

The wind-blasted south face of Pik Korzhenevskaya (7,105m). (1) Northwest ridge (Ugarov, 1953, first ascent of peak). (2) Southwest spur to south ridge (Dobrovolsky, 1966, 5B). (3) Southwest face to south ridge (Tsetlin, 1966, 5A, today's normal route). (4) Variation. (5) South face (Ol'Cha, 2018). (6) South Spur (Romanov, 1961, 5B). (7) South Rib (Bozhukov, 1966, 5B). Not all routes are shown. *Expedition Photo*

spent two days moving up the Moskvina Glacier and the broken icefall, in temperatures down to -30°C and wind gusts up to 80–90 kph. In similar conditions they progressed to 5,800m on the 19th, and the next day climbed past a shoulder at 5,900m toward the center of the face. Then, after five pitches across crumbling rock (60–80°, with a few small overhangs), followed by an ice wall and a horizontal traverse at 60°, they reached the base of the large hanging glacier that descends from the summit.

On January 21 they made their way with difficulty through four ice steps on this glacier slope, camping for the night at 6,450m. The next day, their sixth on the route, they left the tents and headed for the summit, negotiating large crevasses and then avalanche-prone slopes between 6,650m and 6,800m. At 12:30 p.m. they were on the summit in a wind of 50 kph and temperature between -35° and -40°C. The team was safely in base camp by midday on the 24th. The route has been named Ol'cha in memory of a friend, Olga Goroganina. 📑 📷

— *INFORMATION SUPPLIED BY* **ANNA PIUNOVA**, *MOUNTAIN.RU, RUSSIA*

LYAP NAZAR, FIRST SKI DESCENT (2009)

In August 2009, Peter Schön and Andreas Riesner made the first ski descent of Lyap Nazar (5,990m). This peak, recently renamed Afzalsho Olimov by local authorities, lies just south-southwest of the well-known Pik Revolution (now officially Quillai Istiqiol, 6,940m) in the Yazgulem Range. The two Austrians skied the northwest ridge and west couloir, with sections of at least 50°.

— *INFORMATION FROM* **PETER SCHÖN**, *AUSTRIA*

Bivouac on the southeast ridge of Ghaintar Chhish, one of two peaks attempted by Dutch climbers above the Dasbar Valley. At right is the Ghamobar massif, with a high point over 6,500 meters. *Menno Schokker*

KACHQIANT

A RARELY SEEN BEAUTY IN THE HINDU RAJ IS CLIMBED

BY BAS VISSCHER

INSPIRED BY FLORIAN Tolle's report in *AAJ 2008,* Ruud Rotte, Danny Schoch, Menno Schokker, and I left the Netherlands on June 3 for the Dasbar Valley in far northwest Pakistan. We were possibly the first climbers to visit since Tolle's French team in 2007.

We hired 30 porters in Nialthi and reached a base camp at 3,600m, where we planned to stay three and a half weeks. Beautiful, unclimbed Kachqiant, named by the late Bernard Domenech, was our main goal, but we also wanted to explore other mountains. Acclimatization trips quickly showed the snow to be very soft during daytime; climbing on snow was only possible at night. We made an advanced base at 5,000m, at the foot of Kachqiant's northeast ridge.

After two weeks of acclimatization and exploration, Danny, Menno, and I attempted the northeast ridge. It was a big struggle. The wind was extremely cold and the snow very powdery. Our progress was slow, and at 5,450m we decided to retreat.

Subsequently, Menno and Ruud went for the southeast ridge of Ghaintar Chhish (a.k.a. Gainthir Chhish, 6,273m), whose main peak had only been climbed from the far side. The southeast ridge rises to an unclimbed eastern summit at about 6,200m. They packed a tent and food for four days, but at an altitude of 5,800m they decided to retreat—the rock was very poor and there were many wet snow avalanches.

Danny and I went for a final try on Kachqiant. Regaining the previous high point proved difficult, but there was less wind. An extra camp, lots of food, and thick down jackets were parts of the new strategy. At 2:30 a.m. on July 1, we left our tent at 5,500m. The snow was very powdery and unconsolidated. A lot of exhausting wading followed, though some of the snow overlay bulletproof black ice. There were a couple of 70° ice pitches, but these were easy compared to the sections of

deep snow. Our progress was very slow, but luckily the conditions improved on the final ridge.
At 4 p.m. we reached the summit. What a happy
moment! Maps quote a height of 6,015m; the
GPS on our satellite phone indicated 5,990m. We
graded the ascent TD- (1,000m, mostly 50cm of
steep powder snow on black ice, with five sections of
60–70° ice and a knife-edge corniced ridge).

Taking no risk, we descended the ridge
entirely by rappelling from Abalakov anchors
with our single 60m rope, finally reaching our
tent at 1 a.m. We were completely exhausted and
next day rested many hours in the sun. When the
temperature cooled, we descended the tricky ridge.

Kachqiant from the north (2007 photo). The Dutch
climbed the obvious northeast ridge falling
toward the camera (TD-, 1,000m). *Florian Tolle*

The next day we walked out of the Dasbar Valley with smiles on our faces.

The Hindu Kush and Hindu Raj have not been frequented much by Western climbers in recent
years. While we met many friendly people and the reception we received in Nialthi was wonderful,
it was hard to assess the risk. The police in Ghizer District decided to send an agent to stay with
us for our entire time in base camp. Future expeditions will have to make their own judgment.

We had good weather in June, with very hot days and cold nights. Better snow conditions
might be found in September or October, but by that time it could also be very dry. The rock
seems good in the lower valley, and there are some serious walls. Higher in the valley, the rock is
poor. Lots of peaks have seracs, so finding safe lines is not easy.

Probably the best unclimbed goals are the north-northwest ridge of Ghamobar Zom (a.k.a. Dhuli
Chhish, a collection of summits over 6,400m; the highest, 6,518m, was climbed in 1973 by Italians, via
the southwest face and southeast ridge); the southeast ridge of Ghaintar Chhish (6,273m, first climbed
from the north in 1968 by an Austrian expedition); and perhaps Ayesh Bilou (5,000m). Attractive Peak
5,900m is hard to access and might be better from the adjacent valley to the west. [*Editor's note: The
online report has good photos of many objectives in this area.*] 📷 🔍

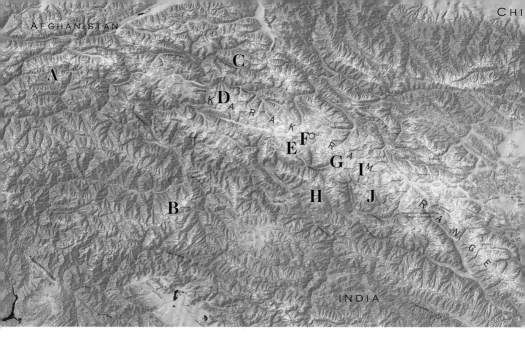

Map of the mountains of northern Pakistan and neighboring countries, highlighting the locations of various reports in this section. (A) Kachqiant in the Hindu Raj. (B) Nanga Parbat in the Himalaya. (C) The Ghujerab Mountains of the Karakoram. (D) Lupghar Sar West in the Hispar Muztagh. (E) The Baintha Brakk group in the Panmah Muztagh. (F) The Choktoi Glacier, where Suma Brakk is located. (G) Hainabrakk East Tower in the Baltoro Muztagh. (H) Kiris Peak in the Shimshak Mountains. (I) Laila in the Masherbrum Range. (J) The Lachit Valley in the Tagas Mountains. A high-resolution copy of this map is available at the AAJ website (search "Carey Karakoram map"). *Dallin Carey*

HIMALAYA

NANGA PARBAT, RUPAL FACE, ATTEMPTED VARIATION TO MESSNER ROUTE

CLIMBING IN ALPINE style, Czech climbers Marek Holeček and Tomáš Petreček attempted a variation to the south-southeast spur (a.k.a. Messner Route, 1970). From below the Merkl Rinne, the steep gully the Messner brothers followed to exit the Rupal Face, the Czechs slanted up to the left following a natural line of weaknesses through rocky buttresses. On September 2, after six days on the face, they reached around 7,800m on the headwall below the crest of the southwest ridge. However, strong wind forced them to descend 400m to find shelter. With increasing wind and a poor forecast, they retreated.

The Messner Route has only seen two ascents (neither in alpine style), the second in 2005 by the late Kim Chang-ho and Lee Hyun-Jo (fixed ropes to 7,550m), who traversed the mountain by descending the Kinshofer Route.

– LINDSAY GRIFFIN

KARAKORAM / GHUJERAB MOUNTAINS

FIFTH KOKSIL GLACIER, CHAPCHINGOL SAR AND OTHER PEAKS

TOMAŽ GOSLAR, MOJCA ŠVAJGER, and I arrived in Pakistan on July 10 with the aim of climbing a high peak in the Hindu Kush. However, due to security issues on the Pakistan-Afghanistan border, our permit was denied and we had to focus quickly on another area, below 6,500m, where a climbing permit was not required. We decided to go to the Koksil Valley, south of and close to the Karakoram Highway. This valley lies within Khunjerab National Park and therefore we had to wait three days for an entry permit.

On the 25th we reached base camp at around 4,190m, close to shepherds' huts in the main Koksil Valley, below the Fourth Koksil Glacier. The weather was bad for the next eight days, but we used the few dry hours to explore. On August 1 we set up an advanced base on the Fifth Koksil Glacier at 5,100m, southwest of the main valley. Over the next few days we climbed the three highest peaks in this cirque.

Looking west from the western rim of the Fourth Koksil Glacier at the Fifth Koksil Glacier and (A) Peak 5,809m, (B) Chapchingol Sar (6,103m), and (C) Peak 5,802m, all climbed for the first time in 2018. The Chapchingol Pass (5,241m) lies hidden in the obvious dip in the ridge running away from the camera. *Irena Mrak*

On August 2 we climbed Peak 5,802m GPS (ca 5,800m on Jerzy Wala's Koksil Valley sketch map, included with the online version of this report) via the south-southwest face. The next day we climbed Peak 5,809m (5,760m on the Wala map) via an east to west traverse, and on the 4th we climbed Chapchingol Sar (6,103m; 6,082m on the Wala map) via the southeast face and northeast ridge. [*The name Chapchingol Sar has been attributed to this peak for some time and appears on the Japanese Miyamori maps published in 2001. However, Google Earth and Gunter Seyfferth (himalaya-info.org) mark Chapchingal Sar I more than 10km to the southwest, on the south side of the upper Chapchingol Valley. This other summit is more frequently referred to as Sonia Peak (6,265m, Seyfferth) and was first climbed in the early 1990s.*]

On the 5th we descended to base camp. Two days later we explored the Fourth Koksil Glacier, where we made the first ascent of a peak of around 5,500m on the western rim. The only previous ascent from this glacier basin appears to be Peak 5,830m GPS (5,720m on the Wala map), on the eastern rim (*AAJ 2014*). By August 9 the weather was bad again and we left the area.

These glacier basins have potential for further exploration. While the peaks may be not particularly high, they are beautiful and demanding in their own way, because of the remote situation. 📷 🔍

– IRENA MRAK, *SLOVENIA*

SHUIJERAB GROUP, SHUWERT VALLEY, BANAFSHEH, SOUTH FACE

ON SEPTEMBER 18, Philip De-Beger and I set up base camp at 4,864m at the entrance to the East Shuwert Valley, not far from Shimshal Pass. There was a fair amount of snow, but this cleared over the next few days as we set up an advanced base in the East Shuwert Valley. On the 22nd we made an ascent of Peak 6,040m (36.462939°N, 75.750659°E), the highest in this valley. Our route on the south face was on snow slopes at alpine PD, probably the first ascent of the peak. Our Shimshali guide later suggested the name Banafsheh Sar, which means Violet Peak, after a flower that grows in the area. [*Editor's note: The online report includes a historical summary of ascents in the Shuwert Glacier area.*] 📷

– PETER THOMPSON, *ALPINE CLUB, U.K.*

The big peaks at the western end of the Hispar Muztagh. (A) Peak 6,220m. (B) Lupghar Sar (7,215m). (C) Lupghar Sar West (7,157m), showing the 2018 route on the west face. (D) Distaghil Sar (7,885m). (E) Momhil Sar (7,414m). (F) Trivor (7,728m). (G) Khunyang Chhish (7,852m). *Hansjörg Auer*

SOLO ON LUPGHAR SAR WEST

A NEW ROUTE UP A 7,157-METER PEAK IN THE HISPAR

BY HANSJÖRG AUER

ON JULY 7 I reached the summit of Lupghar Sar West (7,157m) via the previously untouched west face. (This peak was first climbed in 1979 via the southwest ridge.) Completely on my own, and after making some good acclimatization loops around base camp, I climbed from base camp for seven and a half hours to a good bivouac spot at 6,200m. Next morning I climbed a line on the left side of the west face to reach the steep northwest ridge. I followed this past some very loose rock and reached the summit at 11:30 a.m. (Just below the summit cornice, I found an ancient piece of rope, presumably left by a climber in 1979.) The descent proved both complicated and tiring, but nevertheless I made it safely down to base camp at 8 p.m. the same day.

It hadn't been easy to find the right approach to the base of the mountain. The upper Baltbar Glacier is pretty wild, and falling into a crevasse is the last thing you want to do on your own. I used my acclimatization forays to learn more about the approach, and luckily found some nice climbing as well, which was good for my motivation while adapting to the thinner air. I felt stronger than on previous expeditions, which was pretty cool.

I had planned to make two bivouacs on the ascent but decided to push to the top on day two and leave all my gear at around 6,900m, where I reached the northwest ridge. The climbing itself was not too hard—I would say 50–55° ice and M3/M4 on the ridge. But the rock quality was really bad. Halfway up the ridge I was sure I had made a big mistake in leaving the rope below, but in the end all was fine; I tried to stay really focused on the downclimb. My rack included a 60-meter 5mm rope, three ice screws, two cams, two nuts, one beak-style piton, slings, and carabiners.

You obviously take more risk when climbing solo, but it feels so great to move light and fast at high altitude on technical terrain. Furthermore, you're much more focused, which often results in better performance. Soloing at high altitude gave me fewer emotions during the climb than I'm used to. I was able to fade out psychologically hard moments and doubts much easier—maybe because my focus on getting to the top was stronger. 📷

An interview with Austrian climber Hansjörg Auer is featured in episode 13 of the Cutting Edge podcast.

HISTORICAL NOTES ON LUPGHAR SAR: *The rarely visited Lupghar Sar massif comprises three peaks on a high summit ridge. The central summit is always quoted as the highest, though some photographic evidence suggests that it is lower than the east summit. Lupghar Sar West was first climbed in 1979 by Hans and Sepp Gloggner. Their route on the southwest ridge, which featured very rotten rock, was repeated in 1979 and 1980 by Japanese. The first of these Japanese expeditions continued east for more than 1.5km along the sharp ridge, with Tatsuo Nazuka, Hitoshi Shimizu, and Yuichi Wanantabe making the first ascent of the central (main) summit. Lupghar Sar East was climbed via the east ridge in 1987 by the Swiss Lukas Cestmir, Edi Furrer and Ruth Steinmann. In 2000, Frenchman Nicolas Sieger is reported to have climbed "Lupghar Sar West II (7,010m)," described as a peak around 2km northwest of Lupghar Sar West. The only high summit in this direction is a peak of around 6,800m a little over one kilometer to the northwest.*

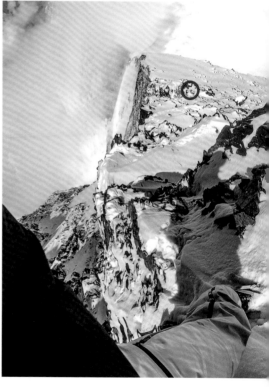

[Top] **A corniced section of the summit ridge of Lupghar Sar West traversed by Auer.** *Hansjörg Auer* [Bottom] **Looking down the steep, loose ground of the upper northwest ridge on Lupghar Sar West.** The red circle marks the author's gear cache, where he moved from the west face (left) onto the ridge. "Halfway up the ridge I was sure I had made a big mistake in leaving the rope below, but in the end all was fine." *Hansjörg Auer*

Alik Berg enjoys some "fine mixed climbing" on the south ridge of Gus Zrakun Sar. *Raphael Slawinski*

GUS ZRAKUN SAR, SOUTH RIDGE

ALIK BERG AND I arrived at our 4,500m base camp on the Yutmaru Glacier on July 14. As often happens on expeditions, neither the final team nor the final objective were what we had planned. At the start, four of us had hoped to explore the largely untouched peaks of the Kondus Valley, but over the winter two team members pulled out, and then, just a couple of months before departure, military authorities refused us a permit for our primary objective, unclimbed K13 (6,666m). We scrambled to find another goal and settled on unclimbed Pumari Chhish East (6,850m Polish map) in the Hispar. I had attempted this peak previously (*AAJ 2010*)—I knew it to be both a difficult and inspiring objective.

Alik and I spent three weeks systematically acclimatizing, starting with day trips and culminating with an ascent of Rasool Sar (5,980m GPS; 5,890m Soviet map), repeating the route I had climbed in 2009 with Eammon Walsh and Ian Welsted. We spent two nights on top to complete our acclimatization.

We now turned to the south face of our main objective, Pumari Chhish East. The shattered glacier below looked impassible, but we were able to find an alternative approach by climbing over a rock spur. From its crest, we could see that the upper half of the south face still looked in good mixed climbing shape. However, it was now late summer, and the snow and ice fields on the lower half had degenerated into wet rock slabs strafed by rockfall. We examined the eastern aspect of the mountain for an alternative route, but found it guarded by batteries of seracs. With just over a week remaining of our scheduled stay at base camp, we cast around for other options and settled on an unclimbed and unnamed peak of 5,980m (GPS) across the Yutmaru Glacier from base camp. [*This summit lies north-northwest of Emily Peak; the Russian map gives it an altitude of 5,936m.*]

An obvious snow and ice rib on the northeast face led directly to the summit, but this had severe serac hazard. Instead we moved much farther left, where a long snow gully rises to the upper south ridge of Emily Peak. We scrambled up rock to the left of the gully, turned right, and continued up the ridge to the summit of Emily Peak, where we bivouacked at around 5,700m. Next day we spent 16 hours negotiating the complex ridge to and from Peak 5,980m, arriving back at our bivouac at midnight. We slept in the following morning before descending south to the Hispar Glacier and walking back around the mountain to base camp. We called the peak Gus Zrakun Sar, after the donkeys that did most of the hard work to get us to base camp (*gus zrakun* is donkey in the local Burushashki dialect).

Looking west across the Yutmaru Glacier from the summit of Rasool Sar. The rounded peak above the gendarme is Gus Zrakun Sar (5,980m GPS). The route of ascent started well left, climbing broken rock left of the obvious long, narrow couloir. The ridge was then followed up right to a small pointed summit—Emily Peak (climbed twice previously from the far side)—and a bivouac was made here both on the ascent and descent. The complex ridge was followed up and right to the summit of Gus Zrakun Sar. The big snow peak on the opposite side of the Hispar Glacier is the highest summit of the Haigutum Group (6,041m on Soviet map). *Raphael Slawinski*

Two days later, in cold rain, we left the meadow where we had spent half the summer. Thanks to the John Lauchlan Memorial Award and MEC Expedition Support Grant for their financial assistance. 📚 📷

— **RAPHAEL SLAWINSKI**, *CANADA, AAC*

BAINTHA BRAKK WEST II, NORTHEAST BUTTRESS, ATTEMPT

ON THE LONG west-northwest ridge of Baintha Brakk (a.k.a. Ogre, 7,265m) lie several impressive summits, including Baintha Brakk West (6,660m) and Baintha Brakk West II (6,540m). Max Ten and I had the latter as our goal and approached up the Biafo Glacier, making base camp at Karpogoro (4,680m) and advanced base five hours above, beside the lake on the Sim Gang Glacier.

To acclimatize we attempted Dom Brakk (5,830m), a snow dome climbed a number of times before, camping two nights on the summit of Peak 5,560m, a minor summit along the way to Dom Brakk. From this top we could view our intended route on Baintha Brakk West II, up the impressive buttress on the right side of the north face. It looked very steep for the first 15 or so pitches, and we decided to switch goals to the northeast buttress, on the left side of the face, because it looked less sheer and had more ice smears.

At 7 a.m. on August 4 we crossed the bergschrund and started up the face. We climbed a steep ice runnel between large mushrooms to reach an ice smear—our proposed line. Closer inspection showed the ice to be too thin, so we traversed 70m left to the base of a second, fatter smear. By this time it was 6 p.m. Twenty meters below the entrance to the smear, we chopped a platform big enough for us to sit comfortably, then put up the tent and went to sleep.

Next morning we climbed two steep and really thin ice pitches, the second of which was the scariest ice lead I've ever done. For 15m a sheet of ice only a few centimeters thick lay unconnected to the rock beneath. Above, we climbed five more pitches to reach the steep upper buttress at 5,800m, where we stopped for the night on a mushroom. In our original plan we had hoped to be here in one day or less.

Next morning we had a conversation. Our satellite phone was not working, we were slow, our acclimatization was obviously insufficient—everything felt wrong. We decided to go down. I hope we'll manage a return match with Baintha Brakk West II. 🗎 📷

— KIRILL BELOTSERKOVSKIY, *KAZAKHSTAN*

[Top] The north faces of (A) Baintha Brakk (7,265m, a.k.a. Ogre), (B) Baintha Brakk West I (6,660m), (C) Baintha Brakk West II (6,540m), and (D) Peak 6,250m. (1) Normand-Pierson attempt, 2015. (2) Belotserkovskiy-Ten attempt, 2018. The 2018 Swiss attempt on Baintha Brakk West I was on the south face (opposite side). *Kirill Belotserkovskiy* [Bottom] Kirill Belotserkovskiy traversing left below a rock barrier to gain the first bivouac on Baintha Brakk West II. *Max Ten*

BAINTHA BRAKK WEST I, SOUTH FACE, ATTEMPT; SIAYH KANGRI HO BRAKK, NORTH FACE

DAMIAN GÖLDI AND Marcel Jaun (Switzerland) attempted unclimbed Baintha Brakk West I (a.k.a. Ogre IV, 6,660m) via the south face. They acclimatized with an ascent of 5,330m Uzan Brakk VI, and then, in a short weather window, they climbed the lower south face of Baintha Brakk West I to a notch at 5,800m, where Jaun became ill with altitude sickness. After spending the rest of the day and following night waiting for freezing conditions, they descended safely to base camp. They noted that the hanging glacier up and a little left of their high point avalanched every hour.

On their way out they deviated into the region of the Sokha Lumba Glacier, on the west side of the Biafo Glacier, due south of Baintha, and climbed a peak of around 5,935m via its glaciated north face. They named this Siayh Kangri Ho Brakk. It's not known whether this peak had been climbed previously. 📷

— *INFORMATION FROM* DAMIAN GÖLDI, *SWITZERLAND*

Fabian Buhl cleaning ice from the cracks of Suma Brakk for free climbing. *Alexander Huber*

THE BIG EASY
THE 56-PITCH SOUTH RIDGE OF SUMA BRAKK

BY FABIAN BUHL, *GERMANY*

AFTER REPEATING Alexander Huber's 2012 route Nirwana (multipitch 8c+) in Austria, I met him in 2016 at one of his lectures to talk about the climb. It soon became clear that we got on well together. We went to South Africa for our first shared adventure, and since then have climbed in the Taghia, the Alps, and Patagonia, always having a good time. The logical progression for me was to go to the Greater Ranges. We decided on a small expedition to the Choktoi Glacier in the Panmah Muztagh, where Alexander knew of an amazing, elegant arête.

This unclimbed line formed the huge south ridge of Suma Brakk (6,166m), a summit first climbed in 2007, via the southern slopes and southeast ridge, by Americans Doug Chabot, Mark Richey and Steve Swenson (*AAJ 2008*). [*This mountain has also been called Choktoi Peak or Choktoi Ri; it was named Suma Brakk by the 2007 team.*] We arrived in Islamabad on July 10. From our comfortable base camp on the Choktoi Glacier we ascended nearly 1,000m to place an advanced base at 5,000m right below the south ridge. As I had no prior experience of altitude, I was waiting for the headaches to strike. Fortunately, I never got handicapped by altitude and was very pleased to see that my body can handle it well.

The south arête rises in three big "waves," and during our first stay at advanced base we climbed the first of these, quickly realizing that the route would take much more in the way of commitment and energy than we first had thought. Although not too difficult, it needed all our alpine trickery and route-finding skills to navigate the enormous sea of excellent granite. From the first col we fixed a descent line directly to the glacier. After this we went down to base camp

Fabian Buhl on the Choktoi Glacier, with the huge south ridge of Suma Brakk rising just to his right. See pages 104 and 105 for a closer look at the upper ridge. The right skyline of the mountain, approached by the obvious snow slope to the col, was the route of the first ascent (Chabot-Richey-Swenson, 2007). *Alexander Huber*

to sit out bad weather and eat our mostly vegetarian meals—a mountain fox had made off with all our chickens.

When the weather cleared, we set off again. Alexander and I ascended our fixed ropes and climbed a long section of relatively horizontal ridge until we found a good campsite at around 5,500m (after a total of 28 pitches from the base) below the second wave of the ridge, which we called Red Pillar. It was the only flat place on the entire arête and had an incredible panorama over the Latoks and Ogres. Even more exciting were the perfect splitters just above, as impressive as those in Yosemite.

Next morning the weather was as stellar as the climbing, pitch after pitch of perfect rock. We thought we might reach the headwall the following day, as the terrain was less steep, but in the morning we woke to the sound of snow on the tent. We decided to give it a go, and found it tricky but OK, constantly changing from crampons to rock shoes. However, upon arriving at the headwall, it was clear this would form the crux of the route and was way steeper than we'd expected. It was also covered with snow. We retreated to base camp again for a rest before a final summit push.

The weather remained bad for nearly a week, and then we waited a further two days of semi-good weather for the mountain to clean its white coat. With a forecast of four days of fine weather, we set off on August 3. As walking during the blazing sun is so exhausting, we hiked to the base of the wall in the last light and jumared the ropes to our camp at 5,500m in the dark. Four hours after going to bed, we were enjoying breakfast and an incredible sunrise.

We reclimbed to the headwall, jumaring a few ropes we had left in place on the difficult pitches above the Red Pillar, and then ascended the first 200m of the headwall. As expected, the cracks were still iced. There was no bivouac spot, so we went all the way back down to our camp for the night.

Next day we climbed back to our high point and continued up a corner system. It was totally iced but still looked the easiest option. I got some really nice mixed pitches before reaching a foresummit. It was already late, as the climbing had taken longer than expected. We rappelled to a col on the far side and negotiated a long snow arête to the main top, a cornice, on which we took turns to summit. There we reflected on our good fortune to complete a line that required all our skills and energy. However, most important, we had an amazing time, with a lot of laughs and no bad moods, in the peaceful and calm Karakoram. It clearly showed me the smaller the expedition the richer the experience.

We descended to our tent and spent one more night there, then continued down in the morning, removing all of our ropes from the mountain. We named our route the Big Easy. It gave around 2,200m of climbing over 56 pitches, with difficulties to 5.10+R A1 M6. 📷 🔍

HAINABRAKK EAST TOWER, SOUTHEAST FACE, HEINOUS BROCCOLI ROBBERY

JONATHAN SCHAFFER AND I climbed a new route on the left side of the southeast face of Hainabrakk East Tower. We climbed ground-up, used no bolts or pins, and made two bivouacs: Heinous Broccoli Robbery (1,100m, 5.11+ A1).

We also climbed Eternal Flame on Trango Tower, as well as a 500m rock route on Uli Biaho Gallery, where most of the pitches had traces of human passage but some were as fresh as a mountain breeze. In addition, we attempted a long route on Great Trango Tower's southern aspect, right of Assalam Alaikum (Cmarik-Kopold, 2005). It's hard to say how far we got. To our high point it was garbage, and the climbing above appeared even worse. We also intended to try a line on Shipton Spire but discovered the glacier had been rendered impassable by climate change.

Big hugs to A.P., A.M., and D.A.—base camp besties with an endless supply of inspiration (and warm clothes). Higher Ground Expeditions smoothly saw us through all things in-country, and of course a big shout-out to Jonny Schaffer, who, for those who don't know, is the *man*.

— PETE FASOLDT, *USA*

Hainabrakk East Tower (5,650m) from the southeast. Routes are around 1,100m in length. Approximate lines of (1) Cmarik-Kopold 2006 attempt to 5,375m, VI/6; (2) Heinous Broccoli Robbery (5.11+ A1, Fasoldt-Schaffer, 2018); (3) The Choice (5.11+ R C3, Lavigne-Meis, 2008); (4) Mystical Denmo (VII+ A2, Kolarik-Rabatin, 2005); (5) Tague It to the Top (5.11 C2, Copp-Pennings, 2000); and (6) For Better or for Worse (5.12a WI3, Baer-Brock-McCray-Schneider, 2000). In 2007, Ko Imai and Hiroki Suzuki linked Tague It to the Top with Mystical Denmo to reach the summit at 5.10 A2. Immediately right of Hainabrakk lies Cat's Ears Spire, and right again, in the background, Shipton Spire. *Jonathan Schaffer*

GASHERBRUM II, SOUTHWEST FACE

ON JULY 16, Felix Berg (German) and Adam Bielecki (Poland) climbed a partial new route on Gasherbrum II (8,034m). The pair followed the normal route up the southwest ridge to about 7,300m, the point where it begins to veer right and traverse below the southeast face of the mountain. Here they moved left along a traverse leading toward the Gasherbrum III–II col. Above this lies the southwest face. The right-hand ridge (southwest spur) was climbed directly to the summit in 1995 by Carlos Carsolio (Mexico), and the left-hand ridge (west spur) was possibly climbed in 1990 by Georg Rudiger Lang, a German climber who was part of a 12-member international expedition. (It is not clear whether Lang climbed this line or the northwest face, a mixed snow and rock wall first ascended in 1975 by Polish climbers.) Berg and Bielecki climbed the middle of the southwest face, finishing toward the west spur and encountering delicate climbing over fragile rock slabs. The two were roped but unable to find much in the way of meaningful belays.

This was the only ascent of Gasherbrum II during the season, and no fixed ropes had been placed on the upper mountain. The pair crossed over the summit and descended the normal route.

— LINDSAY GRIFFIN, *WITH INFORMATION FROM FELIX BERG, GERMANY*

Massimo Faletti climbing on the second day during the ascent of WaterWorld on the northeast face of Kiris Peak. *Maurizio Giordani*

KIRIS PEAK, NORTHEAST FACE, WATERWORLD; SNOW PEAK

GHULAM MUHAMMAD, AN old Pakistani friend and organizer of many of my travels in Baltistan, knows my taste in mountaineering objectives. He had sent me a photo of a beautiful granite wall, which I tried to find using Google Earth within the seemingly infinite geographical area of the Karakoram. Eventually, I discovered that Ghulam's peak could be a mountain east of Skardu, a summit I had noticed many times in the days spent waiting to leave for the mountains or to make the journey home. [*This area, which lies to the south of the Mango Gusor Group, is referred to as the Shimshak Mountains by the Polish cartographer Jerzy Wala and as the "Group West of Thalle Valley" on the Japanese Miyamori map.*] Ghulam called this mountain Kiris Peak and insisted it was unclimbed.

Kiris seemed an accessible objective, without any major logistical problems, so I proposed the idea to Manrico dell'Agnola. While we were both climbing with Luca Schiera in the spring, he told us about his recent trip to Pakistan and showed a picture of a fine "big wall" he had seen. Inevitably, it was almost the same photo that Ghulam had sent to me. This only reinforced my interest, as the wall was now no longer unknown, and we put together a group to visit the Ghoro Valley, home to Kiris Peak.

Once assembled in the valley, I suggested a quick raid to the highest peak in order to improve our acclimatization. On July 8, after an eight-hour trudge across moraine and snow, Massimo Faletti, my wife Nancy Paoletto, and I reached the summit of Snow Peak (5,500m, 35°22'54"N, 76°1'30"E).

With the weather now set fair, it was time to touch rock, so Manrico, Massimo, Cristiano Marinelo, Andrea Peron, and I climbed the first pitches on Kiris Peak, immediately realizing that the rock on this vertical wall, beginning at around 4,800m, was hard, compact, polished granite. The aspect of the face—northeast—and the summit snowcap meant that shortly after dawn the snow began to melt, and drips flowing down the wall rapidly turned into veritable cascades tumbling down every crack and corner. The wall was exposed to strong sunshine until just after midday.

We took a line that was logical and sheltered by large overhangs. There were no comfortable bivouac sites, so we fixed the lower pitches. After two days of climbing, Manrico, Massimo, and I reached a high point and descended to our tent on the glacier. In the morning Manrico complained of an altitude-induced headache. The weather had now been good for a week and we felt we couldn't wait. Massimo and I decided to make a summit attempt.

The two of us completed the

[Top] Massimo Faletti moving up the lower wall of WaterWorld on Kiris Peak (5,428m). [Bottom] The northeast face of Kiris Peak and the line of WaterWorld (at least 600m, with ca 1,250m of climbing distance). The climbers weren't sure which top was highest, so they went to both—the right one was slightly higher. *Maurizio Giordani*

lower wall with one bivouac to gain the left end of a prominent snow band, where we made our second bivouac. The next day we traversed the steep snow band for four pitches and then gained the snow and ice slopes of the northwest face, which led to the summit ridge. On the left lay a top of 5,426m, which we reached, then traversed the ridge southwest for around 150m to reach the slightly higher 5,428m summit (35°20'42"N, 75°59'09"E).

On this clear day, we could see from Nanga Parbat to K2 and K6. There were hundreds of unnamed peaks with no climbing history—future projects for those, like us, who want genuine adventure among the high mountains of the Karakoram. We named our route WaterWorld (at least 600m, around 1,250m of climbing, UIAA VIII A2 65° M3, Faletti-Giordani, July 10, 12, and 13–15). 📷 🔍

– MAURIZIO GIORDANI, *ITALY*

Carole Chambaret skiing the northwest face of Laila with the icefalls of the West Ghondokhoro Glacier behind. A shoulder of Masherbrum is visible in the upper right. See also the photo on p.1. *Boris Langenstein*

LAILA, NORTHWEST FACE, FIRST COMPLETE SKI DESCENT

ON MAY 5, in poor weather, Carole Chambaret, Boris Langenstein, and I (all French) established base camp at Dalsampa (ca 4,200m) on the Gondokhoro (a.k.a. Ghondogoro) Glacier, intent on skiing from the summit of Laila (6,096m). The safest approach appeared to be from the south, where there are fewer crevasses and no apparent serac threat. After putting in a track on the south side of Laila, we decided to try for the summit in one push from base camp.

We left at 1:30 a.m. on the 11th and climbed up to a pass at 5,133m. We then moved up to the left to begin a long traverse to the col on the west ridge of Laila, which gives access to the northwest face at around 5,600m. At 7 a.m. we reached this col, where we had great views of K2, Broad Peak, and the Gasherbrums. We could also now feel the steepness of Laila's northwest face—this was the point of commitment.

After getting established on the face, we began six and a half hours of plodding (without skis) through deep snow on the steepest part of the route. For safety, we tried to stay close to the rocks and kept roped. Laila has a strikingly pointed summit from afar, so we never thought the top would be such a nice chill place. It was an easy flat place to put on skis and get ready for the descent.

We skied the full northwest face, a descent of about 1,800m. The conditions seemed more or less perfect: soft snow but not too warm, and with no wind. The skiing was a real pleasure. We were so lucky to have perfect weather and be able to ski from the very top. 📷

– TIPHAINE DUPERIER, *FRANCE*

LAILA CLIMBING AND SKIING HISTORY: *Laila's first known ascent was in 1987 by a four-man British team via the northwest face. This celebrated face (variously reported as 1,500m to 1,700m high, and rising to 55° at the top) became a focal point for extreme skiers after the millennium. In 2005, Jörgen Aamot and Fredrik Ericsson made the first serious attempt, climbing to within a couple of hundred meters of the summit and then*

Looking southwest down the Gondokhoro Glacier at Laila Peak, with the northwest face in profile. *Tomas Fernandez-Montesinos*

descending the northwest face on skis. (Poor snow conditions prevented them from making the top.) Subsequent attempts by several parties were thwarted by similar problems, notably in 2012 and 2014. In 2016, Italians Zeno Cecon, Leonardo Comelli, Carlo Cosi, and Enrico Mosetti were turned back within 150m of the top. All four decided to ski the northwest face from this point. At around 5,350m, Comelli slipped and fell to his death.

On May 14, 2018, a few days after the successful French descent, an Italian-Swiss expedition, also intent on a first ski descent, arrived at base camp. On May 25, Cala Cimenti, Julian Danzer, and Matthias Koenig reached Laila's summit and started down the northwest face. Danzer fell partway down and lost a ski, forcing him to complete the descent on foot. However, Cimenti and Koenig continued down on skis, following an identical line to the French.

Subsequently, on the 27th, Cimenti and Koenig reached the col (ca 5,700m) that separates Laila from an unnamed 5,809m peak to its southeast. (Climbers have nicknamed this peak Laila's Little Sister.) After a night at the col, the Italian-Swiss duo climbed the northwest face of the unnamed peak and skied from its summit all the way to 4,400m. It is unclear whether this mountain had previously been summited.

– LINDSAY GRIFFIN

LACHIT VALLEY: BABA HUSSEIN; CHHOTA BHAI, CHANGI II

NELSON NEIRINCK (BELGIUM), Jess Roskelley, and I (both USA) spent 25 days exploring the Lachit Valley, from July 22 to August 15. The Lachit is a subvalley of the greater Kondus Valley, a region that until recently has been closed to non-military activities due to the continuing border conflict between Pakistan and India. The permitting process seemed difficult, though the drive from Skardu to the entrance of the valley was a relatively fast seven

Changi II (6,250m) from the southwest, showing the upper part of the 2018 route. *Jess Roskelley*

Jess Roskelley at the summit block of Baba Hussein, a previouly unclimbed 5,800-meter tower. On the left, a high, unnamed spire partially conceals distant Karmading Brakk (6,100m). *Kurt Ross*

hours, slowed only by four or five military checkpoints. Hiring 30 porters, we hiked one and a half days to an elevated grassy area, speckled with edelweiss flowers, at the confluence of the east and west Lachit glaciers. Here, we established base camp at 4,500m. After two days acclimatizing, we hiked up the East Lachit Glacier to scope peaks in the higher cirque, then established an advanced base at 5,000m with easy access to the surrounding mountains.

On July 30 we climbed a 5,800m spire above camp as part of our acclimatization. This involved a long, steep snow climb culminating in two pitches of M6 and a final M7 boulder problem that took us to the summit. We dubbed the tower Baba Hussein after our assistant cook, a small, tough man in his 60s who could be heard singing into the night.

We rested two days at base camp while waiting for rainy weather to pass, then returned to advanced base, and on August 3 headed for the higher of our two main objectives. After negotiating some steep, complex glaciated terrain, we were forced to stop and camp, as temperatures were too high to climb the sloughing icefields above with safety.

Early next morning we climbed a long AI3 icefield to the south ridge, where we encountered steep mixed climbing for which we were not prepared, having carried only a minimal rock rack of one set of nuts and a few pins. We climbed down and sideways across the icefield for several rope lengths until we met a gully that allowed us to skirt the more difficult rock. Exhausted, we rested and brewed for two hours on the ridge before continuing. The climbing involved two pitches of traversing rock with interspersed snow patches, two pitches of WI4 ice, the fixing of a line to descend past a gendarme on the summit crest, and a final stretch of corniced ridge to the top.

We called our route Naps & Noms, and due to the ominous presence of the adjacent K6, named the 6,321m peak Chhota Bhai (assuming another name does not already exist), which means "little brother" in Urdu. [*This summit, at 35°23'25.50"N, 76°33'56.30"E, lies just south of 6,500m Changi Tower, see AAJ 2016.*]

Once we felt rested at base camp, we knew we had energy for another climb. We returned to advanced base on August 9 to attempt an aesthetic peak that had attracted all of us, even though we considered it fairly improbable. We moved camp closer to the base of the south face and then launched the following day.

A surprisingly easy icy gully gave us a welcome boost. Then began more difficult climbing, with a handful of mixed pitches bringing us to easier ground where we spent our first night. With only light bivouac sacks, we were grateful that some looming storm clouds brought no more than light snowfall—the nearby mountains were clearly being hammered by heavy precipitation.

We had intended to ascend a straight, thin, ice line that led directly to the summit, but with the rising heat, the steep line was now more of a slushy waterfall. Regrettably, the following morning we descended with several rappels to reach a massive ice gully that had survived the increasingly hotter days. We quickly pitched out the calf-melting terrain for hundreds of meters, weaved our way through some interesting mixed terrain, brewed up, and then returned to exhausting AI3 climbing until reaching a short summit ridge. The incredible diving board that formed the summit block was a breathtaking reward. We took turns climbing onto this narrow spire and viewing our shadow overlaid onto the steep north face.

As the sun fell, we descended, deciding to follow a different route than that climbed. This turned out to be more difficult than expected. Many easy rappels from Abalakov anchors started things off well, but loose rock on subsequent rappels damaged our ropes in several places. With the shortened ropes and uncertainty about route-finding in the darkness, we opted to sit for a long and disheartening open bivouac. The cold—and the moderately wet bags from our first night out—woke us early next morning. Many 20m rappels eventually put us back on the glacier. We named the route Hard Tellin' Not Knowin', and as far as we know we made the first ascent of this 6,250m peak, which locals referred to as Changi II (35°21'29.42"N, 76°35'29.78"E).

The area around the Lachit Valley is beautiful, and due to lack of tourism it remains relatively pristine and clean of trash. It is a place for all alpine climbers to find interesting first ascents.

— KURT ROSS, USA

[Top] Chhota Bhai (6,321m) and the route of ascent along the south ridge. *Kurt Ross* [Bottom] Jess Roskelley on steep mixed ground during the ascent of Changi II. *Nelson Neirinck*

INDIA

On the Southeast Shukpa Kunzang Glacier, looking west: (A) Peak 6,200m. (B) Karpo Kangri (6,535m). (C) Konto La. (D) Argan Kangri II (6,640m). (E) Argan Kangri (6,789m). (F) Peak 6,210m. *Priit Simson*

EAST KARAKORAM

KUNZANG RANGE, RANGSTON GYATHOK

On July 22 our Estonian expedition summited Peak 6,801m GPS (6,751m on the Indian map; 34°37'06.3192"N, 78°04'38.7084"E), the highest unclimbed peak in the Kunzang Range. [*The Kunzang Range is generally defined as the mountainous region north of the great bend in the Shyok River and south of the Shukpa Kunzang Range and Saser Kangri Group.*] The ascent followed a complex approach to our high camp that required nearly two weeks. Although a road follows the Shyok River to the east of these mountains, it is generally off-limits to foreign visitors, necessitating a long approach from the south.

We left the village of Rongdo (3,200m) on July 9 with 20 horses (15 porters followed the next day) and began our 60km trek to the mountain, initially following the Rongdo Lungpa. After three days we established base camp at 5,387m beside the moraine of the Sagtogpa Glacier.

On the 15th we crossed most of the Southeast Shukpa Kunzang Glacier, passing south and then west of 6,165-meter Mariushri, climbed in 2014 by a Canadian expedition (*AAJ 2015*). The following day we continued to a col leading over to the Phurdupka Glacier. The lowest point of this col is 5,981m, but it was heavily corniced on the northeastern side, so we moved up to 6,041m before making a rappel descent of 180m toward the glacier. This was the first known crossing, and we named the passage Estonian Col. Nine porters made this crossing, the others having gone back when they got ill. (All route-finding and technical climbing on the expedition was carried out by the Estonian members of the team, and we all carried our share of the equipment.)

On the 17th we descended the glacier to 4,878m and established our advanced base at the junction with North Phurdupka Glacier flowing east from our mountain.

After a rest day, we spent the next three days moving up the North Phurdupka Glacier, placing a high camp at 6,298m on the southwest ridge of Peak 6,801m. On the 22nd, leaving two porters and a Sherpa at high camp, Lauri Ehrenpreis, Priit Joosu, Meelis Luukas, Sven Oja, Lauri Stern, Priit Simson, and I, along with liaison officer Stanzing Norbu (a passionate climber with great knowledge of Ladakhi history) and Sherpa Pasang Temba Butia, continued up the ridge in cloudy weather with some snowfall. We moved west onto the face left of the ridge and then, via a 30m ice pitch (WI3), gained a couloir leading to the summit pyramid. Moving left through loose rock, we reached a short knife-edge snow arête, which we followed to the summit.

This peak has been identified by a variety of names: Kunchang Kangri (Google Earth); Phurdukpo Kangri I (Jurgalski); Unnamed Peak I Kungzang (Seyfferth); Mandaltang I (The Mountain Encyclopedia, Hartemann-Hauptman). We are more or less certain this mountain has no common name, nor had it been properly surveyed. We therefore decided to name it Rangston Gyathok, which means "100 years of independence" in Ladakhi and celebrates the 100th anniversary of the Republic of Estonia.

Our return journey to Rongdo was rather more dangerous than the approach,

Rangston Gyathok from the west and the route followed on the first ascent. *Kristjan-Erik Suurväli*

due to continually poor weather and snowfall. Snow bridges were softer, and Pasang, leading the way on the Southeast Shukpa Kunchang Glacier, took five falls into crevasses. 📷 🔍

– KRISTJAN-ERIK SUURVÄLI, *ESTONIA*

RONGDO VALLEY, PHOKTO SCHEYOK (BLACK PYRAMID), SOUTH FACE

IN FAR NORTHERN India, a number of steep-sided granite valleys are enclosed by the "Great Bend" of the Shyok River. Their mountaineering potential was first recognized by Chewang Motup of Rimo Expeditions, and his company has supported all approved expeditions to the Rongdo Valley. Various teams have climbed or attempted mountains in the valley nearly every year since 2012, sometimes mistakenly thinking they were making first ascents (*see note below*).

Our team in 2018 consisted of three climbers: Ralph Eberle (Germany), Tsewang Gyalson (Ladakhi and our sirdar), and me, a British national living in Germany. We were accompanied by liaison officer Abhinav Pandey and four assistants. We took three days to trek with horse packers from Rongdo village to our base camp at 5,375m, covering 25km and ascending 1,895m. Tsewang had visited Rongdo before and suggested positioning our base camp higher than previous expeditions, which turned out to be good advice. Regular rockfalls on one of our objectives, Peak 6,064m, made us focus on the pyramid-shaped peak north of the head of the Rongdo Valley. An India expedition (*AAJ 2014*) and a British one (*AAJ 2016*) had previously attempted this peak but turned back due to poor weather and snow conditions.

On July 21 we ascended the side arm of the Sagtogpa Glacier and sited our advanced base at 5,820m below the south face of the pyramidal peak. We left camp around 5:30 a.m. in improving weather and climbed a very loose rocky rib that was covered with a few centimeters of new snow. This proved heavy going, so we roped up and traversed left into an open snow and ice gully. We reached the left rocky ridge of the gully and climbed along it unroped, then continued for several hours up the snow and ice slopes above. At around 9:50 a.m. we arrived on the southwest top. The eastern summit was clearly higher, so we traversed snowfields and reached the highest point at 10:45 a.m. A GPS established the height as 6,235m.

We initially started down the southeast ridge, but unstable snow slabs made us turn down

Untouched granite in the lower Rongdo Valley. In the background lies the unclimbed peak of Yonchap Kangri (around 6,080m, summit hidden). *Keith Goffin*

a gully on the south face, which we descended with three 60m rappels and downclimbing the rocky rib that formed the eastern edge of the couloir. We arrived at advanced base at 4:30 p.m.

Our Rongdo horseman said the mountain's local name is Phokto Scheyok, which emphasizes its color (Scheyok is Ladakhi for black) and form (Phokto for pyramid or dome).

Rongdo offers many unclimbed 6,000m peaks, including an interesting one near Fatha to the north and the prominent peak of Yonchap Kangri to the south, clearly visible from the shepherds' huts at Doksa. However, both have challenging access. The rock climbing possibilities are endless; from the middle of the Rongdo Valley we observed approximately 10km of 500m-plus rock walls with no existing routes. However, the quality of the granite decreases in the upper valley, and some rock walls are sacred to Buddhists and so should be avoided. 📄 📷

— KEITH GOFFIN, *GERMANY*

HISTORICAL CLARIFICATION FOR TWO RONGDO PEAKS: *In AAJ 2016 we reported the apparent first ascent of Sagtogpa Kangri (6,305m, 34°32'12.66"N, 78°1'44.46"E) by an Indian expedition in August 2015, via a route from the Sagtogpa Glacier to the south, eventually finishing up the southeast ridge. In fact, this was the second ascent, albeit by a new route. In August 2014, Graham Rowbotham and Joie Seagram, part of a Canadian expedition (AAJ 2015), climbed this same peak via the north ridge (AD, 45° ice), approaching from the west. They named the mountain Tara, and their GPS recorded 6,248m on the summit.*

One day before climbing Tara, Rowbotham climbed another peak, solo, via the south face and southwest ridge (PD). He called this 6,167m peak Mariushri. The same mountain was climbed in 2017 by another Indian expedition during a long exploratory traverse (AAJ 2018). They also followed the south face and southwest ridge and, believing they had done the first ascent, called the mountain Nga Kangri (cited at 6,165m).

ZANSKAR

CHILING I, EAST RIDGE

IN AUGUST 2017, Jon Griffin and Tad McCrea (both USA) climbed the east ridge of Chiling I (6,349m). Beginning from a high camp at 5,575m, the pair simul-climbed the ridge in six long pitches over snow and ice up to 70°, with an easy mixed section at two-thirds height. They climbed through a "frozen silver fog" and reached the top just after dark. Here, they opted to traverse the summit and descend the south ridge to regain their camp. The route was named Wantonly Tarnished (600m, 70°).

Griffin and McCrea's ascent of Chiling I was meant to provide acclimatization for another objective, but afterward they both came down with bronchial infections that lasted two weeks. They finished their expedition by packrafting for three long days and 135km along the Zanskar River from Padum to the confluence with the Indus. This, they said, was by far the highlight of the trip.

In 2015, McCrea had hoped to attempt Chiling II but deferred to the American team of Kitty Calhoun, Renny Jackson, Jay Smith, and Jack Tackle, who had made their own plans for the mountain. These four attempted the east ridge, and after six days they reached a point estimated to be 80m below the summit before retreating in extreme cold. This route was completed in better conditions the following year by Oriol Baró and Lluc Pellissa (*AAJ 2017*). These two were well acclimatized from climbs elsewhere and were able to reach the summit in a round trip of just 23 hours from their camp below the route at 5,400m. 📷

[Top] Looking southeast from the approach to Chiling's east ridge, over the upper Lalung Glacier, to unnamed high peaks at the head of this glacier and the next one to the east (a southeasterly offshoot of the Lalung with a snowy col at its head leading to the Pensilungpa Glacier). (A) Peak 6,274m. (B) Peak 6,048m. (C) Peak 6,197m. (D) Peak 6,067m. It is not known if any of these have been climbed. The three Lalung peaks designated by the IMF are off picture to the right. [Bottom] Chiling I (left) and II from the Lalung Glacier to the northeast. The east ridge of Chiling I, climbed in 2017, is marked, as is the 2016 Spanish route on the east ridge of Chiling II. Four Americans attempted a similar line in 2015 and estimate they got to a point 80m below the summit. *Tad McCrea (both photos)*

– LINDSAY GRIFFIN, *WITH INFORMATION FROM TAD MCCREA*

THE CHILING AND LALUNG PEAKS AND THE ENIGMA OF Z2: *The Chiling peaks are located on the boundaries of Zanskar, Kishtwar, and Suru. The climbing history of the area is only roughly documented, and a plethora of names and altitudes have been granted erroneously to many of the peaks, features, and valleys. In the past, the Chiling peaks have variously been referred to as Lalung or Z2, and reported ascents on "Z2" in 1977, 1982, and 2016 were probably of Chiling I or II. Descriptions, coordinates, and a map of the Chiling, Lalung, and Z2 peaks, as designated by the Indian Mountaineering Foundation (IMF), can be found at the AAJ website (search "enigma of Z2").* 📄 🔍

Looking into the south branch of the Mulung Glacier from advanced base camp. (A) Peak 5,631m. (B) Aari Dont (5,557m). (C) M12 (5,652m). *Derek Buckle*

MULUNG TOKPO: AARI DONT, NORTHWEST RIDGE; CHILH POINT, EAST FACE

I FIRST WENT to Zanskar in 2013, inspired by an article by Harish Kapadia in the *Himalayan Journal*, to explore the glaciated regions of the Pensilungpa (*AAJ 2014*). Following a second visit, in 2015, to the Korlomshe Tokpo (*AAJ 2016*), I was tempted back in 2018. This time we chose the Mulung Tokpo after seeing photographs by Kimikazu Sakamoto (*AAJ 2017*), and after some deliberation we eventually selected Peak 5,871m, defined as M15 by Sakamoto, as our primary target. This mountain lies at the junction of the south and west arms of the extensive Mulung Glacier.

Our expedition lasted from August 30–September 29. From Ating in the Zanskar Valley, Drew Cook, Mike Fletcher, Adele Long, Gus Morton, Tony Westcott, and I trekked for two days up the Mulung Tokpo (valley) with our support team, before establishing base camp on September 7 at the junction with the Nabil Tokpo, close to the snout of the Mulung Glacier, at 4,188m.

Over the next few days we explored potential routes onto the glacier, before finally selecting the true right lateral moraine as the lesser of several evils. We subsequently established an advanced base on the moraine at 4,525m. However, extended periods of poor weather precluded a full evaluation of approach routes to M15. A collective decision was therefore made to attempt one or more of the peaks on the southern rim of the South Mulung Glacier, since these offered more straightforward access.

With new targets identified, a high camp was established on the 17th, on the glacier at 5,085m. Two days later, Drew, Mike, and I attempted the north face of Peak 5,631m (height estimated from maps, but possibly a little higher). However, in deep new snow we aborted the climb some 300–400m short of the corniced summit. Gus and Tony had better success, reaching what we called Aari Dont Col (Hindi for "saw tooth," 5,480m) via its north face, before Gus continued alone to make the first ascent of Aari Dont itself via the northwest ridge (5,557m, PD). On the 20th, Drew, Mike, Adele, and I made the second ascent of Aari Dont by the same route, and then Mike and I climbed the mixed face leading to what we subsequently called Chilh Point (Hindi for "Eagle Point," 5,537m, AD).

The next day, after 10 nights at higher camps, the team returned directly to base to recuperate. All the higher camps were cleared the day after. This was a fortuitous decision, as some 40–50cm of snow fell that day and overnight, and three base camp tents were destroyed. With more snow forecast, we and our support staff decided to return to the valley while we still could. Taking only essential items, we endured an arduous 13- to 16-hour descent over 25km in deep snow to reach Ating.

The following day we managed to arrange transport to Padum, only to find that the Pensi La was closed, so there was no way to return to Leh. Two days later, we were able to continue our journey, arriving in Leh in time to catch our return flight. Our equipment was not so lucky. Before our support team was able to return to base camp, hungry bears beat them to it, ravishing the camp. 🗎 📷 🔍

— DEREK BUCKLE, *ALPINE CLUB, U.K.*

LADAKH

KANG YATSE GROUP, SHAN RI, NORTH FACE AND EAST RIDGE

IN AUGUST I guided Pedro Costa, Tiago Faneca, and João Lopes on an expedition to Ladakh. We spent four days on the famous Markha Valley Trek, then established base camp at 4,400m in the Langthang Chu, near the settlement marked as Male, aiming to climb a nearby high peak.

Camp I was made at 5,170m, very close to the snout of the "Male Glacier," which drains a basin to the south of the Kang Yatse massif. This glacier has several peaks on its southern side of which there is no record of any ascents or attempts. On August 30 we moved to Camp 2 (5,550m).

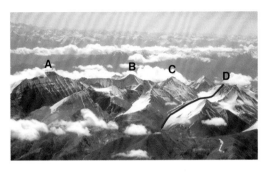

The Kang Yatse group, looking east-southeast in July 2015. (A) Kang Yatse. (B) Dzo Jongo. (C) Ibtsi Kangri. (D) Shan Ri, showing the route of ascent. *Damien Gildea*

The next day we left at 4 a.m. and headed up the glacier, which was seemingly devoid of crevasses, and in three hours we were at the base of our chosen peak. We climbed the north face of the mountain for 300m, via a 55–60° slope, mostly on ice around AI3+ with some easy rock steps, all of which we belayed. We reached the east ridge and climbed another 55° ice slope to gain the summit at 6,198m (33.701860°N, 77.561501°E), at 2:30 p.m.

We downclimbed the east ridge to a small col, from where we managed to descend to the glacier in three 60m rappels, reaching the bergschrund just at dusk. Unofficially, we called the peak Shan Ri ("snow leopard peak" in Ladakhi); we named our route North Face Indirect.

After this my regular partner Daniela Teixeira arrived, and we traveled to the Suru Valley and unsuccessfully attempted two peaks at the head of the Pensilungpa Glacier, south of the Pensi La. Very bad snow conditions and an incoming storm forced us back, so we returned east to Kang Yatse and climbed to 6,000m on the eastern spur before deep snow and dangerous avalanche conditions again forced us to retreat. 📷

– **PAULO ROXO**, *PORTUGAL*

KISHTWAR HIMALAYA

FLAT TOP AND KISHTWAR EIGER ATTEMPTS

RICHARD (REG) MEASURES (New Zealand) and Timothy Elson (U.K.) made attempts in October on Flat Top (6,100m) and Kishtwar Eiger (ca 6,000m), situated above the Brammah Glacier on the southwestern side of the Kishtwar region, in the state of Jammu and Kashmir. Their approach took them up the Nanth Nullah (valley) to base camp in a meadow at Sattarchin (3,400m) at the end of the Brammah Glacier.

Frequent and heavy snowfall stymied their efforts, which included attempts on the north spur of Flat Top, left of the 1980 first ascent route up the north ridge, reaching about 5,300m; the easier east ridge of Flat Top to 5,400m; and the south face of Kishtwar Eiger to 5,700m.

[Top] 2018 attempt on the south face of Kishtwar Eiger (ca 6,000m). *Timothy Elson* [Bottom] The Arjuna group, with Arjuna North, the peak attempted in 2018, at far left. *Marko Prezelj*

Elson's complete report, available at the *AAJ* website, contains useful descriptions of these attempts, their approach, and general travel conditions in this area of Kishtwar. 📄 📷

— TIMOTHY ELSON, *ALPINE CLUB, U.K.*

ARJUNA NORTH, SOUTHWEST FACE, ATTEMPT

IN SEPTEMBER, JOSIE McKee, Caro North, and I traveled to the Kijai Nala (valley) with the intention of climbing the west face of Arjuna (6,230m). We spent 28 days in the mountains and encountered mostly bad weather and difficult conditions.

After nearly losing a bag of vital climbing gear dropped over a cliff by porters into the Chenab River during the approach, we continued trekking up the Kijai Nala for three more days until reaching base camp at 4,000m on September 3. We then spent two weeks searching for a way through the icefall, sitting out bad weather, and shuttling gear to a cave below the upper icefall, before receiving a forecast for four days of good weather.

Since the weather had been so poor, we hadn't been able to move our gear to the base of the peak before our attempt, nor scope a line. After deliberation, we decided Arjuna was not possible for us to climb in its current condition and with the forecast we had been given, so we set our sights on a lower rock peak just to the north (unofficially Arjuna North). There was a line on the southwest aspect that would allow us to climb more in the sun.

In the early hours of the 19th we started up a couloir at 4,900m and soon reached the base of the rock. Our packs were heavy with supplies for three days, but the terrain was relatively moderate. We moved efficiently and climbed seven long pitches, encountering terrain up to 5.10-. There was some rock of incredible quality, the face peppered with solid black knobs. Just before dark, we reached a good place to dig out a tent platform at around 5,450m.

The next day our climbing slowed as the terrain became more complex, forcing us to switch between boots and climbing shoes. After five more pitches, an unexpected snowstorm came in from the west, forcing us to start rappelling. A few stuck ropes and many hours later, we made it back to our camp at 5,450m, where we spent a second night. We finished the rappels on the third day. Knowing that a bigger storm was supposed to come in 24 hours, we descended the icefall all the way back to base camp. The next day a foot of snow fell, ending any possibilities for more climbing. 📷

— WHITNEY CLARK, *AAC*

The Japanese trio took shelter in this cave after crawling four hours through deep snow from their advanced base camp while descending from the 1,500-meter northeast face of Cerro Kishtwar (6,173m). In this foreshortened view, their route, Aal Izz Well, is marked. *Genki Narumi*

AAL IZZ WELL
THE FIRST ASCENT OF THE NORTHEAST FACE OF CERRO KISHTWAR

BY GENKI NARUMI

I GOT A message from Hiroki Yamamoto: "I'm going to India with Yusuke Sato this fall, and I'm wondering if you wanna join us?" Five months before, I had become a father and was on parental leave, spending all my time with my wife and daughter. I didn't think I'd be going on an expedition in 2018, but the photo Hiroki sent was just too beautiful to ignore.

On August 25 we landed in Delhi, just a week after the IMF had granted us a permit for Cerro Kishtwar (6,173m) in Jammu and Kashmir. We drove the notoriously exposed road from Manali to Gulabgarh, and then took a low-cost helicopter to Machail, skipping a day and a half of walking. Three more days on foot took us to base camp at 3,900m, where we arrived on September 2.

Our goal was the unclimbed northeast face, where it appeared there were very few options for a line free from objective danger. Our planned route had an easy but dangerous lower section, where speed would be the key. The middle section was steeper, with a skinny ice pillar and mixed terrain. The headwall was a thinly iced slab.

After six days of acclimatizing and watching movies in base camp under blue skies, we set out for advanced base. The forecast had changed: a 40 percent chance of snow and more than 20cm of snow per night starting in two days. *Dude, should we pretend we didn't see it?* We decided to try to reach the summit in just two days. After all, it was just a forecast—it might be wrong.

Next morning we climbed unroped up a 500m snow gully. Yusuke then led the first ice pillar and then another 250m before handing the lead to Hiroki. The ice got thin and the angle steepened, but we climbed simultaneously, and after 15 hours we chopped a three-out-of-five-star ledge for our bivouac. (Around 70 percent of the tent floor fit on the ledge.) I led another pitch and fixed a rope. We had covered 1,000m that first day.

We awoke before 3 a.m. The forecast was still bad, and we needed to get to the top quickly. We

[Top] Yusuke Sato on steep ice during day one of the first ascent of the northeast face of Cerro Kishtwar. *Genki Narumi* [Bottom] Narumi makes the long wade out to base camp through several feet of snow that fell during their descent. *Hiroki Yamamoto*

left our tent and sleeping bags and started climbing. Fragile ice, increasingly steep terrain, and a tricky mixed pitch led to the headwall. I was relieved to hand the lead to Yusuke, who embarked on some bold climbing up the thinly iced slab covered with soft snow.

The sun went down. As I was jumaring, I tried to shout to the pair above, "Why don't we stop and have tea and sleep?" But Yusuke was focused on the summit.

A short offwidth, a cornice, and then we were on the summit, around 10 p.m. Between the clouds we could see the lower south summit, so knew we were on top. We immediately started down. The summit is only halfway, and our final goal was to meet our families. Yusuke and Hiroki had a preschool event for their sons right after the expedition.

The descent and return to base camp was an ordeal, taking more than three days. We paused after a few rappels to brew tea and doze, but falling snow covered us so quickly that we had to excavate ourselves every 20 minutes. We moved again before dawn. The snowfall stopped for a while, but it was still misty. We reached the site of our bivouac at noon, stopped for an hour, then set off on the first of 20 rappels to the bottom of the face. Snowfall was now heavy and spindrift turned to full avalanches. Around 11 p.m. on our third day on the mountain, we found a relatively safe spot to pitch the tent. It was the first time in 41 hours when we could lie down and sleep.

Next morning we made three more rappels along a relatively safe ridge, reached the glacier, and swam through snow to our completely collapsed advanced base. We rebuilt the camp so we could eat and drink. However, the blast from avalanches reached the tent a few times, and when a particularly large one shook the tent at 8 p.m., we decided it was time to go. The snow was now waist deep. We tried cutting sleeping pads to make snowshoes, but this didn't work so we had to crawl. It took four hours to travel only 200m. We found a rock cave in which we could squeeze the tent and stopped again. Next day the storm abated, but Yusuke had vision problems, probably caused by altitude, and we still sank to our hips in the soft snow, so we waited a whole day for the snow to consolidate. On our sixth day out from base camp, the sky finally cleared and we were able to walk easily down to camp.

We named our route Aal Izz Well after a song from an Indian movie, *Three Idiots*, that we had watched during acclimatization at base camp. We'd watched movies through a long period of perfect weather and then climbed through a storm. Who could be more idiotic than us? 📷

SUMMARY: *First ascent of the northeast face of Cerro Kishtwar (Aal Izz Well, 1,500m, VI WI5 M6) by Genki Narumi, Yasuke Sato, and Hiroki Yamamoto from Japan, September 19–25, 2018.*

HIMACHAL PRADESH

BAIHALI JOT, NORTHWEST PILLAR, ATTEMPT

A BORDER DISPUTE with China dashed our hopes of a permit for Rangrik Rang, but at the last minute Justin Guarino and I obtained permission to attempt Baihali Jot (6,365m). In September 2017 we approached up the Baihali Nala from the Chenab River to the west, and after two days' walk from the village of Shaor we placed base camp at 4,000m. For the next month we saw no one except our liaison officer, a cook and his assistant, and a few shepherds.

We acclimatized by climbing up the northwest spur of Baihali Jot North to around 5,700m. At the time, a cairn near base camp with Asian inscriptions, and another at 5,200m on the spur, made us believe this was the route attempted in 2001 by a Japanese expedition (*see editor's note below*).

We then turned to our main objective, Baihali Jot, and its northwest pillar. We left base camp at 10 p.m. and were at the bottom of the face at 5 a.m. On that first day we mostly simul-climbed 50–65° ice on the north side of the pillar. In midafternoon we spent a couple of hours hacking out a semi-hanging tent site at around 5,550m.

The northwest pillar of Baihali Jot (6,365m), showing the 2017 attempt. *Nick Aiello-Popeo*

The next day dawned cold and clear, and the route continued to be highly enjoyable—technical but not extreme, with steep sections of AI3. At around 6,000m we popped onto the crest of the pillar itself to face a rock wall guarding the summit icefield. At this altitude my calves and forearms were screaming after the first few moves, even though the crux rock corner would probably be rated M4/5 at sea level. A few rope lengths higher, we decided that worsening weather, nightfall, and painful leg cramps were signs we should descend. We drilled the first of around 22 Abalakov anchors and began to rappel into the blackness on our 70m ropes. 📷

– **NICK AIELLO-POPEO,** *AAC*

BAIHALI JOT'S GEOGRAPHY AND CLIMBING HISTORY: *Baihali Jot lies at the head of the Ur Gad (valley), immediately west of the Miyar. Maps have traditionally marked the summit on a northern top (and noted a height of about 6,280m). However, photos and Google Earth show that the northern top cannot be the highest, and the Indian Mountaineering Foundation's list of open peaks (where it is spelled Behali) now designates Baihali Jot as 6,365m and places it on the south summit.*

In 1969 an Indo-British team reported making the first ascent of Baihali Jot. However, expedition sketch maps and photos suggest they climbed the north top via the southeast face and "west ridge" (the peak has a southwest ridge). The main summit was climbed in 1973 by a British Army Mountaineering expedition led by John Fleming, which reached a col at the southwestern head of the glacier, named Pegasus Col, and then climbed approximately northward over a broken rock buttress and up a steep snow arête to Baihali Jot's southern top. (The expedition also made the first ascent of Gurkha Parbat, ca 5,900m, southeast of the col.) "Baihali Jot" was reportedly climbed again in 1992 by a team from West Bengal. In 2001 a Japanese expedition most likely climbed the north ridge of a peak of about 6,000m to the northwest. In short: Baihali Jot (the higher south summit) may have been climbed only once and Baihali Jot North a few times. 📄 📷

SPITI VALLEY, CHEMMA, NORTHWEST RIDGE

An Indian Himalayan Club team comprising Rajesh Gadgil, Ratnesh Javeri, Vineeta Muni, Imran Pathan, and Ashish Prabhu, led by veteran Divyesh Muni, made the first ascent of the northwest ridge of Chemma (6,130m), which was probably also the first ascent of Chemma's main summit.

The climbers approached up the Karcha Nala from Batal, making a base camp at around 4,500m, where the Karcha splits, and advanced base at 4,900m. After a period of poor weather and various reconnaissance trips from a Camp 1 at 5,400m, Gadgil, Prabhu, and the Munis set off on August 2 up the scree of the northwest ridge of Chemma, made a high camp, then reached the summit at 11 a.m. on August 3.

After a period of bad weather, the team also repeated the 1956 route up the east ridge of Ache (6,066m), reached from the 5,800m col between this peak and Chemma. The online version of this report details the history of climbing on these peaks. 📄 📷 🔍

— DAMIEN GILDEA, *WITH INFORMATION FROM* DIVYESH MUNI, *INDIA*

KINNAUR DISTRICT, BASPA VALLEY, PEAK 6,050M, SOUTHEAST FACE

The 2018 route on the southeast face of Peak 6,050m. *Hansjörg Auer*

Austrian alpinists Hansjörg Auer, Max Berger, Much Mayr, and Guido Unterwurzacher traveled to the Baspa Valley in late September, looking for interesting technical objectives. Despite unstable weather during their short reconnaissance and acclimatization period, they succeeded in climbing an unnamed peak of 6,050m (31°27'1.52"N, 78°19'59.67"E), northeast of Sangla village on the long curving ridge between Jorkanden and Raldang.

Starting from near Rakcham village, the climbers ascended northward to a plateau in the Gor Garang valley before turning west and crossing a pass to a camp at 3,200m in the Saro Gad (valley). Above this, the team made two bivouacs, at 4,400m and 5,000m, before taking a reasonably direct line up the southeast face, with moderate mixed terrain, for around 1,000m. They reached the summit at 9:45 a.m. on October 5. There is no record of any previous ascent, and the team was informed by locals that the peak was unclimbed.

— DAMIEN GILDEA, *WITH INFORMATION FROM* HANSJÖRG AUER, *AUSTRIA*

GARHWAL HIMALAYA

SRI KAILAS WEST, FIRST ASCENT VIA SOUTH FACE

While searching for a destination offering a potential first ascent, Alex Gammeter and I heard from two different contacts about mountains in Garhwal lying within the so-called Inner Line, an area of restricted travel near the border with China. On Google Earth, one of the peaks in this group, Peak 6,803m, looked to have sharp ridges and a steep north face. [*Despite being some 4.5km from 6,932-meter Sri Kailas, Peak 6,803m is sometimes referred to as Sri Kailas West; it lies north of the Raktaban (a.k.a. Raktavarn) Glacier at 30°00'27"N, 79°07'44"E.*] However, as we began checking the approach from the north, via Nelang, the last village before the border, we real-

The south face of Sri Kailas West (Peak 6,803m) and route of first ascent. The climbers descended to the left. *Philipp Bührer*

ized the Inner Line was a serious obstacle, and it wouldn't be possible for foreigners to go beyond it. Our contact suggested we look at the south face. The approach would be longer, but base camp could be established in two days from the road at Gangotri, and we only would touch the Inner Line when we reached the summit.

We arrived at base camp, at around 4,500m, on October 8. On the 10th we ascended the Raktaban Glacier and then turned north up the unnamed glacier (possibly called the Shyam-varn Bamak) running down from Sri Kailas West. At 5,100m we finally got a glimpse and saw that it offered all we could ask—in addition, it was not as snowy as its neighbors.

On the 12th we were back at what was now our Camp 1, and the following day we pushed as far as possible toward our peak and set up Camp 2. We spent another day here and then, on the 15th, set off into the blistering cold night. As we progressed, the snow conditions worsened, and we continually broke through an ugly crust. We made a trail to the bottom of the south face and went back to camp for a rest day.

The alarm rang at 2 a.m. on October 20. The temperature was -20°C, but motivation was high. We set off carrying light packs and a substantial amount of fried rice, provided by our cook. By 5:30 a.m. we had reached the face (5,900m) and begun climbing the first snowfield. As the angle increased, the snow became solid. At daybreak we reached a gully system that held some water ice, in some places thick enough for screws. On the final slopes, which were steeper, the snow was like sticky Styrofoam. We passed the final rock band on the left and then reached the west ridge at around 6,700m. The summit crest was one of those "stairway to heaven" beauties, and by 11 a.m. we were taking a lunch break on the summit. It was a great moment.

We descended the west-southwest ridge toward Peak 6,617m (also thought to be unclimbed), but once at the col decided we were too tired to link both mountains, so we traversed Peak 6,617m's south face to a point where we could descend more easily to the glacier. We regained our tent at 5 p.m.

— PHILIPP BÜHRER, *SWITZERLAND*

CHANGABANG, NORTH FACE, RAPID REPEAT (NO SUMMIT)

IN MID-MAY, Léo Billon, Sébastien Moatti, and Sébastien Ratel from the prolific Groupe Militaire de Haute Montagne (GMHM) made the fourth ascent of the north face of Changabang (6,864m) in a scant three days. The French trio followed the line of the 1996 British attempt (Clyma-Murphy-Payne-Perkins) up the bottom half of the face, then moved left and linked with the top half of the 1997 British route, climbed over 10 days by Andy Cave and Brendan Murphy for the first ascent of the face. The second ascent, a new route by a Russian-American team in 1998, was sieged in 20 days of climbing spanning more than a month and a half (*AAJ 1999*).

The GMHM team had their first bivouac on May 11 near the high point of the 1996 attempt, and their second after reaching the east ridge. They continued up the east ridge to the small peak just north of the main summit, named Changabang Horn by the British (they stopped here because of lack of time and incoming weather), and then descended a line to the side of the 1997 route. They estimated their link-up to be around 40 pitches, up to AI5 M6.

— DAMIEN GILDEA, *WITH INFORMATION FROM* SÉBASTIEN MOATTI, *FRANCE*

Malcolm Bass and Paul Figg on the south-southwest ridge of Janhukot in worsening weather during day three of the first ascent. *Guy Buckingham*

JANHUKOT

AFTER MANY ATTEMPTS, THE FIRST ASCENT OF A HIGH GANGOTRI PEAK

BY MALCOLM BASS, *ALPINE CLUB, U.K.*

SUNDENVAN, THE LATERAL moraine meadow under Kedar Dome, is the highest base camp on the Gangotri Glacier. I have probably spent more months living there than most of the summer-resident blue sheep. It has become a place of great peace for me over the years, so it was with mixed feelings that I left it in late May to walk 18km up the glacier toward Janhukot (also spelled Janahut or Janh-kuth, 6,805m). However, I was happy to be accompanied by Paul Figg, who had been down this road before, and Guy Buckingham, a Himalayan veteran reveling in his first trip up the Gangotri. We took it easy, spreading the approach over two days.

I first encountered unclimbed Janhukot looking rather fearsome in a photograph in Rudolf Jonas' account of the prolific 1938 Austro-German expedition to the Garhwal. It seemed to be the type of mountain I had no chance of climbing. The 1938 team maybe thought the same, as they climbed only nearby peaks. Atanu Chatterjee, Sushanta Majumder, Dibya Mukherjee, and Prashanta Roy from West Bengal were bolder, making an unsuccessful attempt in 1989. I saw the peak with my own eyes in 1995, as we made our way up the Gangotri to attempt Chaukhamba I: It looked no less formidable in real life.

By 2004 I was feeling more confident in my ability to get up big mountains, and Marty Beare, Andy Brown, Pat Deavoll, Paul Figg, and I gave it a go. Pat and Marty climbed the broad gully on the right side of the west face to reach the long south-southwest ridge, where altitude sickness forced a retreat from about 6,400m. Andy, Paul, and I retreated in bad weather at around 5,800m on the mixed southwest buttress right of the gully.

Bryan Hylenski, with friends from the USA, India, and Korea, attempted the mountain in 2010 and 2011. They climbed from the east side, where an icefall gives access to a high glacier cwm from which the south-southwest ridge can be gained. They reached about 6,500m. (Hylenski returned in 2016 with John Miller for another unsuccessful attempt.)

Simon Yearsley is always up for a long approach, and, as a veteran of our 1995 Chaukhamba attempt, knew what he was letting himself in for when we teamed up in spring 2014. We had a superb trip, coming close to climbing the mountain via the southwest buttress and south-southwest ridge. We reached the crest at 6,400m, and after a bivouac made the mistake of thinking we could leave our tent and reach the summit in one day. That day faded at around 6,640m, and by the time I got back to the tent I had frostbite in both thumbs and one finger. Despite the lack of summit and minor operations on my digits, I remember this as a great trip (*AAJ 2015*).

On June 3, 2018, as Paul, Guy, and I started up the Mandani Glacier at 1 a.m., heading toward the toe of the southwest buttress, things didn't feel any easier. However, as soon as we crossed the bergschrund, everything changed. We came alive in the cold and swirling spindrift, and briskly soloed the lower 700m, intermittently guided by my fallible memory, to a well-protected campsite at around 5,900m, where we stopped before noon.

Over the next two days, with a bivouac at 6,200m, we climbed a series of hard gray ice pitches and joined the south-southwest ridge. An approaching electrical storm sent us into a

Night view of the southwest buttress of Janhukot (1,700m, ED1 Scottish IV) with the three camps shown. The upper route is much foreshortened and partially hidden in this view. *Hamish Frost*

dither, but we spotted a perfect campsite in a snow bowl just 40m down the west face. That night, comfortably ensconced at 6,500m, we felt optimistic.

In 2014, I had faced hard mixed climbing at 6,600m on a bastion we dubbed the Castle. Our plan now was to traverse the west face below this troublesome obstacle and then follow a twisting gully through a series of buttresses back onto the ridge. We were not pleased to wake to cloud, snow, and even rain. We delayed, then decided it was just like Scotland, and set off into the murk. We fumbled our way across the traverse until we bumped into some rocks, then picked what we hoped was the right gully. Several anxious pitches followed, but our aim was true and the gully ran to the ridge, which vanished into the cloud.

False summit followed false summit. The ridge was narrow and corniced, the visibility poor. We moved together—it all felt very serious. Then, something about the next rise looked different, although we couldn't see beyond. Paul and Guy encouraged me to take the lead, just in case this was the one. For the first 20m it was just more of the same: mist, cornice, soft snow. But then there was a steepening, gray ice, the need for an ice screw, then another, then the ridge dropping away beyond.

Hours later we sat in the dark on our packs outside the tent in the snow bowl, our kit and ropes strewn about us. Clouds had cleared from the peaks just minutes after we reached the summit, and now it was a still, starry night. We would spend the next day reversing most of the south-southwest ridge, then rappel and downclimb the east side to the high eastern cwm, and finally slog back around the mountain in the afternoon heat. But that was all for tomorrow. For tonight all we had to do was eat and sleep. 🗒 📷

SUMMARY: *First ascent of Janhukot (6,805m) in the Gangotri area of Western Garhwal, by the southwest buttress to upper south-southwest ridge (1,700m, ED1 Scottish IV), by Malcolm Bass, Guy Buckingham, and Paul Figg (U.K.), June 3–7, 2018.*

Looking south up the Nying Glacier to the mountains of Nyalu Lek. (A) Nying Himal (6,140m). (B) Peak of around 5,700m. (C) Sharp peak attempted in 2018 to within 40m of summit. (D) Small tooth climbed in 2018 by French party. (E) Shikhan Ri (ca 5,880m, climbed in 2018). (F) Peak 5,975m. (G) French advanced base camp in 2018. *Francois Damilano*

NORTHWEST NEPAL

LIMI HIMAL, FIRST ASCENTS OF LIMI KOTI, SHIKHAN RI, STEPH HIMAL, AND PHASANG PEAK

ACTING ON INFORMATION provided by French guide Paulo Grobel, who had photographed this remote area of Nepal, guide Francois Damilano, Ulysse Lefebvre, and two clients, Guy Perazio and Jean-René Talopp, visited the Nying Glacier, setting up base camp at 4,920m. They located a site for advanced base at 5,275m, and from this camp, on October 9 and with Dhan Magar and Karma Sherpa, made the first known ascent of Shikhan Ri (ca 5,880m on the HGM-Finn map). The route via the northeast face was 700m, F.

In the meantime, a second French group comprising two couples, Julien Desécures and Evelyne Miot, and Grégoire Lestienne and Floriane Pugin, had reached a place known as Talung (ca 4,400m) and then trekked first southeast, then east, up the Talung Valley to set up base camp at 4,950m to the west-southwest of Peak 6,194m, which they named Limi Koti. On October 5, all four climbed the southwest face and west ridge of Limi Koti (30°12'11.12"N, 81°47'5.93"E). The 800m route was AD- (snow to 50°). They returned to base camp, walked out of the valley, then north and east to the Nying Valley, arriving at the other French base camp on the 8th.

After moving to advanced base, Desécures, Lestienne, Miot, and Pugin attempted a relatively small but spectacular peak to the east of Shikhan Ri on October 11, but were defeated 40m from the top by dangerous snow conditions. They retreated and climbed a smaller summit, Nying Tooth (previously climbed by Damilano and Lefebvre), between the unnamed peak and Shikhan Ri.

On the 14th the Desécures group walked up a side valley to the east of base camp, spending the night at 5,300m. The following day they climbed the south face of Peak 6,065m. Their route mostly followed a couloir until around 40m below the top, where a section of rotten rock led to the summit. They named the peak Phasang, the route being PD+/AD- 45°.

The previous day Damilano and Lefebvre had established a camp northeast of base camp at around 5,200m, and on the 15th climbed a couloir on the west face of a peak that forms the end of the west ridge of Phasang. They named it Steph Himal (5,878m) in memory of an old friend of Damilano's, Stéphane Husson [*a noted ice climber and guide who died in 2018 after a fall while guiding*]. The two descended the south face.

Unclimbed peaks of the Limi Himal, both close to 6,000m and close to Limi Koti. *Grégoire Lestienne*

On the 17th all eight climbers left base camp; they returned to Simikot on the 20th. They noted that the area around their Nying base camp appeared to have been visited by previous teams, and some peaks in this glacier basin may have been climbed previously. 📷 ▶

— LINDSAY GRIFFIN, *WITH INFORMATION FROM FRANCOIS DAMILANO, ULYSSE LEFEBVRE, AND GRÉGOIRE LESTIENNE, FRANCE, AND RODOLPHE POPIER, HIMALAYAN DATABASE, FRANCE*

NALAKANKAR HIMAL, PEAK 6,153M, EAST-NORTHEAST RIDGE; PEAK 5,920M, NORTH RIDGE

A FIVE-MAN JAPANESE expedition led by Tetsuji Otsue reached the summits of unnamed Peak 6,153m and Peak 5,920m during an expedition to the remote Takphu Himal in August-September 2016. This was immediately before the German ascent of Takphu North reported in *AAJ 2018*. Their approach from Simikot, across the Nyalu La to Takchhe and up the Sakya Khola to base camp, took 10 days. Details are at the AAJ website. 🗎

— *INFORMATION PROVIDED BY CHRISTOF NETTEKOVEN, GERMANY*

MUGU VALLEY, PEAK 5,467M AND THE MUGU EYE (THE ARCH), ATTEMPTS

INSPIRED BY A photo in *AAJ 2018*, and thanks to a Grit and Rock Award, Cecilia Buil (Spain), Ixchel Foord (Mexico), Spanish photographer Dafne Gisbert, and Anna Torretta (Italy) traveled to the Mugu Valley. They used a helicopter to fly from Nepaljung to Mugu Village, thereby saving around a week of trekking. Their goal was the first ascent of Peak 5,467m (29°44'46.80"N, 82°28'20.10"E), to the northwest of Mugu Village. On the ridge just to the north of this top is a spectacular rock arch, clearly visible from the valley and referred to as the Mugu Eye.

In October the climbers established base camp at 4,200m and an advanced base at 5,050m, below the rock couloir falling from the arch. An attempt was made to climb directly to the arch, but the couloir was deemed too dangerous due to rockfall, and it was too cold to use rock shoes. After a snowstorm covered the wall, Buil, Foord, and Torretta opted for Plan B: a wider, south-southeast-facing couloir to the left, leading more directly toward the main top.

Climbing for one and a half days, with a sheltered bivouac on the wall, the three reached a height of 5,370m, approximately 100m below the summit, before poor rock quality, strong winds, and intense cold forced them down. To that point they had overcome difficulties of 6a A1 M5. 📷

— *INFORMATION PROVIDED BY* ANNA TORRETTA, *ITALY*

Looking southeast from Peak 6,265m at the Koji La lake and (A) Koji La, (B) Koji Kang North (6,275m, climbed in 1997 by a Japanese team via left-hand ridge), (C) a peak of ca 6,600m entirely in Tibet, (D) Myung Thang Kang (6,449m), and (E) Kaqur Kangri (6,859m). In the far right background is Dhaulagiri. *Bruce Normand*

SOLO IN THE KANTI HIMAL
THE FIRST ASCENTS OF THREE 6,000-METER PEAKS

BY BRUCE NORMAND

A CONFLUENCE OF circumstances led to my three partners for a mini-expedition in November canceling their plans. This left me in Kathmandu, fully acclimatized after a successful Takphu expedition (*see p.101*), fully alone, and with four weeks to kill. This hadn't come as a complete surprise, and I had already carried out preemptive Google Earthing that, even with the need for soloing margins of safety, had revealed Rongla Kangri (6,647m) as a worthwhile target. So, after a few days to round up paperwork, a few hours to work out transport, and a few minutes to pack what I could feasibly carry, on October 31 I headed on my way.

This started with two and a half days on public buses to Gamgadhi. I used the bus mainly so I could bring gas canisters with me, but the low cost, local color, priceless experiences teetering around cliff edges, and, in the end, the lack of a functioning airstrip at Rara Lake, all made it seem, in retrospect, like a decent plan.

Given my agenda and the local English-language skills, it didn't seem like a good idea to complicate matters by retaining a porter. My pack leaving Gamgadhi weighed about 25kg. I set a conservative pace up the pretty canyon of the Mugu Karnali. On the third day, the valley turned north and, as I passed through Mugu village, opened into high pastures lining the river. I found a grazing trail heading east through a cedar forest up the Koji Khola and, at the end of day four, arrived at the 5,000m lake directly below the Koji La (5,495m on HGM-Finn map but measured at around 5,470m, due to glacial melt). Despite this pass being an entirely off-limits crossing into Tibet, it sported quite a well-marked trail as far as the flat, icy glacier.

On day five I inspected the Rongla cirque, which from a distance offered no options for reaching the cols on either side of the summit. On day six I set off underneath the southwest face, with intent to cross the west ridge where it merged into the glacier, hoping that a route could be followed up the northwest face. This plan folded when the west ridge turned out to be a vertical choss band, so I beat a retreat to a lower glacier fork and climbed the next summit west from

Rongla. A glacier hike to 5,800m, 400m of 45° southeast-facing névé, and 500m along the north-east ridge brought me to a summit I measured at 6,265m. The wind was moderate and the sky cloudless. I could see that the northwest face of Rongla, although low-angle, had a rocky finish, and thus the east side was going to need a more detailed inspection after all.

With the weather remaining excellent, I set off next morning, planning to summit Rongla Kangri that day. I met the sunrise on the Koji La and continued northwest toward the summit. High-altitude cloud streamers started blowing by, but instead of thickening to spoil the day, they evaporated within two hours. The glacier flattened out and met the cliffs at 5,800m, but there was an option on the far left side of the cirque, next to the southeast ridge, to climb 45° névé all the way to the south top of Rongla Kangri (a.k.a. Kanti East), a border "peak" given the height 6,516m. From there I dropped about 75m down a low-angle ridge and then hiked northeast up snow slopes to the true summit of Rongla Kangri (6,647m), arriving at 1:45 p.m.

On my eighth day out, the weather turned cloudy and cold, and it was a mandatory rest day anyway. For the ninth day I had harbored notions of climbing the southern wall of the Koji Khola to exit onto the flat glacier near Kaqur Kangri (6,859m; climbed in 2002 from the east by Japanese), and then summit a peak close to it. However, by now the difference between south-facing ice glaciers and north-facing, snow-covered ones had not escaped my attention, and I had no desire to push my soloing luck any further. Instead, I climbed just high enough to reconnoiter Churau (6,419m), the dramatic, double-peaked mountain to the west of Peak 6,265m. I then moved my camp an hour down-valley to be ready for another quick start.

Sunrise the next morning found me well up my intended approach, but a hidden glacier trench forced me to change plans, as I could no longer reach the direct south face safely. Instead, I headed to the east ridge, which I reached with only a little heavy trail-breaking, and before the south-facing snow became too soft. I followed the crest over a subsummit to a final 45° snow climb that led directly to the top of Churau. From this angle, the peaks east of Kaqur were more in evidence, reinforcing earlier thoughts I'd had about giving them a closer look.

The next day turned cloudy, with passing snow showers on a strong wind. My welcome in the Koji Khola had expired and I walked out to Mugu. I spent two days exploring the access to the Upper Dolpo via the Chyargo La (5,150m), and getting that closer look, before returning to Gamgadhi at the end of my 15th day out. Another scenic bus tour of 55 unforgettable hours delivered me back to Kathmandu. 📷

[Top] Churau (6,419m) from its east ridge, the route of ascent. [Bottom] Rongla's south top (a.k.a. Kanti East, left) and Rongla Kangri (6,647m) seen from the Koji La. The first ascent climbed the left side of the snowy face on the south peak and then continued along the ridge to the main summit. *Bruce Normand*

SUMMARY: Peak 6,265m by its southeast face and northeast ridge; Rongla Kangri by the southeast ridge of the south top and then the southwest ridge; and Churau by its east ridge; all in November 2018.

DHAULAGIRI HIMAL

The vast south face of Gurja Himal with large serac walls clearly visible toward the left side. *Damien Gildea*

GURJA HIMAL, BASE CAMP TRAGEDY

SOMETIME BETWEEN THE evening of October 10 and the following day, five Korean climbers and four Nepalese staff were killed at their 3,800m base camp below the south face of Gurja Himal (7,193m). This included the team leader, one of the world's most accomplished Himalayan climbers, 49-year old Kim Chang-ho. The other fatalities were Rim Il-jin, Jeong Joon-mo (who was only trekking to base camp), Lee Jae-hoon, and Yo Young-jik, together with Nepalese staff Chhiring Bhote, Lakpa Sangbu Bhote, Phurbu Bhote, and local porter Natra Bahadur Chantel.

In 2017 the highly experienced Kim had made a reconnaissance of the area to select the best place for a base camp from which to attempt the first ascent of the south face of Gurja Himal. His choice was close to the foot of the face. The expedition had approached via Gurja Khani village. A guide had remained here with an ill Korean trekker and was expecting the whole team to return to the village by noon on October 11. When they didn't arrive and no contact could be made with base camp, the guide walked up to within a few kilometers of camp, from where he spotted a body. Next day remnants of clothing and equipment were found scattered 200m–500m below the camp. There was no snow anywhere, but the grass had been flattened, and trees below the camp had been broken.

The face above the site has deep, narrow canyons and watercourses near the bottom, and the supposition is that the wind blast from a large serac avalanche high on the face was funneled through these canyons, causing a catastrophic effect at base camp.

Kim's many high-standard first ascents have been recorded in past editions, available at the AAJ website. He also was the first Korean to climb all the 8,000m peaks without supplementary oxygen, and he set a record for completing this achievement in the shortest time. Gurja Himal was first climbed in 1969 by Japanese and then six times subsequently, all via an approach from the north. ◙

– LINDSAY GRIFFIN, WITH INFORMATION FROM OH YOUNG-HOON, KOREA, AND RODOLPHE POPIER, THE HIMALAYAN DATABASE, FRANCE

MUKUT HIMAL / SANGDACHHE HIMAL

TSARTSE, FIRST ASCENT AND HISTORICAL NOTES

AT 10:45 A.M. on September 25, Koki Ikeda, Daisuke Shimozuru, Yujiro Suga, and Asahi Takeshita (Japan) with Dendi Sherpa, Ngima Sherpa, Penba Sherpa, Tenjin Sherpa, and Bir Kaji Tamang (Nepal), all from a Japanese expedition led by Sachio Nakamizo, made the first ascent of Tsartse (Tasartse, 6,343m).

The compact Sangdachhe Himal lies northeast of Dhaulagiri and the eastern aspect is clearly visible from the Muktinath-Jomsom trail. There are three main summits: Tashi Kang (6,386m), Sangdachhe (unofficially Peak Europa, 6,403m), and Tsartse.

Tashi Kang was brought onto the permitted list in 2002 and climbed in August the same year by a Japanese expedition. From a base camp to the south at 5,400m, they climbed the southwest ridge, then traversed snow to the east to reach the southeast ridge, up which they finished. A German team that repeated this line the following year found the route technically quite difficult, the lower part steep and narrow, while the upper southeast ridge rose to 60° ice.

One of the German summiters, Geotz Wiegand, returned in 2006 to attempt Tsartse (also opened in 2002) by climbing over the summit of Tashi Kang. On his team was the Romanian Constantin Lacatusu. On that occasion the ridge to Tsartse looked too corniced, so the team descended northwest to a 6,177m col and climbed the southeast face of

Looking northeast at Tsartse, as seen from the summit of Tashi Kang. The 2018 team traversed to the snowy southwest face and followed it to the top. *Japanese Tsartse Expedition*

Peak 6,403m, making the first ascent of this summit and giving it the unofficial name of Peak Europa. Wiegand and/or Lacatusu returned four times, from 2012 to 2015, to attempt Tsartse. Altogether this less well-known peak was tried by eight different expeditions, the last in 2016 by Japanese, all via a traverse of Tashi Kang. Dangerous snow conditions were generally the reason for retreat.

The 2018 Japanese team also had a base camp at 5,400m, directly south of Tashi Kang. On September 24 they spent the night in a high camp at 6,000m on the southwest ridge of Tashi Kang. Early next morning they traversed snow on the east face of Tashi Kang to reach the ca 6,000m col on the far side, then climbed the southwest face of Tsartse to the summit. They were back in base camp at 6:45 p.m. the same day. A total of 3,000m of fixed rope was used on this ascent. 📷

— *INFORMATION PROVIDED BY RODOLPHE POPIER, THE HIMALAYAN DATABASE, FRANCE*

ANNAPURNA HIMAL

TARKE KANG AND TARE KANG, CLARIFICATION OF NAMES AND PAST CLIMBS

WHILE RESEARCHING THE south face of Gangapurna and unclimbed peaks in the Annapurna Himal prior to my expedition in 2016 (*AAJ 2017*), I discovered an anomaly: Parties said to have climbed Tarke Kang (Glacier Dome, 7,168m) from the north appear to have reached a different summit than those climbing from the south. I was able to confirm this from the summit of Gangapurna and would like to share the information with other Himalayan climbers.

During a reconnaissance of the Annapurna Sanctuary in 1956, Jimmy Roberts gave the name Glacier Dome to a rounded summit on the watershed just east of the long east ridge of Annapurna. It was first climbed in October 1964 by Mitsuhiro Nishimura and Dorje Sherpa via the southwest and south face. This route has been repeated on many occasions. Later, the government of Nepal renamed the peak Tarke Kang.

Continuing east along the ridge from Tarke Kang, there are two summits before reaching

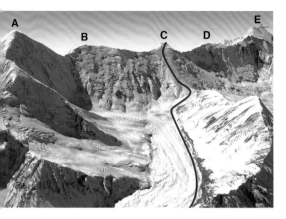

From the northeast: (A) Gangapurna (7,454m), (B) Gangapurna West (7,140m), (C) Tare Kang (suggested new name Tarke Kang Shar, 7,069m), (D) Tarke Kang (7,168m), and (E) Annapurna I (8,091m). The 1981 Italian route up Tarke Kang Shar is marked. Tarke Kang (D) has been climbed from the south (opposite side) numerous times. Its north face is a much steeper and more serious proposition and, as far as is known, remains unclimbed. *Google Earth*

Gangapurna: Tare Kang (as designated on the HGM-Finn map, 7,069m) and Ganga-purna West (a.k.a. Asapurna, 7,140m). Tare Kang is not on the official permitted list, while Gangapurna West was opened in 2014 but remains unclimbed. (Choi Seok-mun and I reached a point 100m from the summit in 2016.)

In 1981 an Italian expedition reported making the first ascent of Tarke Kang from the north. In fact they climbed the north face of *Tare* Kang (that is, Peak 7,069m) to its summit. This route has been repeated by at least five other expeditions. In written reports there is no mention of these parties continu-ing along the west ridge to reach the actual Tarke Kang. As far as is known, the north face of Tarke Kang remains unclimbed.

[*Editor's note: Discussion of this find-ing by Lindsay Griffin of the AAJ, Eberhard Jurgalski of 8000ers.com, and Richard Salis-bury and Rodolphe Popier from the Himala-yan Database has led to a proposal to designate Peak 7,168m as Tarke Kang (as it was historically named) and to refer to Peak 7,069m as Tarke Kang Shar. The name Tare Kang would no longer be used. More details and photos of these mountains are at the AAJ website.*] 📄 📷

– KIM CHANG-HO, *KOREA*

DAMODAR AND PERI HIMALS

CHULU WEST AND CHULU SOUTHEAST, HISTORICAL REVISIONS

WIDELY REPORTED HAVE been the ascents by Carlo Stratta (Italy) on the southwest face of Chulu West (6,419m, see *AAJs 1988 and 1989*). However, these ascents actually took place on Peak 6,429m, a summit that could logically be called Chulu Southeast.

On October 14, 1987, Stratta and Dawa Lama Sherpa climbed the south-southwest face of Peak 6,429m directly to the summit. The snow was in perfect condition, even in the full sun of the afternoon, and Stratta only used two axes for a steep section (70°+) to bypass a serac wall just below the top.

The same two climbers returned in October the following year and climbed two routes on the southwest face to the shoulder at around 6,000m on the southeast ridge. Again, snow condi-tions were optimal and *piolet traction* was not required. They left around 10:30 p.m. on the 7th and climbed a couloir on the left side of the face to the shoulder. After a short rest they rappelled down and then climbed a second couloir, more to the right, back up to the shoulder. From here they continued to the summit.

In 1978, Lhakpa Nuru, Jangbu Sherpa, Peter Lev, and Larry Zaroff climbed Chulu West via a variant to the 1952 Japanese route finishing up the north ridge (the normal route). They "short-cut" access to this ridge by continuing west in the ablation valley, some distance past the place where the normal route ascends steep scree slopes to a col in the ridge, and then climbed direct to the crest via a rock buttress (around 5.6). Lev was guiding Zaroff on this ascent and ropes were fixed; a few old pitons and sections of rope may still remain. Above the buttress they connected with the normal route and followed this to the summit (*see AAJ 1979*). 📷

— LINDSAY GRIFFIN, *WITH INFORMATION FROM PETER LEV, USA, AND LUCA SIGNORELLI AND CARLO STRATTA, ITALY*

DHECHYAN KANG, FIRST OFFICIAL ASCENT; NAGORU FAR EAST, WEST RIDGE

ON MAY 5, Wolfgang Drexler (Austria), Martin Thallmair (Germany), Lawang Tamang, and Yokaci Tamang (both Nepal) climbed Dhechyan Kang (6,019m) above the Thapulghocha La on the border between Nepal and Tibet. After a six-day trek to the lake called Damodar Kunda, the team established base camp closer to the frontier and then climbed the rounded peak easily by south-facing slopes above the pass. The peak was opened for mountaineering in 2014 but had no recorded ascent, though the climbers found evidence of a prior ascent from the Chinese side.

The team then trekked over the Saribung La, climbing Saribung (6,328m) along the way, and on May 11 established base camp at Nagoru Yak Kharka, above which Drexler had climbed three summits in 2013 and 2016 (*AAJ 2017*). The goal this time was a summit he had named Nagoru Far East. From an advanced base at 5,300m, two hours' walk from Yak Kharka, Drexler, Thallmair, and Lawang climbed to the saddle between Nagoru East and Far East early on May 15. From there they turned east and followed rocks and the glacier to the summit plateau. They reached the top at the east end of the plateau at 11:40 a.m. Drexler's full report and many photos of surrounding peaks are at the AAJ website. 📄 📷

— *INFORMATION FROM* WOLFGANG DREXLER, *AUSTRIA*

Looking east at Nagoru Far East from the summit of Nagoru Central. The ascent along the west ridge above the col (reached from the right) is shown. The peak directly behind (6,374m) is unclimbed. Behind this and to the right is Peak 6,524m on the Tibetan border (sometimes referred to as Phungi, but not to be confused with the peak of the same name near Manaslu), while on the far left is part of the south face of Ratna Chuli (7,035m). *Wolfgang Drexler*

The traverse of Himjung (7,092m), seen from the west ridge of Himlung. The Austrian team camped on the glacier shoulder at 6,180m, then continued over Himjung's summit, along the north ridge, down the west spur of neighboring Himlung, and back up to their camp. The round trip was about 21 hours. *Abiral Rai*

HIMJUNG, SECOND ASCENT, TRAVERSE VIA WEST RIDGE AND NORTH RIDGE

AUSTRIANS Vitus Auer, Sebastian Fuchs, and Stefan Larcher, on their first Himalayan expedition, planned to make the second ascent of Himjung (7,092m) via the unclimbed southeast ridge, approaching from the east. The first ascent of this mountain, in 2012, via the southwest face, had been made by the late Kim Chang-ho and fellow Korean Ahn Chi-young. However, the Nepalese authorities refused permission to access the valley to the east, so instead the Austrians set up base camp at 4,800m on the western side of the mountain and looked at other options.

After acclimatizing up to 6,000m on Gyaji Kang and exploring the idea of attempting the southeast ridge of Himjung from the western side, they observed that the unclimbed west ridge was an attractive, elegant line and decided to go for this instead. The intention was to traverse the peak and descend the unclimbed north ridge over a total of four or five days, carrying all their gear. However, renowned forecaster Karl Gabl gave them only a day and a half of good weather, and thus the plan was revised. The three set off from base camp on October 31, and at 5 p.m. the same day they reached a high camp at 6,180m, just before the first steep section of the west ridge.

They set off again at 11 that night, lightly equipped. They simul-soloed up steep névé (55°) through the dark and onto a long, quasi-horizontal section of ridge. Often traversing the 55° flanks of the corniced crest, they crossed a minor summit of about 6,600m, and after six hours had reached the lowest col on the ridge, where they decided to take a break. Unfortunately, with no shelter from the rising wind, in 30 minutes they were forced to start again. They pitched out a steep section shortly below the top, and then, at 9 a.m. on November 1, they reached the summit.

After a good rest on top in a surprising calm spell, they began the long traverse of the north ridge toward 7,126-meter Himlung Himal, eventually descending that peak's west spur. This ends in a brittle rock face, and it took some time for the three Austrians to find a route around it. They gained the glacier at sunset, crossed it to the south, then laboriously climbed back up to the waiting tent and sleeping bags at their high camp, arriving exhausted at 8 p.m., about 21 hours after departing. At 4 p.m. the following day, they were back in base camp. The route, never too technical but very long and sustained, had snow and ice to 55° and a friable rock passage of III. 📷

— LINDSAY GRIFFIN, *FROM INFORMATION SUPPLIED BY HANSJÖRG AND VITUS AUER, AUSTRIA*

MANASLU HIMAL

PANKAR HIMAL, NORTHEAST RIDGE

THE JAPANESE "HIMALAYA Camp" is a project of Yasuhiro Hanatani, the purpose being "succession and progress in mountaineering culture." This camp for young alpinists has been held three times: 2015, 2016, and 2018. In the spring of 2018 we reached the summit of previously unclimbed Pankar Himal (6,264m), a peak on the Nepal-Tibet border east-northeast of Samagaon. Pankar Himal was first brought onto the permitted list in 2014. It is unnamed on the HGM-Finn map but lies just west of Saula (6,235m).

Reo Chikara (22), Yasuhiro Hanatani (42), Ryosuke Matsuyama (21), Daijo Saito (32), Airi Wanatabe (28), and I (29) left Kathmandu on April 11 by chartered bus and started walking the

Members of the 2018 Japanese expedition on the summit of Pankar Himal after the first ascent. (A) Saula (6,235m). (B) Saula South (6,199m). (C) Peak 6,224m. Behind lie Chamar and the big peaks of the Ganesh Range. *Tatsuro Sugimoto*

next day from Soti Khola (700m). We reached the village of Sho (2,880m) on the 20th and base camp at 4,000m on the 22nd.

A large ridge runs south from Pankar Himal. To the west is the Panpoche (Pangpoche) Glacier, while the glacier to the east appears to have no name. We hoped to attempt the peak from the Panpoche Glacier, but the glacier was in a much worse state than we expected, and at 5,000m we realized we would need many more days if we were going to succeed from this side. We decided to retreat and approach the peak from the eastern glacier. We had to change base camp, and on May 3 placed a new camp much lower, at 2,850m, more or less in the main Buri Gandaki Valley.

We now had only three days to climb nearly 4,000m. On May 5 we began our summit push from base camp. We ascended the glacier to the southeast of Pankar Himal to reach the col between this peak and Saula, and then finished up Pankar Himal's northeast ridge. On the 7th we reached our high camp (Camp 3, 5,500m), and a little after noon on the 8th all team members reached the summit. That same day we descended to Camp 1 (4,400m), and on the 9th returned to base camp. 📷

– TATSURO SUGIMOTO, *JAPAN*

ROLWALING HIMAL

KORLANG PARI TIPPA NORTH, WEST TOP

IN 2017 WE made the first ascent of Korlang Pari Tippa South (*AAJ 2018*). In November 2018, I led a small team to attempt Korlang Pari Tippa North (5,738m, according to the Ministry of Tourism), which had appeared slightly higher from the south peak. The rock on the main, eastern top of Korlang Paria Tippa North appeared too shattered to climb safely, so instead we reached the lower west top (5,574m) on November 25. 📄 📷

– BRIAN JACKSON, *EXPEDITION WISE LTD., U.K.*

PEAK 5,840M, SOUTH FACE AND WEST RIDGE

ON NOVEMBER 5, 2017, Tore Sunde-Rasmussen (Norway), Dawa Tashi Sherpa, Tamting Sherpa, and Thundu Sherpa made the first ascent of an unnamed peak of approximately 5,840m on the long east ridge of Dolma Kang (new formal name; previously Tseringma, 6,332m) that runs along the Nepal-Tibet border toward Beding Go (6,125m). The four made a 12-hour round trip from a base camp at 4,750m, the narrow summit ridge giving difficult and exposed climbing. The team thought they were climbing Dolma Kang (6,332m), but detailed analysis of their images by the Himalayan Database confirmed the ascent of the eastern top. A full report and photographs appear at the AAJ website. 🗄 📷

— LINDSAY GRIFFIN, *WITH ADDITIONAL INFORMATION FROM DAVID GOTTLIER, TOBIAS PANTEL, AND RODOLPHE POPIER, THE HIMALAYAN DATABASE*

DRANGNAG RI, SOUTHWEST RIDGE, BIZIPENAK

Drangnag Ri (6,757m) from the west. (1) The route climbed in 2005 by Paul Hartmann and Bruce Normand; Normand went to the summit alone, once the party had reached the southwest ridge. (2) The 2018 Spanish route Bizipenak, up the southwest ridge. *Mikel Zabalza*

MIKEL ZABALZA LED an expedition of the Spanish Alpine Team to the Rolwaling in 2017 (*AAJ 2018*). The following year he returned with a group of friends to attempt the unclimbed southeast ridge of Drangnag Ri (6,757m).

Base camp was established in the village of Na at 4,150m, after which Iñaki Arakistain, Alberto Fernández, Joseba Larrañaga, and Zabalza, all from the Basque country, headed up the Rolwaling Glacier, eventually acclimatizing by summiting a small peak at the glacier head, on the border with Tibet. Inspecting Drangnag Ri, they discovered conditions were much drier than anticipated, so they changed their goal to the southwest ridge, a much longer route but with little in the way of objective danger. They placed a camp at 5,000m, below the ridge, then walked the 12km back down to Na to wait for good weather.

On October 16 they set off up the route. They moved around the west side of the toe of the southwest ridge, then climbed through an icefall to a glacial terrace on the northwest flank, from which they gained the ridge via a steep 150m ice slope. They bivouacked on the crest at 5,700m.

On the second day they climbed over a dome-like tower, after which a horizontal section took them to around 6,100m on the crest, where the main difficulties began. From here to 6,600m the climbing was sustained though never extreme, with sections of ice at AI5, rock to V, and mixed terrain. (One vertical ice pitch was situated at around 6,500m.) They bivouacked at 6,350m, very near the point on the crest where, in 2005, Paul Hartmann and Bruce Normand exited from the west face to the left, after making its first ascent; Normand continued solo to the summit (*AAJ 2006*). The Basques continued up the crest to the top on the 18th, finding the last 200m to be psychologically very hard due to cold temperatures and wind gusts to 70km/hour.

That night they were back at their top bivouac, and over the following two days descended and returned to Na. The team named the route Bizipenak (ED-), which means "experiences" in the Basque dialect. From the toe of the ridge, the route is more than 1,500m high but involves significantly more climbing. The highly experienced Zabalza, for whom this was the 37th mountaineering trip outside Europe, felt it was one of the most beautiful routes he had climbed in the Himalaya. 📷

— INFORMATION SUPPLIED BY **MIKEL ZABALZA**, *SPAIN*

LANGDUNG, SOUTHEAST RIDGE, BIHANA

IN OCTOBER 2017, Jesus Ibarz and Pablo Ruiz were part of a Spanish Alpine Team expedition to the Rolwaling, led by Mikel Zabalza. They decided to return independently in October 2018 and brought along Edu Recio. The goal of this trip was the unclimbed south face of Drangnag Ri (6,757m; the right side of this face, leading to the upper south ridge, was attempted in 2014; *see AAJ 2015*). However, the team discovered this magnificent face is protected by a complex approach, for which they did not have time.

On the suggestion of Zabalza, who was also in the region to attempt another line on Drangnag Ri (*see previous report*), the three went to look at Langdung (6,357m), a peak at the head of the Rolwaling (a.k.a. Ripimo Shar) Glacier, climbed in late December 2017 by a four-person Sherpa team (*AAJ 2018*). The Spanish were immediately attracted to the southeast ridge, the bottom section of which features a triangular buttress of red granite.

It took a day to reach base camp from Na, then a second day to establish an advanced base close to the mountain. On the third day they climbed several pitches on the lower triangular wall, including the technical crux of the route, a friable chimney (6c+). They fixed 200m of rope (which was later removed) and then returned to their tent for the night, where the temperature fell to -16°C.

The next day, October 28, the three left at 3 a.m., re-ascended the lower section, and by the time dawn broke they were already on the upper wall, overcoming pitches of 5+ to 6b. At around 11 a.m. they arrived on the crest of the ridge at about 6,000m. They continued along the well-defined crest over ice and rock of variable quality, finding some of the climbing quite delicate (graded 4 to 5), and their acclimatization for this altitude less than perfect. The ridge seemed never-ending, but eventually, at 4 p.m., they reached the summit, exhausted.

The original plan had been to reverse the ridge, but because of its length they opted instead to descend a gully on the southwest face. This turned into an

[Top] Pablo Ruiz climbing the crux chimney (6c+) on the first ascent of the southeast ridge of Langdung. *Pablo Ruiz Collection* [Bottom] On the upper southeast ridge of Langdung. In the background on the right is Rolwaling Kang (6,664m). Left is the pointed spire of Drangnag Ri (6,757m), while at the far left is Ripimo Shar (6,647m). *Pablo Ruiz*

Marek Holeček on the north ridge of Kyajo Ri just before the bivouac at the Eagle's Nest. Behind him lies part of the southeast ridge of Lungaretse (5,916m). *Zdeněk Hák*

18-rappel descent, the rock becoming progressively worse as they went down. The bergschrund was reached at 11 p.m., and their advanced base regained via the glacier one hour later, after several more rappels. The ascent, which gave around 1,500m of climbing [*700m vertical height from the base of the rock wall*], was named Bihana (meaning "dawn," 6c+).

— *INFORMATION SUPPLIED BY* **PABLO RUIZ**, *SPAIN*

MALAHANGUR HIMAL / KHUMBU SECTION

KYAJO RI, LAPSE OF REASON

Following a tip from Czech mountaineer Martin Otta, Marek Holeček and Jan Smolen attempted Kyajo Ri (6,151m) from the west in the spring of 2017. Approaching via the village of Landen (4,400m) in the valley of the Bhote Kosi, the two climbed 700m up a steep couloir on the left side of the west face to reach the north ridge. They progressed along the very sharp crest a short distance to bivouac on a spot they dubbed the Eagle's Nest, a little above 5,800m. The following morning Smolen suddenly became quite ill, began to vomit, and his brain "reeled." The retreat proved difficult, but they successfully descended the wall, after which there was no strength left for a subsequent attempt.

For a return match in spring 2018, Holeček enlisted Zdeněk Hák, his partner from the 2017 new route on Gasherbrum I (*AAJ 2018*). With two other Czechs, Holeček first spent three weeks trekking in the Khumbu area, crossing high cols and eventually climbing a peak of around 6,500m. When he arrived at Landen to meet up with his climbing partner, Holeček was exhausted. Hák was full of energy but unacclimatized, so the two were evenly matched.

They walked up from Landen to a bivouac at 4,900m, from which they could see the peak was far drier than the previous year, and the line Holeček had climbed with Smolen simply didn't have enough snow. They next morning, May 26, they left at around 4 a.m. and found a barely feasible line further left, which they followed over friable rock to reach the crest of the north ridge around midday. From there they continued along the sharp and exposed crest to gain the Eagle's Nest at around 4 p.m.

The next morning they rappelled 30m on the left side of the ridge and moved onto the northeast face, where névé alternated with broken and sometimes overhanging or wet rock. Most pitches

The west face of Kyajo Ri showing (1) the 2018 line to the crest of the north ridge and (2) the 2017 attempt. The bivouac site at the Eagle's Nest is marked. From there, the Czech route slanted up the northeast face behind the skyline ridge. *Marek Holeček*

proved a struggle, and meaningful protection was almost nil. They crossed the summit as the sun was setting and descended around 300m of the southwest ridge (normal route) before bivouacking. Next day, May 28, they continued down the ridge to the Thesebo Valley and walked out to Namche.

The Czech route up the west face, north ridge, and northeast face, with about 1,200m in vertical gain and more than 1,600m of climbing, was named Lapse of Reason (ED+ M6 WI4+ UIAA III+). 📷

— *INFORMATION SUPPLIED BY* **MAREK HOLEČEK**, *CZECH REPUBLIC*

PHULETATE, RECONNAISSANCE AND ROCK TOWER ON WEST RIDGE

The Khumuche Himal is a chain of peaks on the east side of the Thesebu Khola, around 10km north of Namche. Summits there are approximately 5,400–5,750m, and one stands out: Phuletate (sometimes called Lhabarmatse, 5,597m). In 2008, the Thesebu (a.k.a. Kyajo) valley was visited by a Czech-Slovak team that made the first recorded ascent of Teningbo (5,839m) via its north face (*AAJ 2010*), but no attempts have been recorded for other peaks in this valley. The Czech-Slovak team reported Kapsale, Chhedan, and Phuletate to be worthwhile objectives.

On April 24, from an advanced base camp west of Phuletate at around 5,000m, Alan Tees and I reconnoitered a possible line up the peak. One possibility was a ramp leading to the northwest face, followed by a traverse to a col beneath the north ridge—a long, meandering route. There was no direct access to the north col. From the col, climbing up the north ridge appeared feasible, at least to a shoulder below the twin-summit crown. We pressed on toward the ramp until both of us agreed conditions were too bad—a thin crust covering loose, unconsolidated snow—and then turned our attention to a prominent rock tower on the west ridge. We pushed across the lower reaches of the ridge to gain a minor col (PD+), then climbed the northeast side of the tower on easy ground to gain the top (approximately 5,150m).

After returning to Namche, I made a three-day reconnaissance of Phuletate from the east. The view of our peak from the settlements of Dole and Lopharma was impressive. Although there was far less snow on that eastern aspect and an approach to the north col looked easier, the mountain appeared to show little in the way of a straightforward route. 📄 📷

— **GERRY GALLIGAN**, *IRELAND*

NUPLA KANG, SOUTH FACE AND SOUTHWEST RIDGE

Nupla Kang (6,861m), the snowy peak in back, seen from the west. Most of the 2018 ascent route is hidden by the foreground ridge (the northwest ridge of Tharke Kang), as is the Nup La, from which the climbers began their ascent. The chaotic Ngojumba Glacier is in the foreground. *Damien Gildea*

IN 2017, GARRETT Madison led a commercial expedition that made the first ascent of Tharke Kang (6,710m), a summit on the northwest ridge of Hungchi (7,029m), just southeast of the Nup La (5,848m). The expedition trekked from Lukla to a base camp at around 5,200m by the Gokyo Fifth Lake, and then used a helicopter to fly over the difficulties of the complex icefall of the Ngojumba Glacier to the broad glaciated pass of Nup La on the Tibetan border, near which they established an advanced base (*AAJ 2018*). This use of a helicopter to circumvent difficult or dangerous terrain raised eyebrows among some in the climbing community, who considered it an unsporting departure from the norms of Himalayan first ascents [*see also the note below*].

In the autumn of 2018, Madison employed the same tactics to make the first ascent of Nupla Kang (6,861m), just northeast of the Nup La. On October 31 the team was flown from Gokyo Fifth Lake to the Nup La, where they set up advanced base. The flight also allowed an aerial reconnaissance of a proposed route up the southwest ridge.

On November 2, Ang Phurba Sherpa, Pasdawa Sherpa, Kam Dorjee Sherpa, Tashi Sherpa, and Lakpa Dendi Sherpa, with Ingvild Settemsdal (Norway), Joshua Miller, Kristin Bennett, Ben Veres, and guides Madison and Sidney Pattison (all USA), left camp at 2 a.m., crossed the upper West Rongbuk Glacier, and climbed the south face of Nupla Kang to reach the southwest ridge at around 10 a.m. The climbing on the face had been arduous due to hard snow and ice at 40–60°, similar to the Lhotse Face on Everest, but generally steeper.

Once on the ridge, fixed ropes were placed and the climbing became precarious along the exposed, corniced crest. The first team members arrived on the summit at around 11:10 a.m. The weather was clear and calm, and the intersection of three ridges provided a flat area on which the team could stand, the first such spot since they left camp. They then downclimbed the summit ridge and made many rappels on the face to reach the glacier.

— **LINDSAY GRIFFIN**, *WITH INFORMATION FROM GARRETT MADISON, USA*

EDITOR'S NOTE: *Asked to respond to criticism of the use of a helicopter to ferry the team to the Nup La, avoiding about 650 vertical meters of difficult glacier travel, Garrett Madison said he considered this part of the approach to the mountain, akin to flying to the Kahiltna Glacier to climb Denali. More importantly, he said, "We chose to take a helicopter…for one reason, to avoid the dangerous icefall section of the Ngojumba Glacier. Climbing through this section would require many hours or days exposed to significant objective hazard, both for our foreign climbers and also our Nepalese staff. We wish to reduce the exposure to this risk because we care about their safety. I lost Nepalese staff in the Khumbu Icefall in 2014 and prefer not to experience that again."*

LOBUCHE EAST, SOUTHWEST PILLAR, LE QUATUOR À CORDES

In October, Antonin Cecchini, Laurent Thévenot, Aurélien Vaissière, and I arrived in the Khumbu for a month's climbing. We made base camp at Dzongla (4,800m) and acclimatized by trekking, bouldering, and spending five days climbing up and down the normal route (southeast ridge) on Lobuche East. Our main objective was the north face of Cholatse, but conditions were far too dry, and while searching for an alternative we saw the tremendous rock pillar, 1,100m high, leading straight to the summit of Lobuche East (6,090m).

We placed a high camp at the lake below the start of the pillar at 5,000m, one hour above Dzongla, and started climbing on October 22. It took two big days—the first of 12 hours and the second of 16—to reach the summit. We bivouacked close to the top of the large detached rock tower (ca 5,650m) below the final headwall. Reaching the summit at 6 p.m. on the 23rd, we spent one and a half hours traversing the ridge to the foresummit, and then four hours descending the normal route to Dzongla, where we arrived around midnight. We named the route Le Quatuor à Cordes (1,100m, 6b A2 M4 80°). [*This team approached via the right flank of the pillar, initially using the same line as Eric Brand (USA) and Pemba Norbu Sherpa in 1991. They then climbed up the left flank of the prominent rock tower to its summit, dropped into the gap beyond, and slanted across the headwall to climb the right edge close to the seracs. On the second day, during a section of aid, they found a bolt. It's likely this was from the 1995 Spanish ascent (6b+ with one pitch of aid, Miguel-Miranda-Sanchez), and that on the headwall the Spanish and French routes sometimes share common ground.*]

After this ascent, on the 26th, Laurent and I climbed an ice route on the east flank of nearby Arakam Tse (5,904m). After 600m of scrambling up loose ground, we climbed M5 and ice up to WI5 (around seven belayed pitches) to reach the col south of Arakam Tse, calling our line Pray for Porters. [*A good proportion of this couloir was climbed by a Spanish team in 2013 before they branched right up the northeast face to reach the summit(AAJ 2014).*] 🖹 📷

The southwest pillar of Lobuche East (6,090m), showing (red line) Hiding in Plain Sight (2017), possibly similar to a 1995 Spanish route, (green) Le Quatuor à Cordes (2018) and (yellow) the 1991 American-Nepalese Route. The normal route up the southeast ridge follows the right skyline, though most parties stop at the foresummit. *Steve Fortune*

— SYMON WELFRINGER, *FRANCE, WITH INFORMATION FROM RODOLPHE POPIER, HIMALAYAN DATABASE, FRANCE*

2017 Ascent of Southwest Pillar: In November 2017, also planning to climb the north face of Cholatse, the New Zealand/Australian team of Steve Fortune, Daniel Joll, Kim Ladiges, and Matt Scholes was first drawn to Lobuche East's southwest pillar, which they spent two days climbing, calling their route Hiding in Plain Sight (1,100m, 17 AI3). Their climb probably followed a similar line to the 1995 Spanish ascent. However, the 2017 team also made possibly the only ascent to date that began at the actual toe of the pillar. They came in from the left and kept more or less to the crest of the lower pillar, finding pleasant and solid climbing, but with slabs trickier than expected in double boots. There were three gendarmes, each requiring a rappel on the far side. After their Lobuche East ascent, the team repeated the French route on Cholatse. A full account and more photos are at the AAJ website. 🖹 📷 ▶

— *INFORMATION FROM* STEVEN FORTUNE, *NEW ZEALAND*

Pumori (7,161m), showing the upper part of the Romanian line (right) on the southeast face and their descent of the southwest ridge and west face. Their highest bivouac was at the junction of the two lines. *Zsolt Torok*

PUMORI: A DREAM COME TRUE
ROMANIANS COMPLETE NEW ROUTE UP THE SOUTHEAST FACE

BY ZSOLT TOROK

THE IDEA OF a new line on the southeast face of Pumori (7,161m) had been in my mind since 2015, when I had a chance to study the face in person. I tried it in 2017 with Vlad Capusan (*AAJ 2018*), but we were defeated by poor weather and avalanches. In the autumn of 2018, I returned with Romeo Popa and Teofil Vlad. We acclimatized by climbing nearby Lobuche East and spending two nights at 5,900m, and then installed a camp at 5,660m, at the bottom of the steep glacier below the southeast face.

We left this camp at 2 a.m. on October 13, ascended the glacier to the bottleneck where our line began. [*The Romanian line ascends a distinct mixed shield to the left of the 1986 Scottish Route and all other climbs on the southeast face.*] We then climbed through funnels, sometimes with vertical or overhanging steps, to the first icefield, reaching it via a section of M4. Our strategy when it came to bivouacking was to look for a suitable place in good time, rather than pushing on into the dark. However, on day one we didn't find any good place; in fact our bivouac at 6,050m was wretched, with hardly any room, and we spent a difficult night.

The next day started well and we progressed pitch by pitch up less steep ground, heading for the much feared Ramp, the key passage of the route situated in the upper third of the face. The difficulties soon increased—this was the most satisfying part of the route, spectacular and technical (M5). We entered the Ramp and found an ideal bivouac spot at 6,250m, sheltered by a large rock overhang, and with enough space to flatten snow and create a good place for our two-man tent. It was the only good bivouac site on the whole route. Next morning we started up the Ramp with renewed energy.

The Ramp gave climbing to M6 and spectacular ice. Exiting the Ramp was the hardest section—the ice came to a halt and there was little or no possibility of placing protection in the rock. We slanted left and after another 60m pitch reached the Spider, a 60–70° icefield at 6,450m that offered one place for a tent. We were now above our 2017 high point. This bivouac was not exposed to avalanche, but we failed to consider the wind, which released ice and snow from the walls above. We were not hit but kept our helmets on throughout the night.

Getting out of the Spider next morning gave us the final crux pitch (60m, M6). It was really taxing, as the sun had melted most of the ice. Above, four more pitches up steep, large, organ-pipe ice runnels, with a small section of M4, brought us to the southwest ridge at 6,776m, where we made our fourth bivouac.

On day five we were tired and the weather was poor, so we rested. We set out after dawn on day six, October 18. The sky was relatively clear, but the wind was strong and the temperature low. We struggled to the summit, which we reached at 3 p.m. and then enjoyed 40 minutes of surprising calm. We regained our tent that evening, finding later that the wind that day had reached speeds of 105 km/h.

The following day we descended the southwest ridge and west face in 13 hours, leaving Abalakov anchors, ice screws, snow stakes, and slings over flakes during 1,000m of rappelling. We camped that night at 5,760m and on day eight worked our way through a labyrinth of detritus on the right side of the glacier to reach the valley. We then continued down for eight more hours to Gorak Shep.

We named our route Le Voyage du Petit Prince (ED, M6 AI4 R). The line was committing and comparable to the Eiger north face, with similar features but at high altitude. As Teofil remarked, "Some time ago, establishing a new line on a 7,000er was science fiction, something I read about in books by the early pioneers. I have now lived a dream I hardly had the guts to contemplate." ▣

[Top left] Detail of the upper route on Pumori's southeast face, following the central ramp line up and left toward the southwest ridge. *Zsolt Torok* [Right] Torok climbing steep ice during the 2018 Romanian climb of the southeast face. *Teofil Vlad* [Bottom left] Romeo Popa negotiates difficult mixed terrain on day four of the ascent. *Zsolt Torok*

CHAMLANG, NORTH SPUR, ATTEMPT

DURING THE PRE-MONSOON season, a French team comprising Laurent Bibollet, Lise Billon, Emmanuel Chance, Aymeric Clouet, and Sébastien Corret attempted the unclimbed north spur of Chamlang (7,321m).

From an advanced base at 5,500m on the East Hongu Glacier, four of the climbers reached a col (ca 6,100m) on the long ridgeline between Point 6,439m (the high point at the end of the prominent shoulder on Chamlang's north spur) and Hongku Chuli to the northeast. This gave access to a large glacier running northeast below the various summits of Chamlang. From the head of this glacier, the French climbed directly to the shoulder of the north spur, then followed the ridge up to the steepest section of the spur, where, at around 6,500m, they found a protected bivouac spot. A rough night for some members confirmed that they were not yet acclimatized for a summit push, and when the forecast pronounced bad weather for several days, the team decided to abandon the attempt. The compelling line of the north spur has been the goal of several expeditions. 📄 📷

— *INFORMATION FROM RODOLPHE POPIER, HIMALAYAN DATABASE, FRANCE*

FATAL ACCIDENT ON CHAMLANG: In the autumn of 2018, well-known Japanese alpinist Fumi-taka Ichimura planned to attempt a solo ascent of the north face of Chamlang. Sadly, while acclimatizing on the lower west ridge, he must have fallen. His body was spotted at around 6,000m.

SHARPHU II, EAST FACE, SAMSĀRA

IN OCTOBER, AIVARAS Sajus and I made the first known ascent of Sharphu II (6,328m) via the east face—a route we named Samsāra (1,040m, ED2 AI5 M6). The route height is measured from the first belayed pitch on the glacier, though the sustained technical climbing, above the bergshrund, was 730m.

Sharphu I and II are twin peaks that share a steep eastern aspect. In 1963 a Japanese-Nepalese team climbed Sharphu I (6,433m), the highest of the group, from the south side. It does not appear that anyone had seriously attempted Sharphu II.

We approached via the Kangchenjunga Base Camp trail using porters, donkeys, and yaks. We set up our base camp at 4,550m, west of the small village of Khambachen, in a yak pasture beside the Nupchu Khola. We observed many blue sheep, whistling snowcocks, and royal blue granda-las. Snow leopards and Tibetan wolves have preyed on grazing yak in this area.

After acclimatizing and scouting the peak for a week, we established a high camp at 5,600m at the bergschrund below the east face, and acclimatized there for one more day. The approach to the bergschrund briefly crosses into the run-out zone of active seracs.

The east face has four prominent cliff bands in its lower half and several gully systems that extend to the summit ridge. The shaded aspects of these bands held good ice, but the rock was mediocre. We put together a line by climbing ice and mixed terrain through one gully, then traversing rightward across a snowfield below a dry cliff band into a second gully, which we followed to the summit ridge. We camped once on the face under a full moon and the next night on the summit ridge, with a steady 30 mph wind and a temperature of -25°C. Sharing one sleeping bag saved weight and encouraged shivering.

We summited on October 26 by a short snow ridge, then descended the snowy north ridge. After several rappels past summit rime and cliff bands, interspersed with about 400m of steep downclimbing, we spent a final night on the glacier between Sharphu II and Sharphu VI (6,076m). We descended to base camp on our sixth day after departing.

The adjacent east face gullies hold similar terrain with sections of excellent ice. Although in six days on the mountain we observed only one rockfall incident, it was a significant event directly down the first 200m of our line (after we had passed). Future parties might also consider the steep western and northern aspects of the Sharphus and Nupchu from the Yangma Khola.

Samsāra is a Sanskrit word that means to wander and refers to cyclical existence in Buddhist and Hindu traditions. We thank the Sherpa family that owns the White House in Khambachen for their generosity and assistance. ▣

— SPENCER GRAY, AAC

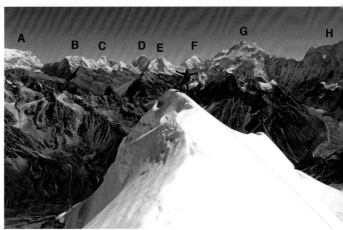

[Top] The east faces of Sharphu I and II across the Nupchu Khola (valley). Samsāra (2018) is marked. The 1963 route to the higher Sharphu I is hidden on the south side. [Middle] Summit morning at 6,260m, with Sharphu I beyond the tent. [Bottom] The summit of Sharphu II. To the northeast are (A) Jongsang (7,462m), (B) Drohmo (6,881m), (C) Pathibara Chuli (7,140m), (D) Kirat Chuli (7,362m), (E) Nepal Peak (7,177m), (F) Gimmigela Chuli (7,350m), (G) Kangchenjunga (8,586m), and (H) Jannu (7,711m). *Spencer Gray (all three)*

CHINA

To reach unexplored mountains northwest of Yushu, three climbers rode four days to reach a camp at 4,800 meters, west of the town of Zhidoi. Here they cached their bikes and headed into the hills. *Nathan Dahlberg*

QINGHAI

MOUNTAINS OF THE MEKONG HEADWATERS

AFTER 14 MONTHS of planning, I landed at Yushu Airport (3,800m) in Qinghai to meet my companions Ben and Jos Hoetjes (New Zealand), who had ridden bikes almost 1,000km from the provincial capital of Xining. It had taken them 10 days and provided valuable acclimatization. Our mission was a lightweight attempt on what we believed, after much research, were the highest mountains in this part of the Qinghai-Tibet Plateau.

This whole project was initiated after reading about the first ascent of Qiajajima in *AAJ 2005*, where the final lines of the report describe "three outstanding mountain massifs in the source of the Mekong River," one of which was "...Sedari (5,770m), and the 5,700–5,800m peaks ranging to the west, where the glaciers are most developed. This massif remains unvisited. No photos of the mountains have been taken."

These peaks lie in the most isolated region of the Yushu Tibetan Autonomous Prefecture. The ranges in this area run roughly southeast to northwest for over 300km, from below Yushu (in the southeast) to above the sources of the Mekong. To the north, west, and south, they drop into the rolling hills of the Tibetan Plateau (often 4,800m high). To the southeast there is no definite end—the mountains drop to below 5,300m and merge with other ranges that stretch toward Sichuan before rising again to over 6,000m.

With just a few blurry Google Earth images and 1950s Russian maps, we planned to explore— and if possible climb—some of these peaks, using bicycles as transport. Traveling light is part of our philosophy, and what I term "velo mountaineering" also increases flexibility in planning and transport, well outside the bureaucratic difficulties normally associated with high Asian expeditions.

In the first two days we rode over 200km, crossing over a 4,800m pass, to reach the town of Zhidoi. The route onward to the west had worried me greatly due to a necessary crossing of the An Yang Gong Chu (Angqiansong River). However, we found a new road had been constructed that bridged the river and considerably eased our travel. One long day took us to the bridge and a camp by the river at 4,650m, from where we could see our peaks for the first time. A second day got us to a second camp at 4,800m, where we left the bikes.

From here, on July 10, we made a traverse of Deception Peak (5,778m, 33°38'26"N, 94°59'22"E). (Altitudes cited here refer to the Tamotsu Nakamura map of the area and differ slightly from an ArcGIS map we used, and which we believe to be more accurate.) This peak was directly above our camp and so named because it proved deceptively difficult.

The next day we moved up the main glacier system to the southwest, which we dubbed Sunshine Glacier, and camped at 5,350m. On

Unclimbed peaks near the Mekong River headwaters. [Top] Looking southeast from Ben Jai Ma (5,876m). [Bottom] Looking east across the upper Fox Glacier. *Nathan Dahlberg (both photos)*

the 12th we crossed west to the Fox Glacier and climbed Peak 5,876m via the northeast face and southeast ridge, naming it Ben Jai Ma (33°34'21"N, 94°55'55"E). The following day, from the Sunshine Glacier, we climbed a peak not shown on the Nakamura map but lying between peaks 5,777m and 5,842m. We named this Constellation Peak (ArcGIS map height 5,797m).

Although we did not have the means to verify its exact altitude, we are now fairly sure from all points of reference, including the summit, that Ben Jai Ma is the highest peak in all the large glacial areas of this region. This includes the Qiajajima Group, approximately 30km southeast of where we climbed; previous reports listed Qiajajima high point at 5,930m, but the massif is significantly lower on satellite and radar-mapped surveys, the highest summit being 5,761m.

Leaving the mountains on the 14th, we spent five days returning to Yushu via Zhidoi, where my friends left me to investigate peaks south of Yushu, which form a southern extension to the mountain system we visited. The names we gave to mountains, valleys, and glaciers are purely for convenience and our sense of fun. We fully expect these to be replaced by local names over the course of further exploration. 📷 🔍

– NATHAN DAHLBERG, *NEW ZEALAND*

NYAINBO YUZE, MANTOU SPIRE AND VARIOUS ATTEMPTS

I FIRST VISITED the Nyainbo Yuze in 2016 (*AAJ 2017*) and soon began planning a return. On September 25, photographer Rachel Ross, Catherine Tao, and I rendezvoused in the city of Chengdu. From there we made a long drive via Jiuzhi to a road-head giving access to a large west-east valley that splits the Nyainbo Yuze. The main valley was surprisingly populated, with nomads inhabiting a plot of land every 500m or so. The culture of these people is so warm and welcoming that, as we shuttled loads into the valley, they not only let us travel, camp, and climb on their land, but also invited us for tea, meals, or to sleep. After staying the night with one family, we employed their horses to get our remaining gear to base camp.

Over the coming weeks we attempted several peaks, and Catherine and I climbed a tower we named Mantou Spire (4,750m), with five short pitches of fun, snowy chaos (5.6 and a few points of icy aid). Unstable weather, powder snow, and icy cracks inhibited our progress on other attempt. I now know, officially, that September is the month to be in the Nyainbo Yuze, not October! [*Details and coordinates of the 2018 climbs, along with advice on climbing in the area, are at the AAJ website.*] 📄 📷

Riding out of the Nyainbo Yuze, looking east into the middle part of the range. This main valley was heavily populated with nomadic families. *Catherine Tao*

— TESS FERGUSON, *AAC*

MUZ TAU (SAUYR ZHOTASY), ATTEMPT FROM THE NORTHEAST

AFTER ATTEMPTING THE peak popularly known as Sauyr Zhotasy (3,840m) from the south in 2017, Eric Kowalski, Alex Tang, and I returned to the China-Kazakhstan border for another attempt in September, along with Libor Jelenek and Wayne Stanley. Due to hassles with security the previous year, we opted for a much longer, but less observed, approach from the northeast, well away from the border. After a four-day approach, we attempted the northeast spur leading to the north ridge, with snow to 60° and two pitches of easy mixed climbing. With afternoon clouds building, we retreated a little over 2km from (and 100m below) the summit. During this expedition, we also learned the mountain's true name: Muz Tau, Kazakh for "ice mountain."

Sadly, a security lockdown now prevents access to the entire south side of the range. Areas free to travel in 2017 were totally closed in 2018. 📄 📷 🔍

— ED HANNAM, *AUSTRALIA*

HUTSA, SOUTHEAST RIDGE AND EAST FACE

WHILE ACCLIMATIZING FOR another objective in the Genyen Massif, Zhang Qingwei, Huang Siyuan, and I saw the pyramid peak of Hutsa (29°54'2.96"N, 99°37'24.03"E). We knew its name and altitude (5,863m) but nothing else. This now became our major goal, but with no information we didn't even know from which side to attempt it.

On October 24 we moved to an advanced base camp at 5,100m, and next day approached the mountain from the south. A fine couloir on the south face was severely exposed to rockfall, so instead we opted for a line to the right that offered 50° névé and led to a col on the southeast ridge. [*This appears to be the ridge to the right of that attempted by Dave Anderson and Szu-ting Yi in 2011 and 2014, while trying to make the first ascent of the mountain. In 2016, Hutsa was climbed twice by a multi-national expedition, once via the west face and once via a hidden couloir on the southwest side; see AAJ 2017.*] After four rock pitches up to 5.10, the terrain became steeper. We avoided an overhanging compact wall by descending to a mixed couloir on the east face and following it toward the upper southeast ridge, with compact snow up to 60–70° and a little WI3. We simul-climbed this until, at 7 p.m. and at an altitude of 5,700m, we cut out a ledge and bivouacked for the night.

The next day a total of four mixed pitches, up to M4+, took us to the summit at 1 p.m. We made 10 rappels on the southwest face to get off the mountain, reaching the bottom by 8 p.m., and were back at base camp three hours later.

– LIU JUNFU, *CHINA, SUPPLIED AND TRANSLATED BY XIA ZHONGMING, GERMANY*

SICHUAN / DAXUE SHAN – MINYA KONKA RANGE

NYAMBO KONKA, NORTHEAST FACE TO SOUTH-SOUTHEAST RIDGE

W.C. FIELDS ONCE said: "If at first you don't succeed, try, try again. Then quit. No use being a damn fool about it." Sound advice for most people, but mountaineers tend to be obsessive.

I first attempted then-unclimbed Nyambo Konka (6,114m), a domed, heavily glaciated peak directly south of Minya Konka, in 2005. I went back in 2009 with a strong four-person team and reached the east-northeast ridge via the southeast face, but the ridge was heavily corniced and we were forced down by four feet of snowfall in two days. Alas, I returned in 2011, failing this time on the southwest face because of insurmountable rotten rock. Nyambo Konka was finally climbed by a large Korean team in 2015, using thousands of feet of fixed line and leaving piles of garbage. I thought their ascent wouldn't bother me and I could put this obsession to rest. I'd already made a damn fool of myself on this mountain, so good riddance. Right? Nope.

I returned to Nyambo Konka in the fall of 2017 with JJ Cieslewicz from southern Utah. With no porters or beasts to hump our loads, we spent four days shuttling gear to the bottom (ca 3,960m) of the northeast face of the south-southeast ridge. We had intended to put two camps on the face, but after one sketchy bivouac on a chipped-out ledge in the middle of an avalanche-prone couloir, we pounded straight up mixed terrain to the ridge. We camped on the crest at 5,550m, a good 2km from the summit, which we reached the next day. We rapped our route in a storm and during the descent found our earlier bivouac ledge had been swept away by an avalanche.

The great British explorer Tim Severin, who sailed a leather boat across the Atlantic and retraced Genghis Khan's route through Mongolia on horseback, once told me that any expedition worth starting is worth finishing. Fourth time's a charm.

– MARK JENKINS, *AAC*

JJ Cieslewicz on the summit of Nyambo Konka (6,114m). Behind and facing the camera is the magnificent southern pillar of Minya Konka (7,556m). In the fall of 2018 this was the target of Nick Bullock and Paul Ramsden (U.K.), but appalling weather prevented any attempt. *Mark Jenkins*

Xiao Hai a little above Camp 3, close to the crest of the northeast ridge, on summit day. The two Chinese climbers' alpine-style ascent took seven days round-trip from base camp. *Li Zongli*

MINYA KONKA, ALPINE-STYLE
A NEW ROUTE FROM THE NORTH TO THE NORTHEAST RIDGE

BY LINDSAY GRIFFIN, *WITH INFORMATION FROM LI ZONGLI, CHINA, AND XIA ZHONGMING, GERMANY*

SUCCESS OFTEN LEADS us to ignore many potential problems; failures amplify our mistakes. —Li Zongli

In 2016, Li Zongli and Xiao Hai (China) attempted the north spur and northeast ridge of Minya Konka (a.k.a. Gongga Shan, 7,556m). Their planned route was significantly independent of the 1998 Korean ascent of the northeast ridge. The Korean expedition approached from the southeast up the Hailuogou Glacier, climbed a steep, rocky headwall to reach the northeast ridge at 5,800m, and then continued up the ridge to the summit. The two Chinese approached first from the east and then the north up the Yanzigou Glacier, from which they reached the crest of the northeast ridge a little above 6,700m.

In 2016 they were more or less blown away by fierce winds at their 6,700m top camp, but learned a lot from this failure. In 2017 they went to neighboring Zhongshan Feng (6,886m), from which they could study their prospective route on Minya Konka. In 2018 they underwent a strict training regime: two months of strength training, two months of endurance, and finally two months of altitude preparation that culminated in sleeping on the summit of a 6,000m peak. Soon after, on October 12, Li and Xiao left Chengdu for Minya Konka. Accompanying them were Achu and Shi Wei, who would carry loads up to Camp 1 at 5,050m, then return to a lower camp at 4,200m, where they would remain throughout the climb.

After rebuilding a footbridge over a river, the team reached Haizi base camp (3,700m) on the 14th. On the 15th it was a long day to reach Camp 1, where they arrived at 7 p.m. It was misty and dark, so it was unclear whether they were in the same location as 2016. Li's sleeping bag and other warm clothing had become wet at lower altitudes, and he was worried there would not be an opportunity to dry them. He and Xiao left at 6 a.m. the next day and climbed a steep 800m slope onto a plateau below the north spur, where they pitched Camp 2 at 5,800m. They arrived by

11:30 a.m., and it was sunny—both were relieved to be able to dry all their gear.

Next day they left at 5 a.m. and spent 11.5 hours climbing a north-facing spur to 6,700m. This is generally a steep snow slope [*quoted as up to 75°*]. In 2016 they had found a flat section that allowed them to pitch a tent relatively easily, but in 2018 it was gone, and they had to construct a platform out of a 50° slope. They dug more than a meter into the slope before securing the tent with snow and ice gear.

Leaving at 5 a.m., they cut up to the northeast ridge, where they met intermittent wind and snow. At 1 p.m. the weather became more unstable, and at 2 p.m., in difficult visibility and high wind, their will began to waver. They persevered, and at around 4:45 p.m., by which time the visibility had dropped to less than 10m, the slope ahead became flat. Soon there was no higher place to go.

Anxious about navigating down the ridge in such poor visibility, the pair set off quickly. The descent became a struggle, and toward the end Li was resting almost 10 minutes every five steps. His eyesight began to fail, and at some stage in the night, when they thought they were close to camp but couldn't find it, they had to take shelter from the intense wind. They found a couple of large rocks at around 6,800m and sat behind them

[Top] Minya Konka (7,556m), showing: (1) 1998 Korean Route up the northeast ridge, approached by the Hailuogou Glacier; (2) 2018 Chinese Route up the north-facing spur and northeast ridge, approached via the Yanzigou Glacier; and (3) 1932 American Route on the northwest ridge. *Google Earth* [Bottom] Minya Konka from the north, showing the Chinese Route up a spur to the northeast ridge. Camp 2 was at 5,800 meters and Camp 3 at 6,700 meters. The right skyline is the northwest ridge, followed by the American team that made the first ascent of the mountain in 1932. *Li Zongli*

until the morning. When dawn finally broke, Xiao found the tent surprisingly quickly. He escorted Li down to the tent and the pair spent the remainder of the day resting, eating, and drinking.

At 8 a.m. on the 20th the two continued the descent with some difficulty. Fortunately, Li's eyesight began to improve, but they still managed to drop a pack before reaching Camp 2 at 5 p.m. The two had hoped to make it all the way down to Camp 1, but, too exhausted to continue, they spent the night at Camp 2 and then reached the lower camp after dark the next day, met by their two friends. On return to base camp Li Zongli had lost 6kg of body weight.

This was likely the ninth ascent of the mountain, seven of which have been via the northwest ridge, the route followed by the American team that made the first ascent of the mountain in 1932. While it is not clear if any ascents of the northwest ridge have been achieved in pure alpine style (perhaps one or two), the 2018 Chinese ascent is certainly the first alpine-style new route climbed on Minya Konka. [*The 1998 Korean Route was not previously documented in the AAJ. A pair of photographs from this expedition are included with this report at the AAJ website.*] 📷

The Sheila Face (northwest face) of Aoraki/Mt. Cook (3,724m), showing (1) The Ministry of Silly Walks and (2) The Pilgrim, both climbed in September 2018. Earlier routes not shown. *Steve Fortune*

SOUTHERN ALPS

AORAKI/MT. COOK, SHEILA FACE, TWO NEW ROUTES

THE SHEILA FACE of Aoraki/Mt. Cook—the northwest face—sits at the head of the Hooker Glacier. Continuously steep and nearly 1,000m at full height, it presents some of the most inspiring technical terrain in the Southern Alps. Helicopter access is forbidden, which means any party wishing to climb in the zone must walk from Mount Cook Village—a trek of between nine and 16 hours, with a good helping of objective hazard and complex glacial navigation. This, combined with the challenges of getting the face in good condition, means the Sheila often goes many seasons without an ascent.

Caleb Jennings was keen to try an impressive unclimbed couloir left of the Central Buttress, so in early September we made the long walk and ski up the Hooker to Empress Hut. September is quite late in the austral winter to try a sunny northwest-facing ice line, but persistent southeasterlies were keeping temperatures low. Still, to be safe, we decided to start climbing at midnight, traveling as light as possible and hopefully being up and out of the couloir before the sun was anywhere near it.

After three or four moderate ice pitches, our route headed up a wall of intermittent ice runnels and blobs. The climbing was engaging but never desperate and well protected with ice screws and rock protection (mostly WI4/5 and M5/6). At the crux, a semi-connected ice pillar presented itself as one option, but with Caleb below I wasn't keen to touch it. Instead, I was able to dry-tool up a crack and turn the roof near the top of the pillar.

After these six or so pitches we found ourselves in a large snow gut (a broad gully), and from here we simul-climbed around 300m on moderate terrain to a notch on a ridge feature, which we followed for seven pitches of easier but engaging mixed climbing (M5, 70°), eventually joining the Central Buttress to reach the summit. We called our climb Pilgrim, 900m, IV, 7 (WI5 M6).

We descended the standard Linda Glacier route, crossed under the Gunbarrels seracs after

dark, and reascended to Green Saddle, from which we were able to rappel Fyfe's Gut on V-threads, returning us to the Hooker Glacier. On the drive home we received a call from our friend Rose Pearson, and after finding such good ice on Cook, we suggested the possibility of climbing another new line farther left on the Sheila Face. Soon Rose and Sam Waetford were following our skin tracks up the Hooker, though clad in snowshoes, the poor souls.

Rose and Sam's route started a few hundred meters higher up Fyfe's Gut than our own, and so their climb began with some brittle ice climbing (WI4) before branching up the Sheila. The southeastern wind flow had ended and temps were on the rise, and even at 2:30 a.m. the pair had to dodge a few rocks while in the gut. Happy to be out of the firing zone, the pair climbed a long pitch up a steep corner with a thin flow of ice. The following pitch involved some insecure mixed climbing, which gave access to a mixed gully that they followed for a few rope lengths to arrive at a large snow ramp at midday. The pair continued up the ramp, and after some more delicate mixed climbing arrived at the summit around 7 p.m.

They descended following our tracks. The next day Sam's knee decided it had done enough bending and he was forced to walk the entire Hooker Valley in some kind of crazy shuffle, after which the pair named their route the Ministry of Silly Walks, 700m, VI, 5 (WI4 M4).

Tragically, Caleb Jennings, my partner on the Sheila Face, was killed in an avalanche on low-angle terrain in Arthur's Pass National Park a few months after we climbed this route. Caleb was an inspired climber and a great friend. The guy you call when you have a plan that clearly involves being wet, cold, and hungry. The kind who looks over mountains he has seen his whole life but shares the same joy he would as if it were his first time. Caleb, I will really miss you. 📷

— KIM LADIGES, *AUSTRALIA*

[Top] **Ice runnels midway up the Pilgrim,** **a new route on Aoraki/Mt. Cook.** [Bottom] **Caleb Jennings rehydrating on the Pilgrim.** *Ladiges Collection*

The southwest face of Mt. Percy Smith (2,465m) and the line of the Promise, soloed by Ben Dare in October 2018. The remote face is rarely seen in winter condition; this photo was taken in 1984. The only previous route is to the left: On the Dark Shore (790m, 23 pitches, with a crux of 17/5.9, Dickson-McLeod, 1993). *Simon Middlemass*

NOTABLE RECENT CLIMBS

SUMMER IN NEW Zealand's high alpine was highlighted by several periods of warm, calm weather, resulting in dry and stable conditions. In March, Ben Dare soloed a new line on the south face of Mt. Sabre (2,162m) in the Darran Mountains: Everlasting Light, 600m, V, 6, (18/5.10a). Dare climbed between the Original Line (Jones-Jones, 1971) and the Campbell-Howard (1973), and in the process claimed the first solo ascent of this face.

In mid-July, the annual Darrans Winter Climbing Meet once again drew a strong crowd to Homer Hut. Unfortunately, unsettled weather and fluctuating temperatures, coupled with intermittent road closures, kept most of the participants pinned down in the hut and sharing stories and whiskey in front of the fire. During one short weather window, Dare managed to sneak out and bag the second ascent and first solo of the south face of Mt. Suter (2,094m)—and by a new route. Elysium, 750m, VI, 6+ (AI5), climbs steep runnels and thinly iced slabs on the right side of the face.

To close out the winter season, Lucas Kirchner and Llewellyn Murdoch made the second ascent of Reunion Invernal (650m, V, 4, Kerkmann-Muños, 2010) on the East Peak of Mt. Crosscut (2,263m) at the head of Cirque Creek. Meanwhile, Caleb Jennings, Alastair McDowell, and Rose Pearson made the first ascent of the south face of Mt. Hutton (2,822m) via Moonshadow, 500m, V, 5+ (WI3 M4+).

The arrival of spring saw a notable surge in activity in Aoraki/Mt. Cook and Westland national parks. Two new routes were climbed on the Sheila Face of Aoraki/Mt. Cook (3,724m, *see report above.*) Evan Davies and Jacob Downie climbed the Grey Hare, 300m, III, 4+ (WI3 M3), on Conway Peak (2,899m), followed soon after by James Warren and Tanja De Wilde with Save Some Ice for Later, III, 4+ (WI3 M4) on the south face of Mt. Barnicoat (2,800m).

Further north, Ben Ellis, Jack Grinstead, and Josh Mitchell climbed a new route on the south face of D'Archaic (2,875m). Their line, Desire, 650m, V, 5 (WI4), follows steep ice through the lower rock band and then snowfields leading directly to the summit.

In early October, Dare made the long trip up to the head of the Hopkins Valley, crossing the main divide of the Southern Alps into the Baker Creek drainage to reach the southwest face of Mt. Percy Smith (2,465m). His new route, The Promise, 700m, VI, 6+ (WI4 M5+ A0), was the second ascent of the face and the long-sought first ascent in winter conditions.

The year closed out with Wiz Fineron, Zachary Orme, and Sefton Priestley adding four new pitches to the route Te Hamo on the Sinbad Gully Wall in the Darran Mountains. Orme and Priestley climbed the first seven pitches in February. (The first two of these had been climbed by a previous party.) The new pitches brought the climb to the top of the wall. The full route has

Wiz Fineron leading the crux ninth pitch of Te Hamo (11 pitches, 31/5.13d), a new route on the Sinbad Gully Wall in the Darran Mountains. *Sefton Priestley*

sustained difficult climbing, partially protected by bolts; nine of the 11 pitches are graded 24 (5.12a) or harder, with a crux ninth pitch of 31 (5.13d). All of the pitches have been free climbed, but the full climb—one of the most difficult of this style in the entire country—had not been freed in a single push as of early 2019. The rock is said to be high-quality granite, and there is much potential for similar climbs on this wall. [*Editor's note: The online version of this report covers numerous other ascents.*]

– BEN DARE, *NEW ZEALAND*

BOOK REVIEWS

EDITED BY DAVID STEVENSON

LIMITS OF THE KNOWN
DAVID ROBERTS. Norton, 2018. Hardcover, 336 pages, $26.95.

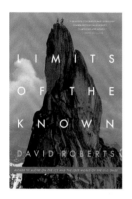

IF I COULD choose a title for this book, I might change it to *No Limits of the Known*, such is the wide-ranging scope of David Roberts' reflections.

Roberts, who was an outstanding climber in his younger years, is now widely acknowledged as the leading chronicler of mountaineering, adventure, and exploration. His books are classics: *The Mountain of My Fear, Escape from Lucania*, and *Moments of Doubt* among them. I've read most of them, always impressed with his command of the English language and his innate understanding of the inner workings of those individuals obsessed with the unknown, with risk.

Now in his 70s, Roberts would, with his typically prolific, over-achieving schedule, be writing at least one impressive volume per year. But things change, and for Roberts, that change has been wrought by a devastating illness. The big C has ripped his world apart, at least on a physical level. Thankfully, that brilliant mind remains, even if his energy levels have waned. One result is this book, a mélange of reflections on the adventures of those he most admires, interspersed with morsels of a deeply personal memoir.

His contemplations of Fridtjof Nansen's epic North Pole expedition, Eric Shipton's Karakoram explorations, and Edmund Hillary and Tenzing Norgay's first ascent of Everest are recounted with authority and acumen. He provides astute perspective to these achievements, which took place before satellite phones, on-demand weather forecasts, and the ever-increasing demands of social media. His tone is nostalgic as he ruminates about a time when there was silence in the hills and there were blanks on the map.

A masterful storyteller, Roberts weaves each historical account into a personal episode that connects him to the protagonists, all the while contemplating the meaning of adventure and asking the big questions: why and for what purpose and for whom. These chapters alone would be worth the price of admission, but it's the personal, self-reflecting elements of the book that distinguish it from much of his other work.

From the start, we have a hint. "For Sharon – Then, now, and forever," he writes of his wife. I know Sharon is his kind, intelligent, and long-suffering (sorry, David) wife, but I can't recall seeing her name appear in one of his books. This is clearly a work that might reveal a more vulnerable, more approachable, tenderer David Roberts. He quickly shoves tenderness aside with some youthful bravado describing his Huntington climb, with its "daunting challenges" and their "seizing" and "blitzing" their way to the top. Aha! This is the David Roberts that we all know and love. But then he pulls us forward to his current situation. Diagnosed with and suffering from an aggressive cancer, he telescopes the narrative: from years to months to days. "I no longer worried about what I might be doing a year from now: what I might be doing in three months seemed a more urgent concern…the question of whether I should ever again hike a favorite canyon in Utah loomed uncertain."

Those canyons mean a lot to Roberts, maybe more than all of those youthful summits. Starting in the 1980s, he began exploring the landscape of the Ancestral Puebloans in the American Southwest, and there he found a kind of reality that challenged his fascination with the sometimes self-indulgent nature of adventure: "However thrilling my canyon play...the game was not about *me*. It was about *them*."

His writing career has been astonishing. Apart from his nearly 30 published volumes, Roberts has written for *National Geographic, Outside, Men's Journal, Smithsonian, Alpinist, Atlantic Monthly, Life*, and more. His assignments have taken him around the world—to lofty peaks and to the deepest caves, all of which have brought richness to his life. In the prologue of *Limits of the Known*, he asks, "Why have I spent my life trying to find the lost and unknown places of this world? And what have the passions of explorers across human history delivered to our understanding of life? The purpose of this book is to grope toward an answer."

I'm not sure he ever fully answers those questions, but his probing eventually brings him much closer to home and the reader closer to the gentler qualities of David Roberts. We learn more about his ongoing medical treatment and the deep friendships that sustain him. He writes, "The forging of friendships too deep for words is almost never the reason we set off into the wilderness to probe the unknown. But in the end, it is what glows in memory."

We also discover much about Sharon, the rock in his life, the manager of his base camp, the one who cares the most, and the one who has traditionally been in the background. He writes honestly about the toll that his life of adventuring has had on her, something that is rarely admitted by those whose high-octane lives inspire and entertain us. And perhaps more fundamentally, he recognizes the dynamic that has shifted between them as Sharon assumes the leadership role in their marriage with firmness and compassion.

He takes the reader through every emotion: the exhilaration of discovery, pride in a summit, anger and frustration at a disease, and tenderness toward those closest to him. *Limits of the Known* proves once again what a consummate storyteller David Roberts is.

— BERNADETTE MCDONALD

TIDES, A CLIMBER'S VOYAGE

Nick Bullock. *Vertebrate Publishing, 2018. Paperback, 256 pages, £14.95.*

When I picked up Nick Bullock's second book, *Tides*, which won the 2018 Banff Mountain Book Festival's Mountain Literature Award, I wasn't sure what to expect. Bullock is known in New England, where I live, as the funny Brit to whom one hands the rack when the climbing gets scary and difficult. But, as *Tides* confirms, his writing chops match his alpine ability. Throughout the book, he balances intense moments (a grizzly bear attack in the Canadian backcountry, a killing storm high on Denali's south face) with a swirling observance rare in alpinism's neon-colored, Instagram-savvy world: the bobbing head of a seal off the coast of Wales, a child in Kathmandu, litter on a rainy run, a flock of starlings. These details are so wrought and vivid they compete with—and sometimes surpass—many of *Tides'* climbing sequences.

Tides covers Bullock's climbing life from 2003 to 2016. Perhaps more importantly, it tackles the relocation of his elderly parents to a houseboat on the United Kingdom's system of canals and waterways, and the fallout of his own relationship with a younger woman. Bullock's unflinching examination of death, of aging, and of the darker side of alpine motivation makes for some heavy reading. It's easy to seethe with jealousy after scanning the newswires and Facebook posts of professional alpinists—I dare anyone to do so after reading this book. Sure, Bullock delivers the moments of alpine glory, but usually with a grain of salt and an awareness I wish more climbers possessed: "I become entranced. I am guilty. But the game we climbers play is trivial. It is not poverty, famine, homelessness, war, destitution, or hopelessness."

The time line and location in *Tides* shift often, as the title suggests. While this is ostensibly to cover the wide swath of climbing Bullock has done, I found the writing shone in the quiet, in-between moments. Often the author dives into the minutiae: "There was always a glimmer of hope in the small unnoticed things of life..." he admits towards the end. A dismal drive to Scotland is given as much weight as the climb the next day: "I turned off the motorway and into the services—one of those strange islands of people in transit. The wind strafed the tarmac and bit back into my face. People stood shivering with smoke trickling from cigarettes clamped between cold fingers. Dead cigarette stubs scattered around tubes of polished steel." When he returns to the U.K. from abroad, Bullock navigates islands within the island. Llanberis and the slate climbing of Wales becomes an oasis; the ribald satisfaction of Scottish winter climbing counters the grimy canals where his parents are moored.

It's moments like these that make Bullock's climbing accomplishments—often oozing with self-deprecation—appear secondary. Without paying ardent attention to the routes described, like a repeat of the House-Anderson line on Mt. Alberta with Will Sim, a reader might think the climbing Bullock tackles in *Tides* is ordinary. It isn't—it's just tempered by an introspection usually removed from such books.

If you're looking for a streamlined mountaineering read in the classical tradition ("I really don't like classics," Bullock admits), look elsewhere. If you're looking for a portrayal of the ups and downs of professional climbing, and of the lost moments in between—all given deft treatment by a seasoned, sensitive writer—this is it.

– MICHAEL WEJCHERT

THE ANDES: THE COMPLETE HISTORY OF MOUNTAINEERING IN SOUTH AMERICA

Evelio A. Echevarria. Joseph Reidhead & Co., 2018. Paperback, 840 pages, $64.50.

IF YOU'RE A longtime fan of this journal, Evelio Echevarria is a name you've likely read dozens of times. That's because, from the late 1950s until recently, the Santiago, Chile, native has been sending in reports about his climbing adventures to whichever *AAJ* editor was in charge. All told, Echevarria thinks he climbed about 100 virgin summits in the Andes. (In an interview last fall, he scoffed when I said "wow," and quickly pointed out that Johan Reinhard, an American climber based in West Virginia, has bagged more than 200 summits, according to Echevarria.) Regardless, Echevarria has now pulled his vast experience—both on the ground and in the research library—into one magnum opus: *The Andes: The Complete History of Mountaineering in High South America.*

This book is a stunner if you're a nerd for facts, figures, altitudes, and dates. At its 828-page heart, it's a door-stopping compendium of data on the mountains of South America, with information on who climbed what and when and how. The big sub-sectors of history are all in there: ascents by indigenous peoples, ascents by explorers, ascents by colonials, ascents by later generations, ascents by women, et cetera. Perhaps what pleased me most about this book were the vast swaths of stories about European climbers' activities in South America—the kind of stories many American readers might not see. And, thankfully, Echevarria puts all those explorations and ascents into context, linking European events (notably the World Wars) to ascents of mountains, walls and towers in the Andes.

The book comes with a text-heavy presentation, but there are enough photos, maps, and delightful little sketches to keep you entertained and reading for the sheer fun that mountain literature can be.

I started corresponding with Echevarria in the late 1990s, when friends and I were headed to South America for climbing goals. His knowledge is limitless and his mind is always two steps ahead of mine when it comes to the next question. Now, readers everywhere can experience something of the Grand Master's knowledge about a mountain range we all know and love: the Andes.

– CAMERON M. BURNS

CHASING DENALI: THE SOURDOUGHS, CHEECHAKOS, AND FRAUDS BEHIND THE MOST UNBELIEVABLE FEAT IN MOUNTAINEERING

JONATHAN WATERMAN. Lyons Press, 2018. Hardcover, 184 pages, $24.95

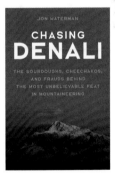

IN THE EARLY 1900s, the town of Fairbanks still bore many of the characteristics of the fading Wild West era. A massive gold strike turned a ramshackle trading post into a boomtown. Prospecting for gold in the rugged Alaskan wilderness required a unique blend of mental fortitude and physical toughness. Extreme cold, barren spaces, and solitude tested the capacities of even the most hardened miner. These "Sourdoughs," as they came to be known, took great pride in their ability to survive and thrive up in the frozen north. In one of North America's most famous mountaineering tales, a group of these men is said to have climbed Denali's 19,470-foot north peak in 1910.

Many Alaskans have long questioned whether a group of upper-middle-aged Fairbanks miners, some nearly clinically obese, could really have raced up the mountain. Coupled with the fact that none of them had any climbing experience, they were reported to have lugged a 14-foot spruce pole to the summit. Spurred by a bar bet, they had ventured to disprove the highly questionable claims of Dr. Frederick Cook, but their own claims soon came under fire.

Jon Waterman knows Denali as well as anyone. It has been an intimate part of his life for the better part of four decades. Not only was he an early climbing ranger on the mountain, he was a member of the team that made the peak's second winter ascent, via the difficult Cassin Ridge. Denali has been Waterman's muse for many books, including *High Alaska* and the must-read for any Alaska climbing aspirant, *In the Shadow of Denali*.

In *Chasing Denali*, Waterman goes into great detail on the history of Alaska around Fairbanks as well as attempts on Denali, then known as Mt. McKinley. Through his own experiences on the peak, he weaves concise analysis and memories from countless trips. I was on the mountain in 2016 when Waterman returned and summited on his 60th birthday. Despite his prior experiences and intimate knowledge of the route, Waterman readily admits that he struggled at certain points throughout his three-week climb. How then could four miners without any mountaineering experience, using rudimentary equipment, dash up the final 11,000 feet (and back) in 18 hours?

Waterman does a fine job of presenting facts and a careful analysis without forcing his opinion upon the reader. "You could never prove that they didn't do it, you could only prove that they did," he told me while we acclimatized together at 14,000 feet. As I finished the last page of *Chasing Denali*, I wished for two things: to know once and for all if aging miners actually got anywhere near the summit and that I, an experienced and trained alpinist, could climb as fast as they supposedly did on a diet of donuts and coffee.

— CLINT HELANDER

INNER RANGES: AN ANTHOLOGY OF MOUNTAIN THOUGHTS AND MOUNTAIN PEOPLE

GEOFF POWTER. Rocky Mountain Books, 2018. Paperback, 330 pages, $22 Canadian.

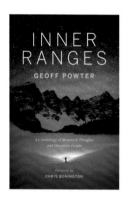

IN THIS MASTERPIECE of mountain writing, Geoff Powter describes his journeys to the crags of western Canada, the significant peaks of the world, and into the inner ranges of his psyche. He encounters a world that can be majestically beautiful at times and shockingly harsh at other times. He writes with understated elegance, humor, and introspection while conjuring up vivid portraits of some of the leading Canadian climbers of this era.

Powter has spent a lifetime balancing climbing, writing, and working as a psychologist. Most works of mountain literature focus on the goal of the summit. Powter's exploration of the outdoor adventure world is bracingly different. His book is a collection of editorials and opinions about the endangered state of adventure, personal tales from a life of exploration and risk-taking, moments of humor, and great sadness, taking the reader into the inner landscapes of those who risk everything for a life in the mountains.

With Powter we rub shoulders with such climbing legends as Barry Blanchard, David Jones, Sonnie Trotter, and Earl Denman. He also explores the mysterious slaughter and mutilation of horses in Alberta, the ongoing Everest debate about self-styled "adventurepreneurs" and the exploitation of the mountain for personal gain, and what it means to climb solo. Throughout the book, Powter continuously brings the reader back to the eternal question *Why*? I sense it is because he truly cares about the mountain world. In his own words: "Mountains have always been the sharpest mirrors for me: They've simplified, purified, and clarified my life, and have reliably shown me the better sides of myself." And of the climbers who go there: "I've watched so many of my friends get so complicated after these climbs, with sadness and emptiness suddenly a part of their lives because it seems nothing will ever match the summit."

Powter's choice of subjects to profile is a superb cast of characters. He writes about dreamers, rock stars, and himself with great insight and candor. There is real intimacy in his portrayals, and he has the rare ability to get his subjects to open up and share their stories with him. Powter has done his time in the mountains, fallen into the omnipresent crevasse and grappled his way back again, in his quest for understanding.

Inner Ranges is one of the most reflective, well-crafted, self-aware climbing books to come out in recent years. It made me feel like I was on a long, often dangerous journey high in the mountains. It was a joy to read and a very thought-provoking book.

— TOR TORKLIDSON

MYSTERIUM

Susan Froderberg. Farrar, Straus and Giroux, 2018. Hardcover, 271 pages, $26.

"There are climbers who climb primarily to enter a deepening mystery," Professor Troy scrawls in his journal in the opening chapter of *Mysterium*. "For this woman or man, the long haul up the mountain contains the ecstasy of devotion. No seeker forgoes the slope."

Mystery, philosophy, and devotion are at the heart of Susan Froderberg's *Mysterium*, a novel loosely based around the events of the 1976 American-Indian Nanda Devi expedition. The story of the original climb began to unfold in 1974, when Nanda Devi Unsoeld (daughter of Willi Unsoeld, of Everest fame) approached H. Adams Carter, editor of the *American Alpine Journal*, with the idea of organizing a climb of the mountain in observance of the 40th anniversary of its first ascent. The 1976 expedition, co-led by Willi and Carter, succeeded in establishing a new route up the northwest face. As the first party of climbers (John Roskelley, Lou Reichardt, and Jim States) returned from their ascent, Devi and her father moved up to Camp IV, where she fell ill and died. Just over ten years later, Roskelley published his account of the climb in the book *Nanda Devi: The Tragic Expedition*.

In an essay at the publisher's website, "How I Came to the Story," Froderberg described how, during a 2008 trek in Bhutan, she became enamored with the mountaineering stories of her guide, John Roskelley. "[He] was full of anecdotes," Froderberg recalled, "but he was reticent about incidents having to do with the Nanda Devi expedition. His hesitancy to speak about the Unsoelds or what happened on that trip fascinated me all the more." Above all, Froderberg wondered: "What would it be like to be [Willi Unsoeld]? What would it be like to be Devi?" Later, she wrote, "I realized I would have to write the book I had been hoping to read."

In Froderberg's novel, the young heroine is Sarasvati Troy, named for the fictional peak of Sarasvati (also known as Mysterium). Her father, climber and widower Professor Troy, teaches philosophy but "doesn't care to discuss dead wives." Other character names and details wink at the historic record: There is the scholarly New Englander "Virgil Adams," who also edits the *AAJ*, and a reference to a "William Hilman," who, with Adams, completed the first ascent of Mt. Sarasvati twenty-five years prior. (H.W. Tilman and Noel Odell made the first ascent of Nanda Devi in 1936.) Other members of the anniversary expedition include Dr. Reddy and his son, Devin; Wilder Carson, a young mountaineer whose tough exterior hides his grief for his lost twin brother; and Wilder's wife, Vida, a yoga instructor who pleads caution in the mountains.

As with the story of the 1976 Nanda Devi expedition, cultural and generational differences create some tension within the Sarasvati party. Some favor the more traditional tactics of the "siege" style of expedition, while others prefer to climb in alpine style. Early on, they debate whether men and women—romantic partners in particular—can successfully climb together in the high mountains.

During the course of the expedition, each character is forced to grapple with the mystery driving their own desire to climb—a question that, though nearly as old as climbing itself, takes on a new luster under Froderberg's ambitious pen. Richly imagined in beautiful, at times ornate prose, Froderberg conjures a high alpine landscape where the mysteries of life glimmer on the horizon: "Snow particles sparkle and waft about…like angelic dust, stellars of icy crystals becoming tiny mirrors of the miracle of existence."

Yet in electing to frame her novel partly around an already well-known story, Froderberg has opened the door to critiques of the work for both its breadth and lack of imagination. Readers will question whether the novel is too deviant from or too similar to accounts of the historic 1976 climb. In their introduction to *One Step in the Clouds: An Omnibus of Mountaineering Novels and Short Stories* (1990), Audrey Salkeld and Rosie Smith observed, "Climbing is considered by its adherents to be somehow too *sacred* to fictionalize. Its vivid real-life dramas and intense loyalties, its acts of heroism, and the all-too-frequent encounters with violent death are too precious, too poignant, too much part of some private lore and myth to become the raw material of fiction." In a 2019 editorial for *Alpinist* 65, Katie Ives suggested, "If the best mountain fiction still appears threatening to some, perhaps it's because it's inherently subversive."

Mysterium abounds with mountain passion and philosophy, but in the end, a problematic oversight confounds its ambition. In its portrayal of the expedition staff, the book fails to subvert one of the deeply colonialist tropes of traditional Western mountaineering narratives: the marginalization of expedition workers. The low-altitude porters, the narrator informs, "wear…the dirt they are covered in like a second layer of skin;" nevertheless, "despite their hardships," they are "the most cheerful bunch on the trip." When one of the workers slips on talus and falls 1,000 feet, his death barely registers on the narrative: There is no mention of who he was or what loved ones he might've left behind—the climbing party never even appears to learn his name. With these oversights, ultimately, *Mysterium* fails to do what literature does best: in the freedom of imagining new worlds, to reach beyond the familiar to find beauty, to stimulate empathy, to stare into the depths of silence and startle the void.

— PAULA WRIGHT

MY LIFE IN CLIMBING

UELI STECK. Mountaineers Books, 2018. Paperback, 224 pages, $21.95.

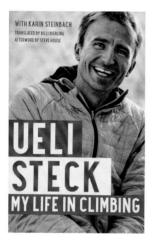

MY LIFE IN Climbing is a terse and passionate record of the late Ueli Steck's drive and determination to reach summits quickly and prolifically, with partners and often alone. The book expresses the anxieties, uncertainties, joys, and passions that attend one whose career, and maybe sense of self, depend on pushing the limits of novelty on mountains, most of which, of course, were previously climbed, by many routes and in many styles.

Steck long dreamed of soloing Everest's West Ridge, linking to Lhotse, and possibly over Nuptse in a push. While acclimatizing for an early attempt at this feat in spring of 2013, Steck's team of three marched, perhaps a bit casually, across a "construction zone" where many Sherpas were fixing lines to the South Col. The Sherpas angrily confronted the three unroped and unanchored friends, even punching Simone Moro. Unnerved in many ways, the climbers headed home.

Steck's solo of Annapurna's south face in the fall of 2013 was both lauded (with a Piolet d'Or, his second), and doubted. First climbed in a British siege, the face offers almost two vertical miles of intense alpinism. After his partner bailed, Steck impulsively crossed the 'schrund, and reported summiting 28 hours later. High on the climb, a dropped camera carried away any unambiguous verification. Though some witnesses reported Steck's headlamp very high on the route, for many his Annapurna was tinged with doubt: no camera, no GPS track, no sightings on the summit. Steck's responses were rational, within the limits of belief, and were generally accepted, but some remained unconvinced and, as he suggests in his book, drove him a bit deeper into himself. [*Editor's note: Ed Douglas thoroughly examines this controversy in "What's Eating Ueli Steck," collected in* The Magician's Glass *(Vertebrate Publishing, 2017)*].

The chapter "Shishapangma" offers more intensity and mishap. Near the summit in 2014, Steck was along with four other climbers when an avalanche was triggered, which carried three of the five far down the mountain, two of whom were killed. It was reasonable for Steck and his remaining partner to be wary of the avalanche's hang-fire and of adjacent slopes. However, their response was questionable: After spotting a survivor (Martin Maier) who was initially mobile but then assumed dead, far below, it was incumbent upon them to investigate. And they did not. (Maier would miraculously self-rescue.)

The final chapters show Steck differently, in his familiar Alps. These later tales allow us to sense his joy as he climbs the Eiger's north face repeatedly, each time ever more quickly, until setting the current record of 2 hours, 22 minutes, and, incredibly, 50 seconds. Another goal was to link all Alpine summits above 4,000 meters, solely under human power, which he did, mostly alone, over a 62-day span of climbing, skiing, biking, and running.

Like no other, Steck blended a mixture of athleticism, alpinism, and ambition seamlessly and nonchalantly. Published just after his death from a fall on Nuptse in 2017, while preparing for another attempt at the Everest-Lhotse-Nuptse linkup, *My Life in Climbing* certainly doesn't answer every question one would want to ask Steck, but it will likely provide the most personal insight into this singular climber that we will ever have.

— CARL TOBIN

IN BRIEF

The Eight Mountains, by Paolo Cognetti (Atria Books, $24), a novel of a friendship in the mountains, was the grand-prize winner at Banff and a finalist for the Boardman-Tasker prize. *As Above, So Below*, by Chris Kalman (chriskalman.com, $24.99), is a gem of a novella set in Patagonia, with drawings by Craig Muderlak. A Banff finalist in the Fiction/Poetry category, Kalman was also a finalist in the guidebook category for *The Index Town Walls* (Sharp End, $32.95), a rare double. *Legendary Maps from the Himalayan Club: Commemorating 90 Years of the Iconic Institution*, by Harish Kapadia (Roli Books, 34.95), offers a collection of maps, many hand-drawn, from both the familiar (Shipton and Tilman, Herzog, Bonington) and the wonderfully lesser known, particularly to North Americans. A truly beautiful collection assembled by a true Himalayan explorer. *End of the Rope: Mountains, Marriage, and Motherhood*, by Jan Redford (Counterpoint Press, $26), is a woman's memoir about the long arc toward finding balance among passions and responsibilities, including climbing. *Vantage Point: 50 Years of the Best Climbing Stories Ever Told*, by Matt Samet and the editors of *Climbing* (Falcon Guides, $26), lives up to its promise, representing "the living breathing history of our dynamic sport, [an] archive of accomplishment and courage and perseverance and tragedy." A regular *Climbing* reader for most of these years, I was surprised how many of these I had missed. "The Black Dog," a collection of five short essays in the magazine on "the dark manifestations of the climber's mind," from 2008, is unflinching in its look into our collective mirrors.

— DAVID STEVENSON

IN MEMORIAM

These tributes have been edited for length; the complete articles are at the AAJ website: publications. americanalpineclub.org. Here, readers will find articles about other climbers who passed recently, including Ed Boulton, Robert Failing, Roberts French, Bruce Gilbert, and Don Wallace Jr.

JIM BRIDWELL, 1944 – 2018

THE WORLD HAS lost a great climber, friend, and mentor.

Jim Bridwell made huge contributions to the world of climbing. He was adept in free climbing, big wall, and alpine climbing, establishing over 100 first ascents in Yosemite Valley, Alaska, and Patagonia. He, along with John Long and Billy Westbay, was the first to climb the Nose of El Capitan in a day. He helped to create the famed YOSAR rescue team, with a core of skilled climbers. In 1979, Jim and Steven Brewer did the first alpine-style ascent of the infamous southeast ridge of Cerro Torre (and first ascent to the true summit by this route). Two years later, he teamed up with Mugs Stump and climbed Dance of the Woo Li Masters, the first route up the massive east face of the Mooses Tooth in Alaska. Jim was a visionary, always pushing the limits of the sport and upping the ante.

I was able to visit "The Bird" a few weeks prior to his passing at the Loma Linda hospital, an hour from his home in Palm Springs, California. Entering the hospital to visit with my friend of 43 years, I reflected back on the time when I first met this giant of the climbing world.

As a teenage climber who was obsessed with the sport and its host of mythical characters, Jim was to me what Michael Jordan was to basketball. I had just tied in to lead the first pitch of New Dimensions in Yosemite Valley, my first 5.10 crack climb, when Jim appeared out of the bushes and struck up a friendly conversation. I would have been star-struck had the task at hand not been so forbidding. With my eye on the prize, I hastened my departure. Lacking the fitness to hang out and place lots of gear, I opted to go fast in the relatively secure hand crack. Just short of the belay, I made the rookie mistake of stepping on my rope and then careened 40 feet through space. Discouraged and humiliated, I pulled back into the crack and finished the lead.

Jim had asked if he could have a tow, and he followed my lead in his Converse high tops, waltzing up the route like it was a Sunday afternoon stroll in the park. When he reached the belay, he looked me sternly in the eye and said, "You know, kid, you'll do alright if you just remember not to step on the rope." We laughed, high-fived, and from that day on we were friends. I never could have imagined the adventures we would share: the first ascent of one of El Cap's most famous aid routes, an attempt on the east face of Mooses Tooth, fruitless bushwhacks in search of climbable ice in the Tahoe basin, being involved in a startup clothing company, and of course just the daily perils of living in Tahoe in the early 1980s, a time of big hair and immense indulgences.

It was a long walk through the hospital and my mind wandered back to the spring of 1978, when Augie Klein, Bill Price and I were fixing pitches on the Pacific Ocean Wall to begin the third ascent. This was Jim's testpeice and reputed to be the hardest big wall climb in the world. We were all under 20, so this caused a stir in Camp 4. Jim would check in with us each day after we fixed another pitch, asking our opinions and giving us gear beta. He also asked me to look at a potential new route to the right of the P.O. Wall. Even from our close vantage, finding climbable features there was like spotting a gnat on a football field from the nosebleed section.

Jim's personality and grit permeated the entire Pacific Ocean Wall, with stretches of gear barely able to sustain body weight for unfathomable distances. On the Nothing Atolls pitch, I cleaned after Price led a very long seam of tied-off knifeblades. The final one was rusty, bent, and partially ripped out of the placement. This was the pendulum point for a big swing to the left, and instead of placing a bolt there, the Bird had decided to make it spicy not only for the leader but also the follower, who was staring at a 100-foot swing should the piton fail during the lower-out.

After seven days we topped out. Jim met us on the trail down, looked straight at me, and asked, "What'd you think?" Instinctively I knew he was talking about the potential new line, not the route we had just climbed. Two days later we were fixing pitches on what became Sea of Dreams. Dale Bard was brought into the mix a few days later while we were unwinding at a party at the employee annex.

Our goal was to put up the hardest route we could, period. Each successive pitch became one in a string of crux pitches. Just before reaching the Continental Shelf, Jim asked if he could lead the long traverse off the ledge—a 100-foot section of blank rock textured like a pimpled-face teenager. His hunch was that it might be spectacular. Knowing full well that he could easily pull rank on me, I protested that we had agreed to swing leads and this one was mine. He thought about it for a few seconds, smiled, and said, "OK, you've got it." That was so Jim. His respect for his partners empowered greatness. The pitch became known as the Hook or Book.

Throughout the climb, Jim had an uncanny ability to recall details from his study of the potential line through a telescope, even when the next section wasn't visible to him. In the lead, Dale or I would explain the terrain we were seeing, and Jim would shout up that we needed to head over to a certain flake that led to a seam or some such thing. It was like he was reading a topo etched in his mind.

Although I had spoken with Jim regularly, I hadn't seen him face to face for at least 20 years. When I entered his hospital room, the beaming smile and glint in his eye brought back a flood of love and memories. His body resembled little more than a scarecrow. He wore a very hip, cool-blue wool hat that matched his blue hospital gown. Immediately we started reminiscing. Rolling in the memories of near misses and telling lies that were truths. He was heartened with all the love from friends that had poured out through visits and phone calls. Jim shared with me that he had accepted Jesus as his Lord and savior when he was 18 and had been ordained, which also legally kept him from participating in the Vietnam War. We shared two small containers of Häagen-Dazs strawberry ice cream that I had smuggled in at his request. Delight radiated throughout all 125 pounds of his frail body. He was totally at peace with leaving the world if the cards played out that way but stubbornly wanted to finish up some writing, chiefly an autobiography. Although he got out of the hospital for a short spell, things went from bad to worse, and he was soon on life support. Jim left us on February 16, 2018.

Jim's life exemplified pushing the boundaries of his God-given gifts and helping others pursue their limits. He was always focused upon the horizon of what could be. I miss my friend—even his half-hour political rants and off-the-wall commentaries on humanity. "Those who fail to plan, plan to fail" was one of his favorite Benjamin Franklin quotes. Even in his last days, Jim was certain of the plan.

— DAVE DIEGELMAN

Steve Grossman

CHARLES COLE, 1955 – 2018

IN 1975, AS a sophomore engineering student at the University of Southern California, Charles Cole saw *The Eiger Sanction,* a Clint Eastwood thriller that featured dramatic climbing scenes. With his native passion and intense focus, he threw himself into the sport. After buying some pitons and a rope at Sport Chalet, he strong-armed a friend into joining him. They drove up a road on Mt. Wilson looking for a rock outcrop. I recall him telling me, "It took me awhile to figure out that you pound the pitons into cracks and not directly into the rock."

A man of extraordinary intelligence and athletic ability, Charles hurled himself into rock climbing. I experienced his drive first-hand. My first climbing trip to Yosemite, in 1978, happened to correspond with the first for Charles. He had never done a big wall of any sort. Within two weeks of arriving in the Valley, I was with him when he topped out on the Salathé Wall on El Capitan. Over the next month, Charles climbed the west face of the Leaning Tower, south face of Mt. Watkins, and northwest face of Half Dome. Then he recruited me to do the Shield on El Capitan, a route that, at the time, had been climbed only a few times. When we reached the top and he undid his homemade, one-inch-webbing swami belt, I was horrified to see he had tied it with a square knot. "Have you been doing all those routes over the last two months with your swami tied like that?" I asked. He admitted sheepishly that he wasn't very well schooled in knots.

Charles worked briefly for a major global construction firm in Pasadena, and every Friday evening he raced out to crags at Joshua Tree or Tahquitz, or up to Yosemite. After a year he quit and lived in Yosemite until his credit cards maxed out. He went to business school in Michigan and then took another "real" job. But the lure of the Valley was too strong, and he began living in Camp Four on a semi-permanent basis. It was during those years, in the mid-1980s, that he put up several remarkable routes on Half Dome and El Capitan, including Jolly Roger, Queen of Spades, and Space—the latter two climbed solo. *[Cole also put up spicy free climbs including Run for Your Life at Joshua Tree and Autobahn on Half Dome, climbed with John Middendorf and the author of this article.]*

During the early 1980s, Charles and other Joshua Tree regulars resoled running shoes with stickier "green dot" rubber, allowing them to do classic routes in a casual fashion. Always looking for the technical edge in climbing, he worked with a rubber engineer to come up with something better, which he could put onto shoes of his own making. The early made-in-Taiwan Five Tennies fell apart rapidly, but they were great fun, and what started as a fad became a market segment, the approach shoe. Soon, climbing shoe resolers were ordering sheets of his Five Ten rubber; climbers would even have brand-new shoes resoled with it. By the late 1980s, Charles had a full line of technical climbing shoes as well as a creative line of advertisements, which he loved dreaming up.

Charles was outwardly and unapologetically competitive. (After the birth of his third child, he sent me a postcard: Cole 3, Reno 2.) Although he spent more nights sleeping on the ground than anyone I know, he had no interest in playing the bohemian. He did not drink or smoke pot. He wore polo shirts—and had, in fact, played polo in his youth. He drove a Hummer to piss off environmentalists. Were he capable of lying, he would have said he owned guns and shot bunnies. All of this irritated some in the climbing community. His great success with Five Ten made some people more cordial, and age mellows us all. But he never fit in. He never wanted to fit in.

I never spent a boring day with Charles, despite rainy days, long approaches, and tedious stretches on big walls. His mind was ever active and inventive. He made up crazy songs, debated political theories, and wondered about the role of entropy in the origins of the universe. He had a puerile sense of humor that made my wife understand instantly why we were friends.

My life was changed when I met Charles in September 1978. He infected me with his can-do mentality and his wild ambition. He buoyed me up with his profound loyalty. We did some marvelous things. We failed more than once. We had some close calls. When I heard that Charles had suddenly died, I wept. There's nobody I've shared a rope with who knew me as well as he did.

– RUSTY RENO

CHARLOTTE FOX, 1957 – 2018

Dougald MacDonald

CHARLOTTE FOX WAS strong and good in the mountains, not known for speed so much as being able to go and go and go. She climbed Everest in 1996, surviving the famous nighttime "huddle," with her eyes and contact lenses freezing and patches of frostbite dotting her face and feet, though fortunately she kept all her toes. Her high climbs were mostly guided, but she was prepared: Before Everest, she had also climbed Gasherbrum II (on an unguided expedition) and Cho Oyu. She was the first American woman to do three 8,000-meter peaks and eventually climbed five of them. She had done all 54 of Colorado's 14ers, involving all kinds of terrain and weather. She also ski-patrolled in Colorado for 30 years, in Aspen and then Telluride. She had so much energy she would run or skin up a mountain before a full day of patrolling. In May she had just turned 61 and had recently climbed two 8,000-meter peaks—Dhaulagiri in 2017 and Manaslu in 2016. She had just returned home to Telluride from attempting Baruntse (7,129m) in Nepal.

Charlotte had survived so much up high that it was stunning and profoundly sad that she died the evening of May 24 in a household accident. Friends who were staying at her Telluride home for Mountainfilm returned to the house at perhaps 10:45 p.m. to discover that Charlotte had apparently fallen down one of the steep flights of hardwood stairs in her 4.5-story house, which is entered via the top floor. (She never took the elevator, even when rehabbing a knee injury.) She apparently had died immediately. Somehow the scene, sorrowful as it was, was indicative of her life. Her house was full, with three friends already staying and two more soon to arrive, because she was a giver: generous and open-hearted.

Charlotte gave and gave to the climbing community and many other causes, both from her pocketbook and of her time, energy, and organizational efforts. She was a board member of both the American Alpine Club and the Access Fund, and long involved in Mountainfilm as well. Her final Seven Summits ascent, of Mt. Elbrus in 2014, was part of a benefit for the dZi Foundation for underserved communities in the remote Himalaya. Her alma mater, Hollins University in Virginia, has a Charlotte Fox Climbing Wall. She once treated 14 people to a heli-ski trip in the Selkirks. Friends loved her deep sudden laugh and her cheery gruffness. She had her quirks and faults, was stubborn and did things her way, but she was loving and beloved.

Charlotte experienced much tragedy in her life, including the loss of her husband, Reese

Martin, then 49, who died in a paragliding event in 2004. Earlier, she had been seriously involved with Mark Bebie of Washington State, who died in 1993 on the ice climb Slipstream in the Canadian Rockies. She gained unexpected fame with the attention given to the Everest disaster, but she steered clear of the hubbub, mostly avoiding interviews, movie negotiations, and even the topic itself. I remember asking about her feelings that night in the huddle on Everest, which looked likely to be the end. She laughed, saying, "I thought, 'Well, old girl, it's been a good ride. No regrets.'"

When the end actually came, she was in a good place in her life. A week before she died, Charlotte had told Deb Curtis, of her 8,000-meter peaks, "I'm doin' one more, Curtis." At a dinner with a handful of her friends in Telluride, I repeated a line that Charlotte had said to friends the day she died, "I *love* being 61." At least three people said, "Oh, she told me the same thing!"

— ALISON OSIUS

Royal Robbins | Tom Frost Collection

TOM FROST, 1937 – 2018

ON AUGUST 24, Tom Frost—whose character and influence outshone his remarkable routes—died peacefully after a short battle with cancer.

Frost was the last survivor of the team that made the first ascent of El Capitan's Salathé Wall, the second route up the formation, a climb known for its length and difficulty but also for the excellent style in which it was put up. Eschewing the siege tactics used by Warren Harding on the Nose, concluding in 1958, the Salathé team (Frost, Chuck Pratt, and Royal Robbins) only retreated once from the wall, at one-third height, and placed only 13 bolts on the 3,000-foot route during their 1961 ascent. The climb remains known for its beauty and natural passage. "The biggest surprise of all was El Cap—what a grand place," Frost told me. "We didn't see that from the ground for what it was. It was like a palace."

Frost's best-known ascents were done in the early 1960s, including the Salathé, the second ascent of the Nose, the North America Wall on El Cap, and the west face of Sentinel Rock. In addition to his contributions in Yosemite Valley, Frost established significant routes in the Northwest Territories of Canada and the Tetons of Wyoming. In Nepal, he climbed most of Annapurna's south face (he reached 25,000 feet), made the first ascent of Kangtega, in 1963, and then returned for a new route 23 years later, and filmed (and summited) the second ascent of Ama Dablam.

In addition to his climbing prowess, Frost was a mechanical engineer, and his revolutionary hardware designs contributed to the clean climbing movement in the 1960s and '70s. In 1970, after the Annapurna expedition, Frost borrowed chocks from his climbing partner Chris Bonington and used them for a week on 100-year-old routes in the Lake District. "The cracks were in perfect shape because they didn't use pitons," he said. "I came home and told Yvon Chouinard. I invented the Stoppers and Hexes that came out in the 1972 clean climbing catalog. And that's about it. That's history." Frost also designed the RURP piton and made significant contributions to tools for vertical ice climbing. In the '80s he continued designing but shifted his focus to the co-founding and development of Chimera Lighting for photography, based in Boulder, Colorado.

In the late '90s and early 2000s, Frost, by then living in Oakdale, California, was once again active in Yosemite. With his son, Ryan, he repeated his most significant routes from Yosemite's Golden Age. During this time Frost also started a successful campaign to protect Yosemite's Camp 4 from being impacted dramatically by the national park's rebuilding plan after the floods of 1997; the campground eventually was added to the National Register of Historic Places.

I lived in Yosemite during this period, and after a climb with Ryan, at the base of El Cap, he introduced me to his father. Tom and I stayed in touch until his final months. Over dinners in Yosemite Valley, meetings at his house in Oakdale, and hours over the phone, Frost and I talked about everything from climbing to partners to love. He shared everything from the granular—as in what style of aider he preferred, aluminum or webbing—to the 10,000-foot view of his spiritual relationship with El Cap and the Earth.

In Yosemite, "I fell in with a bad crowd, my kind of bad crowd," Frost joked with a deadpan look before releasing his toothy smile, referring to his lifelong friends Robbins, Chouinard, and Pratt. Frost admired each man for different reasons: Robbins for his vision and ethics, and Chouinard for his business sense—the two worked together for ten years. But it was Pratt, a man of few words, who left Frost with a deeper appreciation and spiritual connection with the vertical world. "He was the most natural climber in the group and he had the strongest spiritual base," Frost said. "It was beautiful to watch him climb."

During his climbs on El Capitan, Frost took a series of black and white photos that have become iconic images of the early days of big-wall climbing. "To have a camera up there in such a pristine place…and to be there with these guys who knew what it was all about. You didn't have to have a lot of conversation. We were just enjoying the climbing. The seven rolls I shot in that week on the Nose were the best of my stuff. That was just a reflection of the whole magic of what was transpiring."

My contact with Frost became most frequent in his final years. During this period he was working on a timeline of his climbs with biographer Steve Grossman and a film crew was documenting him—all of which led to reflection on the routes that had the greatest impact on his life. "I realized I was really happy up there, really at home," he said. "It was that interaction, that intimate association, the struggle of the climb, that close relationship with the rock—El Capitan—and the Earth.… In the process of learning how to climb, the Earth is a mentor, providing the handholds and footholds. In other words, the Earth is here to provide for our lives and our success in life. When we do well and we're pleased with it, our spirit is also well."

If I could take home only one thing from my conversations with Frost it's this: "How you do anything is how you do everything."

— CHRIS VAN LEUVEN

ANDREW HARVARD, 1949 – 2019

ANDREW CARSON HARVARD died in January 2019 after a decade-long battle with younger-onset Alzheimer's disease. His final days were comforted by phone messages from his extensive network of colleagues, climbers, classmates, and friends.

Andy was born in New Orleans on July 29, 1949. His family moved to New Haven, Connecticut, and Andy's love of water, wilderness, and the mountains was ignited by the adventures he shared as a Boy Scout. He became an Eagle Scout at age 14 and continued to draw upon the lessons of leadership, team building, and mentorship throughout his life.

During his years at Dartmouth College (1967–'71), he became deeply involved with the Dartmouth Outing Club and its subsidiaries Ledyard Canoe Club—where he and his close friend

Jed Williamson

Todd Thompson became the first recipients of Dartmouth's Ledyard Medal—and the Mountaineering Club, which elected him president in 1970. That year he was among a small group of Dartmouth climbers who traveled to Peru to participate in an earthquake relief mission and then went on to Bolivia to scale Illampu and Huayna Potosí. Following graduation, he worked for the U.S. Forest Service in Vermont and then enrolled in law school at Boston University, where he earned a JD in 1979.

He was involved in major climbing expeditions to Nepal, India, and China, including Dhaulagiri, Nanda Devi, and Minya Konka. In 1980, he did a solo reconnaissance for a new route on the east side of Mt. Everest, and he became a member of the American team that attempted the 6,300-foot Kangshung Face in 1981. Andy and the team returned in 1983 and successfully put four members on the summit, completing the most difficult route on the highest mountain in the world.

His professional career included serving as assistant attorney general for the state of Washington, senior attorney and litigation counsel for the Federal Reserve Bank of New York, and many years in international agribusiness with Eridania Beghin-Say America Inc. He was also the founding partner with his close friend David Breashears of Arcturus Motion Picture Co., which produced the award-winning documentary *Everest: The Mystery of Mallory and Irvine* (1987).

Along the way, Andy was made a national fellow of the Explorers Club and was on the board of directors of the American Alpine Club for many years. His publications included *Mountain of Storms: The American Expeditions to Dhaulagiri* (co-authored with Todd Thompson in 1974) and *The Forgotten Face of Everest* (National Geographic, July 1984).

Andy returned to his alma mater in 2004, becoming director of Dartmouth's outdoor programs. Here, he aimed to live out his passion and belief that "…learning never ends, and that teaching can flourish outside the classroom." "He was our strongest advocate," said student Chris Polashenski. "He put us in circumstances that taught us to deal with risk and uncertainty."

As a direct result of his undiagnosed illness, Andy was forcibly retired from Dartmouth College in 2008. He went on to participate in several awareness-raising events to increase understanding and support for the fight to end Alzheimer's. He also was the inspiration behind *The Final Climb*, a documentary (nearing completion) about challenge, inspiration, and hope in ending Alzheimer's.

– KATHY HARVARD AND JED WILLIAMSON

HUNTLEY INGALLS, 1928 – 2018

"IN THE EARLY '60s the speed limits were high and gasoline cheap. We thought nothing of running over to Moab or the San Juans for a weekend, where there were superb first ascents for the taking. The anticipation, excitement, and carefree nature of these adventures seemed to be the cutting edge of life." Huntley Ingalls, who wrote these words, has died, aged 90. He explored the desert and pioneered the earliest ascents in the Moab, Utah, area, including Castleton Tower and the Titan. Later in life, he could and often did recall these exploits in vivid detail, captivating new generations of climbers.

Steve Bartlett

Ingalls grew up in rural Maryland. His mother was distant, his father hunted for gold, an obsession that drove the family into poverty. They lived for a while with neither running water nor electricity, chasing away social workers when they became too inquisitive. The household was ruled by Huntley's grandmother, who was stern and puritanical. He struggled at school. "There was constant pressure from both home and school to shape up, be a normal person…but I was appalled at what they regarded as a normal person… something so dull and ordinary that I thought it would be better to be dead." He escaped by taking walks in the nearby forests and fields, finding the natural world "a constant source of amazing and delightful discovery."

After high school he began caving and going rock climbing at Seneca Rocks, and he learned he had an aptitude for staying cool and making rational decisions, no matter what was going on around him. He became, as he wrote later, "attracted to…confronting difficulty, danger, and the unknown."

He spent the summer of 1956 on a "gravity survey" crew out West, exploring for heavier, metallic ore bodies; the ore might be uranium, much sought after for weapons research. Ingalls' crew ranged all over the Colorado Plateau, including Indian Creek, the Moab valley, and Castle Valley. For Ingalls, it was a dream come true: "It was a great job—getting paid to be out in this incredible country." He noted the potential on the towers and cliffs around Moab and climbed Shiprock that fall. But his biggest climbs would have to wait until he found a climbing partner who would give him the confidence to try these unclimbed towers.

Ingalls decided to finish his education at the University of Colorado and in 1959 he moved to Boulder, where he lived the rest of his life. He soon met Layton Kor, who was already demolishing existing standards and expectations on the rock. Ingalls, who preferred to follow rather than lead, had found what he was looking for: "There was an immediate rapport between us, and the next day we climbed the Bastille Crack in Eldorado Canyon. I was amazed, even shocked, by his ability. Here was the man for Castleton Tower." Kor, in turn, spoke approvingly of Ingalls: "One of the great things about Huntley is that he never seemed to have any fear. Even when we climbed on the worst rock…there was no fear at all."

Ingalls persuaded Kor to visit Castle Valley. Once there, the outcome, for Kor in his prime, was certain. Today, the Kor-Ingalls Route on Castleton Tower is one of the classic climbs of North America.

Next, Ingalls turned his attention to the adjacent Fisher Towers. The largest tower, the Titan, was twice the height of Castleton and devoid of any obvious weaknesses. Gloomy precipices and bulbous overhangs were festooned with curtains of flaking dried mud. Two reconnaissance trips in 1961 gained only 50 feet; Kor lost interest and in the spring of 1962 left for Yosemite. With Kor away, Ingalls teamed up with Maurice Horn and Steve Komito to climb another of Ingalls' gravity survey discoveries: North Six-shooter, a beautiful tower in the Indian Creek basin.

Kor renewed his interest in the Fisher Towers project when the National Geographic Society offered sponsorship. Or it might have been when Ingalls finally said, "Well, if you won't climb it with me, I'll find someone else who will!" In May 1962, Kor, Ingalls, and George Hurley climbed the 900-foot tower in four days of effort spread over two trips. Toward the summit they followed a fantastically exposed arête. When they arrived on top, Ingalls recalled Kor exclaiming, "This is a superb climb! So superb I can't believe it."

Emboldened by this success, later the same year Kor and Ingalls climbed Standing Rock, in Canyonlands, with Steve Komito. Here, Ingalls took one of his favorite climbing photos: Kor rappelling, ropes hanging in space, the tower illuminated by a golden light, with menacing clouds massing in the background. Ingalls would carry two Leica cameras on these adventures, so one was always ready. As he would later say, "You can take all the photos you want, but you only ever have *one* chance to take first ascent photos!"

Along with their desert climbs, Ingalls and Kor did a number of other first ascents, including the Shining Buttress in the Black Canyon and Psycho in Eldorado Canyon. Eventually, they reached the limits of what they were prepared to do on the aptly named Mud Wall, in Glenwood Canyon, where, beset by bad rock, poor anchors, and, finally, doubts, they retreated. Their route wasn't completed until 2007.

Ingalls later wrote, "In the early 1960s there were not only unclimbed towers in the Colorado Plateau but untouched areas. Part of the wonderful experience of pioneering these climbs was the feeling of exploration. We were fantastically privileged to be the first."

In the mid-'60s, Ingalls quit a job as a programmer for the National Bureau of Standards and spent over two years on the road. Mostly alone, he traveled around India, Nepal, Afghanistan, and Ceylon (now Sri Lanka). On his return he resumed working at the Bureau of Standards. He still climbed occasionally, but in the early 1980s arthritis caused his fingers to begin curling inward to form tight fists that would never uncurl again.

Ingalls was a true gentleman, considerate, humble, interested in new things and new people, always polite and courteous. With his sharp recall, his journals, and his slide collection, he became the keeper of stories and memories of the partners and friends with whom he'd shared so many trips. It's notable how he would invariably and subtly downplay his own role in these adventures. At a memorial at Neptune Mountaineering in Boulder after his death, dozens showed up and we tried to put this right, sharing stories of Huntley, bright vignettes of a life well lived. I feel fantastically privileged to have known him.

– STEVE "CRUSHER" BARTLETT

RYAN JOHNSON, 1983 – 2018

ON A BLINDINGLY sunny day, March 5, 2018, Ryan Johnson's face radiated with the kind of satisfaction only an alpinist can appreciate. In a video sent to his girlfriend, he was smiling and calm, spinning in a slow circle to show a panorama of Alaska's Coast Mountains. Though he'd reached this table-size summit in the Mendenhall Towers numerous times before, this occasion must have felt exceptional. He and Marc-André Leclerc had just made the first ascent of the Main Tower's 2,500-foot north face, a concave enormity of compact granite. This was one of Johnson's ultimate dream lines, and it wasn't off in some far-flung corner of the world—it was right in his backyard, near his hometown of Juneau.

At age 34, Johnson would have been filled with pride to share this grandest of adventures with one of the world's most famous climbers. Johnson wasn't as well known as Leclerc, but in tight-knit climbing communities across the country, he was widely lauded for his broad skill set, spanning the spectrum of rock, alpine, and especially difficult ice climbing. His knowledge and exploration of the Juneau Icefield and the Coast Mountains were exceptional. In the Mendenhall Towers alone, he had established several major climbs, including Great White Conqueror (2,500', V AI4 M5 A1) on the north face of the West Tower and the first free ascent of the South Buttress Direct (2,000', 5.11a) on the Main Tower.

Clint Helander

Growing up in Alaska's capital city, Johnson was surrounded by the mountains, and he took to rock climbing on nearby boulders and hiking on the ice of the Mendenhall Glacier at an early age. After high school, he made many pilgrimages to Yosemite, the Canadian Rockies, the desert Southwest, and the Cascades. In 2005, he and Stefan Ricci made a fast 51-hour ascent of the Cassin Ridge on Denali. A few years later, he nearly summited Pumori (7,161m) in Nepal and went on expeditions to Kyzyl Asker (5,842m) in Kyrgyzstan and beyond.

After college at the University of Montana, Johnson returned to Juneau. To date, no one has been more instrumental in developing new routes around the city. Thousand-foot ice routes near town such as Tide Line (420m, WI6) and Bathtime with Toaster (400m, WI5) and world-class rock climbs all bear his name.

As a climber, Johnson didn't really care *what* you did. He cared *how* you did it. At Kahiltna base camp, he gave genuine congratulations to a team of young climbers who had just reached their first minor Alaskan summit. To him it was just a walk-up, but it was the hardest thing they had ever done. Even after they left, he was excited for their accomplishment.

After years of selling tours to Princess Cruises tourists, Johnson opened Tongass Crossfit in Juneau. Business was slow at first, but he attained numerous certifications and gained a loyal following in the community. He didn't care if members were the best athletes; he just wanted them to always give their best.

Undoubtedly, Johnson's proudest accomplishment was his son Milo. Ice climbs and trips to Chamonix were replaced with weekends building sand castles and going on toddler hikes. Instead of sending pictures of new routes to friends, he sent pictures of Milo covered in bath bubbles. Ryan was a 5.11 climber but a 5.15 dad.

At the start of 2018, monumental things were happening for Johnson. His family was closer than ever, and by early February, he had already established a five-pitch WI5 first ascent in Suicide Basin with his best friend, Sam Johnson (unrelated). They planned to attempt a new route that spring in Alaska's Hayes Range. His business was expanding, three-year-old Milo was learning how to do push-ups, and the future seemed ever more promising.

"Ryan was a wonderful climbing partner and a thoughtful and compassionate friend," Sam Johnson told me. "He was always there for me when it counted, whether it be to shield me from falling ice, suffer together through interminable open bivies, as my best man, or as a coach through some of the tough decisions of early fatherhood. And my experience is not unique. Many people thought of him as their best friend, due to his openness and encouraging nature."

On the summit of the Main Tower, Johnson's final video shows a man who was relaxed and confident, more at peace than friends had seen him in years. A few minutes later, he and Leclerc started down the east ridge and then rappelled into the Fourth Gully. In a few hours, they should have reached their skis and celebrated what should be regarded as one of the greatest achievements in the Mendenhall Towers' climbing history. They were never heard from again.

– CLINT HELANDER

MARC-ANDRÉ LECLERC, 1992 – 2018

Steve Ogle

FOR MOST EVERYONE who reads this—be it now or in the distant future—Marc-André Leclerc will be remembered the way all young alpinists who left us too soon are: as an amalgamation of their deeds in the mountains, their prowess on rock or ice, their boldness.

In this last regard, Marc-André will be lionized as one of the very best. He was an innovator. He sought knowledge in climbing lore, learned the lessons of his predecessors, and assimilated them into his own unique skill set to push the standards of his time until they could support the immensity of his vision. His approach to not just mountain climbing but to life itself was, as his friend Kieran Brownie told me, "scholarly—a path of intimate understanding."

Marc-André's apprenticeship in the Coast Mountains began in his early teens, under the wing of Don Serl (one of British Columbia's most prolific and skilled alpinists of the past generation). He learned under his own tutelage as well, spending many hours on the kind of steep and vegetated slopes that make most climbers cringe, enjoying himself there, learning how to properly distribute his weight (a lesson he would later find incredibly useful for difficult mixed terrain). It was as if each day lessons were learned and neatly filed in the repository of his mind, organized in such a way that he could pull them up at will when later climbs necessitated. This slow entrance into mountain craft and his dedicated focus allowed him, in later years, to move through terrain in a manner that often toed the line of what most would consider reasonable.

From his quick success in difficult sport, trad, and speed climbs, one gets the impression that Marc-André could have been among the climbing elite in whatever specialty he pursued. But the climbing that enraptured Marc was the sort of alpine excursions (with or without partner) that are really best described as vision quests—near hallucinatory experiences that pushed the evolution of the sport beyond what previous suitors had imagined possible. He made scores of first ascents and groundbreaking free solos around the world, but his solo ascents of Cerro Torre's Corkscrew, Torre Egger's East Pillar (in winter), and Mt. Robson's Emperor Face will be forever remembered as some of the most daring and impressive ascents of his generation.

It is difficult to quantify what made Marc so exceptional a climber, because he eschewed (or transcended) the commonly accepted metrics of greatness. He rated the difficulty of his first ascents in accordance with the stiffest (not softest) pitches of the grade he had ever climbed. Though he was among the fastest in the world in alpine terrain, he had no patience or interest in tracking his time. "Already I have been asked how fast I was, but I honestly cannot tell you," he wrote on his blog following his solo of Infinite Patience on the Emperor Face. "I began when I felt ready and I reached the top at sundown. I also don't know how long the hike back to the road took me, but I do know that descending through the changing ecosystems back into the world of green lushness and deep blue lakes I felt more peace than I would have had I been counting my rate of kilometers per hour."

Marc's prowess was, and I believe always will be, shrouded in the cloak of mystery that surrounds climbers who are so great they've managed to slip the noose of caring about their greatness. While some athletes can—and do—provide detailed breakdowns of how they pulled off their greatest achievements, the epic climbs of Marc-André will forever reside in the realm of legend and rare alchemy. Not science, so much as sorcery. What made him so unique was not his brawn but his gifted brain.

Perhaps nobody was as intimately acquainted with the unique form of alpine asceticism in which Marc participated than his friend and climbing partner Colin Haley—himself one of the great alpinists of his era. "There was no one else I knew of that had a more similar vision of climbing to mine, and especially hard, solo, alpine climbing," Haley wrote on Facebook a few months after Marc's death. "In the last few years it felt like Marc-André and I were the only two players in a very special game…. While I think Marc and I shared equal amounts of motivation and drive, he was the stronger technical climber, and, more importantly, the younger climber, and there's no doubt that if he stayed alive our friendly competition would've only lasted so long, before he left me far behind."

Of course, all of this is beside the point to those who were closest to Marc. I was not one of them, though we were friends. But I have had the privilege to spend time or talk with the nucleus of individuals that were central to his life, including his mother, Michelle Kuipers, his siblings, Elijah and Bridgid-Anne, and of course his life partner Brette Harrington. By and large, we talked less about Marc's climbing achievements and more about who he was as a person: his humility, his sense of humor, his kindness and generosity, his enduring love of Brette and the other important people in his life. In a blog post, Bridgid-Anne wrote about Marc following his death that "he literally changed the world," without alluding much to the climbs that most people would associate with that sentiment. Instead she wrote in great detail about what we tend to think of as the little things, such as how "he would work so hard to understand [me], and even though he didn't really care about gifts, he would put in a lot of effort to find me something that I would like."

His mother, Michelle, told me in no uncertain terms that if I could ask Marc what was the most important thing in the world to him, he would have answered confidently and quickly: "Brette." Not climbing, not mountains, not snow or rock or ice. The woman he loved. Marc and Brette had been nearly inseparable. They made trips to El Chaltén together, to Baffin Island, to Yosemite and the Canadian Rockies. Everywhere they went, they established impressive lines or made free ascents of modern testpieces. Alone, each of them was well on their way to climbing stardom. But together they were unstoppable.

Brette was not with Marc when he passed away, along with Ryan Johnson, while descending from the 2,500-foot north face of the Main Tower in the Mendenhall Towers. She was in Tasmania, about as far from Alaska as a human can be. But she wasn't far from Marc's thoughts. From the summit, Marc sent two text messages, one to Brette and one to his mom. Upon hearing that Marc and Ryan were overdue, Brette and Marc-André's family made the long journey to join Juneau Mountain Rescue on the search effort. Marc and Ryan's gear cache was found, as well as their ropes, but their bodies have not been located.

I did not know Marc nearly as well as I would have liked to. But he was a hero to me just the same. Not for his climbs but for the way he carried himself in spite of his climbs. He could have reacted to stardom in the way that many climbers do—with arrogance, hubris, and solipsism. To most of the world, it wouldn't have mattered. He still would have been a legend, resting firmly on the achievements of his too-short career.

But for the most part he shied from the limelight. During the few times I spent time with him, he was thoughtful, kind, almost diffident, I thought. He had a calming effect on me. In his company, I recall feeling that all the garbage in the world didn't really need to amount to much. That you could just choose to be happy, to be at peace with the world and your place in it instead.

— CHRIS KALMAN

Wick Beavers

JEFF LOWE, 1950 – 2018

EDITOR'S NOTE: *In 2017, Jeff Lowe received a Piolet d'Or Lifetime Achievement Award, only the second American (after John Roskelley) to gain this honor. His many accomplishments have been well documented. In lieu of repeating that long list here, we have adapted remarks given by two close friends at Lowe's memorial celebration in Colorado.*

JEFF LOWE'S FATHER RALPH and my father George were brothers and best friends. They were the source of the adventure gene in our family, imbuing a sense of how to deal with new situations and unexpected events into both branches of the Lowe family. When I watched "Metanoia" [*the 2014 film about Lowe's life, his 1991 solo new route on the Eiger, and his degenerative illness*], the photos of my family and the "other Lowes" filled me with nostalgia. We grew up in houses that were only about a mile apart in Ogden, Utah. Our families skied together at Snow Basin. My sister Alta recalls Ralph taking his van up the unplowed Wheeler Canyon shortcut trying to beat other skiers to fresh powder. When he got stuck, he put 10-year-old Jeff in the driver's seat, since he was lightest, and the remainder of the kids and Ralph pushed the van out of the snowdrift. Our families tended to ski like Ralph drove, resulting in Jeff getting a ski scholarship for college.

I started rock climbing when my family joined Uncle Ralph a couple of times as he was teaching his sons Mike, Greg, and Jeff how to climb. Each of his sons successively set age records for climbing the Grand Teton, at ages 9, 8, and finally Jeff at age 7. Looking back, I think all the Lowes are deeply grateful for the adventures we enjoyed with our families—and the sense it gave us that we could do more than we could imagine.

Jeff and I started climbing together when I had finished college and near the time he was completing high school. We probably did the seventh ascent of the Salathé Wall on El Capitan, in 1969, when Jeff was 18, a kid straight out of high school. Of all the climbs we did together, I think the most memorable was the attempt on the north ridge of Latok I in 1978, during which Jeff became seriously ill just below the top of the unclimbed, 7,145-meter peak. I feared he might die in an open bivouac partway down, but his mental toughness carried him through. I think it was best climb we never did together. [*In July 2018, when Russian climber Alexander Gukov was stranded on Latok's north ridge, Jeff Lowe sent a note via a friend saying, "I am sure Alexander will be safely lifted off." Gukov attributed his survival in part to this message of hope.*]

Jeff has been my finest climbing partner. His vision of the future, combined with his incredible technical skills in all the climbing disciplines, plus the stamina to make that vision come true, made him quite unique in the climbing world. But, personally, I admire even more the grace with which he endured the wasting neurological disease, similar to multiple sclerosis, that took away his physical ability to climb. It was so difficult to reconcile his disabled self with the high- energy kid I remember running around our grandmother's yard. Nonetheless, his spirit shined through. He continued to love life and showed yet more mental toughness in dealing with his illness and overwhelming financial stress. He continued to be productive, writing most of a new book. It was wonderful to visit him, enjoy his jokes, and see his beaming smile.

I was fortunate to be with Jeff on the day he passed away. He and his daughter Sonja had decided that it was time that "he move on from this material plane to the next." He camped outside the hospice facility surrounded by grass, flowers, and trees. Despite being in what appeared to a comatose state, he was responsive to the conversations around him. He did not appear to be in pain. We all loved him and the example he provided as he approached the end, with the same grace, vision, and determination that allowed him to love doing the hardest climbs in the world of his era.

— GEORGE LOWE

OUR LIVES ARE FILLED with choices. We can choose to do absurd things like climb frozen waterfalls or solo a difficult line on the Eiger. What we don't get to choose is whether we die. Given the implacable certainty of our mortality, how we shape and deal with the approach of our own demise is the final illumination of who we are. Jeff saw death as a positive transition to something new and exciting.

Jeff and I climbed together for a few years when our unemployment was a badge of honor, we had nothing but our gear and shit-box cars, and life was simply about climbing and friends. [*Among other climbs, the two made the first ascents of Bridal Veil Falls in Colorado, Moonlight Buttress in Zion National Park, and the Grand Central Couloir on Mt. Kitchener in the Canadian Rockies.*] Jeff's climbing resumé is remarkable, but knowing the man was far more rewarding than knowing the resumé. Jeff left me and many others with remarkable gifts.

First of all, Jeff left me with indelible memories of shared laughter and alpine suffering, the partnership of the rope, and time spent in wild places full of life, power, and indescribable beauty. Jeff had a ruthless yet childlike desire to see what was around the corner or at the top of the next pitch. Together we drank in the warmth of desert sandstone and the bitter cold of frozen ice. In the spaces between climbs, we celebrated life with the other eccentric, unbalanced, antisocial, and bizarre members of our climbing tribe. It was a magical time of life.

Second and most importantly, Jeff gave us a lesson on how to leave this world with dignity and grace. He embraced his own end in the same way he embraced the rest of his life, with joy, humor, and bright, childlike anticipation.

Lastly and above all else, in the love he held for his daughter Sonja and his granddaughter Valentina, he illustrated that the bond of family was a far greater legacy than the sum of a climbing resumé. Jeff's body was in ruins the last few years. At one point I asked him why he didn't put an end to it, and he slowly tapped out on his iPad that it all was worth it when he saw the smile on his granddaughter's face.

Over the last few years of Jeff's life he was both lionized and demonized. In both cases I felt that Jeff, my friend, often went unseen for the person he was. Jeff, I am humbled by your strength, friendship, and your transcendent exit, and as always I can only hope to follow your lead.

— MIKE WEIS

NECROLOGY

In addition to those covered above or in AAJ online tributes, we remember the following climbers who passed away in 2018:

AL AUTEN	BRUCE GILBERT	LISA KORTHALS	JOHN MYERS
STEVE BIEM	DOUG HEIVLY	ANN KRCIK	EDITH OVERLY
MATT BRINKERHOFF	TOM HIGGINS	CALVIN LANDRUS	ALEX REED
CHIP CHACE	CHRISTIAN HUBER	DAVE LANMAN	HALEY ROYKO
BRIAN DANNEMANN, M.D.	HELEN KILNESS	STACEY LI COLLVER	DAVID J. SWIFT
MARCO DEES	TIM KLEIN	JOHN MARTS	JASON WELLS

INDEX

COMPILED BY EVE TALLMAN & RALPH FERRARA

Mountains are listed by their official names. Ranges, geographic locations, and maps are also indexed. Unnamed peaks (eg. Peak 2,340m.) are listed under P. Abbreviations are used for the following: Cordillera: C.; Mountains: Mts.; National Park: Nat'l. Park; Obituary: obit. Indexed photographs are listed in bold type.

the AMERICAN ALPINE club

SERIOUSNESS RATINGS

These often modify technical grades when protection is difficult

PG-13: Difficult or insecure protection or loose rock, with some injury potential

R: Poor protection with high potential for injury

X: A fall would likely result in serious injury or death

YDS=Yosemite Decimal System
UIAA=Union Internationale des Associations D'Alpinisme
FR=France/Sport
AUS=Australia
SAX=Saxony
CIS=Commonwealth of Independent States/Russia
SCA=Scandinavia
BRA=Brazil
UK=United Kingdom

Note: *All conversions are approximate. Search "International Grade Comparison Chart" at the AAJ website for further explanation of commitment grades and waterfall Ice/mixed grades.*

YDS	UIAA	FR	AUS	SAX	CIS	SCA	BRA	UK	
5.2	II	1	10	II	III	3			D
5.3	III	2	11	III	III+	3+			D
5.4	IV- / IV	3	12		IV-	4			VD
5.5	IV+		13		IV	4+			VD
5.6	V-	4	14		IV+	5-		4a	S
5.7	V / V+		15	VIIa		5			HS
5.8	V+	5a	16	VIIb	V-	5+	4 / 4+	4b	VS
5.9	VI-	5b	17	VIIc		6-	5 / 5+	4c / 5a	HVS
5.10a	VI	5c	18	VIIIa	V	6	6a	5b	E1
5.10b	VI+	6a				6			
5.10c	VII-	6a+	19	VIIIb		6+	6b		E2
5.10d	VII	6b	20	VIIIc	V+		6c		E3
5.11a	VII+	6b+		IXa		7-	7a	5c	
5.11b		6c	21	IXb		7	7b		
5.11c	VIII-	6c+	22		VI-	7+			E4
5.11d	VIII	7a	23	IXc			7c	6a	
5.12a	VIII+	7a+	24				8a		E5
5.12b	IX-	7b	25	Xa	VI	8- / 8	8b		
5.12c		7b+	26			8+	8c		
5.12d	IX	7c	27	Xb			9a	6b	E6
5.13a	IX+	7c+	28	Xc		9-	9b		
5.13b		8a	29				9c		
5.13c	X-	8a+	30			9	10a		E7
5.13d	X	8b	31	XIa	VI+		10b		
5.14a	X+	8b+	32	XIb		9+	10c	7a	E8
5.14b		8c	33				11a		
5.14c	XI-	8c+	34	XIc			11b	7b	E9
5.14d	XI	9a	35				11c		E10
5.15a	XI+	9a+	36	XIIa	VII	10	12a		
5.15b	XII-	9b	37				12b		E11
5.15c	XII	9b+	38	XIIb			12c		
5.15d	XII+	9c	39						